P9-APW-836

Public-Private
Partnership in
American Cities

Public-Private Partnership in American Cities

Seven Case Studies

Edited by
R. Scott Fosler
Renee A. Berger

LexingtonBooks
D.C. Heath and Company
Lexington, Massachusetts
Toronto

Library of Congress Cataloging in Publication Data
Main entry under title:

Public-private partnership in American cities.

Includes index.
1. Urban renewal—United States—Case studies. 2. Urban
policy—United States—Case studies. I. Fosler, R. Scott. II. Berger,
Renee A.
HT175.P8   1982   307'.34'0973   82–48016
ISBN 0–669–05834–3   AACR2

Copyright © 1982 by D.C. Heath and Company

All rights reserved. No part of this publication may be reproduced or
transmitted in any form or by any means, electronic or mechanical,
including photocopy, recording, or any information storage or retrieval
system, without permission in writing from the publisher.

Published simultaneously in Canada

Printed in the United States of America

Casebound International Standard Book Number: 0–669–05834–3

Paperbound International Standard Book Number: 0–669–05836–x

Library of Congress Catalog Card Number: 82–48016

Contents

Preface and
Acknowledgments

In February 1982 the Committee for Economic Development (CED) published a policy statement titled *Public-Private Partnership: An Opportunity for Urban Communities*. One of the principal sources of information in the deliberation, analysis, and writing of that statement was a series of case studies undertaken by CED to examine the changing relationships between the public and private sectors in seven cities. So that they may be widely available to scholars and practitioners, those case studies are being published in their entirety in this book.

The planning for this research began in 1978, long before the notion of public-private partnership became as popular as it is today. It seemed, then, that constraints on federal funding would cause more governmental responsibility to shift to the state and local levels, and that the constraints on government at those levels would implicitly place a greater burden on the private sector in dealing with urban problems. Ronald Reagan's election as president and his emphasis on private-sector initiatives has focused public attention on the issue. Debate will no doubt continue over the appropriate balance of responsibility between the federal and state and local levels, and between the public and private sectors. But whatever the resolution of those questions, the forces that are now compelling local communities to solve their problems more creatively with their own resources—whether government, business, nonprofit, or voluntary—will continue well into the next decade.

These studies were begun several years ago, and show the long-term view. They do not try to deal with all of the innovative partnership efforts that have been initiated within the past year with the waxing of interest in this topic, but attempt to establish a historical base for understanding the growing interdependence of public and private sectors in urban areas. We hope that these case studies will provide perspective on the more recent developments as well as insights into the process by which more productive relationships can be forged among government and nongovernment institutions.

The introductory chapter provides background on the research effort and puts the case studies in context. A comparative analysis of the cases is included in the CED policy statement.

The editors of and contributors to this volume wish to thank the many people who gave their time and knowledge generously in the preparation of these case studies.

CED wishes to give special thanks to the following foundations, companies, and organizations whose generous support made the case studies possible: The Ford Foundation, Charles F. Kettering Foundation, and The Rockefeller Foundation; in Atlanta, The Citizens & Southern National Bank, The Coca-Cola Company, The Community Foundation, Inc., Davison's, The First National Bank of Atlanta, Fulton National Bank, Georgia Power Company, International Business Machines Corporation, Rich's, Inc., Sears, Roebuck and Company, Southern Bell Telephone and Telegraph Company, and Trust Company of Georgia; in Dallas, the Dallas Citizens Council; in Minneapolis-Saint Paul, Curtis L. Carlson Foundation, Dayton Hudson Foundation, The McKnight Foundation, General Mills Foundation, and Northwestern National Bank Foundation; in Pittsburgh, H.J. Heinz II Charitable Trust, and Richard King Mellon Foundation.

**Public-Private
Partnership in
American Cities**

1

Public-Private Partnership: An Overview

R. Scott Fosler and
Renee A. Berger

The problems and opportunities of cities have long been matters of keen interest to the Committee for Economic Development (CED). In the mid-1970s a number of the CED trustees grew increasingly concerned about the economic and social conditions in America's urban areas. This concern was especially strong among those chief executive officers whose companies had strong business or traditional ties to their cities. As a result, in 1976 the Subcommittee on Revitalizing America's Cities was formed.

Over the years, CED studies had addressed urban problems by analyzing functions (transportation, welfare, education, health, and so on), structures of government (local, state, and metropolitan), and government management (productivity improvement, management of the public work force). What seemed to be lacking was an approach that cut across these various perspectives to take into account the multiple dimensions of problems and to identify the actions required to resolve them.

The subcommittee's first product was the 1978 policy statement titled *An Approach to Federal Urban Policy,* which recommended a major change in national policy toward cities. It argued that the diversity among urban areas and the limits on federal funds required a more selective policy that targeted resources to priority needs and tailored actions to fit local conditions.

The research and deliberations that produced that policy statement confirmed the belief that the conditions among cities were so different and the problems so complex that greater responsibility in dealing with their own needs would inevitably fall to local leaders, whatever the level and sophistication of federal assistance. It was also apparent that there was a limit to what government could do by itself; greater private participation, in the form of capital, expertise, and leadership, would be required to deal with urban problems.

Yet, little was known about the interaction between the public and private sectors in local communities. To be sure, there were numerous studies of the various aspects of urban society, including its social structure, political institutions, economic development, and government management. Much of the research conducted in the 1960s had concentrated on the social factors underlying urban decline. During the 1970s, interest turned toward economic forces that seemed to help some cities to flourish while others declined. However, none of this research directly addressed the question of how urban communities themselves organize government, business, and community resources to solve problems, encourage productive development, and improve the quality of life.

Evolution of the Public-Private Relationship

During the past two-hundred years, the relationship between the nation's public and private sectors in local communities has changed profoundly. In colonial and frontier communities, such functions as water supply, waste disposal, and fire protection were attended to by households themselves or by private companies. Few streets were paved. The police force typically consisted of the night watch, with a standby citizen militia that handled more serious threats to public order. Communities did take some responsibility for the poor, the physically impaired, orphans, and widows, but the care usually was minimal and provided without elaborate formal structure. Generally, such public concerns were addressed through individual or collective private action. Government meanwhile established the legal framework for private behavior but provided few services.

The twin forces of urbanization and industrialization in the nineteenth century transformed America's cities and prompted the expansion of government. Dense urban populations and industrial activity required more extensive physical infrastructure. Paved streets and bridges were more efficiently built and maintained by the local government. The pollution or exhaustion of nearby groundwater supplies required the construction of dams, aqueducts, and water lines, which, for reasons of cost, planning, and public health, favored government operation or regulation. Rising volumes of residential and industrial waste required the construction of sewers, establishment of sanitation and public-health codes, and regulation of plumbing. Fire suppression gradually became a government function because the failure to suppress a fire in any structure posed a danger to entire neighborhoods or to the whole city. Police forces expanded to manage congestion and to contend with the unrest that resulted from widening class, economic, and ethnic differences. State and local governments sometimes initiated or supported such economic ventures as canals, railroads, highways, and port facilities that no private firm or consortium of private interests was willing or able to undertake on its own.

Most of these responses, however, were ad hoc in nature and frequently inadequate to the task. By the late nineteenth century, large cities with industrial economies were straining under a tradition of government rooted in a formerly agricultural society. American cities functioned, but with congested traffic, widespread poverty, poor housing, unsanitary conditions, and frequently corrupt city governments.

Welfare needs were in large part handled ad hoc, sometimes resulting in the coalescing of volunteer groups. By the turn of the century, fortunes made by large industrialists spurred philanthropic giving. Changes in tax laws further accelerated giving for education, health, and welfare needs.

Many of the great issues and political battles of the progressive era in the late nineteenth and early twentieth centuries revolved around the question of the role of government in organizing and managing a densely populated, industrial city. Housing codes and zoning ordinances were adopted to ensure minimal standards of health and residential sanctity. Stricter standards of sanitation were established to guard against communicable diseases, the causes of which were just being discovered. Chronic complaints about the high cost and poor performance of privately owned utilities (water, gas, transportation, electricity) gave rise to more stringent regulation and/or municipal ownership and operation. As the size and complexity of government increased, attention was also drawn to the need for more efficient government administration, including professional city management, civil service based on merit, the application of scientific management principles to government administration, and modern administrative systems of budgeting, finance, and procurement.

At the heart of the progressive philosophy was the belief that government should play a more effective role in addressing the public needs of industrial urban society. Supporters of this philosophy typically included businessmen whose companies suffered from inadequate support services and a growing middle class of professionals and office workers who chafed under the disorder, inefficiency, and political corruption that characterized many larger cities. Opposition to progressive reforms frequently came from private utilities that resisted government regulation or ownership, business entrepreneurs with little enduring stake in the community, political parties that benefited from the patronage of government jobs, and ethnic and working-class groups that saw the progressive proposals as an attempt by a business and professional élite to maintain or reestablish political control.

The depression of the 1930s accelerated government involvement in urban affairs and shifted the initiative to the federal level. Such programs as social security and subsidized housing relieved local communities and, more specifically, local governments of major burdens. Unemployment was recognized as a national problem requiring the attention of the federal government. World War II temporarily resolved the debate over the role of the federal government in managing the national economy since few disputed the necessity of active federal leadership in stimulating war production. As early as 1942, federal officials began planning for conversion from a wartime to a peacetime economy, fearing a resumption of unemployment and economic decline once the stimulus of war production ended. (This concern prompted the creation of the Committee for Economic Development, a group of business leaders dedicated to sustaining economic growth in a peacetime economy.) The momentum of the New Deal continued after the war and eventually expanded federal activity into virtually every area of urban life, culminating in the Great Society programs of the 1960s and the rapid growth of entitlement programs in the 1970s.

The growth and visibility of the federal government obscured the expansion and transformation of state and local government. With the economic expansion of the 1950s and 1960s, suburban growth, which had been noticeable even before World War II, suddenly exploded. New local governments formed in the suburbs to provide the roads, water and sewer facilities, schools, and other services required to support the growing population. As a consequence, the traditional central cities were drained of middle-class population, jobs, and tax base and at the same time gained a poorer population of rural migrants who were predominantly black. The federal government's response to the resulting problems of poverty, health, education, transportation, unemployment, pollution, and public safety was impressive in magnitude and scope, but seemingly never adequate.

A New Juncture in Public-Private Relationships

Two-hundred years of persistent growth in the number and scope of public concerns and the commensurate expansion of government to deal with them, resulted principally from the practical requirements of organizing an urban, industrial society. The public concerns arose from the fact that the specialized but interdependent activities required for modern urban life did not automatically integrate themselves into a smoothly functioning system, either within urban regions or among the increasingly interdependent regions of a national economy. Moreover, the pursuit of private goals did not automatically take into consideration the broader public interest. It was natural that government, which provided an understandable mechanism for collective action, should be called on to respond to these developments.

The pragmatic use of government, however, gradually evolved into political excess. By the mid-1970s, there was a widespread conviction that massive government programs alone could not deal with persistent problems, or that they were too expensive. The resounding victory of Proposition 13 in California in 1978 dramatized the public's resistance to higher taxes and belief that government was wasteful. Similar efforts to limit taxation or cut spending at all levels of government and in every region of the country verified the national scope of the sentiments expressed in California. In 1978 federal grants to state and local governments ceased their historical climb and began to decline. The election of Ronald Reagan in 1980 and the near unanimity in Congress in 1981 in favor of restraining federal budget growth and accelerating the reduction of aid to state and local governments confirmed the change in public mood.

The same pragmatic tradition that gradually led to a stronger government role in the direct operation of urban functions now needs to be applied to a case-by-case examination of what can work best, whether by government, profit-oriented, nonprofit, self-help, or volunteer organizations or by some new combination of approaches. This is not to suggest either the wisdom of, or popular support for, the radical dismantling of government programs. What it does suggest is the need to rethink the roles of the public and private sectors and their component organizations in carrying out the important functions of urban life.

The Research Design

The CED subcommittee decided that the best way to begin to address this issue was to conduct indepth case studies of successful public-private relationships and to try to identify the reasons for their success. The subcommittee was seeking practical ideas—financing techniques, innovative institutions, effective working arrangements—for coordinating government and private resources in addressing such multidimensional problems as economic stagnation, neighborhood deterioration, and malfunctioning public services. But it was interested in more than techniques. It wanted to understand the process by which the public and private resources of a community could be brought to bear on a wide range of commonly recognized needs. So the subcommittee chose as its basic unit of study, not projects or techniques, but cities.

An Emphasis on "What Works"

The research was consciously biased toward purportedly successful experiences. The subcommittee was concerned over the preoccupation with "urban problems" and was determined to highlight opportunities. "Let's find what works" was the way the task was defined.

Unquestionably, it would have been useful to examine cities that failed in attempts to forge public-private partnerships, those that never tried to do so, or those with unusually adversarial relationships. The subcommittee was aware, moreover, that emphasizing success might lead to describing success that really had not occurred. In general, however, the experiences we examined did reveal some identifiable patterns that constituted successful public-private relationships with tangible benefits for the community. Within our examination of successful experiences, we found periods of discord, such as the interlude between Renaissance I and Renaissance II in Pittsburgh and the period following the Ivan Allen years in Atlanta, which provide contrasts with the more positive partnership experiences.

Defining success is, of course, largely a normative exercise. Some would argue, for example, that the positive relationship between business and government in Chicago during the Daley years was based on political conditions that were destructive of other values. It can be argued that the most perfect public-private partnership is where City Hall is in the pocket of business interests. Even where such political control yielded a productive economy, healthful environment, and generally high standard of living, it could be further argued, such gains are not worth the price of restricted political participation. That economic organizations have political influence goes without saying. However, the contemporary reality of most American cities is that political power is dispersed among numerous groups. And it cannot be assumed that businesses are either homogeneous or single-minded in their interests. The Greater Baltimore Committee, for example, was a leader in pushing for the prohibition of racial discrimination in public accommodations, a step that was being resisted by some businesses.

The Sample of Cities

Several factors were considered in the selection of the seven cities to be studied. The first was tangible accomplishment that clearly required more than the normal degree of public-private interaction. Baltimore's Charles Center/Inner Harbor development and Pittsburgh's Golden Triangle were among the more obvious examples.

A second factor was a city's reputation among the national business community, public officials, scholars, and the media. A key question was, which cities have a reputation for getting organized to bring public and private resources to bear on solving problems or on improving their condition? Opinions regularly placed Atlanta, Baltimore, Pittsburgh, Minneapolis-Saint Paul, Chicago, Portland, Oregon, and Dallas high on the list, with Kansas City, Philadelphia, and Milwaukee close behind. Occasionally cited by people who knew them well were Seattle, Indianapolis, and a number of smaller cities such as Worcester, Massachusetts, and Toledo, Ohio. Specific examples of partnership efforts were cited in numerous cities, including downtown development in Boston and Denver, Renaissance Center in Detroit, community-based efforts in Saint Louis, and numerous small projects in Newark, but usually with cautions about whether these successes reflected exceptional experiences or a broader sense of partnership.

A third factor was endurance. We sought evidence of sustained effort over a period of decades. Here again the Twin Cities, Baltimore, and Dallas seemed to stand out, as did Milwaukee and Kansas City. Pittsburgh offered an example of a highly successful public-private partnership that ended or perhaps was interrupted and then was started anew. Atlanta presented the case of a close public-private relationship that changed abruptly with a new political regime; the extent to which the foundations of partnership were sustained beneath the adversarial climate of the 1970s was unclear.

A fourth factor was diversity of experience. Was there some special feature or combination of factors that seemed to distinguish a particular city from others in its public-private relations? In Pittsburgh, it was the durability of the partnership, apparently tied to the presence of top corporate leadership, that slowed the decline characteristic of other industrial cities. In Baltimore, it was the dazzling transformation of a dingy harbor area into a modern, bustling office-pedestrian-tourist complex in a declining northeastern industrial city with practically no national corporate headquarters. Minneapolis-Saint Paul has long enjoyed a reputation as a place where people in government, business, and civic organizations approach community problems rationally and in a spirit of common interest and public responsibility. In the 1950s and 1960s, at least, Atlanta was seen as a city whose business establishment turned it into a major metropolis and regional economic center. In Dallas, the special feature appeared to be a closely knit business community that recognized the importance of a professionally managed city government and broad community involvement in the planning process. Portland seemed to demonstrate the opportunity for leadership stemming from a nonbusiness, neighborhood base of support in enlisting the business sector in ambitious plans for improvement.

The decision to limit the sample to seven cities was based on the need for manageability and desire for indepth inquiry. Although it was not assumed that the seven cities would be representative of American cities in general, an effort was made to spread the selection by region, type of government, political structure, economic base, and size.

Describing Process

A common research framework was applied in each city stressing process: How and by whom were ideas conceived, what was the incentive for pursuing them, how was support developed and obstacles or opposition dealt with, what kind of organization or mechanisms were required for implementation, what were the results and consequences? Finding the answers to such questions required examining the context of partnership efforts: the historical development of the city, its demographic composition, its economic base and changing economic character, its political system and government structure, and its community organization.

In each city, three or four projects were selected both for their intrinsic interest and to provide a focus for examining the process and its context. Organizations that may have played a role in nurturing the development of a project were also targeted for study. The nature of the projects was broadly defined to include significant efforts that were generally agreed to have improved the economy, quality of life, or community organization of the city.

The Researchers

In each of the cities except Portland, one or two resident researchers were selected to conduct the study. (A list of these researchers appears on page 359.) We purposefully sought researchers with a variety of backgrounds and perspectives. The combination of economics, political-science, sociology, history, and management perspectives did indeed contribute to the richness of the studies. The team of researchers met once in Washington to discuss the research design and later in New York to compare preliminary findings. Researchers also discussed their projects at meetings of the CED subcommittee during the course of the research study.

In each case the researcher had access to CED trustees whose corporations were located in that city. We believed that the insight that could be gained from such access would outweigh whatever bias it might cause.

Macro Determinism versus Local Determination

For the past two decades, urban research has been dominated by a belief that certain key political, social, and economic factors are the principal influences on the growth or decline of a city. Such factors as age, population size, ethnic and racial mix, whether the economic base is growing or contracting, whether political power is concentrated or dispersed, are routinely used as the basis for predicting and explaining conditions in cities. The CED study looked to this tradition of research to explore what factors potentially contributed to public-private partnership.

Initially the attempt to identify factors focused on political structure. For example, Baltimore's revival might be considered due in part to its having a form of government in which the mayor was a strong, central figure. This may also account for part of Chicago's success. But this hypothesis fails to explain why Dallas and Minneapolis are also centers of partnership activity. Furthermore, having a strong mayor does not guarantee constructive relations between the public and private sectors.

From an economic perspective, the presence of large corporate headquarters seemed to suggest a higher probability of cooperation. Certainly, this contributed to the performance of two sample cities, Minneapolis-Saint Paul and Pittsburgh. Baltimore is not a center for corporate headquarters, but it has developed impressive partnership activity. As in the case of political structure, the presence of large corporate headquarters in a city does not by itself guarantee the development of public-private partnerships.

City age certainly favors Portland, a fairly young city; ethnic homogeneity facilitates cooperation in the Twin cities; and the Sunbelt attraction aids Atlanta and Dallas. But Pittsburgh, Baltimore, and Chicago are all old manufacturing cities, are ethnically mixed, and are located in the Frostbelt. However, the studies confirm that these cities all formed productive relationships between the sectors. Thus age, population mix, and geography do not unequivocally predict a city's capacity to effectively coordinate use of the public and private resources.

Although cities obviously are influenced by their political institutions, social composition, and economic structure, we believe the case studies demonstrate that initiative by local leadership can give a community the decisive edge needed to improve conditions. Ultimately, we concluded that civic leaders—people who care about their cities and are willing and able to take action—are the impetus for public-private cooperation that can be the vehicle for overcoming otherwise compelling forces of deterioration.

Common Elements of Local Initiative

The process of forming partnerships can be divided into two stages: setting the preconditions for action and the action itself. Preconditions for action start with the people who recognize that a problem—or an opportunity—exists and who look for a means to "do something." In communities that enjoy strong civic foundations, individual leaders or their organizations have a ready mechanism to effectively focus attention on an issue.

Those civic foundations (which are described more fully in the CED policy statement *Public-Private Partnership: An Opportunity for Urban Communities*) include the following:

A positive civic culture that encourages citizen participation rooted in a practical concern for the community as a whole;

A realistic and commonly accepted vision of the community that takes into account strengths and weaknesses in identifying what the community can and should become;

Effective building-block civic organizations that blend the self-interest of their members with the broader interest of the community and translate that dual interest into effective action;

A network among the key groups that encourages communication among leaders of every important segment and facilitates the mediation of differences among competing interests;

The inclination to nurture civic entrepreneurs, that is, leaders whose knowledge, imagination, and energy are directed toward enterprises that will benefit the community, whether in the public sector, the private sector, or both; and

Continuity in policy, including the ability to adapt to changing circumstances, which minimizes uncertainty and fosters confidence in individual and group enterprises.

In communities where the civic foundations are strong, leadership is still required to make them function. Where the foundations are weak or nonexistent, leadership is especially important to build the foundations or to compensate for their absence. How leadership is recognized by each sector and how it is cultivated are key aspects of the seven case studies.

In many of the cities, one sector appears to play the dominant role, with the other acting to facilitate reaching the goals. Few cities have had strong public- and private-sector leaders acting in unison. Chicago and Baltimore have had powerful, well-organized business communities and a similarly vigorous public sector. Pittsburgh, Minneapolis, and Dallas, on the other hand, had powerful business coalitions working with a city government that viewed its role as primarily facilitative. In Pittsburgh and Atlanta (and perhaps in Baltimore), initiative has shifted from the private to the public sector. In Portland and Saint Paul the initiative for partnership efforts came principally from public-sector leaders.

In other words, leadership that promotes partnership formation does not have to be present in equal amounts in both sectors at the same time. Nonetheless, business leaders with a civic vision need the cooperation of government and citizens even if it is not highly visible. Public-sector leaders too must obtain the cooperation of the private sector. Leadership is not always visible or vigorous; it often comes in the form of government being willing to help or business being flexible in accepting political change. In each of the seven cities, the fact that leadership was present, recognized, and encouraged contributed significantly to success.

Private-sector leaders in these cities were devoted to the vitality of their cities, and saw self-interest and civic interest as closely tied to each other. During the urban crises of the 1960s and 1970s, questions were raised about whether cities should be saved and, if so, by whom. These leaders responded decisively that the city is not only worth preserving but also worth the organization, planning, and hard work necessary for such preservation.

Pittsburgh

Pittsburgh's Renaissance I period owes its origins and support to the Allegheny Conference on Community Development (ACCD). Joel Tarr and Shelby Stewman explain how ACCD provided the agenda, planning, and capacity that evolved into the projects of Renaissance I. Established in 1944 as a nonprofit research and planning organization, ACCD served as the prototype for business civic organizations in other cities, such as Baltimore's Greater Baltimore Committee. The tradition of public-private partnership established by ACCD continues to provide a foundation for Renaissance II in Pittsburgh today.

Baltimore

The Baltimore Citizens Planning and Housing Association (CPHA), a group of concerned citizens who wanted to improve the quality of residential neighborhoods, is characterized by Katharine Lyall as an "incubator for 'civic entrepreneurs.'" CPHA leaders, including James Rouse, were responsible for stimulating business interest in establishing the Greater Baltimore Committee (GBC), which played a key role in downtown revitalization. In 1957, the GBC and the Committee for Downtown (an offshoot of the Retail Merchants Association) jointly raised

$150,000 and contracted with a professional planning group for the development of a master plan for downtown renewal. The result was the eventual development of Charles Center. From its inception in 1955, GBC was composed of executives from the area's largest corporations. In 1979, however, GBC merged with the Metropolitan Chamber of Commerce, expanding its membership to 1,200 and inviting participation from small- and medium-sized firms, a move that early GBC leaders believe may have undermined its effectiveness.

Chicago

Pastora Cafferty and William McCready describe the importance of the Loop, the area of downtown Chicago in which corporate headquarters are concentrated. Chief executive officers belong to the same clubs and socialize with each other; and although they may live in the suburbs, they feel rooted to the city, its central business district, and its neighborhoods. The Chicago Central Area Committee was established in the 1950s when businessmen decided to organize to stop the downturn in retail activity in the central business district. The committee contracted with the architectural firm of Skidmore Owings & Merrill to prepare a plan for the central business district. This became the Chicago 21 Plan, the central feature of which is a $15-billion rejuvenation effort that gave the highest priority to housing development and rehabilitation. Since the plan's inception in 1973, nineteen of thirty-two projects or proposals have either been completed or are underway.

Twin Cities

Also in the 1950s, the Downtown Council was formed in Minneapolis. John Brandl and Ronnie Brooks describe how this organization brought together Minneapolis leaders in the downtown area. In 1959, the Downtown Council retained Barton Aschman Associates to develop a plan that led to the creation of the highly successful Nicollet Mall. The case study also discusses the Whittier neighborhood redevelopment in Minneapolis and Town Square, a downtown project.

In Saint Paul in the late 1960s, Norman Mears, a local corporate executive, developed a master plan for Lowertown, an area on the eastern edge of Saint Paul's downtown. In 1977 the McKnight Foundation funded the formation of the Lowertown Redevelopment Corporation (LRC), a partnership of the foundation, the city of Saint Paul, and the private business community.

Dallas

William Claggett traces the development of the Dallas Citizens Council (DCC) from its formation in 1937 as a means of raising the capital for the Texas centennial celebration. This was a difficult economic period for Dallas, and it was hoped that through rallying the support of top business people, financial stability could be attained. DCC was credited with promoting cooperation between the city's business and public institutions in the 1950s.

The planning for improvement in Dallas took a unique form with the Goals-for-Dallas program, one of the oldest and most comprehensive processes of urban goal setting in the nation. Begun by Mayor J. Erik Jonsson in 1964, the program involved more than 100,000 people in planning committees and neighborhood gatherings over the 1966–1977 period.

Atlanta

Dale Henson and Jim King describe how the Atlanta Chamber of Commerce provided leadership as reflected, for example, in the enormously successful Forward Atlanta program, an advertising campaign to attract business to Atlanta. In the 1970s, initiative shifted to Central Atlanta Progress (CAP), a group composed of the city's top business executives, which has been instrumental in sustaining that city's downtown development.

Portland

Portland proved to be unique among our studies in the unusually active role neighborhood associations played in shaping the city. Indeed, George Barbour cites the lack of an organized downtown-business group as an explanation for the slow progress in revitalizing the central business district. It was not until 1972 that a downtown plan was created. Over the years this plan has been revised, and its process has been notable for the openness of participation.

Thus in each of these cities, leaders from the private sector translated their concern for businesses' success into organizational mechanisms to strengthen the economic base of their cities. But there were parallel forces operating in the public sector. Mayor David Lawrence (Pittsburgh), Mayor Richard Daley (Chicago), Mayor George Latimer (Saint Paul), City Manager George Schrader (Dallas), and Mayor William Donald Schaeffer (Baltimore) were the able government counterparts of private-sector leaders. These political leaders saw the economic vitality of their cities as synonymous with their own political agendas. Though their individual styles differ significantly, each was able to inspire trust among decision makers in the private sector.

For those cities that did not sustain continuous long-term political stability (Pittsburgh and Atlanta) or the benefits of a short-term burst of public leadership (Goldschmidt in Portland), the flexibility and capacity of leaders in the private sector has been important to harboring the tradition of partnership. In some cases, interruptions in the cooperative relationship between the public and private sectors, as Pittsburgh's interlude under Mayor Peter Flaherty showed, have proved useful in expanding the partnership agenda to include social and managerial as well as economic objectives.

The Potential for Public-Private Partnership

The seven case studies demonstrate that although certain factors such as city age, size, economic base, and population mix influence a city's capacity to solve problems, local initiative supported by a strong civic foundation can give a community the ability to mobilize its public and private resources to improve community conditions. The leaders may come from the public or the private sectors, or both; they may create or participate in an organization that has the objective and the capacity to bring about civic improvements; and they share an attitude that their interests and the city's interests are compatible. Although there are often periods of discord, the prevailing atmosphere is one of cooperation. We noted that, while crisis can expedite change and promote a cooperative spirit, it need not necessarily be present to stimulate partnership formation. A civic foundation emerges over time as the support system that sustains the momentum of local initiative. It provides the organizational culture in which success can be achieved and can breed other successes.

Our research design encompassed a range of targets for public-private partnership including improving the environment, strengthening community services, developing minority enterprise, creating jobs, providing housing, and building community institutions, as well as developing the economy. However, the most salient examples of success fell into the category of economic development, and more specifically downtown revitalization. This is not surprising given the fact that one of the principal problems confronting cities in the post-World War II era has been the decline of their economic base.

The *process* by which public and private resources were combined to tackle this problem successfully is no less relevant, however, to the problems of neighborhood revitalization and improving community services, which increasingly confront urban areas in the 1980s. The hard-won successes of Atlanta, Chicago, and Baltimore in building intown housing; the experiments in Minneapolis-Saint Paul in trying new forms of service delivery; the accomplishments of Pittsburgh in cleaning up smoke pollution and controlling floods; the initiative of Dallas's business community in building a major public library; and the experience of Portland in tapping neighborhood energies are all testaments to the potential for public-private partnership to address a wide range of urban needs. These examples also demonstrated the importance of including influential and affected groups in partnership efforts that address issues of importance to them. The private sector is composed not only of business but nonprofit organizations, neighborhood associations, community-development corporations, and numerous social and political organizations, all of which have a stake in the community.

To be sure, processes that have been successful over the past several decades are not necessarily applicable to the needs and conditions of the 1980s. Much has changed, and much is changing, and if the case studies teach anything, it is that approaches must be tailored to local circumstance. Nonetheless, the key lesson that emerges from the case studies will be as relevant to the immediate future as it has been to the recent past: Where leaders in the public and private sectors seek the maximum advantage that the special assets of their city provide and the prevailing economic conditions of the time permit, their communities will be better off than if no such effort is made.

2 A Bicycle Built-for-Two: Public-Private Partnership in Baltimore

Katharine Lyall

Anyone who has ridden a bicycle built-for-two knows that while the balance of effort may shift back and forth, one partner coasting while the other pedals on, long distances can be covered only by joint and sustained effort. Baltimore's experience with public-private partnership has been a thirty-year spin over sometimes rough terrain, but the distance covered has been considerable.

The history of public-private partnerships in Baltimore goes back more than thirty years and spans a variety of projects, ranging from economic-development efforts to housing rehabilitation. The success of these efforts can be traced as much to people as to plans. The evolution of two organizations, the Citizens' Planning and Housing Association and the Greater Baltimore Committee, as incubators for civic entrepreneurs has paralleled the major bricks-and-mortar achievements of the redevelopment process.

Downtown revitalization has followed a master plan that is flexible in its details but sustained in its basic outline. It sets priorities and some basic principles to which individual projects must adhere: commitment to good architectural-design standards; respect for the opinions and preferences of local residents as expressed through the neighborhood organizations; support of the city's ethnic and racial diversity as an asset; and a willingness to create innovative working institutions as necessary to carry out final plans.

The focus of this case study is on the evolution of a unique pattern of working relationships between the city's public agencies and the private business community. Neither sector is homogeneous, and both are subject to mutiny within the ranks from time to time. But these facts have given color and personality to Baltimore's renaissance.

Baltimore Today

After spending decades in the shadow of the nation's capital, Baltimore is today coming into its own as a vibrant and revitalized port city. National publicity surrounding the Inner Harbor renovation and Harborplace has given Baltimore a clearer awareness of its own character.

Written with the research assistance of Brian Peters.

17

Baltimore, which sits close to the Mason-Dixon Line, is a blend of southern charm and northern industry. The economy of the metropolitan area is well diversified, with employment about evenly spread over the manufacturing, service, and government sectors. Very few large firms are headquartered in Baltimore, but the city is a regional- or branch-office location for major manufacturing enterprises. Companies in the area include the Bethlehem Steel shipbuilding yards, a General Motors assembly plant, the Noxell Corporation, Bausch and Lomb, Westinghouse, Black and Decker, and other nationally oriented firms, many of which produce for both national and export markets. The major retail department stores—Hechts, Hutzlers, Stewarts, and Hochschild-Kohn—serve both the Baltimore and the Washington markets.

Like most older industrial cities, Baltimore has experienced a decline in population and a decentralization of traditional manufacturing employment opportunities over the past decades, with service- and public-sector employment growing in importance.

Baltimore's distinct neighborhoods give local flavor and organization to a complex social and physical environment. Much housing redevelopment has occurred over the last ten years in areas ranging from elegant Bolton Hill to more modest working-class neighborhoods in South Baltimore. More than a hundred active neighborhood associations work to improve living conditions through self-help programs, political lobbying, and other efforts. Perhaps the best known is the Baltimore City Fair, which is held annually in the Inner Harbor. This event features food booths and neighborhood displays and draws millions of visitors to the downtown area.

As Baltimore experiences the broad ebb and flow of social and economic forces that continuously change its economic base, its daily working and living patterns become more intertwined with those of its surrounding suburbs. This growing interdependence of city and suburbs requires new ways of working cooperatively. Furthermore, the growth of Washington, D.C., only thirty-five miles to the south, exerts a constant pull on the people and resources of Baltimore. Cross-commuting between the two cities is becoming more common as the region's labor force responds to differences in housing costs, job opportunities, and ambience. In these ever-changing circumstances, Baltimore's public and private entrepreneurs form partnerships to plan for, and invest in, development. These joint ventures are investments not just in the future of the city but in the future of the entire metropolitan area.

Contrasts in Public and Private Leadership

Leadership—the willingness to step in and take responsibility for solving a problem or overcoming an obstacle—is much touted as the key to

success in both the public and the private sectors. Yet relatively little is
known about this capacity. Is it an innate and personal skill? Or can it
be learned through observation and experience? It is known what leadership looks like in private business and the different forms it takes among
public leaders. But little is known about the particular skills required for
successful joint ventures between the two sectors and even less about
how this leadership is developed and cultivated.

The literature of business management and of public administration
brims with advice on how to analyze problems, package financial or other
deals, make incisive decisions, and manage activities to achieve a specific
end. But as Michael Blumenthal, former secretary of the treasury and
past president of Bendix Corporation, has noted, there are significant
differences.

> A government bureaucracy, in terms of structure, is the opposite in
> many ways from a private bureaucracy. A government bureaucracy, in
> terms of work load, is an inverted pyramid . . .; the people at the top
> do most of the work and have most of the pressure and cannot delegate.
> In business, you work hard at the top, but you can delegate . . .; the
> tests of efficiency and cost effectiveness, which are the basic standards
> of business, are in government not the only—and frequently not even
> major—criteria. In business, the directors and the shareholders essen-
> tially have a common interest . . .; the Congress's [or city council's]
> interests are much more diverse. Business is simple to succeed in if you
> follow a few simple rules. Government is harder . . .: the principles
> of the top manager are the same, but they do not lead to success in
> government as surely as they do in business. . . . To move within the
> process and still come out with the right decision is the essential dif-
> ference between what you do as a senior executive in the government
> and what you do in business.[1]

Indeed, in some instances it appears that the skills that make for
successful leadership in one sector are sure to produce disaster in the
other. Successful private business leadership is measured on the bottom
line, by profit (or market share). Decisions on how to get there are made
in private, away from the watchful eye of the news media, and various
corrections and changes of tack can be made along the way as long as
the desired result is achieved. The successful businessman is one who
delivers the product. But public leadership's bottom line is much less
distinct, and the accounts are balanced only every four years at the polls.
In the interim, political leaders must balance competing demands and
interests of many constituents, project a vision of accomplishment, and
make most of their decisions in the glare of daily news reporting. Changes
of mind or approach are viewed as indecisiveness or political double-
dealing, even though such corrections, of course, are often called for.
In a very real sense, for public leaders, the process counts as much as
or more than the outcome.

Business leaders are also accustomed to choosing their markets, the arena in which they will perform, carefully. They do not have to satisfy all comers who feel that they have paid in advance for services they now demand. Businessmen can often identify a task that is achievable and then concentrate their resources on producing that result. In contrast, the politician faces a broad array of tasks specified by others that are, almost by definition, impossible to achieve. He or she must then try to show a little progress on every front but can seldom achieve definitive success. Statutes and directives from the courts and higher levels of government often charge local political leadership with "ensuring equal opportunity," "eliminating racial discrimination," or "guaranteeing decent, safe, and sanitary housing for every American"—sweeping objectives that in practice can be tackled only in stages.

These differences in the way public and private leaders go about their business, the constituencies they must satisfy, the publicness of their decision-making processes, and the flexibility they have to correct their course of action along the way would seem to make them strange bedfellows indeed in the business of joint ventures. How they met in Baltimore, recognized a common interest, and managed to sustain it to a successful outcome is the subject of this case study.

Organizations: Incubators for Civic Entrepreneurs

Citizens Planning and Housing Association

In Baltimore many of the leaders responsible for successful joint ventures can trace their interest in, and first-hand knowledge of, urban problems back to membership in a single nonprofit organization, the Citizens Planning and Housing Association (CPHA). Like much of the early interest in housing and neighborhood problems, CPHA's roots lie in the concern with urban social conditions that were documented in the diaries and reports of social workers of the period.

CPHA's constitution states the organization's purpose:

> To foster good city planning, to provide better land use, to improve housing and living conditions, and to correct urban decay in the Baltimore metropolitan area by means of research, education, public discussion, legislation, law enforcement and other methods.

From the beginning, CPHA viewed itself as a group of concerned citizens intent on improving the quality of residential neighborhoods through the use of donated time and talents. In the beginning, the organization had no staff, no budget, and no membership requirements beyond an active interest in civic affairs. Individuals participated as individuals, not as representatives of other institutions or organizations. Among them were people who happened to hold public positions and people from the corporate world.

CPHA has pursued its goals by consciously encouraging citizen participation in a wide variety of civic matters and by grooming individuals for membership on boards, commissions, and public bodies concerned with planning and revitalization issues. Over the years the organization's somewhat narrow original focus on housing and traditional land-use-planning issues has been broadened to include transportation planning, air pollution, the support of a regional planning council, promotion of a city fair as a vehicle for strengthening neighborhood organizations, and more recently, mortgage monitoring to stop redlining, studies of displacement and gentrification, and efforts to find an alternative to rent control.

The impact of CPHA activities has been felt throughout the city in two major ways: through a long series of institutional innovations and changes stimulated by CPHA activities and through the creation over time of a widespread network of individuals with common roots in CPHA and its concerns.

Institutional Innovation and Legislative Change

Early in the century, concerns with the social and health conditions in the city's slums and the publicity these received in the local newspapers led to the establishment of the Ordinance on the Hygiene of Housing. In 1937 the Citizens Housing Council, a voluntary organization, was created to monitor the application and enforcement of the ordinance by Baltimore's Department of Health. It rapidly became apparent, however, that the detailed enforcement of minimum standards of housing, safety, and sanitation was a more complicated task than the Department of Health was able or willing to undertake. Furthermore, it was recognized that many of the problems the Citizens Housing Council hoped to address extended far beyond structural conditions in the housing stock itself to broader issues of neighborhood conditions, population density, and public infrastructure and that these issues required an active planning approach rather than reactive enforcement.

In 1941 the Citizens Housing Council merged with a larger group of professional architects, planners, and university professors to form the CPHA. Immediately, CPHA began to press for a more effective means of dealing with housing code violations. These efforts led to the establishment in 1947 of a special housing court. This was the first court of its kind in the nation and represented an important institutional innovation that was subsequently adopted in many other cities. One year later, in response to CPHA reports and recommendations, the Department of Planning was established as a regular line agency of city government. It was charged with mapping out a strategy for stemming neighborhood blight through preparation of a master land-use plan and provided, for the first time, an official mechanism for directing public attention to the longer-term problems of housing and neighborhoods. Having made a commitment to institutional responsibility for these matters, city government could not be held responsible for taking action or accountable for the results. Moreover, official interest in these issues no longer depended on catching the attention of particular individuals in an administration but was recognized as a continuing responsibility of city government.

CPHA's activity did not stop with these changes in the formal instruments of government. Believing that coping with neighborhood blight required from-the-bottom-up action, CPHA assisted in the organization of some 150 voluntary neighborhood-improvement associations throughout the city. At first, these groups served as the focus of local self-help, clean-up, and fix-up efforts; but gradually, they evolved into powerful and effective advocacy organizations dealing with city government. A recent study of Baltimore neighborhoods identified 104 active neighborhood associations, many of which lobby city agencies for public services and improvements they think essential to revitalizing and maintaining their areas.[2] Some of the larger and more active groups receive grants and enter into cooperative service-delivery arrangements with local and federal agencies. In 1968 the city officially encouraged this cooperative process by agreeing to pay the salaries of six full-time district planners assigned to work directly with the major associations as their intermediaries in dealing with the city's agencies.

Despite these efforts, revitalization efforts began to lose ground in the 1950s, neighborhoods continued to decline, and the exodus of the white middle class to the suburbs began in earnest. Aided by the large federal interstate-highway and single-family-home mortgage-insurance programs, this trend accelerated. The problems of wartime overcrowding and housing shortages gave way to those of abandonment and decay. In response, Baltimore embraced the federal Urban Renewal Program, which provided funds on a scale large enough to finally tackle blight in a serious way and began large-scale clearance and redevelopment programs.

The Redevelopment Commission was formed to carry out these programs in an integrated way. It had the authority to coordinate the activities of the city Housing Authority, the Housing Bureau of the city Department of Health, the Bureau of Sanitation, the police, the fire department, and building inspectors in the renewal neighborhoods. This represented the first real opportunity for the city to confront its slum problems in a carefully coordinated way and with enough money to begin to make noticeable changes. Although there were no private-sector representatives on the commission, the neighborhood organizations that CPHA had helped to create were active participants in the process. By 1956, however, there were public charges of corruption and inaction in the Housing Authority, and it was decided to strengthen the city's capacity by formally merging the Housing Authority with the Redevelopment Commission to form the Baltimore Urban Redevelopment and Housing Agency (BURHA), a volunteer group chaired by Walter Sondheim, Jr. [The idea for a merged and strengthened agency was put forward by the Greater Baltimore Committee in one of its earliest public reports, *Baltimore's Stake in Urban Renewal* (1952), which gave as its purposes: "To reorganize the City Planning Commission and the Department of Planning to make them an integral part of the Mayor's administrative machinery; to speed up the preparation of a comprehensive general plan, to prepare a 20-year development program, to prepare a 4-year capital improvement program, and to concentrate urban renewal planning on a city-wide basis."] And in 1968, with the active support of CPHA, BURHA was merged with the City Bureau of Building Inspection (then part of the Department of Public Works) to form the present Department of Housing and Community Development (HCD).

This consolidation of all the city's physical-development powers in a single department was a bold step, designed to facilitate efficient decision making and timely action on projects. HCD was an extremely powerful agency with control over most of the physical-development and redevelopment activities of the city. Its first commissioner (an appointive post) was Robert C. Embry, Jr., an early and active member of CPHA. Embry held the position for nine years before moving to the Department of Housing and Urban Development (HUD) in 1977 as assistant secretary for community planning and development. His deputy commissioner and successor at HCD, M. Jay Brodie, was also drawn from the ranks of active CPHA members. During HCD's formative years, a third CPHA member, William Donald Schaefer, was serving as president of the City Council; when he became mayor in 1972, the political strength of the mayor's office was added to the administrative strength of HCD to form a powerful and aggressive coalition for revitalization. These individuals knew each other and shared a common philosophy about housing and neighborhood problems that had been formed before they held public office. In addition, both Embry and Schaefer have served long terms in public offce, providing a stability in public goals, philosophy, and personalites that more nearly matches that of their corporate counterparts. This stability and unity of purpose within the public sector has undoubtedly been a key factor in the successful pursuit, with substantial private-sector participation, of long-range development goals.

Clearly, the continuing forum provided by CHPA for the practical examination of specific city problems has produced many alumni who are now in prominent positions in both the public and the private sectors. In a very real sense, CPHA has been an incubator of entrepreneurial talent uniquely suited to join public-private endeavors.

Creating a Network of Civic Entrepreneurs

This network of long-term association has added strength and stability to the pool of potential cooperating partners in Baltimore. The magnitude of this contribution is best illustrated by a roll call of CPHA alumni.

Those in the public sector serving in positions directly or indirectly concerned with urban-revitalization programs include: Mayor (and former Councilman) William Donald Schaefer; M. Jay Brodie, the current city housing commissioner; Robert Embry, the original commissioner of HCD in Baltimore, later assistant secretary for community planning and development at HUD; Walter Orlinsky, president of the Baltimore City Council; Paul S. Sarbanes, U.S. senator from Maryland; Elsbeth L. Bothe, judge of the criminal court; Clarence Burns, Maryland state delegate; and George Piendak, Baltimore's director of finance.

Among the most distinguished members in the private business community are William Boucher III, the executive director of the Greater Baltimore Committee; Walter Sondheim, Jr., chairman of the Charles Center/Inner Harbor Management Corporation; Martin Millspaugh, president and chief executive of the Charles Center/Inner Harbor Management Corporation; Hope Quackenbush, director of the Morris Mechanic Theatre Corporation; James Rouse, chairman of the board of the Rouse Company, the developer of Columbia, Maryland, the Quincy Market in Boston, and Harborplace in Baltimore. (Both Millspaugh and Quackenbush head organizations that depend heavily on city funds and that might therefore be classified as quasi-public institutions.)

The current members of the CPHA board of governors include individuals associated with the Baltimore Department of Planning, the Baltimore Convention Center, the National Council for Urban Economic Development, the Baltimore Health Department, HCD, the Multi-Family Housing Service, the U.S. Social Security Administration, the Baltimore City Department of Human Resources, the U.S. Department of Justice, the Regional Planning Council, and the Maryland Service Corporation. Board members in private-sector positions are associated with Chase, Fitzgerald and Company (real-estate agents), Baker Watts and Company (stockbrokers), McCormick and Company, the Greater Baltimore Committee, the Rouse Company, Baltimore Federal Savings and Loan, Bache and Company (brokers), Associated Jewish Charities, Oella Company (real estate), Semmes, Bowen and Semmes (attorneys), and Gordon, Feinblatt, Rothman, Hoffberger, and Hollander (attorneys).

The honorary board members include the mayor of Baltimore, a district court judge, a U.S. senator, two members of the current City Council, two delegates to the Maryland State Legislature, the executive director of the Greater Baltimore Committee, the assistant secretary for community planning and development at HUD, the director of the Morris Mechanic Theatre, the chairman of Charles Center/Inner Harbor Management Corporation, and a number of architects, lawyers, and professional planners.

These individuals serve as individuals, not as organizational representatives. Neverthelss, they constitute a network of professional information and contacts that reaches wide and deep. It is difficult, of course, to analyze the precise effect of such a network on any given project. But it is abundantly clear that these aware and experienced individuals constitute a pool of talent, knowledgeable about the city's needs, and that they are able to rely on each other in joint efforts.

Structure

CPHA currently has about 1,800 individual members, 200 business memberships, and 150 neighborhood-association affiliates. Roughly one-third of its individual members live outside the city, primarily in Baltimore County. Although its origin and main focus are on the city, CPHA has from the start taken a metropolitan view of planning and housing problems and has reached out to residents from the surrounding urban counties in both its educational and its action programs.

In its earlier years, CPHA had no formal budget and operated entirely on voluntary contributions of time and resources raised for specific studies or programs. More recently modest membership fees and corporate contributions have supplied a small core budget sufficient for leasing office space and defraying the cost of an executive director. In 1980 membership fees provided 60 percent of the organization's budget of $150,000; the remaining 40 percent came from the United Way, which CPHA joined in 1974. As a United Way agency, it is prohibited from the unrestricted and direct solicitation of businesses for project funds. Some members fear that although this new arrangement adds to the stability of the budget, that stability may come at the expense of breaking the direct link between

CPHA and those individuals and businesses that in the past have felt a special responsibility for the organization's success.

Most of the work of CPHA is done through a series of committees formed to address single policy issues. In the past, there have been working committees on public housing, rent control, open housing, master plan, zoning, and transportation. Current committees include the following:

City Center. Concerned with plans to renovate the old Lexington Market area for retail uses. A subcommittee is studying proposals for the use of Rash Field, one of the last open spaces on the Inner Harbor.

Self-Help. Produces a handbook describing successful neighborhood self-help projects and providing technical assistance from local individuals.

Committee for a Livelier Baltimore. Supports the Baltimore City Fair and sponsors *Bawlamer,* an informal guide to Baltimore's neighborhoods.

Housing. Concerned with the local pressure for a city rent-control law. Attempts to find alternatives for addressing the problems of low-income renters. A subcommittee is examining the issue of displacement in areas that are being revitalized and the problems of building abandonment, code enforcement, and rising fuel costs.

Metropolitanism. Engaged in evaluating tax-base-sharing proposals for the Baltimore metropolitan region and in examining the financing and use of the city's major cultural institutions.

There are also more specialized committees on zoning, membership, and special events.

The single-issue committee structure has proven to be an extraordinarily pragmatic and flexible tool. It provides opportunities for individuals to work together on problems on which they basically agree without requiring them to subscribe to a whole range of policies advocated by an organization. It fosters a common understanding of a number of the city's problems and a realization that solutions must be politically as well as economically acceptable.

In the early 1950s a number of businessmen active in CPHA became interested in what business leaders in other cities were doing to address urban decay. A committee of top businessmen was appointed to explore ways in which the business community could contribute to revitalization efforts in Baltimore. The group made a visit to Pittsburgh to examine the renewal program sponsored by the Allegheny Conference, a program wholly funded with private monies. The Baltimore group sponsored a public forum on the topic.

With the Pittsburgh model in mind, the CPHA businessmen's committee recommended the establishment of the Greater Baltimore Council, consisting of the chief executive officers of the one hundred largest corporations in the metropolitan area. Direct, high-level participation was required so that members would have the power to commit time and resources to projects without first having to engage in lengthy negotiations.

Conclusions

CPHA has served, however unwittingly, as a powerful and effective training ground for civic entrepreneurs and as an important catalyst in achieving institutional innovation in public agencies and citizen organizations. Its chief tools have been:

> An expert knowledge of city and state agencies and key personnel

> An early and close alliance with the neighborhood organizations, which have grown in strength and political sophistication over the years

> A pragmatic, activist approach to identifying and solving specific problems

> An early commitment to biracial cooperation and programs of special concern to minorities, especially open housing and school desegregation

CPHA's active support for the creation of a single, integrated developed agency, HCD, and the impetus it provided to the establishment of a Greater Baltimore Committee helped set the stage for genuine public-private partnerships in the 1970s. The creation of the Greater Baltimore Committee, in particular, enlarged the vision of what needed to be done beyond housing concerns to encompass strategies for commercial and economic revitalization.

Greater Baltimore Committee

The Greater Baltimore Committee (GBC) has been the vehicle for mobilizing business intiative in support of downtown renewal efforts. The

idea for the committee was generated by a CPHA-sponsored public forum
on the role that business might play in urban renewal. Additional impetus
was provided by a report of the Commission on Governmental Efficiency
and Economy (1954), which documented the decline in the city's property-tax base and predicted disaster within the decade unless something
were done to reverse current trends.

> Many worthy projects were failing, they concluded, not because op-
> position was very strong, but because general support was woefully
> weak. Special interests had stronger voices than the majority who stood
> to benefit. Thanks to these obstructionist factions, plans met with in-
> difference and then with failure. And influential civic leaders who cared
> about improvement were too few to break the stalemate.
>
> The business community was failing to provide the essential impetus
> for change. Instead of adding its weight to new proposals vital to the
> welfare of the community, it refused to look beyond its own limited,
> immediate concerns.[3]

The formation of a committee composed of members representing
the area's major businesses and corporations was pressed by James and
Willard Rouse, Robert Levi, Louis Kohn II, Guy Hooyday, and Hunter
Moss and supported by the chief executive officers of several established
corporations, including A.S. Abell Company, Alex Brown and Sons, and
National Brewing Company. In general, however, the initial reactions
of the corporate leadership in Baltimore were hostile or indifferent. According to Clarence Miles:

> Reactions ranged from disinterest to outright opposition. Some ex-
> pressed concern that the proposed organization would duplicate the
> Association of Commerce [later the Chamber of Commerce], a reaction
> that the group began to consider a standard dismissal. Jim Rouse re-
> members calling on Ted Wolfe, the Chairman of the Baltimore Gas and
> Electric Company and one of the City's outstanding citizens. His re-
> sponse was: "Baltimore is not in bad enough shape yet to support that
> kind of organization." The local press also greeted the rumors of the
> new group with skepticism.[4]

In desperation, the organizers turned to Miles to help generate broader
support from the corporate community. Miles was a lawyer who had won
recent notoriety by successfully negotiating the deal to bring the Saint
Louis Browns to Baltimore's new stadium as the Baltimore Orioles "to
put Baltimore back in the big leagues." He was widely perceived as a
proven winner, someone with shrewd bargaining skills and the best interests of the city at heart. At a meeting with twenty-five key business
leaders called by Miles, James Rouse explained the need for decisive

action by the business community to support the city's renewal efforts and won agreement to form an organization capable of mobilizing such private initiative. Two months later, in January 1955, the first meeting of the CBS was held, with fifty-seven members in attendance.

Structure

The new organization was designed as an élite group consisting of the chief executive officers of the one hundred largest corporations in the Baltimore metropolitan area, who could speak for their firms and make on-the-spot commitments to action. GBC would support individual civic improvement projects approved by a majority of the members.

No specific statement of philosophy was issued, but a pragmatic purpose was stated: to function as "a citizen arm of the government . . . it could provide the necessary business and financial expertise to help implement city projects; it could provide accurate and complete information on their necessity through surveys and studies and overcome opposition; finally, it would exert whatever possible pressure on the government to get approval for necessary improvements.[5] "Our watchword should be *action now*. . . . We must not be content with postponing or leaving undone, by ourselves or by others, anything possible of accomplishment. We want sound planning, but we want action to implement the plans, and we want it now, not at some future time when we may not be around to see it."[6]

The newly formed committee quickly settled on a priority agenda of projects that included the Jones Falls Expressway, transportation planning, port development, and the Civic Center. Lower priority was given to issues of waterfront redevelopment, pollution, and slum clearance.

William Boucher III was appointed executive director, and the committee adopted the CPHA system of working through a network of subcommittees directed to study and make recommendations for action on specific projects. (Archibald Rogers served one year as temporary executive director and was charged with recruiting his successor. There was some initial opposition to the appointment of Boucher on the grounds that he was too liberal politically and was a resident of Baltimore County rather than the city. But it was decided at the start that managerial skills, not politics or residence, should determine the selection, and Boucher was appointed. He served in that position continuously from 1955 to 1981, a period spanning the administrations of six mayors.) James Rouse chaired the Urban Renewal Subcommittee, through which GBC's initial support for the Charles Center and Inner Harbor projects was orchestrated.

GBC had an immediate impact on the development of a privately financed master plan for downtown renewal. Both GBC and its sister organizaton, the Committee for Downtown, firmly believed that private expertise was essential to producing a realistic plan that could be implemented with private support. When the time came to implement the plan, GBC recognized the necessity of focusing on a smaller project, Charles Center, for which private investment and support could be raised quickly. GBC's follow-through on the Charles Center project was an unqualified success, with the city and press giving the organization full credit for its crucial role.

The GBC role in subsequent projects of the Inner Harbor plan was more subdued and behind the scenes. Because many of those development projects were publicly financed, GBC's role increasingly became one of review and communication of the planned development to the private business community.

Tensions developed between the city and GBC over the alleged failure of the committee to deal adequately with the old problems of downtown retail revitalization. Many downtown merchants feared that new retail development in the Inner Harbor would have the effect of shifting the main retail center from its established north-south axis along Howard Street to an east-west axis along Pratt Street, several blocks away. Some of the smaller merchants resented the "grandiose" GBC plans, which they feared could not be implemented without disturbing their businesses. The city argued that it fully intended to revitalize the Howard Street area but could get neither agreement on the physical plans nor commitment from the major retailers to stay in the area if it were redeveloped. (Indeed, during this period, two major department stores, Stewarts and Hochschild-Kohn, announced that they would close their Howard Street premises.)

In an effort to move forward on a retail plan, a steering committee was set up. It was chaired by Robert Embry and jointly financed by the city and GBC. Planning reports from three separate consultants produced conflicting advice, with one being highly pessimistic about prospects for downtown retail revival. As a consequence, a full plan for the area was never developed. The City Council, when asked to address the question, insisted that a developer be found first and that a plan be negotiated with him. GBC wanted a plan before an attempt was made to recruit a developer. The mayor also complained that GBC appeared unable to produce a developer for the project, a task with which it had assisted so successfully in Charles Center. Finally, in 1980, a developer was found, and the project is now under way.

It appears that a division of purpose within GBC itself served to weaken its impact on later downtown development planning. Some members continued to believe that solving the Howard Street problem should be given first priority; others paid more attention to efforts to keep the Orioles in Baltimore, attempting to raise private funds to buy out the franchise and pressuring the city and state to invest in a new stadium to be located on the south side of the Inner Harbor. Gradually, the initial concern of the GBC—the financial decline of the city and its tax base— faded into the background as attention focused on particular projects. (There has been some recent discussion of reviving the old Efficiency and Economy Commission as a vehicle through which the business community could monitor the city's fiscal condition and advocate responsible positions on tax and spending legislation affecting the city. But to date, this step has not been proposed by GBC.)

Change and an Uncertain Future

In 1979 GBC underwent a major structural change as a result of its merger with the Metropolitan Chamber of Commerce. Whereas it began as an elite group of top corporate executives, socially and professionally well known to each other, GBC now has 1,200 members from small- and medium-sized firms. Many of these members do not know each other and are not well known by the GBC working staff. Their concerns are often quite different from those traditionally espoused by the committee. They tend to be more interested in matters affecting the climate in which small business operates and see their interests as regional, rather than city oriented. They also represent a younger group, on average, than the original GBC membership. (GBC has enjoyed great stability in its membership, with an estimated 30 percent of its original one hundred members still active after twenty-five years. This has the strength of long-term personal and working relationships, but it also has the weakness of insularity from new ideas and fresh personalities.)

This change in structure is a major challenge to GBC. Will it be able to evolve into an effective instrument for the mobilization of a broader spectrum of business support in civic affairs, or will it waiver in purpose and fade? There is at present no other organization in Baltimore capable of stepping into the role played by the GBC as a conduit for private-sector action on public projects. If the transition cannot be made, the city will lose a major partner in the redevelopment process.

One step in the direction of successful adaptation was taken by the establishment, in 1979, of the Economic Development Council (EDC), an autonomous organization within GBC charged with advancing a private business economic-development agenda for the city and the metropolitan area. The council operates within the general framework of GBC, but it has its own budget and board of directors. EDC efforts to date have focused primarily on marketing and on integrating the marketing efforts of the several jurisdictions in the Baltimore metropolitan area. Attention has also been given to coordinating local strategies with the state's marketing efforts at home and abroad.

Projects

Charles Center/Inner Harbor

The Charles Center and Inner Harbor development programs are the earliest and largest efforts at downtown revitalization in Baltimore. Each is really made up of many projects that are part of an overall plan for center-city redevelopment adopted in 1959.

Charles Center consists of a unified complex of office buildings, apartments, hotels, and a theater connected by pedestrian plazas, walkways, and retail shops and served by several underground parking garages. Altogether, the thirty-three-acre area, located in the center of the commercial district, comprises 2 million square feet of office space, seven-hundred apartment units, and seven-hundred hotel rooms.

The Inner Harbor project covers a much larger area, extending west and south around the harbor and north and east to include the city hall area. Whereas Charles Center is organized around three self-contained plazas, Inner Harbor encompasses the waterfront and the neighborhoods that surround it (Federal Hill, Otterbein, and so on). The Inner Harbor plan includes development immediately surrounding the harbor (Harborplace, the Convention Center, the Maryland Science Museum, the National Aquarium, the World Trade Center), a campus of the Baltimore Community College, parking facilities, and high-rise housing a block or two from the waterfront. Commercial facilities include the U.S. Fidelity and Guarantee Building, offices of IBM Corporation, and a Hyatt hotel. The plan also involves substantial areas of rehabilitated housing in adjacent neighborhoods.

These two projects provide fascinating insights into the shifts in focus and funding between the cooperating public and private sectors over a period of more than twenty years. Charles Center was undertaken on private initiative, and the individual buildings were built largely with private capital (except for the Federal Building, which was constructed with federal funds). The individual projects represented relatively low-risk commercial investments that required planning and coordination but no special subsidies for financial success. The Inner Harbor program has been chiefly an initiative of the public sector, requiring considerable federal- and local-government financing. Its scale is much larger, and the kinds of individual projects involved, many of them public nonprofit properties, entail much higher-risk investment that often requires special tax breaks and subsidies. These subsidies are justified by the projects' spillover effects: the stability they will give to real-estate values and the tax base in the area and their inducement to subsequent private investment in housing, retail facilities, and job growth. Thus the Inner Harbor program may be thought of as leveraging on a massive scale.

Although the working relations between the public and private partners have not been uniformly smooth, the principle of cooperative planning and action was established early and has perhaps made long-term development efforts successful in Baltimore in a way that has been rare in other cities.

Charles Center. Baltimore's business community was the first to call public attention to the issue of central-city decay and its impact on downtown economic activity and property values. (CPHA had earlier expressed concern with housing and neighborhood blight and the impact of slum conditions on health, crime, and social conditions, but little attention was paid to the implications for economic activity. Thus, although the concern with neighborhood blight dates back to the 1930s, the connection with economic decline was not made until the 1950s.) In the beginning, concern was strongest among the downtown retail merchants, who felt most directly the loss of the middle-income market as a result of rapid suburbanization of population. But it was not long before concern spread to the rest of the downtown business community. Traffic congestion and parking problems, insufficient public transit, and physical blight and deterioration were recognized as undermining other kinds of business activity as well.

The Master Planning Process. By 1957 alarm at the eroding business climate and declining property values was so strong that the Committee for Downtown (an offshoot of the Retail Merchants Association) and the GBC jointly raised $225,000 from their members and contracted with the Planning Council (a private nonprofit professional planning organization created by, and part of, GBC) for the development of a master plan for downtown renewal.

The plan, presented eighteen months later, traced the problems of the central business district to physical and demographic changes, including population decline, physical blight, and growing transportation inadequacies. In the best urban-renewal tradition, it called for clearing twenty-two acres in the heart of downtown and the construction of a federal office building (for which funds had already been appropriated by Congress), seven other office buildings, an eight-hundred-room hotel, a transit terminal, 400,000 square feet of commercial space, 4,000 underground-parking garage spaces, and three small parks. (The original version of the plan also supported an expressway network around the central business district that would carry traffic around the center to a connection with the Jones Falls Expressway on the southeastern edge of the city. This proposal was ultimately dropped because it became the subject of strong controversy and the committee did not want to delay progress on the other portions of the plan. As it turned out, this was a shrewd decision; the expressway controversy precipitated many vigorous battles between the city and various neighborhood groups, who were finally successful in blocking other proposals.) It was estimated at the time that the total plan would cost $127 million over ten years. Of this, $110 million (86 percent) would be privately supplied, and $17 million would come from city resources.[7] Later the estimates were revised to $180 million with $145 million from private and $35 million from public sources. It was a bold plan, and its announcement eclipsed the city's own urban-renewal scheme, which had been in process for some time.

The city's proposal had two flaws that doomed it in the contemporary political climate. First, it ignored the downtown district, focusing primarily on plans for housing rehabilitation. Clark Hobbs, chairman of the Baltimore Redevelopment Commission, referred to the downtown as "the hole in the doughnut." Louis Azrael, writing for the *News-Post* in August 1957, said that "even this ambitious program leaves downtown as a step-child, benefiting only indirectly." A reporter from Dallas noted that "so far the Mayor [D'Alesandro] has indicated that he is more interested in residential rehabilitation than in the downtown area, but businessmen are hopeful he will throw his support to the plan that evolves." Second, it proposed a controversial network of expressways and radial highways ringing the central business district and connecting the Jones Falls Expressway (newly under construction), to be supplemented by express-bus service to the center. The proposed highways would have cut through established neighborhoods and, in some later versions of the proposal, would also have chopped up the business district itself, cutting off portions of it from the harbor waterfront. Campaigns were launched by some in the affected neighborhoods who objected to both the displacement of individuals and the physical destruction of the neighborhoods. Finding no solid constituency to support its own renewal plan and faced with a competing and largely self-financing master plan for downtown redevelopment, the city joined forces with the private sector for the first time.

Certainly, the prior announcement of the GBC plan (and the activities of GBC and the Committee for Downtown) had helped to shift the spotlight from residential slum clearance to the problems of the city's commercial core. (The GBC plan noted the need for residential redevelopment in the Bolton Hill and Harlan Park neighborhoods but gave top priority to the Charles Center project.) In combination with a publicly stated commitment to implement the plan primarily with private investment funds, these initiatives put the business community up front in the renewal process. The city declared itself ready to cooperate but retained its concern with residential renewal.

Implementation. GBC now turned its attention to problems of implementation. It soon became apparent that accomplishment of this plan was going to be a slow process and that some dramatically conspicuous project was necessary to sustain public interest and attract private capital.

The Charles Center project, described in the planning documents as a "small pilot area, to be financed by private capital," was proposed for thirty-three acres at the center of the downtown-renewal area. In that area would be built private-office towers, a theater, a hotel, a retail square, and the federal building for which funds had already been approved. The total cost was estimated at $127 million, including $20 million for the federal building, $25 million from a public-bond issue for land acquisition floated by the city ($17 million of this would be recouped from subsequent resale of the land to private developers), and about $90 million in private development resources. Planners estimated that the city would lose roughly a half-million dollars in taxes on properties purchased or taken by eminent domain but would ultimately gain more than $2 million a year in new property-tax revenues when the project was complete. (This turned out to be a conservative estimate.)

The scheme was immediately hailed by Mayor D'Alesandro and Oliver Winston, director of BURHA, as "a vivid demonstration of the merging of public and private interests seeking to solve downtown renewal problems." Endorsement was equally swift from both of Maryland's U.S. senators and from the governor. However, the City Council, which had not been fully briefed on the project, adopted a wait-and-see attitude.

A GBC development committee was immediately named "to take Charles Center out of the realm of imagination and give it reality." With the exception of the mayor and Walter Sondheim, Jr., then chairman of BURHA, this committee was composed entirely of private businessmen. The members were Robert B. Hobbs, chairman of the board, First National Bank; Thomas Butler, chairman of the board, Mercantile Safe Deposit and Trust; S. Page Nelson, chairman of the board, Savings Bank of Baltimore; Charles Phillips, chairman of the board, U.S.F&G; and James Rouse, president of Rouse Company. Pending voter approval of the bond issue, Charles Center became an official project of BURHA. Responsibilities were assigned as follows: The *city* was responsible for land acquisition and site clearance. (The original Charles Center proposal stated: "The growth potential of the region cannot be tapped as a resource for downtown's revitalization without the application of the urban renewal powers of the City to create the opportunity for downtown investment.") In later stages of the plan, it was also made responsible for the construction of the parks. The *private sector* was responsible for finding developers able and willing to take on the project and for identifying possible tenants for the office building and for raising $90 million in private investment funds.

Like other early cooperative efforts, Charles Center required planning, coordination, and contributions of funds from both sectors. However, public and private funds were not mingled within any single investment. Instead, elements of the plan were apportioned out to the various parties, with each responsible for completion of his particular "building block." If a precise moment can be identified at which Baltimore committed itself to public-private efforts, it may be this first formalization of the specific responsibilities for each of the participants in the Charles Center project.

The early impetus for downtown renewal was associated primarily with the major department stores (Hutzlers, Hechts, Hochschild-Kohn, and Stewarts) and dominated, at least in the minds of outside observers, by the interests of retail businesses. However, it soon became apparent that there was no uniform set of private-sector views or commitments to Charles Center. Several local firms located in the redevelopment area were reluctant to commit themselves to the success of the project. Notable among these were the C&P Telephone Company and the Baltimore Gas and Electric Company (one of the few firms within the Charles Center site to have its building left standing by the plan). Both companies were ambivalent to the prospect of making a commitment to future investment in corporate facilities in the center. C&P would say only that the company would "consider Charles Center along with other localities when the times comes to make such a decision in the next six or seven years."

This lack of unanimity points to an important distinction masked by the expression public-private partnership. Such ventures involve two spheres of interest that are organized in very different ways. A local government can adopt and enforce, however laboriously, a common set of policies through its agencies, but a large group of unrelated business firms have different structures, serve different markets, and have no compelling method of coordinating their views or positions on any given issue. A GBC or a "committee for downtown" can attempt to provide this leadership, but it is always a fragile venture, subject to perpetual renewal.

The Charles Center ordinance was formally approved by the City

Council March 23, 1959, and J. Jefferson Miller, who headed the Committee for Downtown throughout the master-plan process, was appointed to oversee implementation of the entire project. Shortly thereafter, a national competition was held for the design and construction of a high-rise office tower to be known as One Charles Center. Among the bidders were Metropolitan Structures Corporation, with Mies van der Rohe, and a local group, the Blaustein team with Marcel Breuer. Metropolitan Structures was the winner, but the local team bought a site just across the street and announced that it would put up a *second* office tower, which was completed and came on the leasing market almost at the same time as One Charles Center. Despite competition for tenants, both buildings filled quickly and within a year paid more property taxes than the city had previously received from the entire Charles Center area. Both buildings were privately financed.

The much discussed Federal Building became entangled in bureaucratic problems. The House of Representatives, which had approved the original funding, subsequently killed a leaseback provision under which the government would have leased the structure from a private operator, and required direct purchase instead. The leaseback was considered crucial to the financial viability of the building as part of Charles Center because it would enable the city to continue to collect real-estate revenues on the property; but a federally owned building would be tax exempt. There followed prolonged negotiations with Franklin Floete, head of the Government Services Administration, who reported that he was ''in favor of putting a federal office building somewhere in Charles Center, but does not want the precise site dictated to him.'' These obstacles were eventually surmounted, and the Federal Building was completed with federal funds in 1967. By 1973, the Morris Mechanic Theater, the Baltimore Gas and Electric addition, the Hilton hotel, Mullen Towers, the center plaza, overhead pedestrian walkways, and underground parking garages had been completed. Both the Hamburgers Store and Vermont Federal Savings and Loan successfully relocated within the area, and Sun Life cancelled a previously planned move to Baltimore County opting to stay in its original location. Charles Center became Baltimore's first successful public-private renewal venture.

Inner Harbor. Whereas Charles Center's focus was on clearance and commercial redevelopment financed chiefly from private investment, the Inner Harbor program also included mixed-income housing, office buildings, cultural facilities, and waterfront recreational development. By the mid-1960s, both public attitudes and general economic conditions had changed to create a climate in which the kind of investments envisioned by the plan were riskier and required substantial preliminary public investment to attract private funding. Business leadership had carried the initiative for Charles Center, but public leadership had to assume major responsibility for the Inner Harbor effort. Charles Center had been implemented as a self-contained project with clear boundaries and good prospects for financial success. Inner Harbor was a broad effort to change the overall climate for living and working in downtown Baltimore and would be subject to the political vagaries of highway planning and to the neighborhood alarm those plans fostered.

The partnership had worked so well for Charles Center, however, that many of the same people and organizations were asked to participate in Inner Harbor. Theodore McKeldin, governor during the construction of Charles Center, was elected mayor in 1962; and in his inaugural address, he immediately committed his support to "a new inner harbor area, where the imagination of man can take advantage of a rare gift of nature. . . ." He followed up by asking GBC and the Committee for Downtown to cooperate with the city's Planning Commission in producing a general plan; this time with all three partners contributing to its financial support.

"The Inner Harbor Concept" is the title of a document, issued in September 1964, that set out a series of projects in two phases:

> The creation of a mall on which would front "a host of new city government structures." The Maryland Port Administration's World Trade Center tower was to rise from the foot of the mall on the waterfront.
>
> Construction of 3,700 dwelling units in the downtown area.
>
> Extension of Charles Center southward by constructing 600,000 square feet of new office space.
>
> Development of the west edge of the harbor to include such facilities as a marina, the Maryland Science Center, and a theater.
>
> Construction of a new campus for Baltimore Community College, new cultural facilities, and some fifty-five acres of parkland.

The total plan was expected to cost $270 million over thirty years, including $180 million in federal funds, $58 million in city resources, and $22 million in private investments. The ratio of public investment to private was thus almost exactly the reverse of the Charles Center precedent.

Response to the plan was cool from the public at large, some city councilmen, and the press. The reasons lay partly in the plan itself and partly in the process by which it had been produced. The major difficulty arose because accessibility to the Inner Harbor required rerouting traffic directly through two of the city's most historic districts, Federal Hill and Fells Point. The proposal was for the central business district to be divided into "superblocks"—for development of shopping areas, a convention center, a financial district, and so on—and encircled by an "East-West Expressway." This new expressway ring would pass south of the harbor and join the Jones Falls Expressway at the edge of Little Italy, one of Baltimore's most distinctive ethnic neighborhoods. Organizations in these (and later in other) neighborhoods joined together to mount an increasingly effective opposition to stop the expressway. Consultants were retained and alternate routes proposed, but to no avail. Opposition continued to grow. Spokesmen for GBC and the Planning Commission supported the expressway and argued that some rerouting of traffic was essential to getting the Inner Harbor projects off the ground. The City Council, beseiged by citizen resistance, opposed the highway and argued for exploring mass-transit options, including a subway, an option that David Wallace, director of the Planning Council, insisted was not feasible. Some observers even argued that the Inner Harbor should be preserved for trade and shipping and that the expressway should be routed across the northern edge of the harbor, between the city and its waterfront.

A second source of popular opposition arose in response to the proposal for a "mall of government buildings" along the waterfront. Some public officials, such as Eli Frank, Jr., president of the Board of School Commissioners, stated publicly that they did not care to move from their current locations and resented being pressured by the Inner Harbor planners to relocate there. When other city officials made it clear that proceeds from a bond issue already on the ballot for that November would be used to start construction on the municipal mall, the issue was soundly defeated. However, the voters in that same election approved funds for further planning and preliminary work on redevelopment of the Inner Harbor proper. Attention then turned to construction of the World Trade Center tower, and the mayor announced his intention to start seeking state funds for the project.

Heavier reliance on federal funding for portions of Inner Harbor required a rethinking of the housing plans for the area. Originally, the plan called for the construction of subsidized and middle-income housing as a tool to help stop "white flight" to the suburbs. William Boucher III, executive director of GBC, called the Inner Harbor "the most important project Baltimore has ever undertaken . . . because it will change the environment enough to get people living again in the center city. No longer will they have to run to the suburbs to get a decent neighborhood to live in. Making downtown compete effectively with the suburbs as a place to live can be one of the most significant things to happen in this

century in the life of a city.''[8] But federal guidelines directed that federal
dollars be used for those with the greatest housing need, mainly low-
income and minority families. In 1967, the Christ Lutheran Church,
located just west of the harbor, announced the first firm commitment to
housing in the area, a nursing home-apartment complex to be built with
a combination of private funds and federal housing subsidies (for the
apartment building). Later the city modified its housing plans to include
substantial rehabilitation of existing houses under the Homesteading Program. In addition, more emphasis was placed on visitor attractions (Harborplace, the aquarium, and the convention center) to lure middle-income
families downtown for recreational purposes. (The city did not abandon
its dream of providing middle-class housing that could compete with
suburban living opportunities. It carried this purpose over to a later project, the Coldspring new town in town and into Inner Harbor West in the
successful Otterbein homesteading and Harbor World townhouse developments.)

Implementation. The city contracted with Charles Center/Inner Harbor
Management Corporation to manage the mechanics of the development
process. J. Jefferson Miller had agreed to serve as chief executive officer
of the corporation for a token payment of $1 a year. The Charles Center/
Inner Harbor Management Corporation was established by the city as a
quasi-public organization to manage land acquisition, site preparation,
construction, and package-development deals. The principals, Martin
Millspaugh and Miller, were veterans of the earliest Charles Center planning, as well as skilled private-sector entrepreneurs. The establishment
of this nonprofit corporation is another in the long string of pragmatic
institutional innovations that contributed to Baltimore's development success. It is described by Millspaugh as follows:

> Charles Center/Inner Harbor Management provides the city with skills
> and experience needed for large commercial developments but not nor-
> mally found in the civil service ranks. It operates within a framework
> established by the mayor and the Departmentof Housing and Community
> Development; unlike a city agency which has a permanent function,
> Charles Center/Inner Harbor Management provides a specialized service
> to the city on a contractual basis. The city advances the corporation
> money on a monthly basis, through which the corporation pays its own
> expenses. The total cost to the city of the management of Charles Center
> and Inner Harbor redevelopment projects has been less than two percent
> of the total public funds involved. The city's capital investment has
> been paid out of ten local bond issues approved by voters and appro-
> priated for the realization of individual projects.[9]

Walter Sondheim, Jr., chairman of the corporation, described its
work this way:

We initiate and supervise planning activities, prepare detailed prospec-
tuses for offerings of land, oversee the process of developer selection
whether by competition or other means, and negotiate agreements with
developers, but each of these functions is subject to some form of city
approval. . . . We submit a yearly budget for our operations, but have
somewhat more freedom in the administration of those funds, once they
have been approved.[10]

The freeze on federal grants imposed during the Johnson administration delayed the receipt of federal funds until 1968. While it waited,
the city took options on the land, set up a relocation office to help
displaced businesses, and drew up plans for Inner Harbor West (forty-
four acres of high-rise offices and public housing intended to be a "showcase for new techniques in moderate income housing").

Just as federal funds were being released to the city, Robert Embry
was appointed commissioner of the newly consolidated HCD. Projects
then began to move fast. U.S.F&G and IBM announced that they intended
to construct office buildings in Inner Harbor, voters approved a $5.7-
million bond issue for the Baltimore Community College's campus, and
HUD allocated an additional $7.9 million in grants to the city. Other
developers began to inspect the area and examine investment possibilities.

At first, the public waterfront improvements (the pedestrian walkway
and clearance of pier warehouses) stood alone, testaments to the enormous
gamble the city was taking; but by the mid-1970s, there was substantial
private investment in the residential neighborhoods. Harborplace, the
Rouse marketplace development that mirrors the Quincy Market in Boston
and is the latest project to be completed, opened with national fanfare
on July 2, 1980. The available evidence to date suggests that the city's
gamble with large-scale redevelopment has indeed paid off.

Obstacles Encountered in the Charles Center/Inner Harbor Process. As
a complex set of efforts, the Charles Center/Inner Harbor projects encountered the usual share of unexpected problems, political obstacles,
and practical difficulties. Many were resolved quickly, but several posed
more persistent problems.

*Opposition to a New Network of Expressways and Radials through the
City to Relieve Traffic Congestion in the Central Business District.*
Traffic congestion and parking were identified early as key elements in
the decline of downtown retail activity. All parties agreed that a long-
term solution had to be found before solid planning for redevelopment
of the area could proceed. The enthusiasm of private investors depended
both on the future accessibility of office and retail space in the central
city and on a reasonable assurance that new buildings would not be
immediately supplanted or cut off by a new expressway loop.

Several solutions were offered that did not require elaborate express-way construction, including a proposal for express-bus service to a central terminal in Charles Center and the construction of a subway or other rapid-transit system. The proposal for express-bus service was vigorously opposed by the Baltimore Transit Company (BTC), a privately owned enterprise that believed such service would be too costly. It was backed up in this by GBC and other members of the business community who argued forcefully and publicly for $1 million in subsidies to BTC to enable it to provide better central-city service. However, the mayor's Committee on Mass Transit came to a different conclusion, issuing a report that suggested that BTC would soon go out of business in any case and recommending public ownership of an integrated transit system as the best solution. This suggestion was strongly opposed by some on the grounds that it was ''socialistic.'' (Until its assets were purchased by the Metropolitan Transit Authority in 1969, the privately held Baltimore Transit Company was responsible for bus service within the city. Although its decisions were often not in the best interests of downtown, it was kept afloat by municipal and state tax abatements and not insignificant political support from the business community.) Similarly, suggestions that rapid-transit alternatives should be seriously considered were brushed aside by officials such as Henry Barnes, the city's director of traffic, and David Wallace, then serving as director of the Planning Council, who stated flatly that ''mass rapid transit here can't work.'' (By 1975 the official view had changed, and Mayor Schaefer was arguing for the construction of a subway system, which is now underway.)

Nevertheless, vigorous neighborhood opposition was expressed to the routing of the proposed East-West Expressway, to the site of the inter-change with the Jones Falls Expressway, and later to the proposed location for a bridge across the southern tip of the harbor. This resistance was expressed both by active neighborhood organizations in the affected areas and by members of the City Council, which would have to pass an ordinance providing for the condemnation and taking of the necessary land.

Throughout the controversy, the business community, speaking through the Committee for Downtown and GBC, supported the express-way plan as necessary to the long-term development of the area. Similar arguments were made by Philip Darling, director of the city Department of Planning.

As neighborhood resistance grew more organized and more effective, additional studies were commissioned to find more acceptable alternative routes. But because the neighborhood organizations had not been included in the original planning or offered any part in the largely private-sector-generated Charles Center plan, they felt no special commitment to finding a mutually satisfactory solution. Instead, the expressway proposals were seen by many as a callous effort on the part of the downtown business community to improve economic conditions for itself without regard for the damage its methods might wreak on residential communities.

Clark Hobbs, then chairman of the Baltimore Redevelopment Commission, writing in *Baltimore Magazine,* said:

> The stability of business and maintenance of property values in downtown Baltimore are threatened no less than were business and property values in downtown Pittsburgh. Vide—Public transportation had deteriorated and solution of the problem is left to the Transit Company unassisted by interest dependent upon the preservation of downtown business. . . . Be it said for the municipal government that there is no lack of awareness on its part of the menace to our inner city. It is far ahead of the citizenry in recognition of the dangers that beset us and the need for doing something to remove their threat. . . . The private citizens who ought to be supporting programs that would be beneficial to the community as a whole sit back on their haunches blandly unconcerned and leave their public servants to face, unsupported, the abusive denunciations of yapping obstructionists.[11]

Although a supporter of the plan for a system of radial highways, Henry Barnes, the director of traffic, succinctly expressed the underlying view of the opposition:

> The retail business of downtown can be saved if the merchants will stop spending their millions of dollars in the outlying areas and use that same money toward providing for the comfort and convenience of those customers who prefer . . . the downtown district.

Ultimately the neighborhood efforts proved sufficiently strong and well managed politically to defeat each of the proposed expressway routings; even the Jones Falls Expressway has not been completed. This may well be a blessing in disguise for Baltimore, for its downtown redevelopment has been able to go forward, and some of its most historic neighborhoods and residential areas have escaped the fate of extinction suffered in so many other cities. These neighborhoods have become a major asset in the 1980s.

If there were a lesson in this experience for both the business community and the city officials, it was that future planning must find some way to take into account the interests of the neighborhood organizations and concerns for residential redevelopment. What began with a narrow concern for eliminating blight and improving property values in the commercial center was widened to accommodate the interests of the community as a whole.

Dispute over Whether Redevelopment Projects Should Be Located in Cleared Urban-Renewal Sites in the Inner City or on Vacant Sites Elsewhere. A corollary issue was the proper size for the renewal area. Should it be limited to the few blocks composing the central business district? Or should it be extended to include an area nearly twice that size, reaching around the western and southern shores of the harbor and northward to City Hall.

In the early 1950s, a debate arose over the proper location for the proposed Civic Center. Mayor D'Alesandro, seeking a site that would permit quick construction with a minimum of hassle, opted for a location in Druid Hill Park, a city-owned public park. However, GBC, CPHA, and the Association of Commerce argued that the Civic Center and other projects should be used to help achieve long-term redevelopment goals and therefore should be sited on cleared land in the Inner Harbor, even if this might mean some administrative delays. The dispute was finally settled by litigation, and the Civic Center went up on cleared land in the redevelopment district, thus setting an important precedent for future projects.

Major D'Alesandro rebounded with a proposal that the entire central business district be declared an urban-renewal district. This step gave the city powers of condemnation and made it eligible for federal funds, thereby guaranteeing that future development efforts would be on a scale large enough to have a significant impact. The combination of these two outcomes—establishing the principle that civic projects should advance the general development scheme and broadening the urban-renewal area—provided an important boost to future success.

Resistance of Smaller Businesses to Being Displaced from the Central Business-District Renewal Area. The master plan for development of Charles Center candidly identified 371 establishments that would be displaced and specified that they would be compensated for the appraised value of their physical assets but not for the goodwill or other intangible assets that are often especially important to small firms. The plan noted that

> [for] the small firm whose business has been declining and for whom relocation may mean extinction . . . , there is perhaps no real solution, but the agency will give them fair and sympathetic understanding and treatment, within the limits of available resources and the time schedule that is adopted.

(An inventory of available space within the city was assembled and made available to relocating firms.)

A parallel problem arose when, in response to the Inner Harbor plan, the Merchandise Association stated that unless the city was able to relocate them together in the central area, "the entire wholesale market is doomed." Some efforts were made to arrange relocation aid to defray the costs of moving to a new location and to encourage wholesalers to move to the new state-owned market house in Jessup, ten miles away.

Recent research on the importance of small business suggests that, especially in central cities, firms with fewer than twenty employees may account for as much as 80 percent of all new employment generated in these areas. In recognition of this fact, more recent redevelopment plans have included specific attempts to recreate small local retailing opportunities through the city's "shopsteading" program, and more attention is finally being paid, through the Baltimore Economic Development Corporation, to business-retention strategies. (Some have expressed concern that the current subway construction in the business center may touch off another wave of small-business displacements.)

Citizen Opposition to the Proposed Siting of Harborplace on One of the Last Open Spaces Fronting the Harbor. By the time the Harborplace markethouse project was announced, Baltimoreans had become accustomed to seeing the empty spaces in the Inner Harbor fill up with office towers, the World Trade Center, a convention center, and the Maryland Science Center. They had developed strong habits of using the remaining open space on the north and west sides of the harbor for personal as well as civic events. The most conspicuous of these is the Baltimore City Fair, a well-established tradition that brings millions of people downtown to the Inner Harbor each fall.

When it was announced that part of the Harborplace Market would be located on one of the waterfront's last open spaces, objections were heard from many quarters. The restaurant owners of Little Italy, only a few blocks away, mounted additional opposition, fearing that the Harborplace restaurants and concessions would destroy their business. The debate was finally brought to a head in a referendum vote, and Harborplace was overwhelmingly approved. (A side result of the referendum was to reserve Rash Field and the other remaining open spaces for recreational uses.)

The draw the Harborplace Market now provides for tourists and residents alike has certainly increased the number of people who come downtown, although it is still too early to assess the net impact of Harborplace competition on other businesses. But there is no doubt that the issues raised in 1979 concerning the value of open space versus the economic payoffs from further retail development would surely have amazed the original planners fifteen years earlier.

Some Changes in the Partnership Approach. Because the Charles Center and Inner Harbor projects have been such complex undertakings, they illustrate an interesting evolution in partnership arrangements.

Charles Center was spurred largely by private initiative and depended primarily on private investment; it entailed relatively low-risk projects that required no special subsidies or tax breaks.

Inner Harbor was initiated jointly, but with the city taking the lead and with a more nearly equal contribution of public and private funds. The scale and types of projects constituted a high-risk strategy for inducing long-term private investment, and many components required special tax breaks or subsidies.

In Charles Center, public and private funds were kept separate in distinct projects; the financial deals were relatively simple. The federal funds came from one-time, project-specific grants.

In Inner Harbor, public and private funds are mingled in the same projects (as, for example, with Urban Development Action Grant funds), and the financial deals are far more complex. Federal funds come largely from continuing entitlement programs such as Community Development Block Grants.

Charles Center was justified by both the public and the private sectors chiefly on the grounds of the improvement it would make in property values and tax base.

Inner Harbor projects are justified not only by tax-base additions but also by the employment and minority opportunities that they create. Quality-of-life improvements are also given more weight.

The Charles Center plan was assembled and implemented with virtually no grassroots citizen participation. It was produced and managed as a professional exercise and announced to the public largely as a set of faits accomplis.

The overall Inner Harbor concept and the individual projects had considerable citizen participation, both negative (neighborhood protests of the expressway proposal) and positive (the consultation of neighborhood organizations with HCD on housing needs), and ten bond referendums were approved to support individual projects.

The GBC development committee, charged with implementing the Charles Center plan, consisted largely of bankers and businessmen and included the mayor and the director of BURHA.

The Inner Harbor steering committee reversed this pattern. Its membership included only one private businessman, William Boucher III, executive director of GBC. (It did, however, report to the all-private Planning Council.)

The management mechanism used to guide development of joint projects over the past twenty-five years has grown in complexity and sophistication. The Charles Center/Inner Harbor Management Corporation was established in 1965 as a quasi-public corporation with a contractual budget from the city and a professional staff capable of arranging complex deals and financial packages.

In short, success has bred more complex arrangements and more sophisticated means for handling them. There has been a distinct shift of initiative from private to public leadership that is partly a result of the expanding scale of projects, partly a desirable result of the city's growing capabilities, and partly a consequence of apparent decline and uncertainty of purpose at GBC, the vehicle for coalescing private-sector actions. These adaptations appear to have allowed Baltimore to get on with the business of winning a daring gamble for downtown revitalization.

Coldspring

In the 1950s, efforts to come to grips with housing problems through the city's urban-renewal plan were eclipsed by the privately sponsored master plan for downtown and the subsequent drive to implement and complete Charles Center. The Inner Harbor plan, produced in the mid-1960s, originally called for construction of a substantial amount of middle-income housing as a drawing card to attract and retain middle-income households in the city, but federal housing programs required that greater attention be given to the housing needs of low- and moderate-income residents, and the Inner Harbor plans were modified accordingly.

Nonetheless, the problem of "white flight" continued to plague the city. (Recent results from the 1980 Census indicate that the outmovement continues, with Baltimore losing 122,000 residents in the 1970s.) Mindful of its weakening tax base, the city decided to try once again to mount a development program aimed at creating middle-income housing and neighborhood options that could compete with what suburbs had to offer.

Coldspring Newtown was the first major project initiated by HCD. Planning for the project began late in 1969. The completed plan, adopted in January 1972, called for 3,780 new housing units to be constructed on 385 acres of open land in the northwest sector of the city, land originally slated for the expansion of Cylburn Park. The city would acquire the land, pay for detailed plans, build the necessary infrastructure, and act as mortgagee in financing the final sale of the completed units. In addition, the city would provide a short-term construction loan at favorable rates to the developer. The city, therefore, was the senior partner, with the junior partner, the developer, functioning primarily as builder and general contractor.

A land-disposition agreement between HCD and the developer (New-town Corporation, a subsidiary of the F.D. Rich Construction Corporation), placed a 10-percent ceiling on the developer's profit and stipulated several conditions:

Careful attention to architectural design and aesthetic appeal

30 percent of all units (approximately 1,200) to be set aside for moderate-income buyers under federal Section 8 and 236 programs

Substantial subcontracting with local minority contractors

The contract was signed in early 1975, after a year of negotiations. Meanwhile, the city had retained Moshe Safdie, the renowned architect-designer of Habitat 1967 in Montreal, to prepare the detailed plan for the site. There was a special compatibility of purpose between Safdie and the city that undoubtedly led to a good working relationship. Moreover, Safdie took a more active role than is usual for a project designer in such ancillary efforts as negotiations with neighborhood groups and development of the environmental-impact statement for the project. (This was the city's first real attempt at preparing an environmental-impact statement. Under the terms of federal housing programs at that time, HUD was responsible for preparing environmental reviews, but the city decided to prepare its own for Coldspring in order to speed up the funding process. It is estimated that the environmental review was completed for less than $20,000 and was accepted by HUD essentially without change. It is doubtful that the same review would be acceptable for a federally assisted project today because of the much more detailed current requirements for the statements.) Here is how Safdie describes the experience:

In 1970 we were invited to become the master planner for Coldspring. But, in commissioning us to do the job, the city gave us a number of what I considered at the time unusual instructions and guidelines. For example, we were told that the city is deeply committed to integrating racial and income groups in communities it is building. But it also recognized that this has to be done extremely carefully so that the right balance of various income groups and racial groups is maintained and in order to keep a project from going all the way to low-income or all the way to upper-income. All of this was a rather delicate balancing game. We were told that the city had no intention of pursuing a project over the backs of community objections in the heavy-handed way of projects in the 1960s. Therefore, if the project was to be realized, it was through a rather intensive community participation effort. And at the same time we were told that the city had stated, without embarrassment, that Coldspring was to be in part aimed at attracting middle-income families to live there instead of going to the country or coming back into the city from the country. That meant a high level of amenities in order to seduce them back. As architects committed to certain social structures, to environmental quality, to amenities, we found ourselves perhaps for the first time in our experience completely sharing the objectives of our client.[12]

Implementation. Financing for the Coldspring project came almost entirely from public sources: federal funds from HUD and Economic Development Administration totaling nearly $30 million to date, city tax-exempt mortgage-revenue bonds in the amount of $11 million (proceeds reloaned to individual homebuyers at 7½ percent, and city general-obligation-bond revenues of $5.5 million, which were loaned to the developer at 7½ percent for construction financing.

A much-publicized problem led to the city's taking a $1.5-million loss on the construction costs of the project. The city had insisted, as a condition of the deal, that the developer subcontract with three local minority firms for much of the masonry and electrical work. The intention was not only to provide immediate jobs but to strengthen the experience and track record of minority contractors for future bidding on housing construction in the city. It soon became apparent, however, that lack of experience with a project of the size of Coldspring would weigh heavily on the early pace and costs of the construction. Work was done imperfectly and had to be redone, imposing costly delays that pushed up all the other costs of the project. Because the employment of local minority subcontractors had been insisted upon by the city and because the city did not wish the developer to lose interest in completing the project, it agreed to absorb the overrun. (The developer, F.D. Rich Construction Corporation, was from out of town and could not have been expected to be familiar with the work or credentials of local minority firms. The $1.5-million cost overrun was covered by the city from its Block Grant funds, a use that was disputed but finally accepted by HUD.)

The Coldspring Planning Committee was established, with representatives from the major local institutions, neighborhood organizations, universities, and citizens from the area. This committee provided a vehicle for airing concerns about the project and for citizen input and suggestions for improvements in the design. Of particular concern was the appropriation of land originally planned for park expansion, the provision of adequate schools and public facilities so that Coldspring would not cause congestion in neighboring areas, and the number of units set aside for moderate-income buyers. The openspace issue was resolved by the negotiation of a twenty-two-acre buffer zone between the project and the existing park. The level and location of public services called for in the plan were reviewed by the committee to its satisfaction. And the number of moderate-income units was set at 30 percent of the total, a figure that the Park Heights community thought ''too low'' but that the real-estate community, concerned with marketing the units, warned might be ''too high.'' To ease this latter fear, the agreement provides that the moderate-income units will be phased in in later stages of the project, after a market has been established for the rest of the units. (It was also tacitly agreed that in exchange for community support of Coldspring, the city would produce a development plan for the Park Heights area.)

To date, 490 units in Coldspring have been completed or are in process; 125 have been sold at prices ranging from $33,000 to $58,000; the balance in process will sell for $75,000 to $105,000. It is interesting that Coldspring so far appears to be achieving some measure of its intended purpose of attracting and retaining middle-income homeowners. Although the numbers are still quite small, the emerging patterns are revealing; half of all buyers in Coldspring are coming from outside the city and half from elsewhere within the city. Seventy-five percent of the buyers were formerly owners, only 25 percent were renters; 25 percent are minority families; 32 percent are female-headed households. Given the purchase prices, it is apparent that none of these are low-income households.

At least two unique features may have made it possible to start this major housing in Baltimore in the mid-1970s: The unified HCD was able to concentrate, in a single agency, all the powers required to approve major physical-development projects, and the requirements for federal environmental-impact statement were considerably more lax than those used today. The first condition still exists, but the second, the impact-statement requirements, has altered dramatically and would surely slow down such a project proposed in the 1980s.

More recently, skyrocketing interest rates and the general slump in home buying have slowed the Coldspring project. In May 1981, the city once again agreed to provide a $1-million ''bridge loan'' (at 10-percent interest) so that construction could begin on the substructure for a condominium tower (75 units) and a Section 236 building for the elderly (150 units). The funds will be loaned to Baltimore Economic Development Corporation, a quasi-public corporation, which can contract for the construction without competitive bidding, thereby speeding up the process to assure that the substructure is ready when final plans for the towers are complete. The substructure will ultimately be sold in part to the Section 236 syndicate and in part to the condominium association for the tax write-off. Commenting on this arrangement, one of the city's financial trustees noted, "Costs are escalating at such a rapid rate, I doubt if we will undertake any further stages in the future. Whether the private sector would be able to come in, I don't know."[13]

Without future private investment, the Coldspring project will come to a halt, consisting of only 600 of the nearly 3,800 units originally envisioned.

Some Speculative Conclusions

There is no doubt that Baltimore owes much of its current shape and vitality to the results of public-private partnerships. Such joint ventures have both a theoretical and a pragmatic justification. The theoretical justification lies in the economies of scale inherent in undertaking revitalization on a sufficiently broad front to encourage corollary development; marginal investments simply cannot turn the tide of urban decay or capture the imagination of other potential investors. In addition, fiscal pressures on public budgets and increasing competition of public and corporate borrowers in the capital market naturally lead to more careful planning of major investments and efforts to leverage public expenditures with private monies. Future urban revitalization will, of necessity, depend even more heavily on shared planning and resources.

Baltimore has a tradition of civic activity on the part of its business sector, that dates back more than thirty years. The organizations and personal networks developed over that time have borne fruit in a series of successful joint ventures that have transformed the face of the city as well as the attitudes of its residents.

The Lessons of the Baltimore Experience

Experience with public-private cooperation suggests several lessons. First, public-private cooperation is a way of pooling risks, particularly for large projects and during periods of national economic slump or uncertainty. The Baltimore business community also recognizes that it needs to face up to a changing urban economy. For example, during the 1950s and 1960s, when retail markets began moving to the suburbs and the central city began showing signs of decay, businesses had to ask themselves what was happening to both their product and their labor markets and precisely how they should, or could, adapt for survival.

During the 1970s, Baltimore continued to lose population and employment opportunities to the surrounding suburbs, inflation became a persistent problem, and the city became increasingly dependent on grants and aid from other levels of government. For the first time, the federal government articulated a national urban policy that encouraged public-private partnerships and targeted federal aid specifically to improve the economic base of distressed central cities. The ability of business leaders to recognize sweeping changes in the structure of the city economy enabled them to confront the need for a new way of tackling projects of mutual interest seriously.

Second, public-private partnership is a continuous *process*, requiring a stable network of interpersonal relationships developed over a considerable period of time, a fairly even *balance of capacities* in the two sectors (so that they can act as equals and not as substitutes for one another), and the ability to bring about *institutional innovation when needed*.

In Baltimore, strong entrepreneurs and leaders emerged from both the city agencies and the business community. Similarly, a tradition of institutional innovation is traced by the activities of CPHA, which assisted in creating an extensive network of neighborhood improvement associations; through the city's creation of the first integrated department (HCD) to deal with housing and community-development issues, which was given broad powers to affect all physical development activity in the city; and, most recently, by the creation of a series of quasi-public agencies such as the Charles Center/Inner Harbor Management Corporation and several trust funds to manage economic-development projects. The private sector has also responded by establishing the EDC unit of GBC to focus private marketing efforts in cooperation with state and local development programs.

The ability to take the plunge and establish a new organization or restructure an existing one as needed is aided immeasurably by the considerable stability that Baltimore has experienced in both its political personnel and its major business leaders. The city has had only two mayors and three heads of BURHA/HCD over the last fifteen years and nearly one-third of the founding members of GBC are still active members in that organization today, some twenty-five years later.

Third, there have been some noticeable changes in the structure of public-private cooperation. In particular, there is an apparent shift of the private-leadership role from a few élite big businesses to smaller firms and neighborhood organizations. In part, this parallels the maturing of GBC as an élite organization and its merger with the Chamber of Commerce, whose members are less concerned with monumental improvements in the central business district and more concerned with smaller-scale improvements in neighborhood commercial opportunities.

The focus of many cooperative revitalization efforts now appears to be on producing a continuous flow of smaller improvements. The fate of such large proposed projects as building a new sports stadium or converting the city's old power plant to a luxury hotel seems more in doubt. There may also be some sense that it is time to balance some of these larger successes in the downtown business area with greater visibility for projects that more directly affect the living conditions of city residents in their neighborhoods.

Fourth, the concept of partnership itself has become more sophisticated. In the public sector, for example, there is a shift in philosophy away from a view of public activity as grants giving toward a view of public activity as investment. This has meant that governments at all levels have begun to ask what the return (broadly defined) is on alternative investments, how public monies can leverage additional private investment, and what trade-offs need to be made between new investment and maintenance of existing facilities.

The projects themselves have become more complex financially and managerially and require more flexibility and quicker response times on the part of public agencies. In addition, the justification of the public interest served by such complex projects becomes more complicated, especially when they entail indirect means such as the subsidization of private developers to generate the promised benefits in jobs, income, and a stronger tax base.

Martin Millspaugh put it neatly:

> In the years since we developed the first buildings in Charles Center, the nature of the public/private partnership has changed. Although it has always been a three-way partnership between the city, the private business leadership and the developer (who might be either public or private), the roles played by the three partners have become more equalized in recent years.
>
> In the early years, the cooperative planning effort between the city and the business community organizations was the dominant thrust. The developer fitted himself into the planning framework and received the combined support of both the public and private sector leadership.
>
> Now that city planning objectives have become an accepted fact, the changing nature of the urban economy has placed much more emphasis on the developer, and on our skill and adaptability in working out the terms of the actual deals between the city and the developer. The arm's length transaction is pretty much a thing of the past; we are now creating joint ventures of immense complexity utilizing the assets of both the public and private sectors to make something happen which neither could do alone. For instance, the Hyatt Hotel was a tax shelter for the developer and the city provided a "soft" second mortgage. In the Camden Yards it is a matter of leveraging the land belonging to both

the private and public partners. In other cases, it may be a land lease, an assigned option, revenue bonds, mortgage insurance, or underwriting portions of the front end costs, or a combination of some or all of these things.

This is where the flexibility or quasi-public characteristics of a non profit corporation are of paramount value. Still, the quasi-public nature of the corporation preserves control by the city in all areas where public policy is involved.[14]

Fifth, public-private efforts have been crucial to successful grants-manship on the part of the city. Baltimore has an extraordinary grants-manship record, with some two-thirds of its operating revenues coming from state and federal aid. Some of this is formula or entitlement aid, but Baltimore does best in capturing discretionary funds, such as UDAG and EDA monies, that are allocated by competition with other cities. Some of this success reflects the leadership and personal contacts built up between city officials and federal agencies over the years, but much can be attributed to the fact that the city has been in position to be aggressive and take the initiative.

The early development of a master plan for the redevelopment of Inner Harbor, a plan agreed to by both the city and the private business community, allowed officials to know what they needed, how it fit with the larger development plan, and how to deliver on funds received. Applications for funds reflecting private-sector commitments present a more promising opportunity for leveraging federal investments. The fact that Baltimore had its ''horizontal'' governmental relationships worked out well before the advent of ''vertical'' grants programs has allowed it to use federal programs rather than being led by them.

Sixth, stable local political leadership has given joint ventures a degree of reliability not common in many cities. Baltimore has had only two mayors in the last fifteen years, D'Alesandro and and Schaefer. Mayor Schaefer is just beginning his third term; when that is completed, he will have provided twelve years of continuous leadership under a single set of development policies and objectives. Schaefer's management style encompasses close personal attention to the neighborhoods and neighborhood associations and a willingness to ''sell'' the city in business circles. Most recently he has established a series of quasi-public trusts that allow the city to do business more nearly like its private partners— faster, more flexibly, and with less public participation. This innovation reduces the role of the City Council and avoids the usual disclosure and review procedures that are part of the normal budget process. The city's private partners like this innovation, citing Baltimore as one of the easiest cities in which to do business, but there is considerable uneasiness among some with regard to the appropriateness of committing large amounts of public money in this fashion. Ironically, the functions of these quasi-public groups appear to be supplanting the role played earlier by GBC in bringing private developer and city together.

Seventh, civic entrepreneurs from both sectors have played critical roles in establishing a tradition of public-private partnership in Baltimore. They have provided a sense of urgency about a problem and the will-ingness to lead the way to an early commitment to action. They have given stability to long-term projects through commitments to see the projects through independent of political change. And they have had the imagination to seize on creative solutions and the power to articulate these objectives persuasively to varying audiences. Just as the importance of the single great entrepreneur has declined in most corporations, to be replaced by a technocratic management system, so, too, there are indi-cations that the initiative for major redevelopment projects may be shifting to groups and more institutionalized methods of launching projects and ideas. No single individual can assemble or finance projects on a scale large enough to have a major impact on the city's economic base; everyone must have multiple partners, some public and some private, to succeed.

Challenges for the Future

The effectiveness of future public-private partnership efforts in Baltimore will depend on several challenges now facing the leadership of both sectors.

> The successful transformation of GBC from an élite, big-business club to a larger, more diverse membership with a broader agenda. If this, or the emergence of a replacement organization to serve as a focal point for mobilizing business action, does not occur, the city may pursue its plans directly with individual developers in ways that are less and less like partnerships.

> Adaptations to the public-sector fiscal crunch and a reduction in the volume of grants from higher levels of government. The main chal-lenges here are the city's ability to reattract or retain middle-income residents and to create new jobs to replace the losses that loom ahead in the automobile, steel, and government sectors, all major sources of employment in Baltimore.

> Revitalizing of retail activity in downtown Baltimore.

> Adaptation to the loss of political representation that will result from reapportionment under the 1980 Census. This will entail forging an

effective and informed metropolitan coalition that recognizes the
economic interdependence within the metropolitan region and acts
with a common purpose with respect to economic and public-service
problems such as waste disposal, environmental quotas, specialized
police and fire laboratory facilities, development of an energy-effi-
cient transportation network, and joint labor-force training and placement.

Acknowledgments

Special acknowledgment and gratitude go to a number of individuals and
organizations that supplied many of the historical details that enliven this
report and add to its accuracy. Without their willingness to discuss and
reflect on their experiences and to open both their personal and their
institutional files, this effort would not have been possible. I am grateful
to Bernard Berkowitz, Physical Development Coordinator for the city;
Jay Brodie, Commissioner of Housing and Community Development;
and Larry Merrill, Program Manager for Coldspring, for advice in selecting items for review and especially for discussion of the Charles
Center and Coldspring projects. Barbara Bonnell and Walter Sondheim
provided valuable information on the Charles Center/Inner Harbor Management Corporation and its projects, and James Rouse reviewed and
offered comments on the discussions of Charles Center/Inner Harbor and
GBC.
    Nancy Winkler's thesis "Baltimore's Unelected Leaders" lent color
to the political history of Charles Center. Nancy Roberts, Executive
Director of CPHA, and Bea Haskins of the CPHA staff, were especially
helpful in providing information on the background and early functions
of that organization in spawning civic leadership in Baltimore. William
Boucher III and the staff of GBC were helpful in tracing that organization's role in redevelopment efforts.
    In addition, the historical files of the *Baltimore News American* and
the Baltimore Region Institutional Studies Center were particularly rich
sources of information, yielding details that otherwise would have been
missing from the public record of Baltimore's revitalization efforts.

Notes

    1. Michael Blumenthal, "Candid Reflections of a Businessman in
Washington," *Fortune,* January 29, 1979, pp. 36–50.
    2. Ralph B. Taylor, Sidney N. Brower, and Whit Drain, *Toward*

a Neighborhood-Based Data File: Baltimore, A Map of Baltimore Neighborhoods (Center for Metropolitan Plannning and Research, Johns Hopkins University, October 1979).

3. Greater Baltimore Committee, *Opening Days: Memoirs of Clarence Miles* (Baltimore: 1980), p. 19.

4. Ibid., p. 20.

5. Ibid., p. 27.

6. Ibid., p. 31.

7. GBC Planning Council, *Charles Center Proposal* (Baltimore: 1958), p. 17.

8. "Inner Harbor Progress Report", *Baltimore Magazine* (July 1965), p. 32.

9. Roberto Brambilla and Gianni Longo, *Learning From Baltimore* (Institute for Environmental Action, October 1979), p. 55.

10. Ibid., p. 63.

11. *Baltimore Magazine* (October 1954), pp. 11–12.

12. Brambilla and Longo, *Learning from Baltimore*, pp. 125–127.

13. Charles L. Benton, Jr., "City Gives New Loan, Warning to Coldspring," *Baltimore Sun* (May 28, 1981), p. 1.

14. Brambilla and Longo, *Learning From Baltimore*, p. 63.

3

Four Decades of Public-Private Partnerships in Pittsburgh

Shelby Stewman and
Joel A. Tarr

Although the roots of public-private partnership in Pittsburgh lie in the nineteenth century, the earliest plans issued both by the private sector and by public-private groups were not always carried through to fruition. The reasons for this are complex, involving financial stringency, public inertia, and failures of private and public leadership. Before Renaissance I, public-sector partnership initiatives usually involved specific projects, such as park development, but leadership and planning stemmed from various voluntary associations (the so-called third sector), which provided the vehicles through which influence and expertise were applied. In order to understand present-day Pittsburgh, then, it is critical to see how Renaissance I (1945–1969) differed from previous attempts at private-public partnership, what changed during the Interlude (1970–1977) and during Renaissance II, which began in 1978, and what similarities or differences exist between these periods of development.

Evolution of the City

During the nineteenth century, the city of Pittsburgh evolved from a military post and commercial center to one of the nation's leading industrial cities. As early as 1850, a larger share of Pittsburgh's population was involved in manufacturing activities than that of any other city in the nation. Cheap fuel and geographical advantage provided a firm base for growth. In the 1870s, the region's first integrated steel mills were constructed, making Pittsburgh synonymous with steel. The availability of the nation's best metallurgical coke gave the city a price advantage over competitors, and entrepreneurs constructed huge mills along the river valleys.

In contrast, throughout the twentieth century, manufacturing growth in the city and the region has declined as the region's advantages—cheap mineral fuels and access to growth markets—weakened. Since the end of World War II, the city's overall manufacturing employment has gone down in absolute as well as in relative terms, a pattern that characterizes other older manufacturing regions. Accompanying the disappearance of blue-collar manufacturing jobs has been a shift to white-collar and service employment: in 1940, manufacturing employment in the four county Pittsburgh SMSA was almost 50 percent of the total work force or approximately 320,000 workers; in 1981, manufacturing employment had shrunk to less than 25 percent of the total work force.

From a demographic perspective, Pittsburgh has experienced periods of growth, stability, and decline. From 1870 through 1940, the population of the city grew from 86,075 to 671,659. Growth was rapid up to 1920; after that date, it stabilized, and the rate was slower than that for the nation as a whole.

Since World War II, the city's population has declined rapidly, from a high of over 700,000 in 1950 to 400,000 in 1980. At the same time, the remainder of the four-county Pittsburgh standard metropolitan statistical area (SMSA) has gained about the same number of people. Demographic stability appears likely for the area's future.

Like most other cities, Pittsburgh grew by annexation and merger with contiguous territory as well as by immigration and natural increase. Since World War II, however, almost no annexation or consolidation has occurred; suburban townships have jealously guarded their independence. Cooperation between the many government units within Allegheny County has been difficult to achieve. Moreover, within the city itself, rugged topography has combined with ethnic and workplace residential patterns to create a strong neighborhood pattern that has often worked against urban cohesion. Topography has also created a unique central business district (CBD), a true central place on the Pittsburgh peninsula, where the Monongahela and Allegheny Rivers join to form the Ohio.

Until this century, Pittsburgh's government was characterized by fragmentation. The city was chartered in 1816, and until 1911 it was governed largely by a two-chamber city council elected on a ward basis. The councils were the dominant forces in policymaking, and the mayor had little power. However, new charter acts changed the council to a single-chamber body elected on an at-large basis. In addition, executive and legislative power was separated, and the role of the mayor, who now controlled a number of executive departments, was strengthened.

Public-Private Partnership before Renaissance I

Private-public partnerships are not unique to the twentieth century in Pittsburgh. In the nineteenth century, the city aided private firms in constructing railroads and began helping housing developers by providing sewers, streets, and water in new subdivisions. But the most vigorous period before Renaissance I of public-private rationalization and revitalization of urban areas came early in this century. At that time three citywide voluntary organizations—the Civic Club of Allegheny County, the Chamber of Commerce, and the Civic Commission—became involved in urban-improvement projects. The leaders of these organizations were largely corporate and financial leaders or their wives. Their aim was to improve the inferior social, environmental, and political conditions that were by-products of the city's industrial development.

These organizations, working through the city government, attempted reform in areas of their choice. As historian Roy Lubove notes, the voluntary organizations "defined the issues and areas of intervention" for city government.[1] The Chamber of Commerce and the Civic Club, for example, led the way in environmental areas such as flood and smoke control and water supply and sewers; the Civic Club also specialized in planning, charity reform, and housing. The Civic Commission worked on transportation and tax reform. A fourth group, the Voter's League, led the way in City Council and education reform.

In a few of these sectors, such as adjustment of an outmoded tax system, centralization of educational administration, and revision of the electoral system for the City Council, voluntary associations, in cooperation with the city administration, were able to bring about the institutional changes they desired. In other areas, however, such as smoke and flood control, city planning, transportation, and housing improvement, reports were written, commissions appointed, and in some cases, regulatory bureaus established, but little substantive change was made. The forces of localism, vested economic and political interests, weak enforcement capabilities, and inertia prevented change in spite of corporate and financial leaders' support for it.

During the interwar years, voluntary business and civic organizations continued their involvement with urban problems. One important area of concern stemmed from the dispersal of population throughout the metropolitan area and the fragmentation of governmental authority. A number of business leaders believed that for the region's economy to operate efficiently and economically, governmental reorganization was needed. Central-city business leaders who lived in the suburbs led a movement for a dual-level government in Allegheny County that would improve both suburban quality of life and central-city vitality without sacrificing local autonomy. There were several versions of this plan in the 1920s, with most providing for a metropolitan board that would serve metropolitan needs while local municipalities remained responsible for local needs, but they could never get the vote needed for passage.

A private-sector effort to rationalize government involved the attempt of the Citizens Committee on City Plan (CCCP) to develop a general city plan. CCCP was founded in 1918 and chartered as the Municipal Planning Association in 1920. Its objective was the production of "an orderly, scientific, comprehensive, program of city building." Between 1921 and 1923, it produced a six-part plan, with sections on playgrounds, major streets, transit, parks, railroads, and waterways. The plans for recreation and streets were adopted by the City Council but had only a limited impact. They ran afoul of the reality that implementation required action by the public sector and by institutions with a political rather than an administrative focus. (Allegheny County was actively involved in construction of large public works such as bridges, tunnels, and highways in the 1920s but it generally ignored the CCCP plans.)

In the late 1930s, CCCP (now renamed the Pittsburgh Regional Planning Association, or PRPA) devoted its attention to the Golden Triangle, Pittsburgh's compact central business district. In 1939, PRPA, under its new director, Wallace K. Richards, employed the New York planner Robert Moses to prepare a highway plan for Pittsburgh with a focus on the central business district. This plan was similar to those produced earlier by planners from CCCP and the County Planning Commission, recommending the creation of a park at the Point, Duquesne Way along the Allegheny River, a crosstown boulevard, and a parkway east to Wilkinsburg along the Monongahela River. These projects were to become the basis for the physical plans of the early Renaissance period. (Duquesne Way was started in 1940 and completed in 1943.)

Also in 1939, the Chamber of Commerce created its Golden Triangle Division. The object of this group was to build public support to halt the decline of real-estate values within the Golden Triangle by improving it as a business environment.

Another important organizational development was the creation, in 1935, of the Pennsylvania Economy League. It had as its aim the provision of plans for the effective management of cities and counties. Funded by contributions from the business community, the league provided research reports for the government sector. Its early work with city and county government built a reservoir of trust on the part of public officials concerning the objectivity of its recommendations. The Economy League, along with PRPA, later became the prime research groups for the Allegheny Conference on Community Development, the key mover behind Pittsburgh's Renaissance I.

The decade preceding World War II was critical in setting the stage for the postwar program of urban revitalization. Deteriorating social and economic conditions in the city generated by the Great Depression and long-term economic decline provoked serious responses. New organizations emerged, new business leadership developed, and action began on the two major environmental problems: smoke and floods. (Individuals such as Richard King Mellon began to play more active roles. Mellon, for instance, was chairman of the Chamber of Commerce Golden Triangle Division; in 1941, he became president of PRPA.) Their solution was key to further urban-revitalization efforts and required significant private-public cooperation.

Origins of the Allegheny Conference on Community Development

When knowledgeable Pittsburghers discuss Renaissance I, they talk about the Allegheny Conference on Community Development (ACCD). ACCD was not only the critical private-sector organization during the period, but its key planning and action organization as well. To a large extent, the agenda of projects that came to constitute Renaissance I originated with ACCD and its closely linked research and planning affiliates, PRPA and the Western Division of the Pennsylvania Economy League.[2]

The idea for such an organization has been attributed to several individuals. Wallace K. Richards, executive director of PRPA from 1937 to the present, seems to have perceived the need for an umbrella civic association composed of the city's top corporate leadership. Richards was close to Richard K. Mellon, PRPA president, and supposedly broached the idea to him just before the outbreak of World War II. Mellon was "interested," but the war delayed any action. According to Park Martin, however, the idea for the conference originated with Dr. Robert E. Doherty, president of the Carnegie Institute of Technology (now Carnegie-Mellon University). Doherty was seriously concerned about the region's future and conceived of the need for a "super planning group" to organize a postwar reconstruction. He and Dr. Edward R. Weidlein, president of the Mellon Institute of Pittsburgh, journeyed to Washington in early 1943 to present the idea to Mellon and his brother-in-law, Alan M. Scaife. "As a result of this meeting," Martin writes, "Mr. Mellon evidenced his interest and support of the idea".[3] Doherty and Weidlein returned to Pittsburgh and invited a select group of business, civic, and political leaders to an organization meeting, at which basic agreement was reached on the desirability of a planning organization.

Early in the history of the conference, a sponsoring committee was created. Its ex-officio members included selected public officials, a fact that reflected the realization that the support of elected officials was necessary to accomplish anything substantive. Twelve standing committees were appointed to investigate the following areas:

research coordination, housing and neighborhood development, legal advisory, legislation, demobilization, development of skills, economic problems, land use and zoning, financial resources, cultural development, health and welfare, and public improvements.

In 1945 the conference described itself as a "citizen's group of the Allegheny Region whose purpose is to stimulate and coordinate research and planning looking to a unified community plan for the region as a whole, and to secure by educational means public support of projects that are approved by the Conference as parts of that overall unified plan." Publicly, the conference took the position that it would work through existing agencies, acting on its own only in the absence of an agency relating to a particular problem; privately, however, Doherty maintained that the "long-existing agencies have not arrested the trends or solved the problems."

In February 1945, Park Martin became executive director of ACCD. From 1935 to 1945 he served as chief engineer and director of the Allegheny County Planning Commission and had developed the county's first long-range improvement program. He questioned whether the conference could succeed in its ambitious plans and whether the community's corporate leadership was firmly behind it. He believed that the determining factor was the position of Richard King Mellon and his willingness to be publicly identified with the conference and its policies. The two men met, and Mellon agreed to become involved after his retirement from the army.[4]

Martin's selection as executive director and the election in December 1945 of Arthur B. Van Buskirk to the Executive Committee signified a movement by the conference toward a more action-oriented stance. That is, although ACCD would continue to sponsor planning and research, it also began to concern itself with coordination and implementation. Van Buskirk's appointment was also significant because of his relationship with Mellon. Van Buskirk was a lawyer who was a governor of T. Mellon and Sons, the inner sanctum of R.K. Mellon's personal interests. According to Leland Hazard, an important conference figure, Van Buskirk's "voice on the executive committee of the Conference was the last word." Van Buskirk was an exceptionally able man in his own right. He sensed, said Mayor David Lawrence, "the necessity of uniting public and private action for Pittsburgh's advancement." The other Mellon confidante on the committee was PRPA director Wallace Richards, an idealist who provided many of the creative ideas for Renaissance projects; he too was aware of the need for positive private-public interaction.

The Executive Committee was the "real guts" of the ACCD. An important early policy decision was that its members were elected as individuals and could not send a substitute in their place. Originally, the

Executive Committee contained only a few corporate executives, but this changed after 1945, and the committee became primarily a business group, made up of the leaders of major corporations and banks.

Martin was especially valuable in that he provided a bridge between the conference and the city and county governments. He had been active in county affairs for a number of years, knew the important politicians in both parties, and realized that the various conference projects could be implemented only by elected public officials. Because he was known and respected by the politicians and also held the confidence of the corporate members of the conference, he was able to create trust between two groups that had often been suspicious of each other, if not in actual conflict.

The Rise of a Civic Statesman

Renaissance I was built on an unlikely alliance between a Republican-dominated group of corporate leaders and a Democratic political boss. Democratic control in Pittsburgh was actually a relatively new phenomenon. Except for a brief period early in the century, the Republican party dominated the city from the Civil War until the Great Depression. The leading figure in the Democratic party was David L. Lawrence. Just as R.K. Mellon came from a family with a tradition of civic involvement, Lawrence descended from a tradition of involvement in Democratic politics.

When Lawrence consented to run for mayor, he issued a seven-point program that included a statement saying he would aid and support the ACCD plan for the improvement of Pittsburgh. Lawrence demonstrated soon after his election that this was not merely campaign rhetoric. He appointed Park Martin to the City Planning Commission, thus allowing Martin to serve as a link between the Planning Commission, the mayor's office, the City Council, and the conference. Before the election, Lawrence had also formed a friendship with Wallace Richards. Thus by the end of 1945, he had established good relationships with two key persons in ACCD. The groundwork had been laid for one of the most significant instances of private-public partnership in the history of American cities.

Lawrence had always been thought of as a politician, but during the years of his Pittsburgh mayoralty (1945 to 1961), he rose to the level of civic statesman. The conference gave full credit to the administration for its accomplishments, and Lawrence did not play politics with the various projects. Yet his very skills as a politician—his sense of timing and his ability to work with other people and with the electorate—were what made it possible for him to play the statesman's role needed for successful partnership.

Renaissance I

The years that followed the election of David Lawrence as mayor and the formation of ACCD witnessed the development of Renaissance I. During these years, environmental improvements were made in smoke and flood control, the rebuilding of the Golden Triangle was generated, and plans and projects for economic and physical changes throughout the Pittsburgh region were set in motion. The partnership lasted approximately twenty-five years, until the election of a new mayor with a different set of priorities and goals.

Although the conference's focus had been regional, its initial projects were almost all centered on the Golden Triangle. Public officials agreed with this approach. Mayor Lawrence believed that the downtown district furnished a tax base, thus supplying municipal services for the remainder of the city; he also felt that the status of the city as a corporate headquarters center had to be maintained.

Redevelopment could not proceed without the state passing legislation that would allow activity in the areas in which the conference hoped to become involved. The Housing and Redevelopment Act was passed by the General Assembly in 1945, independent of any conference involvement. At the beginning of 1946, the ACCD Executive Committee authorized preparation of a nonpartisan state legislative package that became known as the "Pittsburgh Package." These bills were composed in cooperation with the Economy League, PRPA, and the Lawrence administration. Conference representatives held numerous sessions with members of the legislature, especially the Allegheny County delegation, to explain the package. (During the session, the conference tried not to lobby for bills as an organization but rather only as individuals. Following the session, however, the secretary of the treasury informed the conference that because of its lobbying activities in the General Assembly relating to the Pittsburgh Package, it was losing its status as a tax-free educational and charitable trust. At the request of conference officials, Mayor Lawrence interceded with the secretary and obtained a special hearing for conference officials. As a result of the hearing, the conference's tax-free status was restored.) Pressure was also applied by lobbyists who represented various large Pittsburgh corporations involved in the conference. Eventually, eight of the ten bills introduced were passed. They involved county smoke-control legislation that extended jurisdiction to railroads; county refuse disposal; expansion of county planning-commission control

over suburban subdivision plans; creation of a Pittsburgh parking authority, a county transit-and-traffic study commission, and a Department
of Parks and Recreation; expedited the Penn-Lincoln Parkway; and broadening the Pittsburgh tax base to include sources other than real estate.
Two bills were defeated: one proposed state responsibility for Pittsburgh
bridges, the other amended the Public Utility Act so that the county could
file to appear before the Public Utility Commission in mass-transportation
cases where the county interest was secondary.

The most controversial bill was that providing for the Parking Authority. Its opponents (especially the Pittsburgh Real Estate Board) argued
that parking was a private matter and that public agencies, especially one
with the right to condemn and acquire property, should not be in the
business. Eventually, the bill passed, was tested in the courts, and was
found constitutional. The conference planners utilized the special-purpose
authority mechanism as a means to promote their plan on a number of
occasions. They favored it because it was not bound by the debt limitation
on municipalities, involved a user fee, and avoided political difficulties
stemming from fears of metropolitanism and the normal course of democratic politics.

In addition to the Pittsburgh Package, the General Assembly passed
a critical piece of legislation in 1947 facilitating downtown renewal by
permitting insurance companies to invest in redevelopment areas.

Environmental Partnership: Smoke and Flood Control

The basis for any sort of physical development must be a certain level
of environmental quality. Without the improvements that took place in
the areas of flood and smoke control, there would have been no Pittsburgh
Renaissance.

Smoke Control

The problem of smoke pollution in Pittsburgh resulted from a combination
of urbanization, industrialization, topography, and the availability of low-
cost bituminous coal, which was used for domestic and commercial heating, processing raw materials, manufacturing goods, and providing fuel
for transporation. By the early nineteenth century, Pittsburgh had already
achieved a reputation as a smoky city.[5]

From the 1890s on, especially after a relatively brief period of clean
air resulting from the exploitation of local sources of natural gas, voluntary
associations such as the Civic Club applied pressure on the city councils

for smoke control. Between 1892 and 1917, ordinances were passed regulating smoke emissions from industrial, commercial, and transportation sources, and the Bureau of Smoke Regulation was created in 1911 to enforce them. However, the ordinances largely failed to control the smoke nuisance to any appreciable degree because they defined standards of air quality very broadly; the Bureau of Smoke Regulation had only a small staff and did not attempt to enforce the statutes rigidly; and most critical, no attempt was made to control domestic sources of smoke.

To achieve smoke control in Pittsburgh required a sustained citywide campaign that would convince a substantial proportion of the public that the benefits of smoke regulation would outweigh the costs. In 1941 a movement began that was to result in the most powerful smoke-control ordinance to that time. Two elements distinguished this campaign from earlier ones. First, Saint Louis had passed a smoke-control ordinance in 1940 that appeared to have solved its problem by requiring both industry and domestic consumers to burn smokeless fuel or use smokeless technology; and second, three individuals representing key elements in Pittsburgh's decision-making structure were prepared to use the Saint Louis experience to convince Pittsburgh that it too would have smoke-free air.

The three individuals, who might appropriately be called ''entrepreneurs'' for the collective social good of smoke control, were Abraham Wolk, a lawyer and City Council member; Edward T. Leech, the crusading editor of the city's most influential newspaper, the *Press;* and Dr. D.I. Hope Alexander, director of the Pittsburgh Department of Health. Wolk was responsible for organizing the political coalition necessary for passage of the 1941 ordinance, convincing Mayor Scully that it was to his advantage to support the legislation. Leech used his paper ''like a war club'' to advance smoke control. And Alexander made smoke control a public-health crusade, emphasizing the damage that smoke was doing to the health of Pittsburghers. The campaign that followed was marked by full cooperation among public officials, voluntary associations, and the media. The media hammered on the lesson of Saint Louis and the high costs to the community of smoke pollution while the voluntary organizations (especially the Civic Club and the League of Women Voters) conducted a countywide campaign of public arousal and education. Councilman Wolk headed the Mayor's Commission for the Elimination of Smoke, which represented business (the coal interests), labor (the United Mine Workers), education, the media, government, voluntary associations, and the health professions. The commission played a critical role in getting various interests to compromise on the issues.

At the end of the commission hearings, a final report was prepared for the mayor; it was signed by all members of the commission and listed the names of two-hundred voluntary organizations supporting smoke control. The report held that smoke elimination in Pittsburgh would "bring about a new era of growth, prosperity and well-being" by improving urban conditions, halting population loss to the suburbs, attracting light industry, and creating new industrial activity.

The commission recommended requiring all fuel users to burn smokeless fuels or utilize smokeless mechanical equipment; establishing a timetable for implementation over the period from October 1, 1941, to October 1, 1943; and creating the Bureau of Smoke Prevention, which would have the power to impose fines and to seal equipment that was in violation of the law. It concluded its report by noting that only public cooperation and determination would result in enforcement of the law and smoke-free air. Chairman Wolk introduced a far-reaching ordinance based on the report in the City Council, and it was approved overwhelmingly.

Of course, passage of the ordinance did not guarantee implementation, and involvement in World War II delayed the timetable. Air quality in Pittsburgh during the war was extremely bad, and the need for smoke control after the war became even more urgent. The most critical step was enforcement against domestic consumers. In order to maintain the impetus that had resulted in the ordinance's passage, the Civic Club created a new organization, the United Smoke Council, consisting of eighty allied organizations from Pittsburgh and Allegheny County. The council's function was to continue public educational efforts about the need for smoke control and to extend the ordinance to the county.

Leaders of ACCD believed that without smoke control, their program had no chance of success. A strong relationship with the United Smoke Council made sense and was recommended by R.K. Mellon. The council itself was somewhat adrift. It had been formed out of the Civic Club with input from the Chamber of Commerce, but its leadership had grown increasingly dissatisfied with these organizations. They particularly felt that the chamber, because of the influence of the utilities and industrial interests in its membership, wanted to delay implementation of the smoke-control law.

Negotiations between ACCD and the United Smoke Council began in mid-1944. At this point the critical question of the relationship between the conference and other voluntary civic groups arose. The conference leadership had stated publicly that it would try to deal with community problems through existing agencies. In this case, they proposed a merger, causing concern among the Smoke Council staff that the conference would usurp its territory and among Smoke Council leadership that the conference, because of its industrial corporate membership, would compromise on early implementation.

In December 1945 the two groups reached an agreement. The council was renamed the "United Smoke Council of the Allegheny Conference on Community Development,'' and the conference accepted financial responsibility for smoke-control efforts. The Smoke Council also agreed to allow the Conference Executive Committee to decide policy matters. This last point was of vital importance because Smoke Council leadership had wanted implementation of the law in December 1945, whereas Martin and Richards argued for an October 1, 1946, deadline. The heads of the council finally accepted the 1946 date, although not without some concern that their integrity had been compromised.

A search revealed that supplies of low-volatile fuel were inadequate to meet the deadline without causing hardship throughout the city. ACCD therefore recommended extending the date by one year. A compromise plan calling for the later date was prepared by Van Buskirk and agreed to by the mayor, with the understanding that ACCD and the city would cooperate in maintaining public interest in smoke control. Lawrence's agreement was politically courageous because smoke control threatened to impose hardships on low-income families. He believed, however, that Pittsburgh's redevelopment could not proceed without it, and he was prepared to bear the risk of this position.

The critical test for the law came in the winter of 1947. The conference helped the city try to moderate its impact on low-income users by keeping an inventory of low-volatile coal and arranging for release of metallurgical low-volatile fuel by the steel companies if supplies ran low. (Coal strikes that winter exacerbated the situation.) On its part, the Bureau of Smoke Prevention followed a policy of education and cooperation in enforcing the law against domestic and industrial fuel users rather than insisting on rigid adherence. The result of the law, aided by an unusually mild winter, was a much cleaner city. Air quality in the city continued to improve in the ensuing years as homeowners shifted to clean and cheap natural gas for fuel, and railroads adopted diesel-electric technology to replace coal-burning locomotives.

The conference also played an important role in securing a countywide law. State legislation permitting the county to control smoke from all sources except railroad locomotives had been passed in 1943, but it was clear that railroads would have to be included to make a county law effective. In 1946, country, borough, and township officials declared in favor of a countywide program, and the Smoke Council gathered 48,000 signatures to demonstrate citizen support. An amendment to the county law that would include railroads was prepared by Theodore Hazlett, attorney for the conference, as part of the Pittsburgh Package.

When this amendment was introduced in Harrisburg, it was opposed by the lobbyist for the Pennsylvania Railroad. The Pittsburgh-area railroads were in a difficult position on the question of smoke control. They hauled more tons of coal than any other product and also were the largest consumers of coal. They realized that it was to their advantage to shift to diesel-electric locomotives but preferred to proceed with that equipment change at their own pace.

This delaying action by the railroad resulted in direct intervention by R.K. Mellon, one of its directors, to demand that it halt its opposition to the law. Benjamin Fairless, president of United States Steel Corporation and a conference member, also interceded. Faced with this opposition, the railroad ceased its lobbying, and the enabling legislation passed. The county commissioners appointed the seventeen-member Smoke Abatement Advisory Committee under the chairmanship of Edward Weidlein, director of the Mellon Institute of Science and president of the conference. Weidlein had great experience in the air-pollution field. Under his direction, county legislation was prepared and passed in 1949. The appointment of Weidlein to this committee followed the pattern set by the conference of having the "top echelon of the City's industrial, commercial, and educational life actively lead and participate in the community program."

The case of smoke control illustrates two types of public-private partnerships. Leadership in securing the passage of the smoke-control ordinance in 1941 was taken primarily by public-sector figures, with critical cooperation from voluntary associations. The media coordination of the community campaign was shared by several voluntary organizations instead of one leader. Implementation of the 1941 ordinance and the passage of the county ordinance in 1949 reflected a somewhat different pattern. ACCD absorbed the United Smoke Council and furnished direction on all aspects of the smoke-control question. With regard to implementation of the city ordinance, it provided technical information, made the necessary compromises between interested parties, set the date for implementation, and acted to ease the hardships caused by the fuel transition. In the case of the county law, the conference counsel wrote the critical legislation, and its president provided leadership to the commission that wrote the law. At key points involving the passage of the legislation, conference figures, especially R.K. Mellon, intervened to block opposition. From the public sector, Mayor Lawrence extended his influence and support for implementation of the ordinance, thereby risking political defeat. However, he consistently followed conference advice and leadership with regard to technical questions, timing, and goals.

Flood Control

Flood control presented a different type of problem, involving a larger number of factors and requiring the action of city, county, state, and federal officials.[6] However, the initial leadership was again taken by a voluntary business group, the Pittsburgh Chamber of Commerce. Under the direction of H.D.W. English, a dynamic insurance executive, the chamber appointed the Flood Commission in 1908. In 1911 the commission was expanded to include city and county officials. Financing was provided by assessments on property owners affected by floods, contributions from the chamber, and city and county funds.

The Flood Commission ultimately issued a report calling for a multipurpose approach to flood control and inland-waterway development, including construction of seventeen reservoirs at the headwaters of the Allegheny and Monongahela Rivers. These proposals, however, were hindered by federal inaction in inland-waterway development and multipurpose flood control. From 1911 to 1940, the flood-control program made limited progress at the federal level: Congress approved acts committing the government to flood control, and the Army Corps of Engineers showed a willingness to support a comprehensive program. In 1935, after the Public Works Administration had led the way with the construction of the Tygart Dam and Reservoir in West Virginia, the corps, in compliance with the Rivers and Harbors Act of 1927, submitted a plan to Congress calling for construction of nine reservoirs above Pittsburgh at a cost of $44,215,000.

The urgency of flood control was reinforced by the disastrous Saint Patrick's Day flood of 1936, which put much of the Golden Triangle under water. Expanded pressure on Congress to make flood-control appropriations was applied by a coalition of private groups operating through the chamber's Citizens' Committee on Flood Control and the Tri-State Authority, under the direction of State Senator William B. Rogers. By 1940 the Corps of Engineers had begun work on nine reservoirs. However, World War II caused Congress to delay the projects.

As in the case of smoke control, a renewed campaign for action to complete the reservoir system was necessary after the war. Who would provide direction for this campaign was a critical question in the postwar period. The chamber, a large body representing a variety of business and regional interests, was often beset by infighting and personal rivalries, and the ACCD leadership did not have a great deal of confidence in it.

At a meeting between the chamber leadership and Martin and Richards from the conference, it was decided that out of twenty community issues that were conceivably of concern to both groups, seventeen would be allocated to the conference and only three to the chamber. The chamber, however, retained leadership on the flood-control issue. As one prominent conference staff person said, it was "the only thing on which the chamber could unite that was the kind of a problem on which everybody suffered and so there was no division of interests." To reduce conflict between the two groups, chamber leaders, including two members of its Flood Control Committee, were brought into the ACCD executive committee. Coordinating their actions with area congressmen and Mayor Lawrence, the chamber launched a campaign to secure congressional appropriations for the building of the remaining reservoirs. In 1960 construction began on the last and most controversial dam (creating the Allegheny Reservoir), completing the plan laid out in 1936.

High-Rise Office Buildings and Park Development

Point Park and Gateway Center

Redevelopment of the Golden Triangle involved a very different set of legislative, funding, and implementation requirements. Urban redevelopment required the power to condemn private property (eminent domain), private and public investment in buildings and physical infrastructure, and extensive negotiations between the two sectors. The basic plans were produced by the technical staffs of the conference and its affiliated groups, PRPA and the Economy League, or by consultants retained by the conference. The city itself did not have either the technical staff or the funds to hire consultants. City representatives participated in planning sessions, but the conference formulated the essential program and submitted its plans to the city for approval and implementation. This arrangement required trust between private and public parties and agreement on common goals. The ultimate motivation was economic: to utilize public powers in coordination with private planning and investment to revitalize the economies of the city and the region. A more democratic planning process might have produced a different set of plans and goals, but there were few voices in the postwar period offering other options.

Point Park and the redevelopment of the section of the triangle that abutted it (later known as Gateway Center) are often described as having been developed in sequence—the park first and then the center. Conference planners, however, conceived of them as a unit. The idea of a park at the Pittsburgh Point that would involve the reconstruction of Fort Pitt had deep roots. During the war, R.K. Mellon and Attorney General James Duff convinced Governor Martin of the wisdom of a state project. The governor made the announcement in 1945, just before the Lawrence election. In recognition of the importance of ACCD in the planned redevelopment of Pittsburgh, the secretary of the Pennsylvania Department of Forest and Waters requested that the conference accept responsibility for implementing development of Point State Park. The conference created the Point Park Steering Committee; its key idea men were Arthur

Van Buskirk and Wallace Richards. The committee recommended to the state that a thirty-six-acre park be created at the point, requiring the clearing of this land under the Redevelopment Act.[7]

Abutting this area was a twenty-three-acre commercial "wasteland" that included the Wabash Railroad station and freight terminal, warehouses, and some sixty other buildings. Richards visualized the possibility of utilizing the 1945 state redevelopment law to also acquire this land, especially after fire leveled much of the railroad property in March 1946. The Point Park Steering Committee appointed the Point Redevelopment Study Committee, which recommended that the area be redeveloped. State law permitted municipalities to establish redevelopment authorities to acquire and clear land in sections certified as blighted by the City Planning Commission, and in July 1946, Van Buskirk and Richards asked Mayor Lawrence to appoint and chair a five-member Redevelopment Authority. Lawrence said that if the conference, the Chamber of Commerce, and the newspapers asked him to do it, he would accept; and when the necessary letters were obtained, Lawrence consented.[8]

A bill creating the Urban Redevelopment Authority (URA) was drawn up by the conference technicians and approved by the City Council in November 1946. Lawrence proceeded to name himself as chairman, Van Buskirk as vice chairman, and Lester Perry, retiring head of the Carnegie-Illinois Steel Corporation, Edgar Kaufmann, department store owner, and Councilman William A. Stewart as members. Republicans outnumbered Democrats five to three, which the mayor preferred because he felt it would establish confidence on the part of potential developers. Theodore Hazlett, counsel for the conference, became counsel for URA; and John P. Robin, the mayor's executive secretary, became its executive director in 1948.

Shortly before the creation of URA, Van Buskirk, Wallace Richards, Park Martin, and Charles J. Graham met with the president of the Metropolitan Life Insurance Company in New York to inquire about the possibility of having Metropolitan become redeveloper for the site. He declined the offer. The delegation next went to see Thomas Parkinson of Equitable Life Assurance Society. Parkinson immediately asked what the city planned to do about floods and smoke. When told of the positive developments in these areas, Parkinson agreed to start negotiations.

Richards and Martin had originally planned for apartment buildings in the redevelopment area facing Point Park, but Equitable's real-estate advisers recommended that the area be developed for high-rise office structures, and the members of URA agreed. Pittsburgh was a headquarters city, and its big corporations needed space, but no new office building had been constructed in the triangle in eighteen years, and office occupancy had reached 99 percent in May 1946. Equitable agreed to pay

Pittsburgh $12 million for the remaining structures on the site and $2 million to URA to use the public power of eminent domain. The latter was Van Buskirk's idea and provided funding for the authority for years to come. (The first funding for URA came from the sale of a $150,000 bond package to the three Pittsburgh foundations.)

Parkinson stipulated that the major corporations headquartered in Pittsburgh would have to take twenty-year leases on at least 60 percent of the space in the new buildings to be erected by Equitable. Acquiring · these leases proved somewhat difficult, and R.K. Mellon and Van Buskirk pressured corporations to make long-term commitments. R.K. Mellon met with two chief executive officers who were reluctant to sign and said, ''The Mellon family is not going to redevelop this city so far as finances are concerned, if companies like yours are not going to play a major role.'' The corporations finally signed after Van Buskirk had agreed to reduce Equitable's payment to URA from $2 million to $1 million so that Equitable could lower the rents. The long-term leases gave Equitable tenants for its space and assured the city that these corporations would keep their headquarters in Pittsburgh for some time. All of the corporations that originally signed the leases are still in the city.

Before the park or office-building construction could begin, the city Planning Commission had to certify the site as "blighted," according to the terms of the redevelopment law. The condemnation of the structures for commercial purposes (corporation headquarters) was a liberal interpretation of that law. It changed the purpose of redevelopment from one of eliminating slums and creating new housing to one of changing land use to "conform to a better plan in a more functional city." The declaration of the land as "blighted" was also pioneering; now, standards that concerned economic and architectural land uses had to be developed because the normal health and welfare standards no longer applied. The use of the redevelopment law for these purposes was ultimately tested in the courts and found constitutional. Building actually started in 1950, before the conclusion of litigation. Three cruciform, stainless-steel office buildings were constructed (1952–1953), followed by a state office building (1957), the Bell Telephone building (1958), an underground garage (1959), a Hilton hotel (1959), a twenty-two-story office building (1960), the IBM building (1963), and the twenty-seven-story Gateway Towers Luxury Apartments (1964). Point Park was completed as planned in 1974.

Mellon Square Complex

While negotiations for Gateway Center were proceeding, U.S. Steel, the Mellon Bank, and the Aluminum Company of America announced plans to build new headquarters structures in the upper triangle. This significant announcement reaffirmed the commitment of these large corporations to remain headquartered in Pittsburgh. It also made Equitable concerned about being able to attract enough tenants for the contemplated Gateway project. At this time R.K. Mellon announced his willingness to secure tenants for Gateway Center.

Influenced by the design of San Francisco's Union Square, which provided a sense of greenery and openness plus an underground garage in the midst of the high-rise complex, Mellon proposed that a park with an underground parking garage be built in the area abutted on by the two proposed office towers. Because the city could not afford the cost of acquiring the property for the park, which would be located in an extremely high-value area, Mellon offered to pay for the land if the city would construct an underground parking facility. The Mellon Foundations made a gift of $4 million to the city to acquire the land; the city then made an agreement with the Parking Authority to build and operate the underground garage. The Parking Authority, in turn, contracted with the Morrison Knudsen Company to build and operate the garage while the city built the park on top. At the end of a forty-year period, the garage was to become city property.

The land for Mellon Square and the parking garage was acquired through the Pittsburgh Parking Authority, which had been created as part of the Pittsburgh Package. The original agreement was that the city would build the park, but difficulties arose over the possibility that different contractors might end up building the garage and the park. To avoid this, the agreement with the city was amended to provide that the Mellon Foundations would build the park and then give it to the city; this avoided the necessity of having competitive bids. The foundations in turn gave the money for park construction to the conference, which made the necessary construction arrangements. Work on Mellon Square Park began in September 1953 and was completed in 1955. (The city lost $2,459,740 in taxable properties because of the park, but it made taxable gains of $17,457,185 from the adjacent new office towers and the expansion of the abutting Kaufmann's Department Store.)

Summary

The environmental, high-rise, and park projects of the early Renaissance period and the lower hill renewal and Civic Arena were the primary physical manifestations of Renaissance I. But it involved a much broader range of projects—from sewage-treatment plants and garbage-collection improvements to housing and industrial-park development. (For a list of other Renaissance projects, see table 3A–2. Table 3A–3 provides a summary of the partnerships.) Each included in varying measure the mix of public-private involvement at goal-setting and planning stages.

In the development of the Point Park, Gateway Center, and Mellon Square projects, the leadership role played by members of the conference Executive Committee, its staff, and conference-affiliated research groups in goal setting, planning, and implementation is clear. The role of the public sector was primarily a facilitating one but still of immense importance; the public representatives were the indispensable members of the team. In recognition of this, Park Martin established a public-relations policy of never "frontrunning the public official." He realized that "the Conference does not have to be elected to anything. The public officials who were supporting the Conference's program did have to come up for re-election."

Mayor Lawrence played several different roles. One concerned the relationship with city and state legislative bodies. He established a policy of informing the City Council about activities that were underway. Every Monday, he would hold a closed-door conference with the council to discuss an agenda; he would not introduce any new ordinances until all differences were resolved. As a result, the bills necessary for implementing various projects, such as URA, had no opposition. In the case of the state legislature, Lawrence used his influence with the Allegheny County delegation as well as with politicians from the rest of the state to gain the approval of the Pittsburgh Package and other bills of interest to the city and the conference.

Lawrence was also important as a participant in negotiations concerning redevelopment. He was chairman of URA and worked with the city Planning Commission to obtain certification of the redevelopment areas. He was close to various professionals for the civic groups, such as Wallace Richards, Park Martin, and David Kurtzman (Pennsylvania Economy League), and thought of them not as representatives of powers to be bargained with but "as people having a special knowledge of a special subject area in which cooperative programs could be developed for the benefit of Pittsburgh."[9]

John P. Robin, the mayor's executive secretary, was the chief liaison officer for a number of the projects involving the conference in the late 1940s and early 1950s. Robin noted that he was Lawrence's representative in the "channel of communications" that opened between the private and public sectors, often meeting with Mellon's representatives, Wallace Richards and Arthur Van Buskirk. Robin served as executive director of the Urban Redevelopment Authority, working closely with Theodore Hazlett, counsel for the conference and URA.

The mutual trust and respect between private and public helped eliminate conflict. Personal relationships developed between key staff members on both sides. Van Buskirk said that in thirteen years of working closely with Lawrence, the mayor never broke a promise or did anything contrary to the public interest. Such relationships could only have been the product of trust and the sharing of common goals.

The Interlude

Four forces of change characterized the Interlude period (1970–1977):

> The crescendo of the civil-rights movement into a national emergency exemplified by race riots in major cities across the nation. Racial tensions were approaching the breaking point if not the flash point.

> The difficult fiscal conditions several northeastern and north-central cities faced—like those in New York, Boston, and Detroit today— were increasing.

> The large-scale physical or brick-and-mortar development projects in the form of high-rise office buildings were winding down because the supply of large-scale, high-grade office space had far outstripped the demand.

> A new mayor, Peter Flaherty, was elected. He had run on an "I'm nobody's boy" platform and promised new leadership, indicating a potential change in management philosophy, work habits, and staff, at least at the level of major departmental directors.

We do not mean to suggest that development came to a halt in the Interlude, nor that public-private partnerships came to an end. Rather, although the Renaissance I partnerships were being dissolved, a major new type of partnership, appropriate for its time, was being shaped: social and organizational partnerships between the public and private sectors. (This type of cooperative endeavor continues today.) Three specific areas of change emerged: new links with the black community, the reformulation of "urban renewal" in the area of neighborhood housing, and the improvement of management within government. All three involve organizational infrastructure; the first two deal with social infrastructure, and the third with managerial infrastructure.

The Pittsburgh story, particularly the Interlude, contains some important lessons for successful partnerships. The axiom that individual battles are not nearly as important as winning the war applies to the continued revitalization of America's cities. Generals change in both the public and private sectors, and with such turnover of leaders, there are inevitably changes in personalities, work habits, and development strategies. In addition, there are important differences between private and public projects. Two major brick-and-mortar development projects during the Interlude were rapid transit and the convention center, both large-scale public investments. The convention center required both private and public cooperation, whereas the transit project was largely dealt with by multiple levels of government because of a disagreement between the mayor and the business community over the mode of transit.

Organizational Infrastructure

Social Partnerships

For a partnership to exist, two or more parties need only to engage in business together and share the profits. But another definition includes participation as a necessary part of the description. These definitions are relevant at this point because the partnerships we are dealing with are social ones. Physical infrastructure—transportation systems, energy, water, and waste disposal—is a common issue in any discussion of preconditions for development. Less common is the recognition of the need for an infrastructure that is sound organizationally. Yet if it is considered in connection with neighborhoods, crime, education, health, and hope (with respect to job opportunities), organizational infrastructure is clearly an essential precondition for development.

Links to the Black Community

Important new public-private partnerships were developed in the 1960s to help fill the need for educational and job opportunities for the black population.

NEED. In 1963, seventy-six black students who had been admitted to college approached the Education Committee of the Urban League of Pittsburgh seeking financial help for tests, tuition, and the like. As a Community Chest organization, the Urban League could not raise money, and it had to turn the students down. Consequently, two members of the Education Committee (Marian Jordan, a black woman, and Florence Reizenstein, a white woman) resigned and went to Fletcher Byrom, chief executive officer of Koppers Company, seeking corporate support for an idea that they called the Negro Education Emergency Drive (NEED).

Byrom's challenge was that if $100,000 could be raised from individuals, he would be willing to solicit corporate funds. In 1964, $70,000 was raised from community efforts; efforts by a special committee of chief executives from Koppers, Westinghouse, Alcoa, and Edgewater Steel; and remission of tuition by colleges. By 1965, the goal was reached; and in 1966, Byrom enlisted corporate support. The community efforts in 1964 and 1965 were sufficient to generate continued corporate support, which amounts to $250,000 to $300,000 a year.

Since 1963, NEED has awarded 16,806 grants to between 4,000 and 5,000 students. The grants were $250 initially and now range from $300 to $500, depending on need. They are viewed as seed money, enabling the students to obtain federal loans, work-study jobs, and so on. NEED serves as an ombudsman between high schools and colleges. Its funding has always been entirely private, with the partnership between the corporate community in the form of funding and the black community in the form of talent.

PACE. In early 1968, as racial tensions were mounting, black leaders met at Pittsburgh's Loendi Club with business leaders selected by ACCD. As a result of this meeting, the conference set up a grants program, and the United Fund (now the United Way) set up a special committee *within* its purview to disperse funds in a nontypical way, enabling the fund to respond immediately to the problems of the black community. This was the Program to Aid Citizen Enterprise (PACE).

A committee of whites and blacks held approximately fifteen meetings deciding how to create and manage such a United Fund agency. The black community ultimately selected the council to manage PACE with an initial budget in 1968 of $400,000 (in 1981 it was nearly $800,000). One measure of its efficacy is that eight United Way agencies got their seed money from PACE. In 1980 the United Way reevaluated PACE and decided that such an intermediary organization was still needed.

NAB. In early 1968, President Johnson requested the assistance of business leaders in solving the unemployment problem of the urban poor by providing jobs and training. In Pittsburgh, Donald C. Burnham, chief executive officer of Westinghouse Electric, was selected to head the National Alliance of Businessmen (NAB) Program. Also in 1968, ACCD organized its Employment Committee; the chairman was Burnham. This was an important precedent; the Employment Committee chairman continues to chair NAB, and the conference's Employment Committee, which represents major companies in the area, still serves as the NAB committee employment. The working staff for this committee comprises the vice-presidents of human resources (or industrial relations or personnel) of each company.

One of the distinctions of the Pittsburgh NAB program has been the continuing involvement of the conference and hence the major corporate officers. After the first nine years of the program (1968 to 1976), the cumulative number of disadvantaged hires stood at 31,521, with a 60-percent retention rate with the initial employer, one of the highest retention rates in the country. In addition, in 1971, NAB began a job-placement program for Vietnam veterans; and by 1976, 15,702 vets had been hired. By 1976, total NAB hires had exceeded 47,000.[10] Perhaps most important, the NAB commitment by the conference continues through the present.

MELP. In June 1968 the ACCD also organized an Economic Development Committee to help minorities own and manage their own businesses. The Minority Entrepreneur Loan Program (MELP) was developed in cooperation with four major Pittsburgh banks. The program provided equity money in the form of a subordinated loan to enable a minority businessperson to obtain a loan from the Small Business Administration (SBA). Generally, SBA would loan up to 80 or 90 percent of the amount needed. Hence, the MELP program not only made obtaining a loan possible but also provided a loan leverage of 4 to 1 (at 80 percent) or 9 to 1 (at 90 percent) beyond the MELP loan. Like NAB, MELP was directed by a committee of chief executives.

In 1970 the conference organized a skills bank to assist the minority entrepreneurs; and in 1972, the Business Research Center (BRC) was established to aid and promote minority businesses. In 1973, BRC formed the Regional Minority Purchasing Council to assist corporations in locating minority suppliers with whom to place contracts. BRC now has an online computer system listing over 10,000 suppliers to respond to major corporate inquiries.

Between 1968 and 1976, MELP made over $15 million in loans and loan commitments to 650 entrepreneurs. The failure rate was about the same as the national average for all new businesses, about 50 percent over a five-year period. In 1977, the conference ended the program, but not without providing ongoing operational support through BRC to the enterprises spawned. (It is a practice of the conference to be involved in operational programs only temporarily. The conference views its role as that of a catalyst. However, organizations that continue operational missions have often been created by the conference and continue to work alongside it.) Today there are more than two hundred additional minority-owned enterprises in the Pittsburgh region as a result of the MELP program.

Neighborhood Revitalization: Neighborhood Housing
Services

The second form of social partnership that developed during the Interlude
pertained to neighborhoods.[11] In July 1968, the Central North Side Improvement Fund, soon to be renamed Neighborhood Housing Services
(NHS), was incorporated, a result of two years of work by neighborhood
citizens' groups, the mayor's office, and financial institutions. According
to Roger S. Ahlbrandt, Jr., and Paul C. Brophy, NHS can be thought
of in two ways: as a citizen-based effort to improve the neighborhood
and as a revolving loan fund to improve housing in the area. It is the
neighborhood aspect that distinguishes this program from most housing-
related programs and clearly places it in the social-development category.

The genesis of NHS is twofold, with links between citizens' groups
in the Central North Side (CNS) and Mayor Joseph Barr on the one hand,
and the same citizens' groups and financial institutions on the other. The
neighborhood was facing a crisis. Ahlbrandt and Brophy describe the
situation as follows:

> In 1966, citizens in Pittsburgh's Central North Side decided to save
> their neighborhood from urban renewal—renewal and highway clear-
> ance projects had affected three adjoining neighborhoods—and a 1954
> Master Plan designated the Central North Side as a clearance area. In
> 1966 the Central North Side was obviously declining. Its 3,900 housing
> units were aging and in disrepair. The incomes of many of the residents
> in the area were low, and the population was increasingly elderly. The
> investment mentality in the area was pessimistic. Slum clearance seemed
> inevitable. (p. 127)

Three citizens' groups, two of which were local, began to mobilize.
Citizens Against Slum Housing (CASH) initiated a citywide effort to
improve housing, and the CNS Neighborhood Council and the North Side
Civic Development Council concentrated on the North Side.

In 1966, after many meetings between the citizens' groups and the
city administration, Mayor Barr decided that CNS would remain residential. Upon receiving a positive response from the citizens' groups
regarding the mayor's suggestions for developing alternatives to a federally assisted code-enforcement program, the city agreed in 1967 to
designate CNS as a code-enforcement area without federal funding. One
year later, with the aid of the mayor, a group of citizens prepared a
proposal to establish a revolving loan fund for high-risk residents to be
used alongside the code-enforcement program, as well as for more general
housing improvements. This proposal was funded by the locally based
Sarah Scaife Foundation. In total, over the six-year period from 1969 to

1974, the Scaife Foundation granted $600,000; because of the revolving nature of the loan program, this resulted in loans and grants of $813,644 to 339 households. In conjunction with the revolving loan fund, in 1968 and 1969, the city Planning Department issued a detailed program of capital improvements in the CNS, much of which was implemented by the next mayor, Peter Flaherty. Over the 1968–1974 period, the Department of Recreation invested almost $400,000 in parks and playground development in the CNS area; the Department of Public Works invested over $1 million in street repaving, streetlights, and tree planting; and 222 unfit structures were demolished. Thus the city invested more than $1.4 million in physical infrastructure in this neighborhood.

In 1966 the citizens' groups were also meeting with financial institutions. After Mayor Barr's decision to keep the area residential, thirteen lending institutions agreed to make loans available to owners qualifying for conventional loans. It was the realization that many CNS residents would not qualify for such conventional loans that prompted the grant proposal to establish a revolving loan fund for nonbankable residents. Subsequent discussions between the citizens' groups and the lending institutions resulted in an agreement to fund the administrative costs of the revolving loan fund and to provide data-processing services on the loan accounts.

NHS's board of directors consisted of fifteen persons; most were CNS residents, but there were also representatives from financial institutions, community agencies, and the city and county. The primary goal of NHS— to stem decline in the CNS neighborhood—was made operational through the use of flexible internal procedures. Loan criteria were not rigidly defined; the primary purpose of the review process was to determine whether the applicant was bankable and, if not, whether there was a reasonable chance of repayment; each applicant was examined on an individual basis; and both the interest rate and term were quite flexible, depending on the applicant's situation. The loan fund was administered by a loan committee of three citizens and two bankers. (The bankers' participation provided an evaluation of whether the applicant was bankable; if so, the individual was referred to a participating financial institution. The board of directors reviewed the loan committee's decisions and ratified the loans.)

The social partnerships pertaining to NHS and this neighborhood's revitalization involved four parties: citizens, government, financial institutions, and private foundations.

Citizens were not only committed but also organized. They were the heart of this program. They pressured the city to recognize and then raise its level of commitment to the neighborhood. They were the primary force in enabling NHS to obtain funding, in obtaining the community's acceptance of the code-enforcement program, and in the continuing internal operation of NHS via its board of directors.

Government responded in several ways: It listened to neighborhood groups and then reversed an earlier decision designating the neighborhood as a renewal area to be cleared. It helped devise a program with public-private administration (loans and code enforcement) outside of standard operating procedures and without federal funds. It aided in getting funding for the loan program from private sources and it committed capital resources to the physical infrastructure of the neighborhood, providing not only streets and lights but also trees and parks.

The two most direct activities of financial institutions were funding of the revolving loan fund's administrative costs and providing technical and data-processing services on the nonbankable loan accounts. Moreover, the involvement of bankers on the board of directors and on the loan committee was important in establishing credibility to the larger set of participating institutions and in making the loan process not only credible but also operational in the identification of bankable applicants. Perhaps equally important, the long-term viability of any neighborhood requires participation by lending institutions, and it was discovered that the direct, personal involvement by representatives of such organizations was an important key to increasing lending in such neighborhoods. Only those banks with personal involvement on the NHS board increased their lending practice within CNS.

The Scaife Foundation provided $600,000 for the revolving loans to nonbankable persons.

Several organizations, although perhaps not partners, were of assistance in enabling the yet-to-be-proven NHS idea to gain sufficient credibility to obtain foundation funding: the Home Builders Association of Western Pennsylvania, the Pittsburgh Chapter of American Institute of Architects, the Pittsburgh History and Landmarks Foundation, and ACTION-Housing.

The following key features of the NHS model have been identified:[12]

The Program Is a Local Program. Program policy, administration and implementation is the responsibility of those on the local level.

The Program Is Nongovernmental. Control is vested in the board of directors of a private corporation that consist of citizens and financial institutions. There are no government regulations to follow, and therefore, the board has freedom and flexibility in its operation of the program.

The Program Is Nonbureaucratic. Each program develops its own priorities and policies.

The Program Is a Self-help Effort. The involvement of local citizens is regarded as extremely important. NHS operating costs are funded entirely through local sources, and local contributors supply much of the high-risk fund. Emphasis on local funding is part of the self-help element of the NHS model.

The Program Is not a Give-away. The high-risk loan fund is a revolving-loan fund; even for high-risk applicants, there must be a prospect for repayment.

The Program Targets Specific Neighborhoods. The NHS program addresses itself to neighborhoods that are basically sound, though deteriorating. Concentration of the program's efforts into an area small enough to be manageable is important.

The degree of public investment, Ahlbrandt and Brophy pointed out, depends on the state of neighborhood decline. With regard to transferability to other neighborhoods and cities, they offered the following observations:

> In selecting neighborhoods for revitalization programs, a number of factors must be taken into account: (1) residents must exhibit a desire to stay in the neighborhood; (2) homeownership must be sufficient to give evidence of a stable population base; (3) the level of income in a large portion of the community must be high enough to support adequate property maintenance expenditures; and (4) neighborhood change in surrounding communities must be supportive of efforts to upgrade the area in question. (p. 153)

The principal significance of NHS in Pittsburgh was not its dollar value (less than $1 million) but the partnership that evolved and the associated individual, organizational, and financial commitments by all three of the principals (citizen's groups, local government, and financial institutions). Without a high degree of citizen involvement, there would be no neighborhood. Clearly, NHS's program was not sufficient on its own. It required an active partnership in the form of both code enforcement and capital infrastructure for the loan aspect of the process to work. Finally, it was found that while the number of conventional loans within the neighborhood continued to increase yearly from 1969 to 1973, the increase was due solely to the lending institutions with direct involvement on the NHS board. To bring actual lending practice into line with good intentions, it is apparently necessary to have the personal involvement of representatives of each financial institution. One banker noted that such personal commitment increases the lending agency's social consciousness as well as a much earlier identification of the positive changes in the neighborhood, resulting in more flexibility toward extending credit within such a neighborhood. It may well be that this type of program can succeed where others involving many more dollars have failed. (Important spinoffs have resulted from the Pittsburgh NHS project. The Urban Reinvestment Task Force was created in 1974 by the Federal Home Loan Bank and the U.S. Department of Housing and Urban Development. One of its aims was to develop NHS programs in forty cities. A summary of the social private-public partnerships is provided in table 3A–4.)

Managerial Partnerships

There is nothing particularly innovative about efforts to make government operations more efficient or about the use of private-sector-loaned executives within government. Thus the important question is: What are the basic conditions under which loaned private executives contribute to substantial gains in managerial efficiency in government operations? The Pittsburgh example provides important clues.

ComPAC

In the 1975 election of county commissioners, one of the major campaign issues raised by two of the candidates, James Flaherty (brother of the mayor) and Robert Pierce, was that they would bring efficiency to county government. The new president of the Chamber of Commerce, Justin Horan, had been successful in his first program venture (increasing state funds for roads and highways), and one of the major corporate leaders, Edgar B. Speer (U.S. Steel), chaired that effort. Horan's aim was to reinvigorate the chamber, making it an action-oriented, problem-solving organization. Thus he was looking for new and important programs that were regional in nature and that affected the business climate of the region. Horan contacted the two candidates, told them that he recognized the need for more efficiency in government, and asked them how they were going to bring it about. They agreed that if they won the election, they would come to the chamber for assistance because it represented the business community. Horan in turn indicated that he would help organize that community to aid them.

Three persons at Mellon Bank—James H. Higgins (chief executive officer); J. David Barnes (senior vice president and head of corporate planning); and John B. Olsen (who then worked for Barnes)—were the second source of the idea. They recognized the good intentions of the newly elected commissioners but worried about their lack of managerial experience at this scale of operations. After reviewing a white paper on the subject of what the private sector could do (drafted by Olsen), Higgins decided that it made sense for the business leadership to volunteer if the county commissioners were interested in such an arrangement.

The two ideas intersected at the Chamber of Commerce, where Barnes was on the board and Horan was president. The timing of this opportunity for action was important on both sides. During Mayor Peter Flaherty's first term in office, the partnership between the city administration and the business community had basically dissolved. Thus the time was right for the business community to signal that it remained ready to be a constructive partner with government, and from the county government's perspective, the election of two new commissioners opened a window for such a new initiative.

Credibility for the ComPAC project was established from the county's side when all three county commissioners requested assistance from the business community at the annual meeting of the Greater Pittsburgh Chamber of Commerce in April 1976. Credibility on the part of the business community was established once the ComPAC board of directors (all chief executives of major Allegheny county corporations) was selected.

Three stipulations were agreed upon for participation: (1) The chief executive must serve personally, with no surrogates or representatives. (A similar practice had been utilized by the conference Executive Committee.) (2) By virtue of serving on the ComPAC board, the chief executive was, in fact, committing the name and support of his corporation; therefore the ComPAC cochairmen could request individuals by name from the corporation to work on a task force. (3) Each chief executive would assume responsibility for one task force. Support in the form of funding for the management of the program was provided by nine local foundations, a rather common occurrence in Pittsburgh once the corporate community is committed to a task. Time commitments for the loaned executives were absorbed by their corporations. (The estimated value of this time was more than a million dollars.)

ComPAC was organized into nine task forces: purchasing, cash management, personnel, computer services, management information/program budgeting, record management, construction management, financial management, and business/industrial-development services. One of the distinguishing features of this loaned-executive program hinged on the initial expectations regarding implementation or results. The measure of a task leader was the number of recommendations implemented, not the number of recommendations made. In each final task-force report, the first page chronicled the implementation as of that date. Moreover, each task force also continued to meet for six months to two years after the final report was issued, to monitor the results independently, and to report to the ComPAC board and the county commissioners on implementation. After the ComPAC staff went out of business in mid-1978, the county clerk also continued to monitor the implementation schedules. All the recommendations were adopted by the Board of County Commissioners, and over 70 percent were implemented. It was estimated that almost $3 million in one-time savings and another $3 million in annual savings would have resulted from full implementation.[13]

Several other features of the management structure of the project are worth describing. Two codirectors for ComPAC were hired full time to manage the project, with clerical and research assistance where needed. They developed a procedures manual and also coordinated and monitored the three phases of each task force: (1) development of a mission statement, (2) analysis of the problem and recommendations for solution, and (3) implementation monitoring. Once a chief executive officer assumed responsibility for a task force, he selected an executive from his corporation to work full time as the task leader. The task leader and ComPAC managers then developed a mission statement for the task force, including the statement of the problem and how to organize to solve it (the major questions to be answered, the products to be delivered, a timetable for the products, and the individual executives to work on the task force). Each mission statement was presented first to the county commissioners and then to the ComPAC board. Once it was accepted, the chief executive heading the task force would contact the corporations about those selected. The task force was then put into operation, and analyses were conducted. During this process, frequent meetings were held with the county commissioners. Finally, mid-term and final reports were presented to the ComPAC board of directors.

Two additional management features stand out. First, it was stipulated by ComPAC that the work should not result in firings. Where opportunities for reduction were identified, transfers and reassignments should be made to positions vacated by attrition. Second, because it is important to start with a success, the first task force (purchasing) was chosen strategically. It met three criteria: (1) It dealt with a problem everyone in the county government experienced; success would therefore be widely recognized. (2) It concerned an area in which the business community clearly had expertise. (3) An initial success would have a spillover effect, making the work of subsequent task forces easier.

Among the *keys* to the success of ComPAC, two points seem most critical: commitment from the top and emphasis on implementation. The first involves individuals who expect results and have the resources to get results. The second places the emphasis of the entire efforts on such results, not plans or recommendations for action.

Other Seeds of Renaissance II

Other seeds of Renaissance II were sown during the Interlude, partly
through public-private partnerships and partly from independent action
by the public sector. Among these seeds were fiscal soundness, more
efficient organization and employment practice, two large-scale public
projects (rapid transit and the convention center), and emphasis on neighborhoods.

Development often extends across many years, and one political
figure may reap the benefits from the seeds planted by a predecessor.
This is the rule, not the exception. Thus, just as Peter Flaherty had the
Pittsburgh National Bank and U.S. Steel high-rise office buildings completed during the initial years of his administration, 1971 and 1972, the
rapid-transit system and the convention center were projects brought to
the consensus stage during his administration but to be completed during
the 1980s, well beyond his term of service.

In 1969, Peter Flaherty was elected mayor of Pittsburgh. He had run
on an "I'm nobody's boy" platform, without ties to labor, the Democratic
party leadership, or the business community. Three principal goals guided
his administration: To balance the budget, to restore the neighborhoods,
and to provide new leadership. The first goal was to be met without
increasing taxes and therefore meant reevaluation of the city's employment needs. This meant reorganization and significant labor cutbacks.
The second goal indicated a major shift in management philosophy, with
substantially more emphasis placed on neighborhoods and less on the
central business district. The goal of new leadership without ties to labor,
party, or business meant that the rethinking of management and employment practices could occur without dealing with debts and obligations to
either unionized or party-placed employees and also that a shift in emphasis from the central business district to neighborhoods could occur.
Perhaps most important, it also meant that the style of cooperative management on a "business-as-usual" basis, which had developed during
Renaissance I, would no longer be adhered to. The leadership goal meant
not only a change in philosophy but also major staff changes, particularly
among departmental directors, who were responsible for conducting much
of the business of city government. Hence, the task of reestablishing
working relationships between the private and public sectors would have
to be accomplished not only at the top but also at the staff level.

The decline of cooperation between the conference and the mayor
stemmed from two sources: different agendas and different ideas on a
new transit system. A third source of difficulty was in the adjustment by
both sides to the philosophy, staff, and work habits of the new city
administration.

The conference's top priorities appeared to be dealing with the serious racial tensions that surfaced during 1960s and development of a rapid-transit system to the south and a more adequate transportation system to the east. These did not match the mayor's priorities of fiscal soundness, more efficient employment practices and organization, and emphasis on neighborhoods.

The conference and the mayor also differed in their thinking about the *mode* of rapid transit and the project timetable. The mayor gave other issues higher priorities. This lack of emphasis on transit was a big factor in the conference's negative view of the mayor. The *Press,* as well as the conference, was committed to the Skybus (an elevated, rubber-tired, electrically driven, operatorless, people-moving vehicle) before Flaherty was elected, and that commitment continued. Flaherty, however, was reevaluating the transit-system proposals.

The third source of difficulty was in the adjustment by both sides to a new style of operation. The mayor had promised new leadership and that meant a shift in departmental operations. To do this, Flaherty replaced the directors of all departments, including those involved most directly with planning and development, the Planning Department and the Urban Redevelopment Authority. The shift in emphasis to neighborhoods also corresponded to a distaste for development projects that resulted in population displacement. Equally important, the platform issue of ''I'm nobody's boy'' evolved into an initial arm's-length relationship with the conference and therefore with big business.

The initial inability of the conference to come to grips with a major shift in political behavior and management philosophy meant that its offers of help were not viewed as such because they were not attuned ''to the new mayor's mode of leadership'' in terms of personality, work habits, philosophy, and staff. The position that had worked well with his predecessors—''Mr. Mayor, here's what we think you ought to do''— did not work with Flaherty. The staff link had also been cut, severing long-term ties at the levels where business is normally conducted. To add to the difficulty of rebuilding those bridges, the conference hired the fired planning director.

There is little doubt that the partnership was dissolved during the first years of the Flaherty administration at the mayor's initiative. But there is also strong evidence that even without such an arm's-length posture, it would have been difficult to continue joint ventures because of non-overlapping agendas, different priorities, and major disagreement on a public-investment project (transit). The disagreement over transit lasted six years and especially tainted the positive developments that were realized or set in motion during that period, including the joint efforts to develop the convention center.

The most dramatic events of the Flaherty program included a balanced budget and employment reorganizations and cutbacks. In labor practice, Flaherty restored the full workday for all employees (it had not been uncommon for some employees to work from ten to three), stopped labor union abuses (teamster drivers being required to drive pickup trucks for plumbers installing water meters for example), and initiated the payment of pensions for nonuniformed new recruits on a sound actuarial basis. (Funding the pension program was initiated in order to maintain a high bond rating for the city. Nonuniformed employees made up over 50 percent of the city's work force.) Flaherty reduced permanent full-time employment by over 10 percent in the first year and by 27 percent over seven years, mostly through attrition. Reorganizations occurred across the work force. For example, a centralized computer facility was introduced, the water department was automated, garbage routes were revised, better garbage trucks were purchased, police officers were replaced by nonuniformed staff in clerical and communications jobs, and the planning staff was consolidated.[14]

For all their differences, the mayor and the conference did succeed in working together on one project: the Convention Center. In 1973 Mayor Flaherty was reelected, winning both the Democratic and the Republican primaries. In the same year a new conference president took over, giving the mayor the opportunity for a new initiative. Moreover, in 1974 the state threatened to withdraw the funds for building a convention-exposition center, thus giving the conference a window for an initiative. The conference organized the Exposition Hall Coalition Committee, with representatives from business, labor, and civic agencies, thereby reaffirming its interest in and support of the center. Concurrently, the mayor appointed the Mayor's Convention Advisory Committee to study the overall convention project. The main issues were size and site.

In cooperation with the mayor's committee, the conference retained consultants to assess whether Pittsburgh could compete successfully in the national exhibition-convention market. In August they reported that it could; and in September the mayor's committee agreed on size, site, and operation by the Public Auditorium Authority, with Robert Dickey III (chief executive of Dravo Corporation and president of the conference) as the chairman of the authority. All sides viewed Dickey's participation on the mayor's committee, the conference's sponsorship of an outside study, and selection of Dickey as chairman as breakthroughs.

The site was largely determined by the state, and the state's deadline for action triggered the breakthrough. Moreover, both sides had changed, which was equally important. Flaherty had already made his largest labor cuts, and the city's agenda could be partially revised. The initiative to Dickey, who was in effect a symbol of the conference, demonstrated a new spirit of trust and cooperation on the part of the mayor. Furthermore, the reelection of Flaherty had sent a signal that the conference would have to adjust to his style of management and leadership. In 1973, when Dickey assumed the presidency of the conference, it too had begun to revise its agenda, winding down the strong emphasis on social development and turning once again to physical and economic development. Its 1973 annual report indicated this shift in emphasis:

> It would be good to report that the work in the Golden Triangle is complete now that so much has been achieved. The truth is otherwise: the work is only in mid-passage. (p.2)

The report also contained an explicit statement on the need to recover the ability to work together:

> In frankness, we must admit that the Pittsburgh urban region no longer is setting an example to the nation in how these problems [urban infrastructure and urban governance] are identified, in how analysis is made, in how a consensus is reached, in how action is taken. We suggest that it is time to recover these skills which were so pre-eminent in the high period of the Pittsburgh renaissance. (p.1)

The second major public-investment development brought to consensus during the Flaherty administration was the rapid-transit system. This time the principal participants were all public: city, county, state, federal and Port Authority Transit (PAT). In 1974 the Transit Task Force was established with the goal of reaching consensus on a rapid-transit mode. The chairman of this task force was John P. Robin, a PAT board member. (Robin is almost universally heralded as being the chief idea man or visionary of Renaissance II. He was executive secretary to Mayor Scully at age twenty-four and then to Mayor Lawrence in Renaissance I. He was also the first executive director of URA. He is now on the board of PAT, chairman of the board of URA, a member of the Mayor's Development Council, and a program advisor to the conference.)

Robin had seen that a decision on the Skybus was hopelessly deadlocked. He therefore sought the formation of the task force; its members included both those for and against Skybus. Its objective was to reach a unanimous decision on selecting a consultant to recommend a transit mode. The task force was also operating under the threat of cancellation of federal funds. The key to the process was devising a method for selecting the consultant. Robin suggested that the task force use a practice similar to that for selecting jurors. Each member would have one no vote "without cause." This preemptory challenge eliminated any suspicions of a setup. Dismissals "for cause" were also permitted. This eliminated all who could be conceived as having had special relations with PAT in the past that could therefore prejudice their view. This process produced a short list. Secret ballots were then cast, with the low ballot eliminated on each round until a final selection was made. The federal government then agreed to provide $500,000 to $700,000 for the consultant's study. The consultant recommended a light-rail vehicle (LRV) in 1976. Construction of the LRV began in 1981 and is scheduled for completion in 1984.

The keys to this project were a deadline for reaching consensus imposed by the major funding source, a recognition of an impasse, and the devising of a reasonably objective method for reevaluating fixed positions. The latter was the most critical because it eliminated suspicions and established a basis for trust. Although the private sector was not a participant in the final decision, it did play a critical role in obtaining funding at the federal level and thus was important in ultimately developing a rapid-transit system.

A third phenomenon of the Flaherty years was the emphasis on neighborhoods. During the 1960s, the bulk of federal-aid money had been spent in the central business district, but Flaherty decided that downtown and neighborhoods should each be allocated 50 percent of federal funds. The visible impact of the emphasis on neighborhoods, when compared with high-rise complexes is for the most part more difficult to identify. Whatever its positive effects, this policy resulted in no showpieces. Flaherty instituted a home-improvement loan program from Community Development (CD) Block Grant money along the lines of the NHS program but without neighborhood targeting. He also emphasized parks and recreation as another means of bolstering neighborhoods. The conference, in its 1975 annual report, acknowledged the results of Flaherty's neighborhood emphasis while reminding him of the need to give attention to the downtown area:

The Mayor and his staff have provided leadership in rebuilding and improving parts of several Pittsburgh neighborhoods. Downtown, in a sense, is another neighborhood, everybody's neighborhood. It is time to plan and act together, private and public, entrepreneur and shopper, employer and employee. Plan, set a course, and pursue it to its conclusion. Downtown and its environs are uniquely suited for development. The next twenty-five years could make the last twenty-five appear as only a beginning. The Allegheny Conference is dedicated to that purpose. (p. 7)

Having achieved a joint success on the Convention Center in 1974, and having seen the Equibank high-rise office building completed in 1975 and the LRV consensus reached in 1976, the conference noted:

It is too early to say that a second Pittsburgh Renaissance is at hand;
it is fair, however, to say that there is a very good chance one is in the
making. (1976 Annual Report, p. 1)

Some of the specific bricks-and-mortar developments of the Interlude
underscore the fact that it was an interlude in partnerships founded in the
Renaissance, not a cessation of development. In 1975 preliminary draw-
ings of the Convention Center were rendered; in 1977 construction began,
and in February 1981 the center was opened. Other developments included
the Scaife Gallery (1974), the Equibank high-rise office building (1975),
and proposals (1976) for the development of Station Square (a renovation
of the Pittsburgh and Lake Erie Railroad buildings into restaurants and
shops, as well as the construction of a new hotel), with construction to
begin in 1977.

As of 1976, some discussion had already been conducted between
Mayor Flaherty and U.S. Steel regarding the Grant Street East property
and the development of a high-rise office building. The conference had
also approached Mayor Flaherty about conducting a study of street patterns, especially Grant Street, with the idea that it could become a "grand
avenue." Thus there are several indications, including the Convention
Center success and the personal trust that developed between Robert
Dickey and the mayor, which suggest that much of the development in
Renaissance II would have occurred under Mayor Flaherty had he continued in office, but there are also strong indicators that some of the
developments, with their subsequent spinoffs, would not have occurred.
Nor is it likely that there would have been a Renaissance spirit created
to infuse the process. Clearly, the major distinction between the Flaherty
years and those of Richard Caliguiri, who followed him, is not between
development and no development. Rather, the difference lies in the spirit
and flurry of activity.

Renaissance II

In contrast with the years of the Interlude, there was no flashpoint in
racial tensions in 1977; there was no budget deficit. Instead, the city was
fiscally sound, with tight employment practices and a lean labor force.
The newly elected mayor, Richard Caliguiri, had run on an "It's another
Renaissance" platform, indicative once again of a major change in management philosophy and work habits. As in Renaissance I, on the other
hand, there was an extreme shortage of high-grade office space. Over
the 1945 to 1952 period, Pittsburgh's office occupancy rate was 99 percent, a level it reached again in 1980. By 1977 the tightening trend was

becoming quite evident. In addition, the conference was once again con-
centrating its attention on planning and development on a grand scale;
and the Chamber of Commerce had once again become action oriented,
as it had been during Renaissance I in regard to the flood issue. Both in
Renaissance I and in Renaissance II, the outgoing mayor initiated several
major development ideas, but control had not brought them to the implementation or completion stage.

The major differences between the two Renaissance periods are just
as important as the similarities. In Renaissance II, most of the market
demand is met not by one massive high-rise office complex but by a
series of *independent* high-rise office complexes, each requiring different
levels of public involvement. There is no longer one business leader who
speaks for the business community and one political leader who speaks
for the Democratic party; today each is more heterogeneous. At the height
of Renaissance I, the sophistication in planning and development skills
was almost entirely with the private sector, which was therefore the prime
initiator; today the city is more often the planner and initiator of public
investments. Furthermore, the environment is not a major issue at the
moment; the most dramatic environmental achievements occurred in Renaissance I. The public sector also has a different focus for major development in Renaissance II: rapid transit and the Convention Center.
Moreover, there is now a tradition of successful public-private partnerships, particularly between the conference and the city. And there is a
newer tradition of social-developmental partnerships to build on involving
the black community, the neighborhoods, and the internal operations of
government. This has led to the recognition of a second front for Renaissance activity.

High-Rise Office Complexes

The dramatic symbols of Renaissance II, like those of Renaissance I, are
the high-rise office complexes. This is probably due largely to their grand
scale in comparison with other developments.

When Richard Caliguiri was elected, his primary goal was to make
a second Renaissance happen on two fronts: the neighborhoods and the
central business district. This view constituted a major change in philosophy, especially in terms of priorities and organization. A Renaissance,
according to Caliguiri, is a spirit, an attitude, a coming together of the
public and private sectors to discuss and work out a plan or an idea for
changing Pittsburgh. Caliguiri's executive secretary, David Matter, adds
that the new mayor brought with him a new attitude and a new direction:

We were going to pay attention to development activities in this City

and we were going to try to foster and stimulate activity . . . ; we
would have a council or a committee [the Mayor's Development Coun-
cil] if you will, in place and prepared to work with corporations, to
work with developers who are willing to invest in our City. And I think
that came from a realization that the City couldn't do it alone. We just
didn't have the resources. . . ; if we were going to make a go of it,
we'd have to stimulate vast amounts of private capital with modest
amounts of public money. I think we've been fairly successful in doing
that, and it was only by first having the willingness and energy to do
it, that could help facilitate it.[15]

Caliguiri, it is agreed, both coined the term and sold the idea of Renaissance II.

Caliguiri created the Department of Housing at the beginning of his
administration and launched two innovative, large-scale housing programs, the Home Improvement Loan Program (HILP) and the North Side
Revitalization Program (NSRP). If HILP is continued over the next six
years, as planned, its cumulative investment, shortly after the high-rise
offices are completed, will be nearly $200 million. (The "if" hinges on
federal legislation that may stop the leveraging process described here,
thereby gutting these two programs.) The current policy of the Caliguiri
administration is to distribute 75 percent of federal monies to the neighborhoods and 25 percent to the central business district. This is a substantial increase over Mayor Flaherty's dramatic shift. Thus, if the scale
of housing development is carried through, a neighborhood Renaissance
seems in the making with a private-public partnership as its cornerstone.

Organizationally, Calguiri kept the directors of both the Planning
Department and URA. To fill the strategic slot of URA board chairman,
he selected John P. Robin, who bridges both Renaissances and is an
acknowledged idea man. This choice immmediately paid off. Among
other things, Robin suggested that they form the Mayor's Development
Council (MDC) to facilitate and coordinate development. MDC is made
up of the directors of the Departments of City Planning, Economic Development, Housing, and Public Works, URA, the Parking Authority,
the heads of two external organizations (PAT and the Regional Industrial
Development Corporation), and the URA board chairman (Robin). The
mayor's executive secretary, David Matter, is its chairman. Like the
ACCD Executive Committee, MDC has a no-representative-or-surrogate
rule. This rule is both stringent and effective. Either the director is there,
or the department is not represented.

On the private-sector side, there has been a significant shift in the
conference's agenda, characterized by an increasing buildup of expectations and preparations to participate in another Renaissance. In 1973,
after six years of focusing its major attention on social development and
the black community, the conference once again made planning and

development, in the usual sense of those terms, its main agenda. It has a vivid memory and continuous reminder of its successes in this sphere in the form of Gateway Center and several other major office towers of Renaissance I. In its 1977 annual report, the conference discussed its expectations for a new Renaissance:

> In our introduction to last year's Annual Report, we made what has proved to be a sound bit of prophecy: "It is too early to say," the Report stated, "that a second Pittsburgh Renaissance is at hand; it is fair, however, to say that there is a very good chance that one is in the making." It is plain now that last year's "good chance" has become this year's certainty. Mayor Caliguiri adopted "Renaissance II" as the theme of his successful campaign and his new administration. It is in the early stages of definition and execution, but clearly there is a sense of excitement, of urgency, of a new order of things in the city government. We are confident our second Pittsburgh Renaissance will reach the standards of our past. We would be disappointed indeed if it did not exceed them in its scope, its sensitivity, its application to all parts of our urban community and to all persons in our urban society. (p. 1)

Another principal determinant of Renaissance II was the continuing growth in demand for high-quality office space. At the beginning of each Renaissance period, the occupancy rate was 99 percent.

The result of the Interlude's seeds of Renaissance II, the market, the initiatives, the partial renewal of staff and the reorganization (especially the Department of Housing and MDC) is a spectacular flurry of simultaneous development, estimated in the $2-billion range. Among these projects are Heinz Hall Plaza (an open park adjacent to the opera house), the David L. Lawrence Convention Center, Two Chatham Center (a sixteen-story office tower), Riverfront Center (a twenty-story office tower), Station Square (a restaurant, shop, and hotel complex), One Oxford Centre (a forty-six-story office tower and retail complex), Grant Street Plaza (a fifty-three-story office tower and retail complex), PPG Place (six buildings, including a forty-story office tower), LRV (rapid-transit system connecting South Hills and the downtown district), Vista International (hotel and thirty-six-story office tower), the East Busway (exclusive busway connecting the areas east of downtown and the downtown area), and the produce terminal (a fresh-produce market in the central business district).

The conspicuous and spectacular high-rise office complexes are the key to all this development. These buildings are symbolic of Renaissance II in two respects: in the large growth of office space and employment in the central business district; and in the changing nature of Pittsburgh's economic base, from one dominated by heavy manufacturing to a more diversified, service-oriented base dominated by corporate headquarters.

In 1957, downtown Pittsburgh had 12 million square feet of office space; in 1978, it had 19 million square feet, with an average growth rate of 350,000 square feet a year; by 1985, another 4 to 6 million square feet will be added. Thus the increment in Renaissance II is quite large, almost equaling in seven years that of the previous twenty years. Office employment in the area was approximately 51,000 in 1957, grew to 76,000 by 1978, and is expected to reach between 83,000 and 93,000 by 1985, approximately 180 percent of the 1957 level. [16]

The entire *One Oxford Centre* project was privately initiated. The land was intact and purchased from the county government.

Grant Street Plaza (the Dravo headquarters) involved a complicated four-party agreement between U.S. Steel (the developer), the city, URA, and PAT. It included a land trade, reconfiguration of streets, subsurface rights (subway), and air rights (parking). The threat of condemnation (on grounds of interference with a new street pattern) was used by the city to enable U.S. Steel to negotiate with one remaining property owner. The multiparty land trade enlarged U.S. Steel's development property by approximately one-third. The city obtained a new and more efficient street pattern. PAT gained a more efficient LRV track/midtown station development.

The site proposed for *PPG Place* (PPG Industries headquarters) was not owned by the corporation; it had to be designated as "blighted" by the city Planning Commission. The process is analogous to the case of Gateway Center about thirty-five years earlier; that is, URA would act as the intermediary, using its power of eminent domain to purchase the properties, but the entire bill would be paid by the developer (PPG). The city administration's support throughout this bargaining process was critical. Without it, PPG would not have seen the project through. The final development entails several surrounding structures that form a larger complex of restaurants, shops, and open spaces.

Unlike the other high rises, the Vista International project originated with the city and is a combination hotel and office building. The importance of the hotel to the city administration is that it is intended to be adjacent to the Convention Center. URA purchased the property and then developed a marketing strategy to obtain bids. It commissioned a market study, which was then made available to potential developers. The winnowing-down process ultimately produced four actual submissions or proposals, and the developer selected proposed a hotel–office-building complex.

In summary, these four high-rise projects ilustrate levels of public involvement with private developers that range from almost no participation to a role of prime mover. The overall results are bound to equal or surpass development in Renaissance I. Moreover, Renaissance II is characterized by a larger commitment to the architectural design of the building and its situation on the street, as well as to leisure activities in the high-rise office towers. Instead of a mere workplace, a much more vital area will be the result. Two smaller office buildings are to be completed before any of the larger high-rise structures, giving them an initial edge in Pittsburgh's extremely tight market.

This all has triggered a wide range of spinoff developments, including the rehabilitation of historic buildings and new construction. For example, estimates of development advances in the First Side area as a result of PPG Place suggest a twenty-year jump in the area's development beyond what would have otherwise occurred. Discussion and planning for other large areas are also occurring; the conference and representatives of the Penn-Liberty area, which includes the Allegheny riverfront, were, for example, involved with similar talks in 1981.

The continued development of high-rise office buildings, however, means far more than increased office space and jobs. Two of the towers are headquarters buildings, indicative of a long-term economic and employment commitment to the city by growing firms. The long-term, twenty to twenty-five-year growth in office employment has occurred at the same time heavy manufacturing (steel, in particular) employment has declined. That this shift has taken place over several decades rather than all at once has been fortuitous. The high rises are representative of the continued vitality of the central business district and of the shift in the city's economic base.

Organizational Infrastructure

Social Partnerships

Four social partnerships involving the black community were initiated in the 1960s. Three of these—NEED, PACE, and NAB—continue at the same or greater levels of support.

NEED is funded by the corporate community at $250,000 to $300,000 a year and has its own staff. It currently supports over eight-hundred black students at the college level. The NEED grants are supplemental to other sources of income. This program has a solid eighteen-year record and has aided around 4,500 black students.

PACE is a special United Way agency with a mission to serve as an intermediary between the black and white communities. Its council has always had its roots in the black community, and it carries its mission out within the United Way framework, demonstrating the need for and use of flexibility within an organization's operating procedures. (In other cities, a Black United Way was formed.)

The special character of the Pittsburgh NAB stems from its continuing strong organizational and operational support by the conference. The NAB program also has a thirteen-year history of accomplishments, averaging over 3,000 disadvantaged hires annually with a retention ratio of 60 percent with the initial employer. The commitment of corporations and their chief executive officers not only provides facilitation within the major corporations of the region but is also a signal of leadership to the entire business community.

Having recognized the importance of social renewal and development, the conference is currently also involved in the public schools and in health-care planning. It has sponsored a study of the capital needs of the hospitals in the county to determine the impact of major capital investments on health-service costs. It has also created the Trustee Forum, a group of trustees from all the hospitals in the county who meet regularly to learn about the needs and problems of the region's health-care institutions, and the Health Policy Institute (within the University of Pittsburgh), an analytic and policy unit for guiding the development of the regional health-care system.

A number of programs are operated through the conference's Education Fund. A program of minigrants (up to $1,000 each) supports teachers in developing programs. The Partnerships-in-Education program is a joint venture of the conference, the Chamber of Commerce, and the school system. Under this program, a corporation selects a high school and provides staff and assistance to the school. In addition, the conference staff has served on committees dealing with important Board of Education issues. Recently, for instance, in a move directly relating the present to the past, Robert B. Pease, the executive director of the Conference, chaired the Community Advisory Committee on Public School Desegregation. The conference also sponsored a public-relations campaign with television-spot announcements, providing a phone number to call for information on busing, integration, and other critical issues. The bottom line was that, thanks to the organizational infrastructure that had been developed, the desegregation plan was carried out without a serious incident.

Social development efforts are also taking place in the *neighborhoods*. Partial spinoffs of the NHS model have been HLP initiated in 1978, and the North Side Revitalization Program (NSRP), a mortgaging program begun in 1979. The ideas behind both belong to Paul C. Brophy, director of the city's Department of Housing, and David Gressel, a financial consultant under contract with URA who works closely with the Housing Department. Brophy is also the primary mover behind their implementation.

Since 1975 Pittsburgh had offered low-interest rehabilitation loans to homeowners with incomes under a specific level. Within three years, 1,700 loans had been made, but the processing time was a particular problem, and demand outstripped supply. Therefore, in 1977 the city decided to pursue a different policy. It dropped the administration and servicing loan business and let lending institutions take over. A series of discussions between the housing director and the lending institutions resulted in an agreement with thirteen lenders. Two factors related to the public partner were important in this outcome: The prior NHS positive experience had provided a successful working precedent, and the lenders were able to use their standard operating procedures and forms, making it possible to process this program through their operational computerized data systems.

The city sought to leverage its Community Development Block Grants allocated to housing with the issuance of tax-exempt bonds by URA. In 1978 and 1979, bonds were issued totaling $21.8 million. In the first year, over 2,400 loans were made. These loans are citywide, rather than targeted toward neighborhoods, a policy that involved both political expediency and equity.

The NSRP program, on the other hand, is targeted toward six North Side neighborhoods (including CNS) and pertains to mortgaging and, where necessary, associated rehabilitation. The partners in this program are the neighborhood groups, the lenders, the city, and URA. Again the lending institutions originate and service the loans, and URA leverages the money through tax-exempt bonds (in this case, residential mortgage bonds). The program was made possible by $8.1 million in funding, which provided public funds for improvements in physical infrastructure and for rehabilitation subsidies. Citizens' groups from the neighborhoods worked with the city to obtain the UDAG base, and URA floated $23.5 million in bonds. The total mortgage loan portion of the funding is $28 million within these targeted neighborhoods.

The URA mortgage bonds are used to provide below-market-rate first mortgages to investors and homeowners to buy and construct or refinance and rehabilitate. URA owns the mortgages, which are generally secured by private or government mortgage insurance, and the lenders originate and service the loans for a nominal fee. The second part of the package is a second-mortgage or equity-participation loan provided by UDAG and CD funds. There are two types. Deferred equity-participation loans (20 percent of principal) are used to reduce the first mortgage and are due without interest when the property is resold. Installment equity-participation loans are used when the costs of rehabilitation exceed the after-rehabilitation appraised value. This type of loan is provided at the same interest as the first mortgage, and the same lender originates and services both.

The neighborhood groups formed an alliance called the North Side Development Alliance, which monitors the program, provides feedback and advice to the city on its performance, and oversees a neighborhood and marketing program (financed by UDAG) that informs the residents, invites their participation, and markets the mortgage program to potential outside buyers. Monthly meetings between the city and the neighborhood federation assure adequate feedback to the city.

The city has overall responsibility for the NSRP program, for the implementation of the associated physical infrastructure, and for administration of the rehabilitation component. As in the NHS program, all properties are inspected for compliance with codes prior to the loan closing, thereby ensuring that the proposed work will correct major code violations. Perhaps the most novel aspect of the program is the full partnership participation of the private financial institutions, which administer this below-market-rate, subordinated mortgage program within their standard operating procedures. URA is the primary funding source because of its ability to issue tax-exempt bonds.

Managerial Partnerships

Two types of spin-offs from ComPAC occurred during Renaissance II. First, other cities and counties adopted the ComPAC model: the city of Pittsburgh; Allentown and Lehigh Counties in Pennsylvania; Cincinnati and Hamilton County, Ohio; and Jefferson County, Kentucky. Just as the Allegheny County commissioners asked the Pittsburgh Chamber for assistance soon after their election, Mayor Caliguiri requested chamber assistance after his election. This request was the result of prior communication from the chamber. Upon Caliguiri's election in 1977, the chamber sent him a letter of congratulations and offered assistance in achieving greater efficiency of internal operations for the city with a ComPAC-type program. It also invited him to the next board meeting. At this meeting, the mayor requested that a program similar to ComPAC be developed. Thus the Committee for Progress and Efficiency in Pittsburgh (ComPEP) was organized. ComPEP, funded and managed along the lines of ComPAC, launched four task forces: purchasing, computer service, risk management, and fleet management.

A second outgrowth of ComPAC was the organization of the Ad Hoc Committee on Economic Development; its organizer was Fletcher Byrom. Upon ComPAC's completion, Byrom pledged to convene a steering committee (AHCED) to fashion a regional agenda for community economic development. This committee has been meeting for the last three years, engaging people in conversations; it brought in experts from other communities, assessed data, and constructed a framework for both short-term and long-term agendas. It aimed to devise a strategy for building consensus and, ultimately, for making decisions in the nine-county region of southwestern Pennsylvania.

The chamber subsequently moved on to other managerial partnerships, in particular, the development of budget forecasting for the city, the county, and the Pittsburgh Public School Board.

Comparisons of Public-Private Partnerships in Renaissance I and Renaissance II

Three basic types of public-private partnerships dominate the Pittsburgh story: environmental, organizational (both social and managerial), and bricks and mortar. Perhaps the most novel is the development of social partnerships and the elevation of this dimension of organizational infrastructure to a prominent place in the total view of development. Moreover, the Pittsburgh story also illustrates the environmental prerequisites for bricks-and-mortar development. In addition, it offers some lessons regarding the adjustment process when political leadership makes major changes. A list of projects by type of partnership is presented in table 3–1.

Public-private partnerships in the two Renaissance periods can be compared in terms of seven dimensions: facilitative management structures, initiators and implementers, relative share of planning-and-development expertise, reason for development, timing of development, redefining development to include social partnership, and organizational development.

Facilitative Management Structures. In both periods, there were clearly observable mechanisms to foster and coordinate development. Perhaps the most effective facilitative mechanism was that of overlapping organizational memberships at the executive and board levels. A few of the more important examples are listed in table 3–2. Organizational overlap also occurs through individual staff careers. For example:

The director of the Allegheny County Planning Commission became executive director of the conference (Renaissance I).

Table 3–1
Overview of All Projects, by Type of Partnership

Type of Partnership	Individual Project
Environment	Smoke control
	Flood control
Organizational	
Social	Black-community links
	NEED
	PACE
	NAB
	MELP
	Neighborhood housing
	NHS
	NSR
Managerial	Internal government operations
	ComPAC
	ComPEP
Bricks-and-mortar	High-rise office complexes (Renaissance I)
	High-rise office complexes (Renaissance II)

The executive director of URA became executive director of the conference (bridges both Renaissances).

The executive secretary to the mayor became the executive director of URA and later president of RIDC and then chairman of the board of URA and planning advisor to the conference (bridges both Renaissances).

The executive director of ACTION-Housing became director of the city Housing Department (Renaissance II).

The director of public relations at the Chamber of Commerce became the mayor's urban renewal coordinator, then director of city planning, and subsequently director of development for the conference (Renaissance I and Interlude).

Sometimes this sequential overlap backfires, as it did when the director of city planning moved to the conference after being replaced. However, in virtually all the instances just cited, especially those involving simultaneous overlapping organizational memberships, the facilitation of communication and planning proved quite helpful. It removed competition and prevented different organizations from working at cross-purposes by keeping the executives and their staffs informed and their

Table 3–2
Overlapping Organizational Membership

Renaissance I	*Renaissance II*
United Smoke Council head became chairman of the Conference Smoke Abatement Committee.	NAB Jobs Program chairman became the chairman of the Conference Employment Committee.
Two members of the Chamber of Commerce Flood Control Committee became conference executive members.	Two Conference Executive Committee members became members of the board of directors of the Chamber of Commerce.
Conference Executive Committee member was chairman of the PAT Rapid Transit Committee.	Conference planning advisor was also on PAT board of directors and is chairman of the PAT Rapid Transit Committee.
Vice-chairman of URA and chairman of Point Park Steering Committee was on the Conference Executive Committee.	Chairman of URA is a conference planning advisor.
Counsel for the Conference was counsel for URA.	
Conference Executive Committee member and director of PRPA was chairman of the Parking Authority.	President of the conference is chairman of the Public Auditorium Authority.
	Three members of the Mayor's Development Council (MDC) hold linkage positions: URA chairman of board and conference planning advisor, PAT executive director, president of the Regional Industrial Development Council (RIDC).

work coordinated. The sharing of ideas across the private and public sectors was enhanced in both directions, and artificial boundaries were removed. Of course, there was an assumption of honesty and openness in such linkages. When such basic assumptions are met, both from the perceptions of the broader community and between the particular individuals involved, this management strategy appears especially useful. Just as the joint memberships between the conference and chamber at the executive level help to coordinate the two private-sector organizations, MDC links multiple city departments, as well as providing links to the private sector.

Initiators and Implementers. Another important comparison involves the initiation and implementation of ideas. The overall comparison is provided in table 3–3. Ten of the sixteen individual projects were initiated by the private sector; three, by the public sector; and three were joint initiatives. With regard to implementation, fourteen are joint and two private (one high-rise complex in each Renaissance, paralleling the high-rise partner-

Table 3–3
Initiators and Implementers of Public-Private Partnerships

Project	Initiator	Implementer
Environmental		
Smoke	City Council	City (administration)
	City Health Department	County
	Civic Club	
Flood	Chamber of Commerce	U.S. Congress
		Army Corps of Engineers
Organizational		
Social		
Black community linkages		
NEED	Private citizens	Black and white community
	Individual corporate chief executive officers	Private corporations
PACE	Black leaders	United Way
	Individual chief executive officers	
	United Way officer	
NAB	President Lyndon B. Johnson	Conference
		Black community
MELP	Conference	Conference
		Black entrepreneurs
Neighborhoods		
NHS	Neighborhood Citizens' groups	Neighborhood Citizens' groups
	Mayor	City
		Financial institutions
		Private foundations
NSRP	City (Housing Department)	Neighborhood citizens' groups
		City
		URA
		Financial institutions
Managerial		
ComPAC	Chamber of Commerce	Chamber of Commerce
		County
	Mellon Bank Executives	Chief executive officers and their corporations
		Private foundations
ComPEP	Chamber of Commerce	Chamber of Commerce
		City
		Chief executive officers and their corporations
		Private foundations
Bricks and Mortar		
High-rise office complexes		
Renaissance I	Conference	URA
Gateway Center[a]		Equitable Life Assurance Society

Table 3–3 Continued

Project	Initiator	Implementer
Mellon Square Towers[a,b]	Private corporations (U.S. Steel Corp./ Mellon Bank, Alcoa)	Private corporations (U.S. Steel Corp./ Mellon Bank, Alcoa)
Renaissance II One Oxford Centre[b]	Private corporation (Oxford Development)	Private corporation (Oxford Development/ E.J. DeBartolo Corporation)
PPG Place	Private corporation (PPG Industries)	Private corporation (PPG Industries) City URA
Grant Street Plaza	Private corporation (U.S. Steel) City	Private corporation (U.S. Steel/Dravo Corporation) City URA PAT Parking Authority
Vista International Liberty Center[c] (Hotel/Office Complex)	City In Process: Private Corporations Vista International Grant-Liberty Development Group City URA	

[a]With associated parks involving partnerships.
[b]Nonpartnership, parallel office-complex construction.
[c]In process.

ships). Also the flood-control partnership is complete when reviewed across the initiative-implementation time span. It was initiated by the private sector and implemented by the public sector. In the NAB jobs program, on the other hand, the initiative was from the public sector, and implementation from the private sector. A helpful comparison of initiators and implementers by category is given in table 3–4.

The predominant role of the corporate community in the Pittsburgh partnerships is clear. It was the initiator in half of the partnership ventures and the joint implementer in three-quarters of the partnerships in this sample in *each* Renaissance period. Other private-sector partners were the Chamber of Commerce, financial institutions, private foundations, and neighborhood citizens' groups. The role of local government increased in Renaissance II in both initiative and implementation. This change has been especially marked on the initiative side, indicating a more active development position and more capable staffing.

Table 3–4
Comparison of Initiators and Implementers, by Category
(Number of Projects)

Individual/Organization	Initiators	Implementers
Corporate community (Conference, chief executive officers, private corporations)	8	11
Local government	5	9
Chamber of Commerce	3	2
Private citizens/neighborhood citizens' groups	2	4/2
Financial institutions		2
Private foundations		3

As in the case of the NHS program, when several groups form a viable ongoing private-public partnership, results differ from those of other, more singular, and even larger-scale efforts. In addition, NHS was more than just a housing program; it was concerned with neighborhood housing, and it is the neighborhood emphasis that is its second distinguishing characteristic. NHS linked the city, neighborhood groups, lenders, and a private foundation to provide loans to nonbankable homeowners. The gap in the marketplace was filled by initiatives, management structure, and funding from the private sector supported by ideas, enforcement powers, and development of associated physical infrastructure from the city. The NHS initiators came from both sectors, and so did the implementers.

What is most important about the several partnership forms is that they provide a scale and quality of development that otherwise would not be possible. That is, the involvement of private-sector components such as the neighborhood citizens' groups, the corporate chief executives, and the conference significantly enhances implementation.

Relative Share of Planning-and-Development Expertise. In Renaissance I, the planning-and-development expertise for both private and public development came from the private sector. It was the only game in town. The private sector remains as capable and active in Renaissance II as it was in Renaissance I, but there has been a noticeable advance in planning-and-development skills within the public sector. In Renaissance II, the public-sector planning-and-development staffs are capable in their own right. Also the private sector must come to the public sector for guidance and approval; and in some instances, the public sector sets criteria and standards.

Particularly important in Renaissance I were private research-and-planning institutions such as PRPA and the Pennsylvania Economy League. In Renaissance II, there is much more of a balance in such skills. Through the use of both sectors today, the outcome should be an improved one; certainly, it will be shared in more instances. One final point: The increase in expertise on the public side has not meant a corresponding decrease in participation by the corporate community; business participation in planning and development of initiatives and implementations has remained the same in both periods. What has changed is that the public side has become more of an equal partner.

Ethos for Development. Some lessons can be learned from comparing both periods of high development (Renaissances I and II) with a more normal period (the Interlude). Perhaps the most important of these lessons concern sustaining partnerships in the face of changing political leadership. There are five keys to the "ethos" of partnerships:

Commitment from the top, both private and public.

Subordination of personal or business interests.

There must be a bond of trust between the private and public executives and staff and also between the private-sector individuals and organizations. To be responsive to both the citizens and the "sunshine" element of that trust and to the developer regarding confidential information involved in the development process is the task of the public sector.

Willingness on the public side to cooperate and create a climate or atmosphere for development.

Willingness on the private side to adjust to the style of leadership and management of the elected officials. Partnership styles and structures may need to be changed. Because holding political office is generally more unstable than holding a chief executive position, more adjustments may be necessary from the private side than from the public side. Such adjustments may include a new mode of operation, new staff, a new agenda, and new ground rules. The need to develop strategies for making such adjustments should be anticipated.

Timing of Development. Without a market for large-scale development, none should be expected. In the high periods of both Renaissances, dramatic developments in the form of multiple high-rise office complexes were generated largely in response to market demand [a 99-percent occupancy rate for high-quality office space, whereas, during the Interlude demand was slack (a low point of 80 percent occupancy)].

Deadlines also prompt action. In the cases of the Convention Center and rapid transit, the achievement of consensus was aided by a deadline for funding. The race riots of the 1960s served notice of a different kind of deadline, prompting response toward the cause, not just the symptoms. In Renaissance I, the Equitable Life Assurance Society required movement on the environment (smoke and flood control) before it would consider its high-rise development. And in Renaissance II, two corporations deciding to build or to move to a new office complex did so in response to their lease expiration.

Opportunities offer another development window. Two major types have been significant in Pittsburgh: the turnover of key leaders and the achievement of a success. The election of new public officials (for example, mayor, county commissioners) obviously creates an opportunity for partnership. Similarly, a change in executive leadership of a key private organization (for example, president of the conference or the Chamber of Commerce) makes new initiatives possible. The demonstration of a successful partnership project (such as ComPAC, the consensus on the Convention Center, and the breaking the deadlock on rapid transit) often generates new opportunities. Such new developments themselves act to create a new atmosphere, at least for a while. Moreover, timely opportunities are best seen by those expecting or looking for such openings. In this regard, the entire Renaissance I success, with its grand scale of development, established an expectation for such planning-and-development partnerships. This tradition served as an important base from which to start a second Renaissance.

Redefining Development to Include Social Partnership. One of the critical differences between Renaissance I and Renaissance II lies in what might be called a "redefinition of development" to include social development, as well as bricks-and-mortar and economic development. Private-sector realization of the importance of this broader definition became more apparent during the late 1960s and the Interlude. Especially significant, however, is the continuation of a social-development dimension alongside the physical- and economic-development mission in Renaissance II. This has occurred in both sectors. The private sector has continued its partnerships with the black community and extended its attention to education and health, and the city has expanded its Renaissance definition to include two fronts: the central business district and neighborhoods. There was housing development by both sectors in the

latter part of Renaissance I (for example, ACTION-Housing). What seems
different in Renaissance II is the emphasis on neighborhood in conjunction
with housing, changing the character of such housing development.

Organizational Development. When major development occurs, especially when it involves public-private partners, new organizations may
be expected to arise, and reorganizations may be expected to occur. On
the private side, for instance, Renaissance I was partly generated by a
new organization, the conference. It was also partly a result of a change
within the conference from a focus on planning and research to emphasis
on planning, research, and implementation. Organizations spawned by
the conference spawned in Renaissance I were RIDC, ACTION-Housing,
and Penn's Southwest Association.

On the public side, new authorities were created that were very
important to Renaissance I: the Parking Authority, URA, PAT, and Allegheny County Sanitary Authority. Similarly, the city created the Department of Economic Development during the Interlude and during the
start-up period of Renaissance II. The prime coordinator facilitation
group, MDC, was also formed at this time. Virtually all participants,
public and private, view MDC as an important agent in Renaissance II.

One of the keys to Renaissance II is the city's fiscal soundness. This
economic vitality stems, in part, from two types of major reorganization
during the Interlude: the tightening of employment practices and the
restructuring of departments. Both tactics resulted in major reductions in
the city's full-time labor force and enabled the city to hold the line on
taxes and maintain a good bond rating. The Interlude also produced the
development of new analytic capabilities within the public sector (county)
through ComPAC. Moreover, an organizational spinoff of ComPAC and
ComPEP resulted within the city during Renaissance II. Additional developments are underway in the form of budget forecasting for the city,
county, and the city's public schools.

Summary

Renaissance I was the product of the unique coalition between Richard
King Mellon and ACCD on the private side, and Mayor David Lawrence
and the ruling Democratic party on the public side. To a large extent in
this partnership, the private sector led the way in a series of environmental,
physical, and institutional changes. The Interlude was marked by the
disintegration of the partnership that had produced Renaissance I. The

conference turned away from bricks-and-mortar projects and became involved in the social realm. Perhaps the most critical change was the election of a new mayor, Peter Flaherty, who had a different agenda and a different set of priorities. During Flaherty's first term, the original public-private partnership was in disarray; but by his second term, aspects of that partnership were being restored. Renaissance II, currently in progress, represents a restoration of the partnership but differs from Renaissance I because of the leading role played by the city, because the private side of the partnership has several centers of influence, and because of the new tradition of social development, which was established during the Interlude.

Thus public-private partnership in Pittsburgh has taken several forms and has had impact in institutional and social areas as well as in physical development. These partnerships have been critical in the city's past and can be expected to play an equally important role in the future. As the Pittsburgh story clearly shows, leadership in a partnership can evolve from either side, but the full-fledged involvement of both partners is critical to success.

Acknowledgments

This chapter is based largely on two sets of interviews conducted with public officials (past and present), chief executive officers of major corporations, and administrative officials and staff of various private voluntary organizations involved in Renaissance I, the Interlude, and Renaissance II. The first set of seventy-eight interviews deals with Renaissance I and the early years of the Interlude and are housed in the *Stanford Balfour Collection in Oral History* at the University of Pittsburgh. The second set of twenty-six interviews, dealing with the Interlude and Renaissance II, are in possession of the authors. The authors would like to thank the various persons interviewed from the private and public sectors for generously devoting their valuable time to this project.

Notes

1. Roy Lubove, *Twentieth Century Pittsburgh: Government, Business and Environmental Change* (New York: Wiley, 1969). This discussion of the pre-Renaissance period draws heavily from the Lubove volume.

2. The origins of ACCD and its activities to 1958 are traced in Park H. Martin, ''Narrative of the Allegheny Conference on Community De-

velopment and the Pittsburgh Renaissance, 1943–1958'' (1964) and supplemented by interviews with Renaissance figures in the Stanford Balfour Oral History Collection, Archives of Industrial Society, University of Pittsburgh Library.

3. Martin, ''Narrative of the Allegheny Conference on Community Development and the Pittsburgh Renaissance.''

4. Ibid., p. 7.

5. For a fuller discussion of this issue, see Joel A. Tarr, ''Changing Fuel Use Behavior and Energy Transitions. The Pittsburgh Smoke Control Movement, 1940–1950—A Case Study in Historical Analogy,'' *Journal of Social History* 14 (Summer 1981):561–588.

6. This section is based largely on Roland Smith, ''The Politics of Pittsburgh Flood Control, 1908–1960,'' *Pennsylvania History* 42 (January 1975):5–24 and *Pennsylvania History* 44 (January 1977):3–24.

7. A good discussion of the origins of Point Park can be found in Robert C. Alberts, *The Shaping of the Point* (Pittsburgh: University of Pittsburgh Press, 1980).

8. For Lawrence's role, see Stefan Lorant, *Pittsburgh: The Story of an American City*, 2nd ed. (Lenox, Mass: Author's Edition, 1975), pp. 373–447.

9. Interview with John P. Robin, *Stanford Balfor's Oral History Collection* (Pittsburgh: University of Pittsburgh, September 20, 1972), p. 24.

10. These data were obtained from ACCD annual reports.

11. This section is based largely on Roger S. Ahlbrandt, Jr., and Paul C. Brophy, *Neighborhood Revitalization: Theory and Practice* (Lexington, Mass.: Lexington Books, D.C. Heath, 1975).

12. Roger S. Ahlbrandt, Jr.; Paul C. Brophy; and Jonathan E. Zimmer, ''Neighborhood Housing Service Model'' Unpublished paper, ACTION Housing, Pittsburgh.

13. William Dodge, ''Public-Private Cooperation in Improving Government Operations'' *M.I.S. Reports* 12 (January 1980):5–12.

14. In a speech given on July 8, 1975, to the U.S. Conference of Mayors in Boston, David Rockefeller, chief executive officer of the Chase Manhattan Corporation, cited Pittsburgh's fiscal and employment policies as an example of efficient performance (*Greensburg Sunday Tribune*, July 13, 1975).

15. Interview with David Matter, May 26, 1981.

16. Pittsburgh Department of City Planning, ''A Downtown Development Strategy,'' August 1979.

Appendix 3A
Pittsburgh's Public-
Private Partnerships

Table 3A–1
Environmental Public-Private Partnerships

Project	Basic Objectives	Who Initiated Idea	Major Participants and Their Responsibility
Smoke control	To clean the air to improve quality of life, improve health, cut cleaning drudgery	Voluntary associations—Civic Club City Media	Media—publicity about evils of smoke, benefits of control
			Voluntary associations—PR, coordination, political support
			United Smoke Council—director and coordination
			Conference—goal setting, and implementation
			City—to pass and implement law
			County—application of control legislation to county
Flood control	To stop flooding of the CBD area, and the river fronts allowing redevelopment	Chamber of Commerce	Chamber of Commerce—lobbying, organization
			City—political to obtain federal support
			State—state senator heads private/public committee in 1930s
			U.S. Congress—passage of flood-control bills, appropriations
			Corps of Engineers—construction of dams

Table 3A–2
Additional Renaissance I Projects

Projects to 1969	Initiation Date
Sewage Collection and Treatment (Allegheny County Sanitary Authority)	1945
Greater Pittsburgh Airport	1946
County Mass Transit	1947
Playground and Zoo Improvement	1948
Jones and Laughlin Steel Corp.	
South Side Expansion	1949
Hazelwood Expansion	1952
Lower Hill renewal and construction of Civic Arena	1951
WQED	1951

Table 3A–1 Continued

Partnerships	Management Structure	Period of Implementation	Benefits	Spinoffs
Media Conference City County	Conference Smoke Abatement Committee City Bureau of Smoke Prevention County Air Pollution Control Bureau	1946–1949	Cleaner air, clothes, buildings, homes Better health Environment to attract management and professionals	Gateway Center Office Complex
Chamber City State Federal	Chamber of Commerce Flood Control Committee U.S. Congress Corps of Engineers	1938–1965	Prevent floods at the Point and along river fronts, enabling CBD development	Gateway Center Office Complex Riverfronts development

Table 3A–2 Continued

Projects to 1969	Initiation Date
Regional Industrial Development Commission	1955
ACTION HOUSING	1957
North Side Industrial Development	
Chateau Street West	1960
Woods Run	1967
East Liberty Renewal	1961
Allegheny Center Renewal	1961
Stadium Project	1963
U.S. Steel Building	1965
Heinz Hall	1967

Table 3A–3
Physical/Bricks-and-Mortar Partnerships: Renaissance I

Project	Basic Objectives	Who Initiated Idea
Gateway Center Complex	To construct a high-rise office complex in a parklike environment	Conference Point Park Committee on Point Redevelopment
	To construct a park for recreational and historical purposes at the Point (Point State Park)	PRPA City Conference
Mellon Square Complex	Construction of 41-story and 30-story office towers	U.S. Steel/Mellon Bank Alcoa R.K. Mellon
	To construct small park in high-rise area and an underground-parking garage (Mellon Square Park)	

Table 3A–3 Continued

Major Participants and Their Responsibility	Partnerships	Management Structure	Period of Implementation
Conference: assure corporate tenants for office buildings	Conference	URA	1946–1952
URA: to assemble land	URA	Equitable Life Assurance Society	
Equitable Life Assurance Society: to construct the three office towers			
State: funding	State	Point Park Steering Committee	1946–1974
Conference: to appoint the steering committee to design and manage the park	Conference		
Corporations: to construct towers	None	City	1949–1951
Private foundations (Mellon): to purchase land and construct the park	Private Foundations (three Mellon foundations)	Parking Authority	1949–1950
Parking Authority: to assemble the land	Parking Authority		
Mellon-Stewart: to construct and operate garage	City		
City: to operate the park			

Table 3A–4
Social Public-Private Partnerships

Project	Basic Objectives	Who Initiated Idea	Major Participants and Their Responsibility
Black-Community Outreach			
NEED	To provide small (seed money) grants to minority students for higher education	Two women: Marian Jordon (black) Florence Reizenstein (white)	Two women who originated idea, corporate members of an ad hoc committee on black/white relations and community leaders—initial fund-raising drive to raise $100,000
			F. Byrom CEO Koppers Co., Inc.—enlisted corporate funding support ($250–300,000)
PACE	To provide an intermediary United Way agency to relate more directly to the problems and needs of minorities	Black leaders Corporate CEO	Black leaders, headed by K. Leroy Irvis—negotiated the management structure (PACE Council) and selection procedure for council members
			United Fund Committee headed by Fletcher Byrom—negotiated the management structure (PACE Council) within the United Way framework
NAB	To help solve the chronic unemployment problem of the urban poor by providing jobs and training	President L.B. Johnson	Joint NAB Jobs Committee/Conference Employment Committee—CEOs of major corporations—to set reasonable job goals, ensure commitment of job offers to meet such goals, and maintain high retention rate
MELP	To help establish black-owned and operated enterprises	Conference	Conference Economic Development Committee—CEOs of major corporations: to provide financing and management of the loan program
			Financial Institutions—to originate and service the loan program.

Table 3A–4 Continued

Partnerships		Management Structure and Style	Period of Implementation	Benefits	Spinoffs
Corporate community (funding)	Black community (talent)	Incorporation of organization; NEED (Herman Reed, Executive Director)	1963 to present	16,806 grants 4,000–5,000 individual students supported	—
United Way (funding, management structure)	Black community (identification of problems, needs, and talent to direct and manage such an agency)	Creation of United Way Agency PACE (Ray Bates, Executive Director with PACE Council to serve as its Board of Directors	1968 to present	Supports 35–40 organizations per year in such areas as health, culture, recreation, college-career orientation, half-way	Eight United Way Agencies received their seed money from PACE
Conference (jobs)	Black community (talent)	Conference Employment Committee became the NAB Committee	1968 to present	Over 31,000 disadvantaged persons hired between 1968–76 with retention rate of 60 percent	Extension of some programs to help Vietnam veterans from 1972 to present (over 15,000 additional hires between 1972 and 1976)
Conference—(funding, executive management) Financial Institutions— (operation of loan program) Black Community—(talent)		Conference Economic Development Committee and Financial Institutions along with special Skills Bank to assist new entrepreneurs	1968–1976	Over two-hundred minority owned and operated businesses in region at present spawned by this program	Creation of Business Resource Center, to provide technical and management aid to minority businesses

Table 3A–4 Continued

Project	Basic Objectives	Who Initiated Idea	Major Participants and Their Responsibility
Neighborhood			
NHS	To improve the neighborhood in the Central North Side (CNS) and to establish a revolving-loan fund for nonbankable homeowners to improve CNS housing	Neighborhood Citizens Groups Mayor	Neighborhood Citizen's Groups—to change the city's designation of the CNS as an urban-renewal area with a commitment to keep it residential; to obtain commitments from financial institutions to remove red line around CNS for bankable individuals; to obtain funding for nonbankable homeowners in the CNS; and to design a management structure to implement the program. City—to help obtain private funding for the loan program; to designate the CNS a code enforcement area and allocate public funding for and carry-out development of the CNS's physical infrastructure—parks, street repaving and lighting, tree planting, and demolition of unfit structures. Financial institutions—funding administrative costs of the revolving-loan fund and providing data-processing services for the nonbankable loan accounts. Private foundation (Sara Scaife Foundation)—funding revolving loans ($600,000 total)

Table 3A–4 Continued

Partnerships	Management Structure and Style	Period of Implementation	Benefits	Spinoffs
Neighborhood Citizens Groups—City—Financial Institutions—Private Foundations	Incorporation of organization: NHS (Thomas A. Jones, Executive Director)	1968 to present	Revitalization of CNS neighborhood with evidence of increased financing by lenders involved on NHS Board of Directors	HILP—City/ URA loan program using private lenders to originate and service loans

NSRP—City/ URA neighborhood mortgage program using private lenders to service first and second mortgages

NHS adopted by HUD as a national model for neighborhood revitalization with a target of forty NHS cities |

Table 3A–5
Managerial Public-Private Partnership

Project	Basic Objectives	Who Initiated Idea	Major Participants and Their Responsibility
ComPAC	To bring greater efficiency to internal government operations	President of Greater Pittsburgh Chamber of Commerce, Justin Horan	Chamber of Commerce: to facilitate and formalize commitment from the top
			Private and Public: to house the staff
		Three executives of Mellon Bank— James H. Higgins, J. David Barnes, and John P. Olson	Corporate CEOs: to personally serve on the Board of Directors and serve as task-force chairmen with a commitment to loan their corporate executives when called upon
			Loaned executives: to provide private expertise to specify task-force problem, recommend solutions and see that they are implemented
			County commissioners: to demonstrate a commitment to the ComPAC idea and see that its recommendations are implemented
			ComPAC codirectors: to prepare initial briefs and to help develop a procedures manual for task-force operation; and to coordinate and monitor each task force until its completion

Table 3A–5 Continued

Partnerships	Period of Implementation	Benefits	Spinoffs
Chamber of Commerce Corporate Community County Commissioners	1976–1978	Task-force results in the following areas: purchasing, cash management, personnel, computer services, management information/program budgeting, construction management, financial management, business/industrial development services Estimated one-time savings of $3 million and recurring savings of $3 million/year	Use of ComPAC model in the city of Pittsburgh (ComPEP) Allentown and Lehigh Counties in Penn. Cincinnati and Hamilton County, Ohio Jefferson County, Kentucky Extension of the ComPAC development task force to an ongoing ad hoc committee on economic development consisting of corporate CEOs in the Pittsburgh area

Table 3A–6
Physical Bricks-and-Mortar Partnerships: Renaissance II

Project	Basic Objectives	Who Initiated Idea
Grant Street Plaza	Construction of a fifty-three-story Office Complex with shopping, restaurant and leisure activity; Midtown Station—main subway terminal of LRV in CUD	U.S. Steel Corporation City
PPG Place	Construction of forty-story office complex with six total structures including shops, restaurants, an open plaza and winter garden	PPG Industries, Inc.
Vista International	Construction of twenty-story hotel and thirty-six-story office complex	City URA

Table 3A–6 Continued

Major Participants and Their Responsibility	Partnerships	Management Structure	Period of Implementation
U.S. Steel Corp: to construct the office complex	U.S. Steel Corporation	Four-party agreement among partners pertaining to land, streets, subsurface rights and air rights	1981–1984
PAT: to construct Midtown Station	PAT		
City: to redesign and reconstruct streets	City		
URA: to help restructure land parcels between public and private sectors	URA		
PPG Industries, Inc.: to construct the office complex	PPG	URA	1981–1983
URA: to assemble land under its powers of eminent domain	URA		
City: to set climate, maintain support, and assure land assemblage	City		
City/URA: to purchase land, initiate market study and a market strategy to obtain bids and select developer	City	URA	In process; projected to start 1982
Grant-Liberty Development Group: to construct the hotel-office complex.	URA		
Vista International: to manage hotel	Vista International		

4

The Chicago Public-Private Partnership Experience: A Heritage of Involvement

Pastora San Juan Cafferty and *William C. McCready*

Planning has been an important facet of Chicago's development throughout its history. In fact, it is no exaggeration to say that the city is the result of planned development and technological innovations. This case study examines the planning process and the ways in which public and private actors participate in it.

The nature of the planning process in Chicago makes it very difficult to obtain information about some of the more interesting and current activities. The process is based on trust and personal contact and is therefore frequently difficult to observe from the outside. Consequently, the plans and development programs that are described in this study are those that could be observed and documented. They have been chosen because they demonstrate aspects of the process, but they are of course only examples; they do not constitute an exhaustive compilation of all the economic development activities that go on in Chicago.

The city of Chicago can be thought of as a process rather than a place. This process is an outgrowth of its past and continues to shape its future. The city is not the result of particular people rooted for a long time in a particular place. Rather, Chicago is groups of people rapidly replacing one another. Each shapes the city according to its needs. Today the Mexicans, Vietnamese, and Koreans have succeeded the Poles, Italians, and Slavs. They inhabit the same immigrant neighborhoods and continue to shape them with their culture. Traditions become established, routines become set, vested interests develop, and an air of legitimacy begins to surround the way things are always done. This process gradually results in the creation of a structure that becomes both the result of a tradition and a tool for molding the future.

Public-Private Cooperation for Economic Development

If one defines *economic development* as a rational and intentional effort to increase economic activity in a specific community, the separate and

129

mutually dependent roles of the public and private sectors can be described in terms of those functions performed by each separately and by both together toward that goal.

In general, the public sector is responsible for the infrastructure within which urban economic activity takes place. The transportation system, city services and facilities, and the economic atmosphere (defined by tax rates and other regulatory mechanisms) are traditionally the responsibility of the public sector. The private sector is presumed to be acting in its own interest, and the prevailing philosophy is that the general economic good of the community is best served when the private sector is active and growing, jobs are available, and the economy of the geographic area is vital.

The principal reasons for the public sector's becoming involved with the private sector in economic-development activities usually have to do with that sector's intent to redistribute economic activity within its political sphere. It may be the need for additional jobs in a minority community or for increasing a specific tax base or for coordinating future infrastructure expansions with private-sector requirements and projected uses. The general reasons for private-sector involvement in economic-development activities are different but not unrelated. Private economic activity depends on a solid, stable labor base with appropriate skills; a constant consumer population; stable communities, as measured by housing and school indicators; and stable or increasing property values, which prevent the erosion of private assets.

Public-private cooperation does not necessarily happen in response to specific problems that need to be overcome, although in some cities that is undoubtedly the genesis of such partnerships. It is also the case that such cooperative arrangements grow and develop as part of the natural social structure of urban economic life. That is, various persons within the two sectors realize that they need each other's skills and perspectives, and contacts and relationships are pursued. Chicago is a city in which coalitions are common, and because of the weak-mayor–strong-council form of government, consensus building is the style of political leadership that works most efficiently.[1]

The general research methods used for this case study included personal interviews with many leaders in the public and private sectors, reviews of available documents and existing research reports, and reviews of the relevant historical and sociological literature. These sources were primarily used to develop information about the context within which the development process occurs.

The Context for the Development Process

Since Jean Baptiste Point DuSable established the first permanent settlement on the Chicago River in the 1770s, Chicago has attracted group after group of settlers because of its strategic location. The city was the result of development in 1832 at the northern end of a canal planned by the Illinois legislature to replace the portage linking Lake Michigan with the Mississippi River. The raw frontier town attracted a diversity of inhabitants. Although the canal was not completed for another decade, the plan to build it stimulated speculation in real estate that caused and was in turn affected by the architectural innovation that became known as ''Chicago construction.'' The balloon frame developed by Augustine Taylor and George Washington Snow enabled contractors to build rapidly yet substantially and made it possible for Chicago to make the leap from raw pioneer village to great city in less than a decade. Chicago was to continue to influence American architecture and urban development, contributing not only the steel-frame skyscraper but also the first garden suburbs and planned satellite cities.

In 1850 one railroad served Chicago; six years later, ten railroad lines fanned out from the city, moving grain, lumber, cattle, and hogs. In 1865 the Union Stockyards were organized at the city's southern limits. The Armours and the Swifts supplied the beef, the McCormicks supplied the farm machinery, and the great steel mills supplied the rails to join it all together. The tightly knit immigrant communities of Swedes, Norwegians, Germans, and Irish created distinct districts within the geography of Chicago.

The Great Chicago Fire in 1871 left one-third of the population homeless. Both fine residential neighborhoods and ramshackle immigrant shantytowns were destroyed, along with the commercial and industrial areas. Reconstruction began immediately and intensified the forces that had characterized Chicago's earlier development. Many owners rebuilt their establishments on the same sites. But there was change too. The new construction was generally taller. Residential construction in the central business district was discouraged by a City Council decree prohibiting the building of wooden structures in the area.

Previous limitations on building height were overcome through the invention by William Jenney of the steel-framed skyscraper. This led to the development of the early architectural masterpieces of William Adler and Louis Sullivan. Other technological innovations included the elevator, the caisson foundation, and elevated mass transportation to assist in moving the increasing numbers of people who worked in these vertical avenues of commerce.

The radiating mass-transit routes were linked in an elevated ''loop'' of rails circling the downtown business center. When this elevated loop opened in 1897, it clearly defined the central business district as including State Street, the Board of Trade, and the LaSalle Street financial center. Great hotels, including the Palmer House and the Stevens Hotel, were built to serve the growing convention business. Within the area were offices, housing, the city government, much of the city's medical and dental community, the leading social and political clubs, and the whole-sale and produce markets. Adjacent to it were the city's most important cultural institutions, the Art Institute and the Civic Opera House. The elevated loop had defined Chicago.

What became the epitome of the core-oriented nineteenth-century industrial metropolis was defined by nature as a rectangular area bounded by Lake Michigan on the east, the Chicago River on the north and west, and a vaguely marked border on the south between the lake and the river around Roosevelt Road (later further defined by the construction of rail terminals on the south side). The area is also characterized by a series of train stations that form an irregular U-shaped pattern between the existing waterways and the elevated mass-transit loop.

In 1906 Daniel H. Burnham was commissioned to prepare a plan for Chicago. *Monumental City Beautiful: The Chicago Plan* was adopted by the city in 1910 and set the guidelines for the process of development that was to continue until World War II. The plan was implemented during a quarter of a century of unprecedented building and resulted in a monumental civic center, a lakefront belt of continuous parks and beaches, and a greenbelt of forest preserves encircling the metropolitan area. Landscaped boulevards and an east-west highway lead to the western prairie. The Loop, as the center city came to be called, continued to grow.

During the construction boom of the 1920s when the Michigan Avenue Bridge, the Wrigley Building, the Tribune Tower, Guarantee Trust, and 333 North Michigan was built, this core was broken through. Nevertheless, the Loop remains synonymous with downtown Chicago.

The reshaping of the city affected the relationship between the public and private sectors. In a recent article, Andrew Neil noted that

> business and politics have always mixed well in Chicago. The city has been run by a close-knit coalition of politicians, business leaders and union bosses who know all about power and money. Behind the big-city facade is a small town establishment; it is still possible to meet almost everyone who is supposed to matter in Chicago at one cocktail party.[2]

One of the features of Chicago that makes this ''close-knit coalition'' possible is the extreme concentration of the functions these leaders command in a single area: the Loop.

The extreme compactness of the central business district and its accessibility by train, elevated lines, and later, subway, have played vital roles in the area's development and continued prominence. Within the Loop are located the City Hall and county buildings, the central post office, and the courts, as well as the State Street shopping core, the Board of Trade, and the adjacent LaSalle Street financial center. Clustered around these focal points of activity are the offices of real-estate firms, insurance agents, lawyers, architects, and contractors.

The Planning Process

The intricate process of planning and building has continued in Chicago to this day. Chicagoans who watched the Burnham influence on the shaping of the city for over a quarter of a century have a respect for planning; they also understand the intricacies of the process. Burnham cautioned Chicagoans to "make no little plans." His advice has proved sound. Today representatives of the same business and civic groups who first financed and then worked assiduously to implement the Burnham plan sit on the boards of commissions that have produced the various plans of the twentieth century. It is noteworthy that after a century of building, the process is still an interrelated fabric in which one project is intimately related to another. It is the individuals involved in the process that provide the relationships. They still head the corporations and the great financial institutions within the Loop and meet for lunch at the old clubs overlooking the lake and the great buildings they helped to construct.

The social history of Chicago during the middle 1960s was marked by the movement of many members of the white, middle-class, Protestant population to the suburbs, leaving the inner- and middle-city areas increasingly polarized between the black and European ethnic minorities. As steady resegregation devastated area after area on the south and west sides, the Loop and Near North have been transformed into prospering and well-developed centers of commerce and industry, as well as residentially preferable neighborhoods. As a 1976 report indicated:

It was the declining fortunes of the Loop and particularly of the State Street shopping core during the 1950's that sparked a series of actions by the downtown business community that, with the active support and participation of the city government, helped realize the growth potentials afforded by the growth of the service industries and the continuing concentration of headquarters and administrative functions in the downtown areas of America's biggest cities.[3]

The construction of suburban shopping centers, together with the changing population, declining consumable income, and the unpredictability of urban buying habits, combined to drastically reduce the numbers of shoppers in the central business district. The consequences were dramatic. For example, the 1962 profits for the five main State Street department stores stood at a mere 30 percent of their 1948 level. The crisis was at hand.

In the late 1950s, a coalition of business leaders, civic leaders, and municipal government leaders came together as the Chicago Central Area Committee and began to take steps to revitalize and develop the critical central core of the city. The renewal of the Near North Side, the development of Lincoln Park, Old Town and New Town, the University of Illinois Chicago Circle campus, and the construction of the federal office complex in the Loop were all outgrowths of this coalition and its "development by consensus" style. Major decisions to locate corporate headquarters such as the Prudential and Hancock insurance companies, Sears, Montgomery Ward, and Standard Oil, were also the result of this group's insightful activities.

There is no absence of conflict in the process of development in Chicago; however, it is the nature of the conflict that is important. When the process is endangered, for example, it is seldom by a class of ideologies or the behind-the-scenes manipulation of the power élite. It is more likely the result of organizations that disagree on the most effective methods of accomplishing the goal of serving the public interest. For example, the controversy that swirls around the North Loop development comes, not from irate citizens speaking out at public hearings but from civic organizations such as the Metropolitan Housing and Planning Council, the Chicago Central Area Committee To Reshape Urban Systems Together (TRUST), and the Landmarks Preservation Council disagreeing among themselves and with public officials on the best way to restore vitality to the area.

There is a tension between the political system and the political process, on the one hand, and the requirements of comprehensiveness and consistency in planning and policy, on the other. Tension also arises from the belief that self-government consists, not in giving or withholding consent at frequent intervals on matters of general interest but in making influence felt in the day-to-day conduct of public business. A plan is the conscious and deliberate product of conscious and deliberate problem solving, but in its implementation, it becomes fragmented. However, if the processes of planning and implementation are linked together by the participation of the same individuals, the original intent of the plan will be carried through to its conclusion. In Chicago, in other words, those who plan also tend to be those who build.

Although the historical and social context for planning spans the entire history of Chicago, the period of service of Mayor Richard J. Daley deserves special attention for its role in the creation of the model for public-private cooperation in urban development that exists today. Daley, in an article for *Commerce* magazine in the mid-1950s, made it clear that he considered development to be a two-way street, involving compromises between what corporations wanted from Chicago and what the mayor wanted for the city.[4] He identified four principle themes, each having some special significance for the development process.

The first theme is that the well-being of the central city and the central business district is essential to the well-being of the entire metropolitan area. This meant that the close communication that was possible because of the design of the central area was utilized to provide an efficient development mechanism. Daley's style of political communication was intensely personal, and he translated that into his activities with representatives of the private sector. This personalism was ideally suited to the Chicago development climate, and because of Daley's long tenure as mayor, it also shaped that climate, affecting the process of public-private cooperation even after he had gone.

The second theme was that development required a long-term commitment on the part of both sectors. Daley customarily presented plans and budgets covering five-year segments. This not only provided for cyclical reviews and improvements and adjustments as time went on but also signaled an ongoing commitment on the part of the city to the businesses that operated within it.

The third theme was that the city was not to be the only public partner in the development process; the county also had a role to play. The Cook County government is responsible for much of the infrastructure outside the city limits, and Daley's joint tenure as mayor and political director of the county's Democratic Committee gave him a great deal of leverage in bringing the county into the development process.

The fourth theme was that revenue bonds should be used for development in order to reduce the burden on the taxpayer. These bonds frequently provide start-up funds or funds to match private investments and as such play an important role in the process of development. Mayor Daley was one of the first to follow this course of action.

Under Mayor Daley, the central business district, which had been in trouble as early as the 1950s, began to rebuild and exhibit a vitality once again. Between 1955 and 1977, office space in the area increased by more than 100 percent. Although the future of the area was by no means ensured, the immediate decline that had been threatening was avoided, and progress was begun, providing a base for future development.

Organizations and the Development Process

If the Loop defines the geographic core of the city of Chicago, it is the clubs that serve as the places within that core where civic and business leaders meet informally to form coalitions for change. Clubs and other types of organizations provide the occasions for the personal contacts that are crucial to what has been termed the "heritage of involvement." They are a vehicle through which businessmen are encouraged to participate in *pro bono publico* projects.

The Commercial Club, the Chicago Club, the Standard Club, the Chicago Athletic Association, the University Club, and the Union League Club serve, in varying ways, as the mechanisms by which the leaders of business get to know and trust each other. The Commercial Club is one of the most prestigious, and civic involvement is virtually a prerequisite for membership. The others are similar in nature.

Commercial Club member Thomas Ayers, who assumed the chairmanship of the Chicago Economic Development Commission when it was formed in 1976, carried on the tradition of contributing to the economic development of Chicago. In addition, he played a central role in the development and implementation of the Chicago 21 Plan as a member of the Chicago Central Area Committee.

The Standard Club dates back to the last decade of the nineteenth century. It was founded by a group of Jewish businessmen as a response to anti-Semitism and numbered as members not only the businessmen of the day but also architects and planners. William Adler, Louis Sullivan, and Frank Lloyd Wright were all members and took active roles in club affairs.

Throughout its history, the Union League Club, which was initiated in 1879, has been a service organization acting for the well-being of the city. The league is responsible for such diverse projects as the improvement of the Chicago River drainage facility, the location of Fort Sheridan and the Great Lakes Training Center, and the Illinois Forestry Association.

The clubs are all located within several blocks of each other in the south half of the Loop, the operating territory for the "heritage of involvement." The people who gather in these settings demonstrate and share their concern for their city in a variety of ways, some of which have significant consequences for development activities. All these individuals are motivated by a sense of being responsible about the city within which their companies make their profits.

A common perception is that Chicago is a "big small town" and that its unique character is to a great extent due to the confinement of the Loop and the geographic limitations on corporate interaction that the structure of the Loop reinforces. Almost all the corporations have traditionally had their offices in the Loop. Their chief executive officers lunch together and otherwise see each other frequently.

The coexistence that is promoted by the physical constraints of the

Loop is reflected in the process by which the chief executive officers like to get things accomplished. The Crusade of Mercy (now the United Way) is a good example. When Philip Clark of the Commercial Club started the project, he said he would not head the crusade unless all the club members were committed to it. This "élite" motif runs through all *pro bono* projects in Chicago; the executive commits himself and then asks for the commitment of his peers. They in turn assign people from their staffs to carry out the projects. Thus the staffs are performing for their chief executive officers as well as for their community.

It is this process of working together on the basis of personal relationships and trust that results in the plans that built Chicago. Planning and development are not separate from the day-to-day functioning of the city and the groups that work within it. The city itself can be justifiably characterized as a process. Part of that process is historical and part of it is sociological, but the process that occurs within the limited space of the Loop shapes and molds the future of the city as clearly and definitely as the shores of the lake contain the currents and eddies of the water within.

Another organization that encourages *pro bono* activity and promotes the "heritage of involvement" is Chicago United. The issue of trust is primary in this case. Chicago United is a group of white, black, and Hispanic business people who came together as the result of the turmoil, mistrust, and social upheavals of the 1960s. It is an outgrowth, to some extent, of the movement called the "Urban Coalition," which was formed in 1967 as the result of the outbursts of civil disturbances that rocked Chicago and other major cities.

After John Gardner, founder of the Urban Coalition, addressed the Commercial Club in 1969, Mayor Daley invited a group of leaders to his office to discuss the possibility of building a coalition group. The group's first project, the funding and support of the Black Strategy Center, met with failure, and in 1970, the Urban Coalition closed its doors. As Gaylord Freeman of the First National Bank said in his farewell speech to Chicago United in 1975:

> The fault must be shared by the Center's officers and the business support group. The former had little administrative ability and the latter had expected too much.[5]

This had been the business community's initial effort to engage in planning and development activities with the black community, and although it failed, the unlikely alliance of white businessmen and black social activists did establish a working relationship.

A second, more successful attempt to create a multiracial coalition was the direct result of the work of a committee headed by William Berry of the Urban League and B.W. Heineman of Northwest Industries. The Berry-Heineman report on human problems in Chicago became the foundation Chicago United.

Between 1971 and 1973, the group was a loose-knit coalition of task forces that worked on a variety of urban matters, including police and minority-community relations, employment efforts both public and private, and increased minority access to the Cook County Hospital. In 1973 a not-for-profit corporation was formed, and the first president, Robert MacGregor, was appointed.

Chicago United is unique in two ways: It provides for a public "conscience" for the business community and allows for the development of the trust and informal connections that seem to be a part of the economic and social development of this city. Thomas Ayers and Norman Ross, founding members of the association, describe the process as one of providing a meeting place where the black and white members of the community could get to know each other on a first-name basis. It has also enabled the white business community to support the efforts of the black community to accomplish some of the things they thought were important.

The urban affairs officers of Chicago United call themselves *deacons*, and the story of the origin of that term tells us a good deal about the frustration and lack of trust that had to be overcome in the early days of the effort. As one of the founders and charter members of the organization tells it, the term *deacon* originated in 1968 when a prestigious minority community leader was addressing a meeting of bankers. He noticed that the founder who was telling this story was taking notes, and asked "Are you here as a vice president or a reporter?"

When the man answered that he was there as a vice president, the speaker responded, "You don't have any power. You'll just take those notes back to your boss and he'll make the decisions. I have 5,000 people in my operation. They're my power base. You're just a deacon. I want to talk power."

At that moment, the term was picked up by other minority participants, who claimed that they "didn't want to waste their time on a bunch of deacons," and so on.

The next morning the vice-president who had been singled out as the first deacon met with his corporate superior and greeted him with, "Good morning, Bishop!"

Today the term *deacon* is still used to describe the men and women who participate in Chicago United as urban affairs officers.

The suspicion of the early days had given way to a carefully nurtured and developed sense of trust and interpersonal communication. The twin themes of personal trust and meeting genuine needs run through the workings of the organization. Its economic-development activities are effected through the personal and persuasive influences of individuals. The major achievements have been through such operations as the Business Opportunity Fair, which is responsible for scores of millions of dollars being available from corporate purchasing departments for black (and, increasingly, Hispanic) suppliers and through the location and relocation of corporate headquarters.

Another group is responsible for the "heritage of involvement." The Chicago Central Area Committee, started in 1956 by Holman Pettibone, the chairman of the Chicago Title and Trust Company, was founded to work for the improvement and well-being of the central business district through the continual strengthening and improvement of the area. In a restatement of its principles in 1956, the committee stated:

> The key to the formulation of Central area Planning principles is the recognition that the area is a highly-specialized district whose long-term efficiency and convenience are greatly dependent upon how well its physical form is adapted to its functional needs.[6]

Three principles were identified with regard to the basic physical requirements of the central area. First, it must be *compact and compatible in the use of land*. That is, specialized functions must be placed in the central area in a way that facilitates direct and convenient contact between the many interrelating and interacting economic, government, cultural, and recreational activities. Second, the various communities, neighborhoods, and industrial districts within Chicago must each have *maximum accessibility* to the central area, with linkages to the airports, the interstate highway system, and the rail network. And, third, the central area should provide an *attractive environment* for workers, shoppers, and visitors.

Since its inception, the committee has had members from twenty-eight central-business-district firms, and the board of directors has ranged in size from thirteen to twenty-one members. Altogether, some fifty-three men have served on the board, most of them chief executive officers of major Chicago corporations. The standing committees reflect its range of interests: finance, land use and zoning, physical improvement, beautification, transportation, traffic, government functions and relationships, recreational facilities and cultural development, commercial development, planning and research, promotion of central area, publicity, public relations, and special committee coordination.

In December 1971 a Chicago central-area plan was discussed at a meeting at Charles Luckman Associates, and in February 1972, there was a meeting to discuss the liaison between consultants and city departments concerning infrastructure issues affecting the plan. Representatives from the international architectural firm of Skidmore Owings & Merrill, the Department of Development and Planning, the Department of Streets and Traffic, and the consulting firm of Alan M. Voorhees & Associates were involved. At a May meeting, priorities were established for central-area planning proposals, and two—housing and new communities—received unanimous ratings.

In 1973 the Chicago Central Area Committee contracted with Skidmore Owings & Merrill to prepare a plan. In March 1973 a meeting was held in the office of Lewis Hill, commissioner of the Department of Development and Planning, to discuss progress on the Chicago central communities plan. Three major issues were raised: The extent of detailed planning information for the south Loop and the central business district gave the impression that only these areas were being considered for redevelopment; it was suggested that equal treatment be given to all areas in the plan. Some of the illustrations of existing or planned developments were either inaccurate or incomplete. There were many public-housing developments within the city, but only Cabrini-Green was being given any attention.

Some of these questions were resolved at a meeting with Skidmore Owings & Merrill staff, Chicago Central Area Committee representatives, and relevant city department staff representation.

In this process, planning does not move smoothly from one organized set of goals to another. Rather, it lurches along in a generally defined direction as various issues and actors become involved. It is worth noting that the stated priorities of proposals did not accurately reflect eventual accomplishments. At the conclusion of the 1980 annual report of the Chicago Central Area Committee, after the listing of promotional activities, research papers and projects, and other civic activities in which the committee engaged during the years, there is a statement reflecting the mode of operation that characterizes much of the economic development activity in Chicago:

> Chicago is a city where plans mean action. A record of striking success and accomplishments since 1973 attests to this long-standing axiom. Chicago's civic leaders have developed a heritage of involvement that has carefully shaped the face of the city and continues to do so today.[7]

Three examples have been chosen to illustrate the way in which the process of planning for economic development takes place in Chicago. Each involves a different type of development and developmental process.

These examples do not reflect the local development that goes on in the neighborhoods, nor do they reflect the economic planning and activity that is hidden from the observers. They do, however, give some idea of the overall planning that is so critical to the central-area development.

Chicago 21 represents both commercial and residential development and has resulted from a rather clear and specific planning process. Two aspects of this planning process will be examined: Dearborn Park and the North Loop. The Chicago 21 Corporation is now the Dearborn Park Corporation, but it is still a 6.5-percent limited-liability operation managed by an officer of one of the area's largest real-estate firms. Whereas the North Loop aspect of the plan is still being considered, Dearborn Park has met most of its early goals and has started on a new series of objectives.

The *Stockyards Revitalization Project* provides a look at commercial and industrial revitalization in one of the city's older, stable communities. This development process illustrates both the use of revenue bonds and the benefit of having a stable work force and community organization on which to depend.

The *Chicago Plan for Economic Development* is an overall plan for the entire city and illustrates the process in its broadest sense.

Each example has something different to offer, and each is distinct. Although they generally involve different sets of actors, the style of the processes is unique to Chicago. The sense of personal involvement that the people from both the public and private sectors have stems from the conviction that they are all members of the city in a special way. This heritage stimulates a sense of civic responsibility that makes planning and development possible and practical.

Chicago is a city of neighborhoods, and those primarily responsible for planning and develoment may be considered, sociologically speaking, to make up a neighborhood of their own. The examples discussed here will attempt to delve beneath the statistics, the dollars, and other indicators of the city's infrastructure and get at the spirit and process that stimulates the personal sense of responsibility that seems to characterize much of Chicago's economic development.

No attempt will be made to romanticize the process. Self-interest and economic survival are still principal factors in the development process. However, it is also the case that people feel differently about their involvement in Chicago than those in other places seem to. Those responsible for planning talk about their Chicago experiences as different from those they and their colleagues have had elsewhere. Although this difference is elusive and subtle and difficult to document, it does seem to be responsible for forming the character of the development process in the city.

Chicago 21

The Plan

The Chicago 21 Plan represents a summary of conclusions and recommendations for the development of the central-communities area. It defines the area as bounded by North Avenue, the Stevenson Expressway, Ashland Avenue, and Lake Michigan. The central feature of the plan is a proposed $15-billion rejuvenation that would affect almost every block in this area. Of all the recommendations, the highest priority was given to the development of new housing and the rehabilitation of old housing in the central area. The plan called for the building of a landscaped walkway along the Chicago River, the closing of Meigs airport and its conversion into a park, and the transformation of Navy Pier into a recreational facility with shops, restaurants, and a marina. It also called for refinements in the transportation systems, including converting State Street into a pedestrian mall, the building of a rapid-transit line out to O'Hare International Airport, and a subway along the lakefront from McCormick Place to the Near North Side.

The plan makes two assumptions: that the Chicago central business district should remain the dominant focus of commerce and culture for the entire metropolitan area and that the central communities should serve as the transportation hub, seat of government, office and business center, cultural and entertainment center, and central marketplace.

In 1966, the Chicago Central Area Committee released a document titled *Planning Principles for the Chicago Central Area.* The principles, an update and restatement of those first presented in 1957 by the same group, were incorporated in the city's *Comprehensive Plan of Chicago,* also released in 1966. In 1969 the city commissioned a series of studies by consulting firms, including Real Estate Research Corporation, Barton Aschman Associates, and John D. Cordwell. The studies examined commercial, residential, and recreational land-use and transportation needs. The Chicago Department of Development and Planning released the draft report of the Chicago Central Communities Study in 1970, summarizing the consultants' studies and encouraging well-planned mixed use for the areas. Areas requiring additional study were specified.

Skidmore Owings & Merrill was selected in 1971 as the prime contractor for the project. An advisory group, the Planning Review Committee, was organized to oversee the project. James C. Downs wrote a

letter to the members of the Chicago Central Area Committee urging
them to take responsibility for producing a comprehensive plan for the
central committee. His letter referred to the principles developed in 1966
and expressed the fear that unless the Chicago Central Area Committee
assumed this task, the momentum gained would be lost. In 1972 there
was a meeting between Paul Simmerer from the Mayor's Committee on
Economic and Cultural Development and Jack Cornelius of the Chicago
Central Area Committee and others, the purpose of which was to discuss
central community areas for industrial development. It focused on Pilsen,
Chinatown, and the area immediately west of the Loop. The Planning
Review Committee met with Daniel Shannon of the Park District to
discuss transportation issues related to the central-communities plan. It
then met with Martin Millspaugh and Walter Sondheim of Charles Center-
Inner Harbor Management Corporation to discuss their experiences in
directing and guiding the renewal of downtown Baltimore.

In 1973 a meeting was held with representatives of the Illinois Environmental Protection Agency to discuss the environmental ramifications
of the central-communities plan. This was followed by meetings with
various organizations such as the South Side Planning Board, the Greater
Michigan Avenue Association, the West Central Association, and the
Metropolitan Housing and Planning Council, to discuss aspects of the
plan related to their interests.

The plan was presented to Mayor Daley at a meeting with the Chicago
Central Area Committee and Commissioner Lewis Hill, after which it
was then unveiled to the public by Mayor Daley. According to the status
report issued by the Chicago Central Area Committee on the progress
made under the plan from June 1973 through 1980, nineteen of the thirty-
two projects or proposals are either completed or underway. The plan
gave high priority to new housing, especially in strong communities in
or near the central business district. It proposed the development of a new
town of up to 120,000 residents on 650 acres of largely unused land
being occupied by an old railroad yard south of the Loop. To service
these residents, the plan called for the development of schools, churches,
parks, and shops. The project took its name from the recently abandoned
railroad terminal: Dearborn Station.

Dearborn Park

Chicago's South Loop originally served as a port of entry for newly
arrived European immigrants and blacks, who were drawn to the area
because jobs and housing were available. However, the fire of 1874

Proposed	Status			Needs		
	Completed	Underway	Conceptual	Funding	Legislation	Organization
South Loop/New Town		X		X		
Cabrini Green Improvement		X		X		
New Residential Development		X	X	X		
Distributor Subway			X	X		
Franklin Street Extension	Plans for Franklin Street Subway Cancelled					
Loop Subway			X	X		
Columbus Wacker Extension		X				
Graded-Separated Pedestrian Walkways		X		X		
Improved Air & Water Quality		X		X		
State Transitway Malls	X					
Ring Road System			X	X		
Functional Street System		X		X		
O'Hare Transit Line		X				
Mixed Uses in The Loop	X	X		X		
Extended Hours						
Lake Shore Expansion			X	X	X	X
River Zone		X	X	X	X	X
South Lakeshore (Meigs-Soldier Field)			X	X	X	
Peripheral Parking			X	X		
Lake Shore Drive Improvement			X	X		
Pilsen Conservation and Infill		X	X	X		
Chinatown Expansion			X	X		
Monroe Harbor Expansion			X	X		
Navy Pier Reactivation		X		X	X	
Supplemental Transit System			X			
New Loop College		X				
New Library			X	X		
Loop Lighting and Security		X				
Miscellaneous Traffic Improvements		X		X		
Special Streets		X		X		
Historic Preservation	X	X	X	X	X	
Improved Transit Environment		X	X	X	X	

Figure 4–1. Chicago 21 Update

destroyed most of the area. The displaced European immigrants moved west of the Chicago River, the blacks moved farther south, and the area subsequently became a railroad terminal. Dearborn Station opened in 1885 and was closed in 1971 because of a decline in passenger traffic; coincidentally, commercial investment declined until the area around the station was virtually abandoned.

The concept of redevelopment of the South Loop had been proposed by different consortia of businessmen as early as 1968. Warren Lebeck, executive vice president and secretary of the Chicago Board of Trade, announced the formation of an organization known as the South Loop Improvement Project (SLIP). It had two priorities: immediate short-range improvements, including the reduction of crime, and the long-range rebuilding of structures, including the city's railroad terminals.

In June 1968 Charles Wilson, the head of the Area Development Office of Continental Bank, developed a prospectus for a South Loop development project. This document stimulated a study conducted by Metz, Train, Olsen and Younger, Inc., which was completed in 1969. Charles Strobeck, heading the South Loop Development Company, commissioned the study in conjunction with Continental Bank. It recommended developing a tract of thirty-two acres that would be zoned for mixed office, residential, commercial, and entertainment use.

The revitalization of the South Loop, requiring no displacement, received top priority from the business community. In January 1974, the Chicago 21 Corporation was established to serve as a catalyst for South Loop development programs. It was explicitly stated that the corporation's principal purpose was not to maximize profits but to develop and encourage civic and community-improvement projects. The corporation also wanted to transform a decaying area into a middle-income, residential neighborhood of approximately 8,000 people.

The key actors in this new corporation were Thomas Ayers, chairman (chairman and president, Commonwealth Edison), John H. Perkins, vice chairman (president, Continental Illinois National Bank and Trust Company), Raymond C. Wieboldt, Jr. (president, Dearborn Park Corporation), Ferd Kramer (Draper & Kramer), Donald Erikson, executive vice president and treasurer (senior partner, Arthur Andersen & Company), Warren G. Skoning, vice president (vice president, Sears, Roebuck), and Philip M. Klutznick, chairman of the executive committee (then chairman, Urban Investment and Development Company).

Ayers played an active role in revitalization in the South Loop well before Chicago 21. In a 1979 interview with a *Sun-Times* reporter, he said the idea came when he, Donald Graham of Continental Bank, and Gordon Metcalf of Sears were looking out his office window at "those old rail yards" and someone suggested, "We ought to do something about those yards.''[8] James Downs of Real Estate Research Corporation was commissioned by Ayers, Metcalf, and Graham to conduct a study, and Real Estate Research recommended residential development in the South Loop. Thus the Dearborn Park development seed was planted.

The first order of business for the new corporation was additional planning. In the original Chicago 21 Plan, the area was called the South Loop New Town. However, after the completion of additional planning by Skidmore Owings & Merrill and Urban Investment and Development Company, the project was scaled down from 335 acres to approximately 50 acres and renamed Dearborn Park. The Chicago 21 Corporation obtained the option for this site and purchased it for $7.3 million in February 1977. At that time the name of the corporation was changed to Dearborn Park Corporation.

On July 7, 1977, the City Council approved a planned unit-development ordinance, and shortly afterward the actual plan was approved by the Chicago Plan Commission. A three-hour public hearing was held, at which opposition was voiced. The Pilsen community, in particular, felt threatened. Many residents thought speculators would cause the area to become too expensive, thus forcing them to move. The response of the Chicago 21 group was to offer matching grants to neighborhood planning organizations. Pilsen and East Humboldt Park received funds and began a community-planning effort. Fidel Lopez, an architect who led the Pilsen group, is now manager of the Neighborhood Investment Program and Director of Area Development at the Continental Bank.

Groundbreaking took place on the twelfth of July. By early 1980, 939 units were to be completed (190 for the elderly, 144 townhouses, and 605 condominiums). Financing was accomplished in two phases. By private invitation, thirty-two investors were recruited to invest in the corporation. Shares were privately offered in separate stages; purchase in the first phase assumed willingness to purchase the second. Loans for construction came entirely from two sources, each lending 50 percent: Continental Illinois Bank and Trust Company and First Federal Savings and Loan Association of Chicago. Loans for the purchasers of condominiums were made by a consortium of lenders. These loans were available at 10-percent interest for a term of twenty-nine years for 80 percent of the total purchase price with one and one-half extra interest points being rendered at the time the transaction is completed.

Skidmore Owings & Merrill and Urban Investments were responsible for developing the detailed plan of Dearborn Park. Skidmore believed futuristic style was most appropriate, whereas Urban Investments argued for a more conventional approach to attract middle-income families. The conventional construction approach was adopted, but it was agreed that diversity of design was an essential ingredient of success. For this purpose, four architectural firms were hired, with Skidmore as the coordinating architect.

As of 1981, all 939 of the originally planned units have been built, and all but 22 have been sold. The thirty corporations that bought into the plan for about $500,000 each are still involved, and the Dearborn Park Corporation is now planning to expand with two high-rise buildings in the development area. This project has become a foundation for the revitalization of the South Loop area. The final evaluation is not yet in, but it is clear that progress has been remarkable.

The North Loop

The North Loop redevelopment offers an interesting contrast to Dearborn Park because it is one of the unplanned effects of Chicago 21. The North Loop area was not targeted for redevelopment by the Chicago 21 committee, although it was identified as an area that offered great opportunities for development. In contrast with Dearborn Park, North Loop redevelopment has progressed episodically, without much coordination between the public and private sectors.

A fifteen-acre section of Chicago's central business district called the North Loop is in the heart of Chicago's downtown area. Like many such locales, it is characterized by building decay, less than optimal land use, and low employment levels. The city has designated the North Loop a redevelopment area and has prepared guidelines along which future restoration will take place.

In May 1980 the city of Chicago entered into a contract with the Hilton Hotel Corporation to redevelop a two-block area by building a flagship hotel and apartment house. The contract requires that the existing structures be demolished. The city agreed to complete the redevelopment of the remainder of the North Loop in accordance with the overall development plan adopted by the City Council in March 1979. The contract specifically provides that certain portions of the area will be converted to new uses in order to carry out the revitalization. The timetable provided in the contract calls for completion of the project in the mid-1980s; the cost will be roughly $200 million. In addition, construction has recently begun on the new state of Illinois building. This building and the new Hilton hotel are expected to be the catalysts for the entire North Loop project.

Mayor Jane Byrne announced in August 1980 that Charles Shaw of the Charles M. Shaw Company, a coordinating developer for the project, would be responsible for preparing a plan. A preliminary concept, prepared by Skidmore Owings & Merrill and presented by the mayor and

Shaw to a group of three-hundred business and civic leaders in November
1981, includes many of the ideas expressed in the city's original proposal.
This development plan is intended to accomplish the following objectives
within the redevelopment area: eliminate blight, obsolescence, and del-
eterious land uses; foster economically sound development; retain and
strengthen sound land use; provide for the retention of certain structures
with historic or architectural significance; and develop a multilevel pedestrian concourse.

In order to give potential developers maximum flexibility and encourage and obtain the highest-quality development and design, the plan
will not specify all development controls; rather, controls will be established on a case-by-case basis. Each proposal will be considered as a
planned unit development, and all controls relating to signs and advertising will be specified in the planned unit-development ordinance.

Several structures within the project area, most of which are of historic
and architectural significance, are not to be acquired if the owner or
owners will rehabilitate or maintain them in a way consistent with the
objectives of the plan and the structures' values.

However, civic groups have argued that before the project becomes
a reality, some very important issues must be further explored. These
issues may be grouped into four general areas: use of space, preservation,
design and architecture, and public-sector activity.

Use of Space. Planners will have to decide how space should be used
in the North Loop development area. The proper positioning and mixture
of various uses must be taken into account. The questions of who and
what should be relocated and of what are proper levels of population
density must also be dealt with. Finally, the space uses ultimately decided
upon must be related not only to each other but also as a whole to the
area surrounding the North Loop.

Preservation. Decisions will have to be made about which historically
significant building should be retained.

Design and Architecture. Such elements as complementary facades and
building heights, proper use of open space and traffic patterns, and the
proper mix of old and new structures must be considered.

Public-Sector Activity. This issue seems to be the biggest obstacle to
the future progress of North Loop development. It must be determined
what the major public-sector responsibilities are in addition to the basic
renewal activities. The overall development effort must be properly and
authoritatively coordinated. The city must determine the capital com-

mitment it will make and what (if any) incentives for new construction it will offer. It must also carefully consider which development proposals are feasible and appropriate to the overall plan.

To date, the city has preliminary plans for the North Loop redevelopment project, but these have not been approved by the Plan Commission of the City Council. In spite of this, construction of the new state of Illinois building is under way. Work on the new Hilton hotel is in the advanced stages, and a feasibility report concerning the renovation of the old Selwyn, Harris, and Woods movie theaters has been submitted.

The main elements of the preliminary plan present a view of what is intended in this area; but without a formal ratified redevelopment plan, it is unclear to potential developers what will or will not be officially required in their proposals. The redevelopment of the North Loop is progressing episodically. The newspapers carry stories of "new North Loop guidelines" almost daily. In spite of this uncertainty, however, there is excitement about the project; and consequently the value of real estate along the river is already increasing.

The Chicago Plan for Economic Development

Planning in Chicago is not restricted to physical development. There are a number of social- and economic-policy efforts undertaken by the city, private industry, and civic groups. In the opinion of some observers, some of these would not qualify as real plans at all but rather as loosely connected sets of goals. Others say these are the kinds of plans that stimulate the most exciting growth because they are not rigidly structured. The Chicago Plan for Economic Development is perhaps the most ambitious because it addresses the need of the entire city to retain and attract business and industry and formally involves the private and public sectors in an economic-development commission.

The plan was developed in 1977 to encourage industrial investments in the city. It was started before the death of Mayor Daley and continued to be implemented during Mayor Michael Bilandic's tenure. The Mayor's Commission on Economic and Cultural Development, with Zimmerer and Samuel Bernstein as cochairmen, had taken the initiative on an economic-development plan for the city. The commission was formed at the urging of the business community, and its members were top business leaders personally recruited by Mayor Daley. William Caples, a businessman, became executive director, indicating the major role business was to play. The commission divided its work into four parts, each with a committee of board members: retention of businesses, industrial development, commercial development, and public relations and advertising. The commission initially concentrated on keeping industry in Chicago. Then it developed plans for industrial parks, tax-exempt bonds, programs for acquiring and documenting land values, and financing packages.

Among the principal contributors to the development of the plan were Donald Kane of the commission staff, Lucius Gregg from the First National Bank, and Donald Petkus of the Commonwealth Edison. The banks continue to play a key role.

The goals of the plan are to create new jobs and conserve existing ones for city residents and to stimulate private investments within the city. The plan is an outgrowth of the concern over the loss of industry from the city to the suburbs. Manufacturing work was considered vital to the employment picture in Chicago, and the city wanted to keep its tax base from deteriorating. Industry was leaving Chicago, but neither the public nor the private sector were sure where it was relocating. A study by the Mayor's Commission on Economic and Cultural Development found that more than 90 percent were going to suburbs. The commission decided to review what the suburbs had to offer. However, the formulators of the plan decided the city had to offer more than land. The Chicago plan was designed to offer additional incentives.

The plan's strategy revolved around an initial private-sector commitment of $250 million for an investment fund. This was to be supplemented by the participation of private developers in five target industrial parks within the city: the Stockyards Complex, Goose Island, Lake Calumet, Lawndale, and Northwest Industrial Park. These parks were to be the recipients of federal, state, local, and private money. The idea was that if there was a structure to help potential industries, then the industries would be more likely to choose one of the five parks as its particular home.

There has been no displacement or need for relocation except at Goose Island because the parks were created on marginally utilized land or on vacant property. The city has committed its agencies to the advancement of the plan. So have the state, through loans, and the federal government, through both grants and loans. The private sector assists in the development of the parks, owns the land, contributes private loans, and in the overall marketing of the plan. All the industrial parks are privately owned. Each is promoted privately by the individual development company.

The key elements of the plan are to provide and market the security, attractiveness, economics, and services of the parks. Implementation involves land acquisition and write-downs, site improvements, building construction and rehabilitation, public works and infrastructure improvements, financing, and security arrangements.

The plan is currently using a variety of funding sources, including industrial-revenue bonds. They are more a stamp of approval by the city that does not buy the bonds but grants the designated business a tax-exempt status.

Other funding mechanisms are available but have not yet been used. The revolving-loan program, a pool of money made up of Economic Development (EDA) and Community Development funds is used for smaller loans to companies (loans of about $75,000 to $300,000). The size of the loan depends on the company; the maximum term of such a loan is ten years. The low interest is keyed to smaller companies ($250,000 of Community Development money; $1.5 million of EDA money in place within the last three to four months). Tax incentives have reduced the tax rate on new construction from 40 percent to 16 percent of assessed valuation for a thirteen-year period. The approvals are handled by the assessor's office. The tax incentives are flexible and can be used for rehabilitation.

There is speculation that the forming of the Economic Development Commission was part of the foundation for the Chicago Plan for Economic Development because it was organized about the time that EDA in Washington was changing its grants form. The speculation is that the commission was formed in the way it was to better ensure that it could get federal money. One of the businessmen on the commission, Robert Abboud then of First National Bank, went to Congress in 1977 to secure federal help. Basically, his message was that if the federal government worked with them, the banks would be willing to take part in the solving of Chicago's out-migration problem. In this way business was able to obtain federal money and focus public-sector interest on development opportunities in Chicago.

Once the main concepts of the plan were established, representatives of the commission once again went to Washington, this time to EDA. They said that they had the plan plus a $250-million commitment from the banks if EDA would commit $15 to $18 million. EDA thought the plan was an excellent idea and felt it could be used as a model for other cities. (As a matter of fact, it eventually became a part of President Jimmy Carter's economic package.) They then went to the city, saying that the banks and EDA were willing to commit funds if the city would commit $6 million. Finally this process was repeated with the state.

Part of the reason for the plan's success is the work of the Economic

Development Commission. If an industry has a problem with red tape, the commission staff will help in facilitating a solution. The staff constantly canvasses industries to see what they want and what their problems are. They also work with the Mayor's Office of Manpower to help identify labor pools for particular skills that the industry might need.

The plan is being vigorously marketed. *Chicago: One Town That Won't Let You Down* is the title of a series of pamphlets and flyers published by the commission extolling the city's incentives to business and industry. Other publications such as *Chicago: A Place for Profit in the Machine Tool Industry*, are being targeted to specific manufacturing and retail concerns.

It is impossible to judge the ultimate effectiveness of the Chicago Plan because it is impossible to judge the ultimate effectiveness of industrial development over a mere three years. However, it is significant that there was no significant industrial-park activity in Chicago in the previous ten years, but now there is. The plan has been successful as far as it has gone. The Stockyards Industrial Development in the Bank of the Yards area has been the most successful of the lot.

The Stockyards Industrial Development

The term *Back of the Yards* was actually coined at the turn of the century. It refers to the residential area surrounding the Union Stockyards on Chicago's southwest side. Since the post-Civil War era, Chicago had been a center for hog and cattle slaughtering. The stockyards were instrumental in establishing Chicago as an industrial city, and they provided jobs for immigrants and capital for investors. However, after World War II, because of labor-union strife and a decreased need for workers because of the advent of modern technology, the slaughtering of animals was decentralized into a number of smaller, more modern plants. The industry moved west to such places as Dubuque and Kansas City to be closer to the livestock. New slaughtering facilities were placed in the central states, leaving the stockyards an economically void reminder of the city's vital past.

Currently, Back of the Yards defines the area between Racine and California Avenues, and Forty-seventh Street to Garfield Avenue. The neighborhood is a mixture of Irish, German, Polish, Slavic, and, in the past ten years or so, a growing number of various Hispanic groups. Back of the Yards includes one of the oldest Mexican communities in Chicago. The neighborhood has always had an ethnic mix. Contrary to popular perception, Back of the Yards is *not* made up mostly of Irish families, even though it is near Bridgeport and has been run by an Irish organizer for the past twenty years.

Politically, the eleventh and fourteenth wards make up most of the area. Neighboring Bridgeport, the Irish Democratic domain of political power, has a similar demographic composition. The crime rates in both neighborhoods are low; mortality rates, infectious diseases, poor housing conditions, and dense population are not problems of this working-class enclave of the southwest side.

The person most closely identified with the spirit of Back of the Yards is Joseph Meegan. Although Meegan does not hold an elected political office, he has been the core of the neighborhood as a community organizer for over forty years. Meegan came to Back of the Yards in 1937 after he was appointed director of Davis Square Park. With Saul Alinsky and Bishop Bernard J. Shell, he cofounded the Back of the Yards Council, the oldest community organization in the United States, in 1939.

Over the years, the aim of the council has been to sustain the neighborhood, which is renowned for containing three generations and being very stable. Meegan has said:

> My concern has always been to try to keep people from wanting to move out of our community. However, when new residents move into our area, they become part of our family of people. The block in which I live is comprised of residents representing various nationalities. Many Black families also live in the block where I live. My family now has seven different nationalities among us.

Whether the neighborhood would have as strong an identity without Joe Meegan is questionable. Meegan personifies the industrious citizen who believes that the people who live near you should be regarded as a member of your extended family. There are those who criticize Meegan for losing touch with the needs of the neighborhood, which are changing because of demographic shifts. But Back of the Yards is still a thriving community. It contains the Stockyards, one of the city's largest industrial parks, and is adjacent to the political power base of Bridgeport, making it a very desirable area to develop. Another feature of Back of the Yards that makes it attractive for development is that it has a convenient and stable labor force to draw on.

In 1962 the Department of City Planning published the *Stockyard Redevelopment Study and Proposal,* which listed the following advantages for tenants of an industrial park: choice of site and room for expansion, an efficient work environment, protection against encroachment of undesirable land uses, and provision for access, service, parking, and loading.

Drover's Bank, a neighborhood institution, has been instrumental in lending money to industries moving to the Stockyards. Drover's wants to boost industry and service its accounts. The industrial revenue bonds generate low yields, and the bank does not benefit from them unless it needs tax write-offs. However, like the downtown banks, Drover's is committed to preserving and enhancing its immediate environment. On November 19, 1980, Drover's Bank pledged $5 million for industrial loans.

The northwest quadrant of the Stockyards was declared a blighted commercial area by the city, allowing commercial businesses that locate or rehabilitate to get a thirteen-year reduction in their property-tax-assessment level from 40 percent to 16 percent. Infrastructure improvements amounting to $6 million should be completed by 1982. These improvements include Thirty-Fifth Street construction, Racine and Morgan Railroad Crossing, viaduct repairs, and landscaping. The city offers a wide range of incentives, including industrial revenue bonds, property-tax relief on industrial construction, land-cost write-down, job-training funds, reduced carrying charges on industrial parks through joint ventures, federally guaranteed loans, public-works and infrastructure improvements, sales tax on manufacturing equipment, and on-site improvements.

A limited number of sites are available for industrial parks in Chicago that also offer transportation and a nearby conscientious labor force, the Stockyards is one of them.

However, there is a strong correlation between Meegan's identifiable presence as community leader and the economic development of the Stockyards. Meegan is widely known as an established community organizer, a person with leverage because of his connection with the church, the city, the businessmen's association, and the *Back of the Yards Journal*. It would be accurate to say that Meegan overtly controls the Back of the Yards neighborhood and his leadership has facilitated Back of the Yards recognition as a law-abiding, stable, working-class community, a good labor force to continue to tap.

Additional Economic Development

Infrastructure renovations and expansions are an important aspect of the ongoing development process, and like other economic-development activities, they are taking place in neighborhoods throughout the city. The publication *Chicago '81* produced by the city, is a dependable source of data and statistics about infrastructure activities. Other kinds of development also occur, and these have to be researched separately.

As part of this project, information was collected concerning economic development in each of Chicago's fifty wards. The general source of information was the alderman's or ward committeeman's office. Of 120 projects for which complete data, including funding, were available, 48 were residential, 49 were commercial, and 23 were mixed-use, industrial, or educational. The total funding for these projects was slightly over $3 million. If the projects from the Forty-Second Ward are included, the total rises to 334. This ward is located in the Near North section of the city and is probably one of the most prosperous and well-developed areas of any city in the nation. Over 250 projects have been completed there during the past fifteen years. No funding data were available for these projects, although a great deal of useful data were found in the *Chicago Central Business District Office Building Analysis, 1972 to 1976.*

Several local development corporations in various parts of the city are involved in shopping-district revitalization, residential rehabilitation, and more general development activities such as community marketing. Several other potential developers are seeking certification, and it is anticipated that development will become somewhat more decentralized as this trend continues. The history of such groups can usually be traced to several committed, energetic people in a community taking the responsibility for leadership and forming development corporations. It would appear that the "heritage of involvement" is not limited to those in the central city, although they still account for the majority of development activities.

Currently certified local development corporations in Chicago include: the Lawrence Avenue Development Corporation, Greater Southwest Development Corporation, Great North Pulaski Development Corporation, Lawndale Local Development Corporation, South Shore Area Development Corporation, and Bucktown Business Association Local Development Corporation.

Certification in this instance means that these are eligible for low-interest development loans. There are other local development corporations that are not so certified but that do engage in economic-development activities. These are spread throughout the metropolitan area and are becoming more and more common. Some are independent associations; others are attached to existing community organizations. These corporations, as they become more numerous, will act to further decentralize the development activities to the benefit of the entire metropolitan area. One of the challenges facing the city is to discover ways of supporting such decentralized efforts without either taking them over and subsuming their individuality within larger entities or suppressing their enthusiasm.

Conclusion and Recommendations

The theme of a "heritage of involvement" runs through each example
in this case study in the sense that people from the private sector feel that
it is a part of their responsibility, as well as in their self-interest, to be
concerned about the growth, development, and well-being of their city
and its communities. The commitment to Chicago that forms a base for
the involvement and participation of the corporate and private sector is
critical to the success of development projects and plans.

Six characteristics are singled out in a recent report by the Committee
for Economic Development,[9] as being crucial for the emergence of a civic
process that supports emerging forms of public-private cooperation in
economic-development activities. In any specific setting, some of these
characteristics will be stronger, and some will be weaker. But they provide
a framework for summarizing the nature of the civic process in any one
situation.

> 1. . . . . A civic culture that fosters a sense of community and en-
> courages citizen participation rooted in practical concern for the com-
> munity

The "heritage of involvement" in the planning process in Chicago
is in fact a civic culture. Many members of the business community said
that their feelings and those of their colleagues about belonging to Chicago
are different from their senses of having belonged to other cities. The
assumption that private-sector executives are expected to contribute their
skills and talents toward community projects, especially in the area of
economic development, is an extremely important component in the foundation that supports the emergence of innovative and responsive public-
private cooperative efforts.

> 2. . . . . A commonly accepted vision of the community that accounts
> for strengths and weaknesses and involves key groups in a process of
> identifying what the community can become

For years the "commonly accepted vision" tended to be the vision
that Mayor Daley both embodied and promoted. Civic vision must be
symbolized by the leadership, and one of the powerful aspects of the
Chicago story has certainly been the extent to which the vision of the
city as a central economic core in the heart of the nation was nurtured
by the late mayor. In the past, it may well have been true that the strengths
displayed in the vision outweighed the weaknesses, but it is also true that
some of the weaknesses have now become more apparent. Nevertheless,
Chicago continues to espouse a process in which key groups can be

involved in development. This is not to say that it happens at every turn,
but experiences such as that of Chicago United have demonstrated that
the process can work. The challenge is to make it work better.

> 3. . . . Building-block civic organizations that blend the self-interests
> of members with the broader interest of the community, and translate
> them into effective action

Civic organizations in Chicago have both contributed their input and
expertise to the development process and have provided the network for
the people involved in the process to communicate with each other. It
is frequently impossible to differentiate the way in which such organizations serve their own goals and agenda from the way in which they
serve those of the community as a whole. Although Chicago is certainly
a city in which competing interest groups work out compromises, it is
also true that an astute political leader can influence those compromises
so that the end product serves the broad interests of the community. This
too is a challenge for the future.

> 4. . . . A network among the key groups that encourages communi-
> cation among leaders of important segments and facilitates mediation
> of differences

One of the reasons why clubs are such an important factor in the
development of Chicago is that they provide an additional, more private
network. Privacy is a delicate issue in the context of development. There
is a line between the privacy that excludes public participation and the
privacy that allows personal trust to develop. In an ideal world, the trust
would exist without the exclusion; but in the real world of politics, self-
interest, and economics, there must be some risk of exclusion in order
for there to be the benefits of trust, close communication, and commitment. The style of public-private interaction in Chicago contains the
necessary element of trust, and it sometimes contains elements of exclu-
sivity as well. Another challenge for the future is therefore the gaining
of better insight into the current costs and benefits of this style.

> 5. . . . Leadership and the ability to nurture "civic entrepreneurs,"
> that is, leaders whose knowledge, imagination, and energy are directed
> toward enterprises that benefit the community

Chicago is an unusual case for several reasons, not the least of which
is the long reign of Democratic administrations, especially that of Mayor
Daley. This provided, and still does to a considerable extent, a continuity
of policy that the private sector could depend on from one year to the

next. They can engage in their enterprises without fear that policy will shift abruptly or that the conditions under which they operate will suddenly change. One of the central challenges currently facing the city is maintaining continuity while meeting new needs and demands. There is no more critical element in the public-private model of participation than the confidence of the private sector in the stability of the public context within which it functions. This is the keystone of the civic foundation for co-operation, and to the extent that it is firm, many other innovations and adaptations become possible.

Several approaches can be suggested for future exploration. One is to make the most out of the existing heritage and tradition of involvement. It provides a context that has been reasonably successful over the years. None of the plans in Chicago extend very much beyond a fifteen-year cycle, and many are in the five-year range. This appears to have the effect of encouraging the mutuality and personal trust that characterize the heritage because participants know that progress will be evaluated and that the negotiations and compromises are up for reexamination every so often. This cyclical style seems well suited to the goals of both the private and the public sectors and ought to be maintained and supported.

The resources in the neighborhoods ought to be targeted and added to the developmental plan of the city on a broad basis. The decentralization that has already begun is likely to continue. Chicago is very much a city of neighborhoods, and if economic-development activities are going to benefit people by improving the quality of life where they live, it will have to happen in the neighborhoods. Developing and nurturing the civic entrepreneurs in the neighborhoods will have a positive effect on the well-being of the entire metropolitan area and will assure continued economic progress in the central business district.

Neighborhoods can be typified by the level of effort and investment required to improve them. Some must be rebuilt from the ground up. Others require only superficial modification and assistance because they already have a great deal going for them. Still others—and perhaps these should be targeted first—require immediate help because they are on the edge between being viable and nonviable. Now is the time to assist them, when doing so still requires only a modest investment. If we wait, the investment required will become greater and greater. Developing the indicators and the information needed to identify those neighborhoods and their development "windows" is a principal need. Moreover, it requires the right people and the right organization within the community to be able to use assistance wisely. The window through which they can receive effective assistance to prevent decay and improve conditions may also close rather quickly, so timing is very important in assisting neighborhoods.

Private corporate involvement is as critical in the neighborhoods as it is in the city as a whole or the central business district. Technical assistance and advice may sometimes be all that a neighborhood needs to seize an opportunity for development and improvement. Private-sector organizations, especially banks and other financial institutions, can be of great help in these matters. It may well be that the principal challenge facing the city is to be able to apply the heritage that has been viable for development in the central area to other areas of the metropolitan region.

The heritage has benefited from the participation of many in the private sector, and much of the benefit has stemmed from the fact that the process was both continual and cyclical. It was both private enough to allow for trust and cyclical enough to allow for modifications. The continuity that has typified planning in Chicago is a primary strength of the process and ought to be stressed as the process is decentralized for the good of all communities.

Both public- and private-sector representatives appear to be comfortable with this, but more than that the need to recycle every so often appears to have the beneficial effect of encouraging the mutual trust and interdependence that characterize the heritage-of-involvement style.

Chicago 21 was in a sense a continuation of the 1958 plan submitted to the city by the Chicago Central Area Committee. It is worth noting that in both instances, the Central Area Committee offered to do the planning for the downtown area because that was the only area not addressed by the city's own planning department; therefore, this particular contribution of the private sector to the well-being of the city was all the more important. It should also be noted that Chicago 21 was based on the philosophy that planning should be done in cycles not exceeding fifteen years, a philosophy that had guided planning in Chicago since the days of Daniel Burnham.

Commercial development in the downtown area tended to take care of itself. The great need was for residential development. Thus the residential Dearborn Park project became the first piece of the plan to be implemented. It is also worth noting in this context that the North Loop is in a sense also the articulation of a stated need for residential development in the downtown area. In fact, those who worked on Chicago 21 claim that the planning in the North Loop, as well as the residential development around Illinois Center, is a byproduct of the Chicago 21 process.

A corollary to this observation comes from several of the business and civic leaders involved in Chicago 21: that is, that although Chicago 21 had clear goals and objectives, and Dearborn Park has moderately clear goals and objectives, the North Loop has neither. Essentially it has no frame of reference, and that is one of the major reasons for its difficulties. Because it lacks a frame of reference, these sources say the North Loop has not benefited from the clear public-private sector involvement that worked well in Dearborn Park and was clearly articulated in the Chicago 21 plan.

A clearly defined planning process gave the private sector a feeling of confidence and helped it make investment decisions. It engendered trust within the business community. There is a feeling of control by those planning and developing because dialogues on such subjects as transportation, parking, and parks took place within the planning process. Such a dialogue is credited with convincing the State Street merchants to commit themselves to the construction of the pedestrian mall. The mall had been proposed in the Chicago 21 plan and funded as a transportation project, but it required the participation of the merchants to rehabilitate and remodel their establishments in order for it to work successfully.

The greatest liability of the process followed in this style of planning is that it is élitist. It is by definition exclusionary, with little or no citizen involvement. But this can also be seen as a strength in the sense that those who do the planning are also those who are going to implement it, and they benefit by avoiding the delays and vacillation that frequently accompany community participation.

Although the process of planning in Chicago is élitist, it is a process that has made a strong commitment to neighborhood interests. This is perhaps best demonstrated by the matching grants awarded to such groups as the Pilsen Neighbors Community Council and the East Humboldt Park community to do their own planning. These neighborhoods have built their own development capabilities. (Pilsen has the 18th Street Development Corporation, and East Humboldt Park has the Community 21.) These examples highlight the nature of the problem so often perceived as élitism. The neighborhoods, the planners, and the architects are uncomfortable with the episodic and time-consuming nature of the planning-and-development process at the neighborhood level.

A critical component of the planning process is the relationship between the process and the political volatility of the city. It is difficult under such circumstances to keep the commitment of private developers and/or professional planners. Time and time again political stability enjoyed under Mayor Daley is mentioned as being an important factor in supporting and reinforcing the creative and efficient planning-and-development process by civic and business leaders. Mayor Daley frequently visited Skidmore, Owings & Merrill to look at the Chicago 21 Plan and to discuss the details; at the same time he maintained a discreet public distance from it. Privately "hands on" while publicly "hands off" appears to be the way things get done in Chicago.

The heritage of involvement is the key to the successful planning process, and it is made possible because the personal trust that has evolved over the years between the people responsible for developing and implementing plans has contained, mollified, and overwhelmed the natural tendency to avoid public involvement in the volatile political context that is Chicago's legacy. Those responsible, for the most part, for the planning in 1958 were still around for the implementation in the early 1970s. They were around because they remained confident over the years that their plans and judgments and discussions could be carried out in an atmosphere of personal respect and trust. The maintenance of that trust is the challenge for the city of the future.

The challenge will have to be faced in the context created by the increasing interaction between the public and private sectors all through American society, and this context needs to be understood and interpreted in order for us to identify both the potential pitfalls and the ways around them. A survey of 5,900 jurisdictions conducted by the International City Management Association and the Advisory Commission on Intergovernmental Relations indicated that the most commonly purchased services from the private sector were those relating to the professional expertise in engineering, legal services, and planning expertise.[10]

It is extremely important that the lessons of the past not be ignored or forgotten. Chicago's pattern of planning is unique, but that uniqueness is the result of a delicate balance of factors in a sensitive and volatile political arena. Maintaining the balance is the most important task of city leadership as plans and proposals for future growth are being formulated.

Notes

1. For several excellent case histories of this style, see Edward C. Banfield and James Q. Wilson, *City Politics* (Cambridge, Mass.: Harvard University and MIT Press, 1963).

2. Andrew Neil, *The Economist* (March 29, 1980), p. 5.

3. Brian Berry, *Chicago: Transformations of an Urban System* (Cambridge, Mass.: Ballinger, 1976) p. 71.

4. Chicago Association of Commerce and Industry, *Commerce Magazine*, (March 1956).

5. *Chicago United: Its Origin and Its Opportunities*, (Chicago, Illinois: Chicago United, June 1977), p. 3.

6. *Planning Principles for the Chicago Central Area*, Chicago Central Area Committee (January 1966), p. 3.

7. *1980 Annual Report*, Chicago Central Area Committee.

8. *Sun-Times* (February 25, 1979), p. 3.

9. Committee for Economic Development, *Public-Private Partner-*

ship: An Opportunity for Urban Communities. (New York: Committee for Economic Development, 1982)

   10. Brettler-Berenyi, ''Public and Private Sector Interaction Patterns in the Delivery of Local Public Services,'' *Governmental Finance* (March 1980).

5

Public-Private Cooperation for Urban Revitalization: The Minneapolis and Saint Paul Experience

John Brandl and
Ronnie Brooks

The Context of Cooperation: The Twin Cities

For more than a century and a half, Minneapolis and Saint Paul have dominated the upper Midwest region. Although they are commonly referred to as the Twin Cities, each has a distinct character that developed as a result of its own geography and history. Saint Paul, as the northern terminus of the Mississippi, is a classic river town. It grew as a trading center from which the raw materials of the North and West were shipped to the ports of the South and East. Up river to the west, Minneapolis developed beside Saint Anthony Falls, which became the source of power for the city's milling and manufacturing industries. Today, with a combined population of 700,000, the Twin Cities have become a center for commerce, banking, and high-technology industries. The metropolitan area, which has a population of two million, provides both a growing economy and a strong and varied cultural life.

The strengths of the Twin Cities have been well publicized. Throughout its history, the regions' economic conditions have tended to be better than those in the nation as a whole. The area is somewhat insulated from the most extreme effects of several unfavorable national trends. For example, in recent years, unemployment has been about 2 percent lower than the national average, and labor productivity has remained very high. In addition, the cities have earned a reputation for honest and responsive government, as well as for the residential amenities that contribute to a high quality of life.

However, although the Twin Cities economy is healthy, growing, and diversified at the metropolitan level, it has not escaped the tensions that are common between inner cities and suburban areas. The vast majority of urban development in the last decade has taken place in the outlying areas, reflecting the pull forces of land availability and lower development and operating costs. Other growth in suburban areas can be attributed to the push forces of the central city: cost pressures, old and often outdated physical plants, real and imagined lack of personal security and safety, and lack of land for expansion.

Interestingly, the Twin Cities themselves do not compete with one another for economic development. Instead, both find that their fiercest competition comes from their respective suburbs. Businesses leaving Saint Paul move north, east, or south to suburban Ramsey County; those leaving Minneapolis have tended to move north, west, or south within suburban Hennepin County.

Six characteristics distinguish the Twin Cities and their economy from other urban centers around the country. And in a sense, these characteristics roughly correspond to a sequential history of the area.

Geographic Isolation. The Twin Cities urban center serves a vast, largely agricultural area that stretches into Wisconsin, Iowa, the Dakotas, Wyoming, and Montana. Many local observers are convinced that the sheer distance of the Twin Cities from other metropolitan areas has fostered a sense of self-sufficiency and community.

Ethnic Homogeneity. Over the years, distance and a forbidding climate have dissuaded many from coming to the Twin Cities. Although the Twin Cities possess one of the country's largest urban Indian communities, and Chicanos make up an even larger racial minority, the combined Chicano, Black, and Indian populations constitute barely 10 percent of the metropolitan area's total. Accordingly, the Twin Cities lack some of the richness of ethnically diverse metropolitan areas. However, ethnic homogeneity has probably made it easier for the Twin Cities to perceive and build a cohesive community.

Dominance of Locally Based Firms. The geographic isolation of Minneapolis and Saint Paul contributed to the creation of new business firms in the area, and these firms have thrived. There are more corporate headquarters per capita in the Twin Cities than in any other American metropolis except Boston. Roughly half of the people in manufacturing in the Twin Cities work for locally based firms, the highest proportion in the country. And, remarkably, 90 percent of those employed by companies under "outside" control work in jobs that had originally been created by local entrepreneurs and subsequently sold to outside firms.[1] All but one of the dozen largest private employers were locally founded and remain locally based. In the context of this study, the dominance of such companies is of decisive importance. Independence from distant authority fosters a commitment to place, self-reliance, and concern for those aspects of the environment that are not related to the workplace itself. People have put down roots in the Twin Cities, and there appears to be less turnover among top management than is the case elsewhere.

Diversified Economy. The geographic isolation of the Twin Cities has also contributed to the development of a balanced and diversified economy. Many goods are manufactured locally that might otherwise have been imported from another manufacturing center if one were located nearby. In addition, a large portion of the economy services agricultural producers for hundreds of miles around. In 1980, manufacturing accounted for approximately 25 percent of employment; business, professional, and repair services for 20 percent; finance, insurance, and real estate, for 6 percent; wholesale and retail trade, for 23 percent; construction, for 5 percent; transportation, communication, and utilities, for 7 percent; and government, for 14 percent. This diversity has served as a buffer for the local economy. A recession in one sector of the national economy does not affect the Twin Cities as severely as it might an area that is heavily dependent on a single industry.

Involvement of Business Leaders in Public Affairs. Business leaders in the Twin Cities, which are hundreds of miles from any other major city, have been drawn to participate in local civic affairs both to protect their investments and to create an improved environment for their progeny. This is the personal testimony of contemporary Pillsburys, Daytons, and others whose strict and pious grandparents brought their New England Calvinism with them to the Midwest.

The civic involvement of business leaders is by no means entirely a matter of individual choice. There is conscious and explicit peer pressure to participate in public affairs; the area sees itself as a community. Participation occurs both directly and through a variety of intermediary organizations. On occasion, business leaders hold elected office; but more often they serve on appointed boards and commissions, and many of the first members of the Twin Cities' Metropolitan Council were leading businessmen. The council is now generally regarded as the most effective metropolitan governing body in the United States.

That this governmental innovation has from its inception had not only the endorsement but also the participation of business leaders is a telling sign of an unusual interplay between the public and private sectors. Civic duty and corporate responsibility are widely perceived to extend beyond philanthropy. Corporate public-affairs officials—notably Wayne Thompson, formerly of Dayton-Hudson, Ronald Speed of Honeywell, and James Shannon of General Mills—regularly and publicly preach and practice that philosophy.

Government Accommodation of Major Local Firms. Minnesota is a high-tax state that provides a high level of services to its citizens. Although it is difficult to discern a cohesive policy toward business and economic development, two main characteristics of the state government's business policy stand out. The first is the tax level: Corporate taxes are high, and the individual income tax is both high and progressive. The second is that the most significant tax breaks for businesses are focused on encouraging growth in large, locally based firms. Although Minnesota's corporate income tax rates are nominally the nation's highest, since out-of-state sales are taxed at a lower rate than resident sales, taxes are considerably lower for firms that sell sizable quantities of their products outside the state, as do all the largest Twin Cities firms.

In contrast, Minnesota has never readily provided special incentives to attract new or relocating firms, and empirical evidence suggests that this approach to tax incentives has been wise. A recent study by the Academy for Contemporary Problems concluded that "little correlation exists between fiscal incentives and business location decisions, except possibly in selecting the precise location within an already chosen metropolitan area."[2] But this policy may lead to a major problem. If future trends follow those of recent years, with the vast majority of new jobs coming about not through expansion of existing companies but through creation of new firms, it is not at all certain that past forms of public-private cooperation will be appropriate. Government may need to promote, and encourage, the formation of new companies and reduce the risks inherent in such undertakings.

The Metropolitan Council recently finished an extensive study of growth patterns in the Twin Cities metropolitan area. Several patterns emerged (see table 5–1): Population within the central cities continued to decline through the 1970s, although the number of households increased; and suburban growth continued through as city dwellers moved to outlying areas. This trend is expected to level off and reverse slightly by 1990. The back-to-the-city movement is already evidenced in both Minneapolis and Saint Paul by extensive housing-rehabilitation programs and reclamation of entire urban neighborhoods. Strong housing demand can be anticipated in both central cities and in suburban areas as the number of households increases while family size continues to decrease. A movement toward smaller households made up of two wage earners is indicated both by past local trends and by the Metropolitan Council's forecasts for 1990.

The data in table 5–2 illustrate the impact of these trends on economic

Table 5–1
Population, Household, and Employment

Date Item/Area	Year				
	1950	1960	1970	1980	1990
Population					
Fully developed area	951,729	1,069,482	1,088,928	1,074,800	1,084,700
Central cities	833,067	796,283	744,266	719,000	737,300
Suburbs	118,662	273,199	344,662	355,700	347,400
Households					
Fully developed area	283,481	337,607	368,008	406,000	429,450
Central cities	251,504	264,495	265,175	286,700	302,900
Suburbs	31,977	73,112	102,833	119,300	216,550
Employment					
Fully developed area	n/a	523,385	633,633	714,050	744,820
Central cities	n/a	446,935	477,083	505,000	535,500
Suburbs	n/a	76,450	156,550	209,050	239,320
Persons per household					
Fully developed area	3.36	3.17	2.96	2.65	2.53
Central cities	3.31	3.01	2.81	2.51	2.43
Suburbs	3.71	3.74	3.35	2.98	2.75
Jobs per household					
Fully developed area	n/a	1.55	1.72	1.76	1.80
Central cities	n/a	1.70	1.80	1.76	1.77
Suburbs	n/a	1.05	1.52	1.75	1.89

Source: Metropolitan Council, *A New Urban Policy: Report of the Fully Developed Area Task Force to the Physical Development Committee of the Metropolitan Council* (Saint Paul, Minn.: January 1977), p. 28.

Note: A fully developed area is one in which 85 percent of the land is developed (*n/a:* not available).

Table 5–2
Percentage of Regional Activity, 1970 and 1990

	Population		Households		Employment	
	1970	1990	1970	1990	1970	1990
Fully developed area	58.1	42.4	64.1	47.5	74.5	58.6
Central cities	39.7	28.8	46.2	33.5	55.9	40.5
Suburbs	18.4	13.6	17.9	14.0	18.3	18.1

Percentage Change from 1970 to 1990

	Population	Households	Employment
Fully developed area	(0.4)	16.7	22.3
Central cities	(0.9)	14.2	12.2
Suburbs	0.8	23.1	52.9

Source: Metropolitan Council, *A New Urban Policy: Report of the Fully Developed Area Task Force to the Physical Development Committee of the Metropolitan Council* (Saint Paul, Minn.: January 1977), p. 34.
Note: Parenthesis indicate decline.

development in the central cities. The Metropolitan Council forecasts that employment will continue to shift to the outlying areas and that the central cities' share of employment will grow at a modest rate but will be far outstripped by the growth of employment in the suburban area. These predictions have implications not only for the central cities but also for the rest of the metropolitan region because pressures for roads, sewers, and related infrastructure will continue in the outer suburbs. These trends and the expected need to encourage creation of new firms constitute fertile ground for public-private partnerships and indicate a framework for local economic-development policy.

The economy of the Twin Cities has gone through five overlapping stages: trade (mostly of furs); raw-materials processing (lumber, grain); general manufacturing; high-value-added manufacturing (computers, electronics); and services and management.[3] The last two stages have occurred since World War II. As transportation costs for distant raw materials and to distant markets made raw-materials processing and general manufacturing less competitive, highly specialized computer and electronics firms took their place. (Transportation to the customer is only a small fraction of the costs of these products.) This development depended on, and grew out of, research that had been conducted at the University of Minnesota, an especially fortuitous phenomenon that made the area an international electronics and computer center. High-technology firms found a well-educated, dependable work force in the Twin Cities. And by their own testimony, such firms list overall quality of life as an important consideration in determining whether to locate or expand in a particular area. The Twin Cities have scored high in this regard in numerous national studies.

Currently, the fastest-growing sector of the Twin Cities economy is services and management, including sales of banking, engineering, hospital, advertising, and computer programming services. By 1990 this sector will employ as many people as manufacturing—about one-fourth of the work force. Both the advantages and the problems of growth in this sector are becoming apparent, however. Services and management provide employment for highly skilled and educated people. But as early as 1971, one-fifth of the Twin Cities' output from this sector was exported outside the state.

Until now the Twin Cities economy flourished partly by accident, partly in the face of haphazard government economic policy, and partly because the area offered an enviable quality of life. In the future the Twin Cities might find it difficult to attract and hold economic activity that increasingly is coming about through formation of new firms and that is not tied to the area by geography, tradition, or favorable government policy.

The Concept of Public-Private Partnerships in Urban Revitalization

Economic development is a net increase in the level of economic activity in the community. Most frequently, the term refers to activities within the industrial and commercial sectors of the local economy that yield increases in income, employment, and the tax base. However, opportunities for economic development are not restricted to these sectors.

Economic development may result from actions taken in the public interest by an individual or public actor. Construction of an art museum or theater may begin the process of revitalizing an area by attracting auxiliary development. However, this case study focuses on examples of public-private cooperation in which the participation of both sectors was voluntary and deliberate and in which neither actor could have undertaken the project alone and succeeded.

In the Twin Cities, a distinctive process has evolved for public-private interaction in economic development activities. This process is unique largely because it blurs the distinction between what is public and what is private. In each of the examples, both the public and the private participants behaved in ways that were substantially different from what would have been expected in the absence of a joint effort. In addition, each actor recognized the project as being in its own interest, as well as that of the community.

Projects

The examples described in this case study illustrate the diverse patterns and types of cooperative efforts that exist in the Twin Cities. They involve a great variety of goals, actors, and methods to design and accomplish cooperative ventures. It is to be understood that these are only examples; no attempt is made to list every individual or organization that had a hand in the economic development of the area.

Several criteria were applied to the selection of these examples. Each project had to:

Show conscious and voluntary cooperation between organizations and/or individuals in the public and private sectors. In each case, the interaction influenced the actions of each partner, resulting in accomplishments that neither could have achieved alone.

Reflect factors important in each of the two cities, recognizing not only that the Twin Cities constitute a coherent metropolitan area but also that in several respects the two cities present very different social, economic, and political environments.

Reflect the broad spectrum of public-private partnerships that have developed in the Twin Cities metropolitan areas. Taken as a group, the examples illustrate different contexts, goals, actors, and reasons for success.

Provide, insofar as possible, replicable models of both projects and processes that have proved significant for economic development and revitalization of urban areas.

With those considerations in mind, several leaders in the Twin Cities business community were contacted for their suggestions of appropriate examples for closer analysis. Four project or case examples were selected, two in Minneapolis and two in Saint Paul: a neighborhood-revitalization effort (Whittier); a major downtown-development project (Town Square); a downtown area consisting of several individual projects (Lowertown); and a downtown-support system (Nicollet Mall). Each evolved differently, and each emerged from different leadership patterns. They illustrate the opportunities for creativity in addressing problems common to many of America's older, fully built urban areas.

Early in the project-identification process, it became clear that no list of projects, no matter how extensive, could explain the overall relationship between the public and private sectors in Minneapolis and Saint Paul. For this reason, several representative institutions and established processes are also described in this study to further illustrate urban problem solving in the Twin Cities. Two major sources of information were used: printed accounts and available case literature, and conversations with key participants in and observers of public-private cooperative efforts.

The projects described here should not be viewed as isolated economic or political phenomena. As one Minneapolis business leader observed, a single flotation device will not keep a ship on an even keel; multiple supports are necessary. Similarly, the economic and social vitality of the Twin Cities cannot be attributed to or explained by four projects. True success emanates from the number and diversity of the cooperative activities.

There is a climate unique to the Twin Cities, *a habit of interaction* between the public and private sectors that makes it possible to recognize opportunities and seize them. It is this climate that ultimately explains the frequency, variety, and success of public-private partnerships in the Twin Cities.

Whittier Neighborhood

The Whittier neighborhood redevelopment project is an example of a privately initiated partnership. It has become a model of neighborhood planning and organization. The first steps were taken by the Dayton-Hudson Foundation, and the neighborhood and the city of Minneapolis responded.

Whittier is a densely populated, diverse urban neighborhood approximately two miles south of downtown. Comprising 83 city blocks and 445 acres, Whittier contains a variety of housing styles and lifestyles. A commercial strip runs down its center, and several major institutions form anchors in the community.

In 1975 Dayton-Hudson Foundation made a commitment to a new partnership with the neighborhood. This was the foundation's first attempt at working closely with a community, and it approached the project with care, respect, and caution.

Beginnings. In 1975 national attention was still focused on the plight of urban areas. The Model Cities Program, a product of the Great Society era, had been a failure in most communities. The urban-renewal projects it spawned were credited with destroying as much of the urban fabric as they created. The lesson of the Model Cities experience was that urban communities are complex environments with particular physical, social, and economic needs.

Wayne Thompson, then senior vice-president of Dayton-Hudson, had been given responsibility for the corporation's involvement in the community, which included participation in the Nicollet Mall project, legislative lobbying, public and government affairs, the Dayton-Hudson Foundation giving program, and other civic commitments. Thompson had been city manager in Oakland, California, and had been hired by Dayton-Hudson to continue to strengthen its commitment to the community.

With a loosely defined goal of improving and revitalizing one of the neighborhoods abutting the central business district, the foundation studied several Minneapolis communities. Selection criteria included age of housing, level of poverty, community activism and cooperation, and depth of city and federal commitment to program support. On the basis of these criteria and also because of a recent special private investment in the major expansion and refurbishing of the Minneapolis Art Institute within the Whittier community, Whittier was chosen. Wayne Thompson formally recommended to the foundation board that it adopt the Whittier neighborhood. Numerous exploratory meetings were held, and much groundwork was conducted prior to the final decision, with representatives of the Dayton-Hudson Corporation, foundation members, business leaders, top city officials and neighborhood leaders participating. On the basis of the advice and information exchanged at these meetings, it was decided to approach the Whittier community with a proposal for a partnership. This slow process of building a consensus among the prospective participants proved to be an essential ingredient in forging a successful partnership.

Initially, the neighborhood was skeptical. Whittier had been divided by arbitrary boundaries under the Model Cities Program and had been the subject of previous city-sponsored studies, projects, and programs. Neighborhood leaders were concerned about whether their role in the planning process, including the determination of boundaries, would be significant. There was also some general wariness of the big corporation behind the foundation.

During discussions, the neighborhood identified three major concerns that had to be addressed before it would agree to participate in the planning efforts.

The neighborhood wanted to establish the boundaries to incorporate the *entire* community. (Originally, the foundation had suggested limiting the project to the eastern half of Whittier.)

It wanted involvement in the selection of the consultant who would carry out the planning tasks.

It wanted to approve the work program of the consultant prior to initiation of actual work. Community leaders were particularly concerned to establish a participatory-planning process.

Even though extending the boundaries would virtually double the project size and therefore increase the budget required to complete the necessary planning work, the foundation agreed to it and to the other conditions as well. This was a critical decision because it added substantially to a feeling of trust and respect between the foundation and the community.

Establishing the Process. Team 70, a local architectural firm, was chosen as the planning consultant, and planning was begun in December 1976. According to the original plan, the consultants worked directly with, and received policy guidance from, a twenty-five-member long-range planning committee while being paid by the foundation. The committee was made up of elected delegates from all the existing neighborhood groups.

The committee met weekly. Although Marcia Townley, the foundation's project director, a woman with extensive experience in the fields of planning and housing, attended meetings in order to keep the foundation informed of the plan's progress, she had no vote on the committee. The committee elected Jeff Thomas as its chairman. Thomas lived and worked in the community and was deeply committed to the necessity for broad participation in the process. He was seen as a neutral party, whereas many committee members were considered representatives of one or another special interest. Consequently, he was able to reach out and involve all the forces in the community.

Two surveys were conducted to solicit views on issues, problems, and neighborhood ideas and to help establish priorities. A random survey of single- and multiple-family residential units was conducted. Neighborhood businesses, institutions, and nonprofit agencies were also surveyed to invite their participation.

An intensive series of communitywide meetings involving over six-hundred residents was held. In addition, because the geographic area was so large, smaller subarea meetings were held periodically. Community members identified major neighborhood problems, developed planning criteria, sorted and rated design and social-problem concepts, and reviewed and approved final plans and implementation recommendations. In addition, a housing-conditions inventory was taken of every structure in the neighborhood to determine the condition of housing.

Throughout the development of the Whittier Urban Design Framework, the neighborhood newspaper, *The Whittier Globe*, announced all community and neighborhood area meetings and provided continuous coverage of the project's progress.

The plan was completed in December 1977, one year after it was begun. Because participation had been unusually broad and residents and local business people had written the document, approval at the neighborhood level was virtually assured. The plan took a comprehensive approach and contained both planning frameworks and specific recommendations for implementation in the following areas:

Housing improvements

Commercial redevelopment

Open space development

Pedestrian improvements

Parking and vehicular-circulation improvements

Organizational strategies

After its approval by both the community and the foundation board, the plan was presented to the city of Minneapolis. The city Planning Commission took it "under advisement" and agreed in principle with its goals and recommendations. It was then presented to the Community Development Committee of the City Council, which also responded favorably.

The Whittier plan has subsequently served as a guide for city activity. Several times, neighborhood residents have lobbied the City Council to oppose a specific project because it was inconsistent with the neighborhood plan. To date, these efforts have been successful, and the plan has continued to gain credibility.

Implementation. As an outgrowth of the planning effort, community members founded the Whittier Alliance in 1978 as a local community-development corporation responsible for implementing the plan's recommendations (see Figure 5–1). The Alliance, which is funded by a $1-million grant from the Dayton-Hudson Foundation, is still seeking additional public and private financing commitments in order to accomplish plan objectives. The foundation's grant, committed for over four years (from 1978 to 1982), was intended as seed money to support the alliance

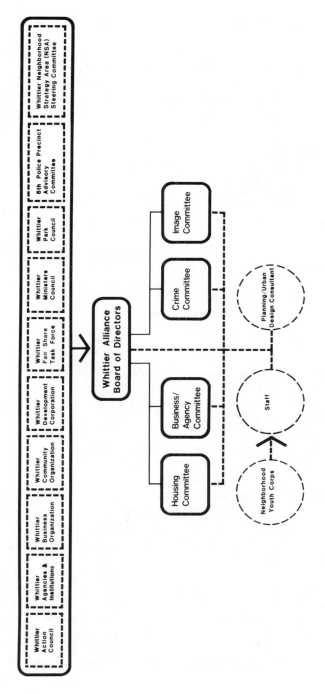

Source: Adapted from *Partners*, John McNamara and Ranae Hanson, The Dayton Hudson Foundation, Minneapolis, 1981, pp. 94–95.

Figure 5–1. Whittier Alliance Organizational Framework

and its individual projects until other resources can be utilized successfully.

Each year, a specific action plan and a corresponding work program
is developed; the projects and plans are subject to year-end evaluation
before the next year's action plan is developed. The alliance has successfully undertaken several specific projects and programs. The action
plan for the first year, for example, included the following projects:

Housing Improvements

    Exterior Rehabilitation Subsidy Program
    Exterior Rehabilitation Loan Program
    Security Hardware Subsidy Program

Commercial Redevelopment

    Business/Agency Committee
    Trash-receptacle construction and placement program
    Lobbying elected public officials

Open space Development

    Boulevard/street tree-planting program

Organizational Development

    Crime Committee
      Crime Prevention Incentive Awards Program
    Image Committee
      Neighborhood carnival in Whittier Park
      Whittier neighborhood garage sales
    Block clubs
      Neighborhood Watch Force Program, including the Operation
      Identification and Premise Security Check Programs

Results. The Whittier Alliance has begun its third year of projects and
programs as of this writing. The planning and implementation processes
are considered successful by both the neighborhood and the foundation.
Homes are being rehabilitated, and block clubs have been formed, fostering community pride and assisting in the control of crime. The community's image is improving. Moreover, in spite of the recession, both
residential and commercial improvements are continuing. However, the
direct economic-development benefits are difficult to assess because it
is impossible to determine how much of this activity would have occurred
in the absence of the Whittier Alliance and without the assistance of the
foundation.

The process itself, however, has become a national model of community-controlled comprehensive planning. Other neighborhoods in Minneapolis have already adopted it. The Dayton-Hudson Foundation has been sufficiently pleased with the experience that it is using a similar process in Pontiac, Michigan, in a neighborhood partnership effort involving the local J.L. Hudson store. Although the Pontiac and Whittier communities are dramatically different in housing stock, socioeconomic characteristics of neighborhood residents, and racial diversity, the Whittier model appears to be both replicable and transferable. Dayton-Hudson is developing the same, strong, mutually respectful relationship with the Pontiac neighborhood that made Whittier a success.

The Lessons of Whittier.

Corporate philanthropic efforts directed toward a neighborhood development can be effective in strengthening a neighborhood and fostering local initiative.

Privately and locally initiated neighborhood economic development can be more effective than publicly initiated attempts. Of course, this is not necessarily so, but the Dayton-Hudson Foundation's current grant of $1 million is small by government standards. The Whittier Long-Range Planning Committee's freedom from red tape fostered enthusiasm, community pride, and hard work.

Foundation money alone was not enough to ensure success of the project. Townley's and the Dayton-Hudson Corporation's knowledge of the neighborhood and Wayne Thompson's persistent belief in the importance of neighborhood economic development meant that the foundation was not merely a distant financier and the neighborhood an unresponsive recipient.

Mutual respect and trust, developed through extended dialogue, were crucial. Had the foundation refused to negotiate directly on the neighborhood's three conditions for participation, it is unlikely that the project would have been able to continue to involve all elements of the community.

Nicollet Mall

A private-sector initiative, the Nicollet Mall in Minneapolis is widely acknowledged to be one of the most architecturally pleasing and economically successful malls in the country. The standard of excellence set for this project by prominent business leader Donald Dayton has since received nationwide recognition.

Nicollet Mall opened in 1967, after a decade of planning, and was the first downtown-shopping street to be closed to automobile traffic in a major U.S. city. Originally eight blocks long, it is currently being extended by four blocks. There have been substantial positive spillover effects on the surrounding downtown area, including new construction of residential and commercial facilities and increased retail sales.

Physically, the mall was a dramatic reconstruction of Nicollet Avenue, the heart of Minneapolis's retail district. It is shared by pedestrians, buses, and an occasional taxi or special-purpose vehicle. Heated bus shelters, a self-service post office, extensive landscaping, and visually exciting fountains and sculptures help to make it an attractive pedestrian transitway.

The Nicollet Mall is an excellent example of a sustained public-private partnership. From its inception, it was a product of the city's business community working with its government. Not only large retailers but also owners of large and small buildings, corporations, financial institutions, and merchants inspired and conceived the project. And although the public sector played a major role in the planning, execution, and routine maintenance of the mall, capital construction and annual operating expenses have been paid in large part by the business community. In fact, private initiative and financial involvement have been especially effective in making street improvements, an area that traditionally has been an exclusively public responsibility.

Beginnings. In 1957 the Downtown Council created Nicollet Avenue Survey Committee, chaired by Leslie Park, head of Baker Properties, a major building owner and manager. The subcommittee was chaired by John McHugh, then vice-president of Northwestern National Bank. The Survey Committee, working closely with city planners, and discussing several general concepts with area merchants, building owners, and tenants, sought ways to improve Nicollet Avenue and thereby strengthen the entire downtown district.

In 1958 and 1959, Minneapolis was nearing completion of its first major downtown urban-renewal project, Gateway Center. Although downtown Minneapolis was not undergoing the decline experienced by many older cities, change was evident. General Mills had recently moved its corporate headquarters to the suburbs. The development of the interstate freeway system was already drawing people to the suburbs and affecting the character of the central city. The first regional shopping center in the area, Southdale, was under development in the southwestern suburb of Edina by Dayton-Hudson, a leading retailer. Although Nicollet

Avenue did not seem to be losing its importance as the preeminent shopping street of the upper Midwest, retail sales were sagging. Taxes were on the rise, and there was little indication of offsetting new value.[4]

The Downtown Council had been created three years earlier to strengthen the downtown area. The organization was made up of individuals representing every facet of downtown life: top executives from major corporations, small businesses and merchants, the corporate leadership of the Minneapolis *Star* and *Tribune*, heads of financial institutions, officials from the utility companies, owners of office buildings, and labor leaders. According to one official, the council's work was to set "aside our difference in some areas" while we "work on accomplishing the objectives where we have mutual goals and interests."[5]

In 1959 the Downtown Council retained Barton-Aschman Associates, Inc., "to work with a permanent Nicollet Avenue Subcommittee on three tasks: first, to make a detailed examination of existing conditions; second, to set objectives; and third, to report upon (not recommend) alternative measures for improvement."[6] The Barton-Aschman report, finished in 1960, stated four overall objectives for Nicollet Avenue improvement:

Make the street more attractive for the pedestrians, and improve pedestrian circulation.

Encourage mass transit by improving the circulation of, and access to, buses along the avenue.

Improve the overall business climate of downtown by making the Nicollet Mall attractive for future investments.

Encourage private investment.

To accomplish these objectives, five alternatives were considered for Nicollet Avenue improvements.

Modification of the Existing Street. This modest beautification program would retain the established mix of automobiles, buses, and pedestrians.

Pedestrian Concourses at Intersections. Each block would be landscaped, and pedestrian bridges would be built above or below street level at each intersection. Autos, public-transit vehicles, and pedestrians would still share the avenue.

Devotion to Pedestrians. All traffic would be eliminated from Nicollet Avenue, and the entire eight-block area would be made a public park.

Block-by-Block Plazas. All traffic would be restricted from Nicollet Avenue itself, but traffic would still be allowed to cross Nicollet at the intersections of each block.

Mall and Transitway. Bus traffic, taxis, and emergency vehicles would be permitted on the avenue, and pedestrian circulation and overall amenities would be significantly improved. This alternative was the Downtown Council's ultimate choice.

Following the publication of the Barton-Aschman report, subcommittee Chairman John McHugh and his fellow committee members personally solicited the advice and support of building owners, tenants, merchants, and other interested parties along the avenue. Their discussions centered on such problems as technical difficulties, the need to keep the buildings and shops open during construction, access to underground facilities, and costs.

Consensus on the preferred alternative of a pedestrian mall and transitway was reached with remarkable speed. But the city, although enthusiastic about the concept, had previously indicated that financing from regular revenue sources would not be possible.

Two of the elements that have contributed to the mall's success were decided on at this time. First, Donald Dayton, head of the largest retailing company in the Twin Cities, helped convince those involved with the mall's construction that it should be elegant, aesthetically pleasing, and of high-quality design. Second, the mall subcommittee and John McHugh were able to convince the various participants that the mall should be built as a permanent emblem for Minneapolis.

Implementation

The conceptualization and consensus-building process took three years. The detailed planning of the mall and the surmounting of technical, legal, and financial difficulties took another three.

Once the Downtown Council had adopted the subcommittee's recommmendation, discussions began with the city for implementation of the plan, and Barton-Aschman was asked to prepare a formal plan for Nicollet Avenue Mall. This formal plan, adopted by the Downtown Council in 1962, made recommendations regarding traffic circulation, design and engineering standards, and landscape architecture for the eight-block, curved route of the mall. The city coordinator's office and the City

Planning Department worked with the Public Works Department, the assessor's office, and the federal government to construct a plan for financing the mall and to resolve technical problems. Thomas Thompson, the city coordinator, and Lawrence Irvin, the city planner, presented the plan to the Minneapolis City Council and the Hennepin County Board of Commissioners, which adopted it, thereby giving it official status.

The city and the business community agreed that although the capital construction costs and the annual operating costs should be borne primarily by the owners of property fronting the mall because they would benefit most directly from the project, some costs should also be carried by property owners on the blocks to each side of the mall. Therefore, an assessment formula was derived that allocated more than half of the total assessed costs to mall-frontage owners, with the remainder to be paid by owners of adjacent property.

During the discussions leading to this arrangement, it became apparent that Minnesota law contained no provision for allowing restrictions on the use of a public thoroughfare or for requiring private businesses to pay annual maintenance costs. In order for the project to proceed, city ordinances needed to be changed, the Hennepin County Board had to vacate the county highway use, and most important, the Minnesota legislature had to change the assessment law to permit construction and operating expenses to be financed by special assessment. Led by the city coordinator's office, city attorneys, planners, and staff aids went to work to change all the necessary laws and ordinances.

Communication and coordination among actors in the public sector took time. The City Council, department directors, key operating staff, the Hennepin County Board, and the county delegation to the Minnesota Legislature all had to be kept informed and up to date on the project's needs and progress.

As part of its commitment to the project, the city sought and received two federal grants for mall construction. An Urban Mass Transit Demonstration Grant of $512,000 paid for some of the construction related to public transit, and an Urban Beautification Grant of $483,500 was awarded to cover some for the landscaping and park amenities. This was the first time either funding source had been used for construction of an urban mall. In addition to seeking funding for construction, the city agreed to an annual payment equal to the routine maintenance budget, which ordinarily would have been allocated to offset operating costs for Nicollet Avenue. Private business owners would be assessed the extra maintenance costs.

Although the mall was originally conceived as a construction project of the Downtown Council, the city was asked to act as general contractor so that more bids on the construction could be solicited in order to reduce costs. Following resolution of the assessment and legal issues, the city agreed to fill this role. Bids were let, contracts were awarded, and construction was finally begun. (Ultimately, construction costs totaled $3,-873,904.)

Results. Thirteen years later, Nicollet Mall is credited with having substantially upgraded, if not transformed, downtown Minneapolis. In the view of those who conceived it, the mall has been a success. Both vehicular traffic flow and pedestrian circulation have significantly improved. Bus ridership seems to have increased, and the mall has certainly made shopping downtown more convenient and pleasant.

Over the years, more than $500 million has been spent directly for new development on the four-block-wide strip adjoining the mall. By 1971 alone, $225 million had been spent for development projects directly fronting the mall. Retail sales in downtown remain strong, and Dayton's mall store remains one of its most profitable outlets. Donaldson's, Minneapolis' second-largest retailer, is currently building a new store on the mall. Many small businesses have also prospered, and new merchants, including several internationally known retailers, have moved into downtown. Although Nicollet Mall cannot be given sole credit for the resurgence of downtown Minneapolis, it has met its original objectives—and gone well beyond them.

Lessons of Nicollet Mall.

> The success of the mall cannot be explained solely in terms of technical, managerial, or organizational innovations or techniques. Rather, it is the result of a community working cooperatively over a long period of time.

> Persistence, patience, and loyalty paid off. From conception to realization, the mall took nearly ten years. Although both public- and private-sector policymakers often felt pressured to make short-term decisions, those pressures were resisted by Park, Gay, McHugh, Dayton, Thompson, Irvin and others involved in the mall's development.

> It was crucial that the issue was *perceived* by many participants as concerning the downtown area and the city as a whole, not merely their own company or agency. Not only would it have been impossible for any one firm to have implemented the project, but it would not have been profitable either.

> Involvement and openness were essential ingredients in the decision-

making process. Examples were the structure of the Downtown Council (where each firm, regardless of size, had equal status) and the procedure followed by McHugh of patiently going door to door to proselytize and seek counsel. Thus individuals and firms were led to decide to take a risk that would be shared by others.

Public- and private-sector participants each successfully took actions normally thought to be the function of the other. This public amenity, the mall, was a private-sector brainchild, the city government became the general contractor, and private firms paid for the maintenance of the street. No rigid distinction was made between public and private. Pragmatic problem solvers worked cooperatively, united by strong goals.

Lowertown

The case of Lowertown involves a three-pronged partnership: the McKnight Foundation, the city of Saint Paul, and the private business community. Lowertown is a 180-acre area on the eastern edge of downtown Saint Paul. A warehouse district built at the turn of the century, it is home to many historic buildings of distinct architectural character. Once an active trading center for rail, lumber and commerce, the area fell into decline during the last three decades. It is flanked by freeways on the north and east and bounded by the curving Mississippi River to the south.

Efforts to revitalize Lowertown began in the late 1960s, when Norman Mears, a philanthropist and chairman of the Buckbee Mears Company, developed a master plan for the area. His ideas included renovating warehouse structures to house specialty shops, offices, and restaurants, and creating linkages to the Mississippi and to Saint Paul's heritage. But when Mears died in 1974, his vision seemed to die with him.

Beginnings. When George Latimer became mayor of Saint Paul in 1976, the city had recently changed its charter to strengthen the mayoralty and its role in city government. A lawyer by profession, Latimer was recognized as a man able to bring people together to accomplish an objective. During his first two years in office, a good deal of the downtown development that had been in the planning stages for a decade was accomplished. One of the projects, Town Square, a mixed-use complex including two office towers, a new department store and retail shops, a hotel complex, a parking ramp, and a new enclosed public park, finally underwent construction. Mears Park Plaza, a 255-unit apartment complex in Lowertown, became the first new housing to be built downtown in ten years. As these two projects became reality, other proposals began to move from the planning stage into financing and construction.

Early in the Latimer administration, the city reorganized its planning and development functions so that it could respond more quickly and competently to development needs, allowing the mayor to follow through more readily on project commitments. The Department of Planning and Economic Development (PED) was created to consolidate four separate agencies. Under the direction of the mayor and city council, PED could respond as one agency to such developer's needs as zoning, financing, project coordination, and management.

During this time the McKnight Foundation was becoming one of the largest foundations in the country. A Minnesota-based organization with strong historical ties to Saint Paul, it was preparing to embark on a more aggressive philosophy of philanthropy. Not content with simply providing grant money, the foundation began to look for a way to make a more substantial impact on the community. The foundation and its executive director, Russell Ewald, began to consider how the foundation might undertake a new type of philanthropy: a program-related investment in Saint Paul's development activities. That is, instead of an outright grant, an investment loan would be made to a project; these monies would be used, recouped, and returned to McKnight to be used again.

Other forces also helped to bring the city and the McKnight Foundation together. The catalyst was David Stanley, then vice president of the brokerage firm of Piper, Jaffray and Hopwood. Stanley was familiar with Saint Paul's aggressive leadership and bold development plans. He also knew Russell Ewald and understood the McKnight Foundation's interest in making more significant investments. The stage was set for the formation of a partnership.

Late in the fall of 1977, David Stanley arranged a meeting between Ewald, Mayor Latimer, and Robert Sylvester, then president of the City Council. Ewald asked the city what it would do with a multimillion-dollar investment. He indicated that McKnight wanted to have a substantial and long-lasting impact on Saint Paul's development, not just to build a concrete and steel monument.

A small working group, consisting of David Stanley and members of the city staff, was formed to prepare a proposal for presentation to the McKnight board of directors. Lowertown was quickly identified as the appropriate project area because of its location, some past involvement on the part of the McKnight board members, and its "ripeness" for development. The dream was to make a "people's place," a downtown neighborhood with housing opportunities for all types of people: young and old, families, all income levels, and a variety of lifestyles. Restaurants, shops, offices, and amenities would round out this urban village and provide both residents and visitors places to work, shop, and enjoy themselves. Development of a historic railroad depot and use of the air rights at the southern end of Lowertown would provide access to the Mississippi River and a link with the city's history. The original concepts of Norman Mears were taken off the shelves, updated, revised as appropriate, and recombined to form the basis of the proposal to McKnight.

The revitalization of Lowertown was an enormous task. Buildings were vacant or significantly underused. Ownership of land was dispersed among many, generally small, businesses and investors. Land assembly would be difficult and implementation of the major program elements would depend on the voluntary participation of various property owners. Even with a major commitment by the McKnight Foundation, it was estimated that upgrading Lowertown would take at least $200 million and approximately ten years. It became clear that McKnight funds would have to be matched with as much money from other sources as possible, including heavy participation by the public sector in securing federal and state grants. In addition, it was essential that the private sector become a full partner in the realization of the project so that the traditional image of Lowertown as an unattractive investment for bankers and private developers could be overcome.

Given the desire to maximize the impact of McKnight funds and the voluntary participation of landowners, the proposal needed to be specific enough to give the project direction, detailed enough to secure the McKnight commmitment, and yet fluid enough to accommodate unforeseen changes.

Implementation. Once the basic concepts were clarified, it was necessary to resolve how they would be carried out. After considering several options, it was decided that the most appropriate vehicle would be a not-for-profit corporation charged with accomplishing the overall goals. This organization would also act as a facilitator and negotiator among the numerous interests in Lowertown: the McKnight Foundation, the city, owners of existing business, tenants, residents, landowners, investors, developers, and preservationists.

In March 1978 the McKnight Foundation announced the commitment of $10 million in program-related investment to revitalize Lowertown. The Lowertown Redevelopment Corporation (LRC) was created to oversee and administer the project and the McKnight funds. The staff of this corporation would work closely with city staff, landowners, area businesses, tenants, and private developers to facilitate development projects.

Incorporated in August 1978, the LRC board of directors reflected the various interests within the Lowertown community. It included the mayor, the heads of two of the largest banks in the downtown area, the president of Burlington Northern Railroad (the largest employer in Lowertown), the pastor of one of the Lowertown churches, a community activist, and a member of the staff of one of the area's congressmen.

The Lowertown concept had to overcome several hurdles. Landowners, business owners, and tenants were suspicious of the large commitment and afraid that they would be forced out of the area. Fear of rising rents, big developers, and land speculators caused early friction between these groups, the city, and LRC. But it became apparent that every effort would be made to assist and protect existing Lowertown tenants and owners, and those tensions subsided.

Unfortunately, most area owners and businesses did not understand the nature of the McKnight commitment and thought that grant money was to be given away to local owners and merchants. When the investment nature of the program was made clear, many owners were disappointed. After the initial disenchantment, however, they began to think of new ways to use the McKnight funds.

The Lowertown dream was also subject to external stresses. As soon as the McKnight commitment became public, land prices in Lowertown skyrocketed. Inflation, rising interest rates, and high-priced real estate tested the economic viability of the basic concept. The notion of using McKnight resources very sparingly to attract large amounts of other public and private resources had to be modified to meet changing economic forces.

Results. A number of accomplishments have already been realized in Lowertown. They include the following:

The first major, mixed-use project has moved from the planning stage to the financing stage, and construction should begin in 1981. This project will entail a total investment in excess of $50 million and include a 392-car parking garage, 250 housing units, a new YMCA, and 150,000 square feet of restaurants and shops.

A major commitment by Control Data Corporation for its first Business and Technology Center has brought several million dollars in new investment to Lowertown and has provided a new home for many small businesses.

Minnesota Mutual Insurance Company has located its headquarters facility immediately adjacent to Lowertown. With assistance by the LRC staff, this building will be integrated into its surroundings and provide an example of the urban village, mixed-use design conceived of in the early Lowertown proposal.

The Park Square Court has been purchased and will undergo substantial rehabilitation in 1981 and 1982. New offices, shops, and restaurants will be combined with established businesses to upgrade existing space with substantially improved amenities. Additional space will be provided for leasing.

Major planning has been completed for the next phases of development along the riverfront and in the northern quadrant. Construction has begun on a new hotel in the north quadrant of Lowertown, and plans are being drawn for an adjacent residential development. In addition, the Union Depot structure situated on the Mississippi River has been sold to private developers for renovation.

Many smaller projects have been provided with technical and financing assistance, design review, and equally important encouragement by the LRC.

In the two and a half years since the commitment of funds by the McKnight Foundation, some net economic-development gains have already resulted. Although it is difficult to assess precisely how much development (if any) would have occurred without the McKnight involvement, it is clear that one of the reasons such private initiatives as Park Square Court, Minnesota Mutual's new headquarters, and the Control Data Business and Technology Center are in Lowertown is the visible commitment by the city and foundation to upgrade the area.

McKnight has led the way in providing an innovative approach to foundation involvement with local government in public-private partnerships for economic development and urban revitalization. As a result, the city of Saint Paul has undertaken additional projects in partnership with foundations. Other uses of the program-related-investment vehicle are being explored by both the public sector and foundations. The business community has actively participated on the LRC board and has helped McKnight and LRC to more clearly understand the pitfalls of inner-city development. Because three sectors—foundations, city government, and private business—have worked together, commitments have been made on individual projects that would not have otherwise occurred.

In addition, Lowertown has been a major component in the Negotiated Investment Strategy (NIS) experiment. NIS is attempting to involve federal, state, and local governments in developing a unified strategy for the investment of public and private dollars to meet jointly defined objectives. As a result of the NIS process, a $4.8-million Urban Development Action Grant was committed for one Lowertown project, and additional smaller amounts were received for street improvements in the area.

The Lessons of Lowertown.

An innovative third sector can have great influence. The McKnight Foundation's central role in the project owes as much to the way in which the foundation participated as it does to the money it contributed. For years the Twin Cities have had an unusual number of generous foundations. Increasingly, they are adding to their traditional philanthropic activities a new role of direct involvement in community activities where the traditional participants need prodding, a sense of cohesion, or ideas.

The major actors from the public, private, and third sectors already knew each other, but today a large downtown redevelopment project is such a complex undertaking that all aspects cannot be known or envisaged by any single participant. Mutual trust is essential and must be facilitated by a habit of interaction among the sectors.

Creation of a not-for-profit corporation, the LRC, facilitated the carrying out of the project. This corporation involved participants from all three sectors. The LRC board included the most influential people from the city's public and private sectors.

Town Square

Saint Paul's Town Square is an instructive example of a public-private partnership for economic-development purposes. This dramatic downtown-redevelopment project includes two office towers, a major retail complex with a new department store and over forty specialty shops, and a major new luxury hotel. Town Square was initiated by the city of Saint Paul in the late 1960s. Plans were conceived, land acquired, and old buildings torn down. The city prepared design and development controls for the downtown area and then sought private developers. After Oxford Properties, Inc., was chosen in 1975, the city continued its participation in the project by sharing the financial burden and becoming a meaningful member of the development team. For example, the city built an indoor park as a project amenity and constructed public walkways and skyways linking the project to other portions of the downtown district. In addition, it assisted in the construction of the project by vacating a major downtown street, granting building permits, and negotiating with major tenants to assure them of the city's deep commitment to the project.

Town Square required a partnership between the developer and the city. Neither could have accomplished the task without the other. For the duration of the projects, including most of the construction period, representatives from Oxford Properties and the city met at least once a week to resolve design, financial, and technical problems and keep the project on schedule. Because the public portion of the construction was inextricably tied to the private portion, construction materials, schedules, and even use of the site had to be closely coordinated.

Beginnings. In the late 1960s and early 1970s, downtown Saint Paul underwent urban renewal. Twelve blocks were cleared, and major new office, retail, and housing complexes were constructed. As part of this process, the block bounded by Cedar, Minnesota, Sixth, and Seventh Streets was acquired by the city. It was originally conceived as a high-density, mixed-use block. Planners sought a focal point for downtown that would link the financial district with the retail and entertainment core. City staff prepared design and development guidelines suggesting hotel, retail, or office use or preferably a combination of these. After the block was cleared by the city in 1970, it sat vacant, awaiting redevelopment. As time went on and various project proposals for the block were rejected, it became known locally as "superhole." Despite the block's strategic location, no development package could be assembled that provided the density and desired mixture of uses and still met the tests of financial feasibility.

The retail picture in downtown Saint Paul worsened during the 1970s as retailers followed the population movement to the suburbs. From 1958 to 1976, the central business district lost $55 million, or 41 percent, of its retail dollar volume. Those numbers represented over two hundred retail establishments, many jobs, and the related tax base. In the downtown area, the office market, which had experienced a surge in construction in the 1960s, stagnated for almost five years, and many other nonretail businesses decided to leave. In addition, there had been no new hotel construction since the early 1960s, a fact that caused conventions to choose locations outside of Saint Paul.

In 1975 Oxford Properties, Inc., a Canadian-based development company, was working with the city of Minneapolis on development of City Center, a major downtown shopping and office complex. Shortly after receiving the commission, Oxford executives were introduced to Robert Van Hoef, vice president of First National Bank of Saint Paul and executive director of Operation '85, a group of downtown corporate leaders. Van Hoef had been heavily involved in the twelve-block downtown urban revitalization effort and was well aware of the tremendous problems that had been encountered. He introduced the Oxford executives to Mayor Larry Cohen and Councilmen Robert Sylvester and David Hozza, who in turn assured Oxford of both the city's and the business community's willingness to assist in any proposed venture. Because Oxford liked the location of the vacant block and the overall development climate in Saint Paul, it began preparation of a development package.

In the early spring of 1975, Oxford initiated contacts with potential anchor tenants and joint-venture partners. These meetings were so successful that on April 23, 1975, Donald Love, president of Oxford, and Curt Carlson, president of the Radisson Corporation, a major hotel developer, announced plans for joint development of two blocks. Radisson would build a major new hotel on one block, and Oxford would put up an office-retail complex on the other.

Oxford, one of three major developers to pursue a plan for this particular site, was awarded tentative developer status by the city late in 1975. The successful proposal included two major office towers, the new Radisson Hotel, and a retail complex that would include a new department store and other shops. Lin Deardorff was named senior project manager by Oxford.

Implementation. Although Oxford had been tentatively declared developer, financial feasibility and project details were still a long way from resolution. Major commitments were needed from a department store and an anchor office tenant if the project was to continue. Radisson Corporation wanted to build enclosed walkways above street level from the proposed new Radisson Hotel to their existing hotel, located more than three blocks away. On the other hand, Donaldson's, the major department store that was considering becoming the anchor retail tenant, wanted dramatic amenities built into the project to lure shoppers back from the suburbs. It became increasingly clear that the Town Square project was of such magnitude and so important to the city that it could not be built strictly with private funds.

The design called for the closing of Seventh Street, a major artery in downtown, and the creation of skyways (enclosed above-ground walkways) that would radiate outward in three directions from the project. The city, working closely with Oxford, began to explore ways in which it might assist or subsidize the public area in the project, including the construction of the skyways.

Throughout 1976 and into 1977, Oxford negotiated to secure the anchor tenants necessary to make the project financially feasible. City project designers worked with the architecture firm of Skidmore, Owings & Merrill as the design of the two-block project began to take shape. It was decided that both blocks would be excavated for a five-hundred-car underground parking garage. In addition, the southern block would contain the new Radisson Hotel, with lobby areas, and meetings rooms. The northern block of the site would house a new department store and retail shops on the lower levels and a glass-enclosed public park on the third floor. Two office towers would contain a combined space of 400,000 square feet of first-class offices, and additional specialty stores would line vacated Seventh Street.

As planning continued, it became clear that the success of Town Square would depend on financial assistance from the city. Mayor Latimer and City Council members were convinced that a dramatic, high-quality project was needed not only to secure the individual office and retail commitments necessary to ensure the feasibility of Town Square but also to change the overall image of downtown and create potential spinoffs of this project on adjacent blocks. Although the public park, skyways, and concourse areas were considered essential design elements, the city decided that they would be too costly to be borne solely by the developer and future tenants.

The city's decision to fund these public areas was essential for receiving the necessary commitment from Donaldson's. Van Hoef, working through Operation 85, and Deardorff sought and received office-space commitments from First National Bank of Saint Paul, Saint Paul Companies, and Northwestern National Bank. These firms did not necessarily need additional office space, but they recognized the effect the project could have on the health of downtown and were willing to assume some of the front-end risk to ensure its success.

In the fall of 1977, Town Square had received enough support from major local corporations to begin construction on the underground-parking ramp. The ramp, which was sold to Oxford upon completion, was financed initially by the Port Authority through the sale of $5.5 million worth of revenue bonds. Oxford's investment in the project totaled approximately $55 million plus tenant improvements, which included the costs of Donaldson's department store, other retail space, and the office towers. The Radisson Plaza Hotel, which costs approximately $15 million, was financed in part by an $8.5-million mortgage package provided by six Saint Paul banks and savings-and-loan institutions. The city of Saint Paul ultimately invested $1.6 million to upgrade traffic and pedestrian circulation around the square and an additional $9 million for the indoor park and public concourses. An Urban Development Action Grant, received from the Department of Housing and Urban Development, covered $4.8 million of these public costs.

In August 1980, Town Square was opened with gala festivities. Although the final cost of the project was almost double the initial estimate as a result of the national recession and the worsening economy, the city's portion of the project had been built on schedule.

Town Square is expected to generate a significant amount of new taxes and employment for the city, and it already appears to have been major stimulus for Saint Paul's sagging retail trade. Moreover, Town Square is having an impact on development decisions on adjacent blocks. In addition to economic spinoffs, some observers already credit the project with instilling a new civic pride in downtown among local residents and business leaders.

The Lessons of Town Square.

> One or a few firms acting out of civic obligation rather than for short-term profits can inspire cooperation from others. When the major downtown banks contracted for space in Town Square, other firms began to understand that their interests were intertwined with the general economic health of Saint Paul.

> Town Square could not have been realized if the public and private sectors had insisted on a sharp demarcation line between the two. The project houses private firms and also contains public walkways, skyways, and even a park. Public and private construction plans were so intertwined that on several occasions, one constructed facilities that were later purchased by the other.

> The structure used was a team made up of the several active partners. This arrangement worked well, engendering trust and facilitating timely decision making.

> The project was facilitated by the fact that the city government was able to act quickly and decisively. This was due as much to the fact that the city government was one with a strong mayoralty as to the individual talents of Mayor George Latimer.

Processes and Organizations

Historically the Twin Cities governments have fostered economic activity by providing infrastructure and granting tax benefits to important industries. In recent years, however, a fundamental change in this pattern has taken place. Partnerships of public and private entities are undertaking economic investments, and private organizations are acting as initiators, evaluators, and implementers of public policy. Indeed, some of the changes wrought by public-private partnerships have become institutionalized.

The Twin Cities have the familiar range of civic organizations such as the Urban League, the American Association of University Women, the Urban Coalition, the United Fund, and the League of Women Voters. But they also have several organizations that are unique. These are characterized by their success in involving business leaders in public affairs in a more intimate and sustained way than is true in other cities.

Citizens League

The Citizens League is probably this country's most successful example of a private, business-oriented, civic research organization. Its beginnings go back to the 1940s when Hubert Humphrey was mayor of Minneapolis and there was a general increase in concern about public affairs. The League was created in 1952, as an outgrowth of years of informal discussions on public issues among civic-minded Twin Cities businessmen. Since the early 1960s, the League's main task has been to identify important issues before they become critical, study them, assess various possible responses, and recommend a preferred approach. More important, however, it is the *mode* of inquiry that distinguishes the organization.

Membership is open to anyone who is willing to pay the minimal annual dues. There are now about 3,000 individual members and 600 supporting firms and foundations. Each year the board of directors surveys League members' interests and then selects from four to six issues for study. These issues may include examination of the structure of metropolitan governance, the financing of higher education, the adequacy of area medical facilities, the role of sports in the schools, the treatment of chemical dependency, transportation problems, welfare reform, and the Twin Cities economy. A task force is formed to examine each topic. Task-force meetings are open to any member who wants to join. These groups meet weekly, hear from invited experts early in the process, and then move to internal discussion. Typically, the meetings are held over a period of six months to a year, until a consensus is reached on what the issue is and what should be done about it. Then a report is written, debated, and sometimes modified by the League board, and widely disseminated. In this fashion, the Citizens League is able to assemble talented people for extended informal discussion without constraints from pressure groups. Its policy decisions, when they are finally reached, are influential both because of the quality of the arguments and because they have the approval of a large, able, and fairly diverse group of people.

Many Citizens League reports have been remarkably influential. A study in the mid-1960s led directly to the formation of the Twin Cities Metropolitan Council, which is, as noted earlier, one of this country's most effective examples of a metropolitan governance structure. A few years later a League report recommended forming a branch of the state university system in the Twin Cities. Metropolitan State University was created soon thereafter to provide people in midcareer with individually tailored programs and credit for work experience. The university, which has no campus, depends heavily on part-time faculty members.

Despite the fact that League activists often hold prominent positions in the Twin Cities corporations, there is a tacit understanding in the Citizens League that individuals speak for themselves, not for their employers. This, along with a tradition of carefulness and consensus, makes it difficult for public officials to ignore League recommendations.

The League process has become institutionalized, and although its immensely talented Executive Director Ted Kolderie resigned in 1980, it is unlikely that there will be a marked change in its mode of operation or its effectiveness. The League cultivates the talents of private individuals and channels their application to public issues. It brings together people from business firms, universities, foundations, and government. In addition, participation in the League fosters an informal network in which people remain in contact outside the League as other issues arise. The League represents a unique and remarkable procedure for ongoing public-private interaction that is open, cooperative, harmonious, and effective.

Minnesota 5-Percent Club

As early as 1945, the Dayton Company maintained a policy of devoting 5 percent of pretax earnings to charitable contributions even though the national average for such contributions has hovered around 1 percent. In 1965, Wayne Thompson, then city manager of Oakland, California, moved to the Twin Cities to work for Dayton's. Thompson was a strong advocate of his firm's corporate contributions policy and clearly saw its value, both to Dayton's and to the community. Largely through his efforts, the Minnesota Five Percent Club was founded in 1971. In addition to Dayton-Hudson's, it included the Minneapolis newspapers the *Star* and the *Tribune*, the First Bank of Minneapolis, and the Northwestern National Bank.

Many other Twin Cities firms had similar policies. When David Koch, chairman and chief executive officer of Graco, Inc., became president of the Minneapolis Chamber of Commerce in 1976, he decided to create a vehicle for recognizing the work of the 5-percent companies. Koch made corporate philanthropy his number-one priority and assumed sponsorship of the Five Percent Club. The Minneapolis Chamber was the first to make corporate philanthropy a primary objective. That year, it sponsored a celebration for 5-percent firms; and to everyone's surprise, twenty-two local companies came forward. By 1981, the number of member firms had grown to forty-four. Moreover, the Two Percent Club, a similar group formed in 1979, had twenty-one members.

The Five Percent Club is noteworthy for three reasons. First, it typifies the private sector's commitment to the community in which it operates. As Kenneth Dayton of the Dayton-Hudson Corporation put it, "I say it is immoral for a company to take profits out of a community year after year without putting anything back in."

Second, the Five Percent Club sets a standard for the wider business community. Membership in the club continues to grow as its standards become integrated into expectations of corporate behavior.

Third, the club's donations give the local community the resources with which to try a wide variety of social and economic experiments such as the Whittier neighborhood-development project. The ability to carry out such programs strengthens the social fabric and enriches the community's cultural life as well.

Minnesota Project on Corporate Responsibility

A most interesting example of institutionalized peer pressure in the Twin Cities business community is the Minnesota Project for Corporate Responsibility. In 1977, after extended informal discussion, a group of executives from the largest local corporations—Thomas Wyman (Green Giant); Peter Gillette (Northwestern National Bank); John Pillsbury (Northwestern Life); Angus Wurtele (Valspar); Bruce Dayton (Dayton-Hudson); and Sandy Bemis (The Bemis Company)—organized a small conference on corporate responsibility. There were fifty participants, thirty-five of whom were chief executive officers. From this conference emerged the Project on Corporate Responsibility.

The project is based on three principles: first, that corporations have a broad societal responsibility; second, that awareness of that responsibility must be diffused from the top down, starting with the chief executive officer; and third, that chief executive officers are the best persons to influence each other. It is not unusual to find middle-level managers new to the Twin Cities who are genuinely puzzled over their chief executive officer's involvement in philanthropic and public affairs.

A most important function of the project is to socialize corporate executives who are new to the area. The project's founders were concerned that as managers from outside the Twin Cities increasingly took hold of large locally founded firms, they might become less concerned with preserving and developing the community. For this reason, the project conducts courses on the general business environment, corporate obligations to stakeholders (stockholders, customers, employees, the community), and the ways in which business people can become involved in public-policy matters. The vast majority of the six-hundred or so who have participated in the courses to date responded favorably to this expanded notion of corporate responsibility.

Like the Five Percent Club, the project does not undertake collective activities (other than its seminars). It is, however, further evidence that there is a widespread perception among Twin Cities business leaders that a firm's responsibilities are manifold and extend to involvement in public affairs. The project is yet another manifestation of the variety of activities in the Twin Cities initiated by the private sector with the public interest in mind. It also provides an additional vehicle through which private-sector leaders can interact and help instruct newer members of the business sector in the community's standards for public service.

Downtown Council

Like many other cities, Minneapolis has an organization of downtown businesses called the Downtown Council. (Its role in the Nicollet Mall project was described earlier.) What sets the Downtown Council apart from similar organizations is its concern for long-term planning and its willingness to undertake some of the activities usually thought to be the sole domain of government.

The council was founded in 1955 when, to the alarm of local business people, both General Mills and Dayton's decided to move out to the suburbs. The council was formed in order to promote and develop the downtown area and thereby stem this tide of corporate relocation. Composed of property owners, tenants, building managers, and others with a stake in the health of downtown, the organization functions through standing committees: highways; pedestrian skyways; Hennepin Avenue; Metro Center '90; riverfront development; daycare; downtown dwellers; housing; hotels; restaurants; bars; nonsupervisory employees; retail trade; promotion; membership development; and government relations. Each of the 350 council members has an equal voice, a fact that clearly has fostered participation.

Through the years, the council has often identified impending problems before they became serious and has drawn up and implemented plans to cope with them. Its two clearest successes are Nicollet Mall and the skyway system that interconnects most of downtown by means of indoor second-story walkways that provide ready access and shelter from the elements.

On numerous occasions, member firms have provided financial and planning assistance when the city was considering policies that would affect the downtown area. The city's "Plan for the 1980's" was drawn up in this fashion. On other occasions, the council contributed funds. For example, the feasibility study that ultimately led to the construction of the attractive new Hennepin County Government Center was financed jointly by the city, the county, and the council.

An especially interesting council activity is the Downtown Development Corporation (DDC), a legally separate entity, founded in 1977. It is composed of twenty-three council firms and administered from the council's offices. DDC guarantees loans by placing letters of credit with lenders who are otherwise unwilling to lend to a developer. After floundering for years, the construction of housing projects in the Loring Park neighborhood between downtown Minneapolis and the Walker Art Gallery–Guthrie Theater complex was made possible because of DDC letters of credit. Over eight-hundred housing units are now completed or under construction. The area is thriving, and the value of completed units is soaring. Although the letters of credit ultimately were not needed, DDC stands ready to step in again if a promising development project might not otherwise be undertaken.

Conclusions

A century ago, Walter Bagehot set out to explain in *Physics and Politics* why the British "excel all other nations."[7] His startling conclusion was that England's success could be attributed, not to climate, geography, genetics, or religion, but to what he called "a polity of discussion." Over the centuries, there had developed an expectation that important issues should be widely and openly debated. A habit of involvement and shared responsibility for the public's affairs by able people was developed. If a mystique exists for the Twin Cities, it is this same polity of discussion, the same habit of interaction.

From an examination of the projects and a consideration of the processes of public-private interaction in the Twin Cities, it is possible to identify the elements that make public-private interaction in the Twin Cities work and that could be replicated in other cities.

An Openness in the Decision-Making Process and a Fair and Honest Government System. Major public-sector actions are widely discussed before decisions are made. There is opportunity for broad participation and widespread confidence that decision makers are generally honest, responsible, and reliable. This not only encourages discussion of major issues but also makes possible greater participation by the private sector.

A Blurred Distinction between What Is Public and What Is Private. The assumption by the private sector of responsibility for the public good has been accompanied by a corresponding willingness of the public sector to support private business projects and has also made possible the rise of a strong third nonprofit sector.

A Widespread Conviction, Embodied in Systematic Peer Pressure, that Corporate Responsibility Extends to Involvement in Public Affairs. Minnesota's elder statesman, former Governor Elmer L. Anderson, a corporate executive, farmer, philanthropist, newspaperman, and public servant, says, "Everyone wants to know that he contributes to the public good." However, what is most unusual about this attitude in the Twin Cities is the determination exhibited by corporate leaders to see that this point of view is reflected in the actions of firms as well as individuals.

Mechanisms for Regularly Bringing Together People from the Several Sectors of the Society. What distinguishes the Twin Cities in this regard is regular and extensive discussion and problem solving on matters of public affairs and the variety of institutions in which such interaction can lead to cooperation among firms.

The Leadership Provided by both the Private and the Public Sectors. In making Nicollet Mall a reality, for example, the government responded to the initiatives of several prominent individuals. In addition, although the key people involved in many projects did not necessarily have the original vision, they nevertheless were able to seize upon that vision and demonstrated a talent for assembling the resources and community support critical for success.

An Innovative Spirit in the Third Sector (Foundations and Not-for-Profit Corporations). Foundation grants for educational, social welfare, artistic, and musical endeavors are, of course, commonplace in the Twin Cities, just as they are in other parts of the United States. But in the Twin Cities, new roles are being devised by the third sector. The Dayton-Hudson Foundation's creation of the Whittier project and the McKnight Foundation's loans for Lowertown are among the numerous examples of these innovative roles.

No single financial, organizational, or managerial device or formula explains the success of public-private cooperation in the Twin Cities. Rather, the story is one of a *habit of cooperation*, a pattern of institutionalized civic-mindedness. Much may be unique to the area, because of its peculiar history and economy. Nevertheless, there also is much that is replicable, that can be applied wherever there is a commonality of purpose and a willingness to commit the human and financial resources necessary to get a task accomplished.

Notes

1. J.R. Borchert, *Entrepreneurship and Future Employment in Minnesota* (Saint Paul, Minn.: Commission on Minnesota's Future, State Planning Agency, 1975), p. 4.

2. G. Cornia, W.A. Testa, and F.D. Stacker, *State-Local Final Incentives and Economic Development* (Columbus, Ohio: Academy for Contemporary Problems, 1978), p. iii.

3. *Helping the Metropolitan Economy Change* (Minneapolis, Minn.: The Citizens League, 1977).

4. Frederick T. Aschman, "Nicollet Mall: Civic Cooperation to Preserve Downtown's Vitality," *Planner's Notebook* (Washington, D.C.: American Institute of Planning, September 1971).

5. O.D. Gay, executive vice president, Downtown Council, personal interview.

6. Aschman, "Nicollet Mall: Civic Cooperation to Preserve Downtown's Vitality," p. 3.

7. Walter Bagehot, *Physics and Politics* (Westford, Conn.: Greenwood Press, 1973), pp. 145–146.

6

Portland, Oregon: A Balance of Interest in Public-Private Cooperation

George P. Barbour, Jr.

Portland Public-Private Collaboration: The Context

In the mid-1970s, the Midwest Research Institute published a study rating the quality of life in the sixty-five largest standard metropolitan statistical areas (SMSAs) in the United States.[1] Portland, Oregon, was characterized as "America's Most Livable City." And in almost any recent popular poll or survey, Portland will generally be near the top of the ratings. The city, which is located on the Willamette River, is often described as "one of the largest small towns left."

The area's scenic grandeur, capped by Mount Hood, and the relative ease of access to the out-of-doors have contributed to its attractiveness. Portlanders, along with other Oregon residents, have demonstrated their concern for their environment by supporting some of the strictest environmental-protection laws in the country.

Hospitality is another Portland characteristic. Business, community, and political leaders alike tend to be open and generous with both their insights and their valuable time. According to the director of the Oregon Historical Society, "Portlanders are generous in allowing newcomers a chance to contribute." Certainly the multitude of neighborhood associations and citizen task forces, boards, commissions, and study groups is tangible evidence that the opportunity to contribute is there.

Most of the public-private debate has focused on the organizational dimension, but such cooperation has an important human dimension as well. When the institutional framework and the corporate or public interests are stripped away, what is left, basically, is people cooperating with people. Portlanders have developed discernible perceptions about how the game is played and by and large subscribe to an ethic that says, "You are expected to contribute." They tend to enter into these cooperative efforts because they want to rather than because they have to do so. When the researchers explained to an interviewee that they were interested in public-private cooperation for economic development, his response was, "Is there any other way to do it?"

Politics of Participation: The Basis for Cooperation

The diversity of Portland is represented by its sixty-eight distinct neighborhoods and fifty-four independent neighborhood associations. These groups participate in neighborhoood planning, provide representation to citizen advisory groups, and gather community input on a wide range of neighborhood issues. For example, it is standard practice to consult with these associations on neighborhood park development, transporatation issues, and housing.

The Office of Neighborhood Associations (ONA), established in 1974, shares responsibilities for coordinating neighborhood programs with the City Bureau of Planning and the Portland Development Commission (PDC). These three agencies form a system for interacting with individual neighborhood associations. ONA provides organizational and coordination assistance to the neighborhood groups; the Bureau of Planning provides planning assistance; and PDC is the vehicle for implementation of many of the projects.

In citywide issues as well, private-sector participation is a way of life. Business leaders, community representatives, labor, and civic associations are generous with their time and assistance. In the last decade, involvement and participation in the activities of the City Club of Portland have had their biggest jump in the club's history. Membership has increased 40 percent in the ten-year period. A community representative from Neighbors North in the Saint Johns area described the phenomenon this way: "Newcomers arriving from the East are so impressed with the openness of our system they can't wait to participate."

There are numerous examples of citizen and private-sector participation and a long history of effective use of committees. The Downtown Plan, first adopted by the Portland City Council on December 28, 1972, was the product of such participation. In 1980 the Downtown Plan Citizens Advisory Committee prepared and revised the goals and objectives. Early in its existence, the committee had formed task forces on housing and downtown neighborhoods, commerce, waterfront, Portland State University/park blocks, and transportation. Each task force was headed by a committee member, but membership was open to anyone willing to attend meetings. Each addressed the problems identified by public response at early "town-hall" meetings and by planning-staff reports. Drafts of goals and objectives were formulated and later edited, reviewed, and approved by the entire committee. The planning guidelines that were incorporated into the 1980 Downtown Plan were developed by the Planning Commission, its staff and consultants, the Mayor's Citizen Advisory Committee, and the City Council.

Another important example of participation is the development of the

Economic Development Policy for the City of Portland. This policy, which was adopted by the City Council on March 6, 1980, was prepared by the city's Economic Development Advisory Committee (EDAC). It covers eight areas of opportunity: public and private partnership; jobs and incomes; business and industry; district economic development; central business district; equalization of economic opportunity; regional coordination; and environment, energy, and transportation.

The willingness of Portlanders to participate in the life of their city has been recognized as a unique and valuable community asset. In *Report on a Vision of Portland's Future*,[2] prepared by the City Club of Portland, the volunteer research committee, in a section titled "Latent Opportunities," noted many taken-for-granted assets. Although most of these were physical and visual, the list included "Portland's concerned and participating citizens."

The Locale: Portland's Economy and Position in Oregon

Many of its residents view Portland as having a small-town atmosphere, but the city is in fact the financial, trade, transportation, and service center for Oregon, southwest Washington, and the Columbia River Basin.

No single industry dominates the Portland economy, and there is no large defense industry or other cyclically unstable sector in the economy that could cause significant fluctuations in employment and income. The largest employer, a locally based manufacturer of electronic display and signal equipment, employs less than 3 percent of the local labor force. The manufacturing base continues to diversify, with impressive growth in recent years in the machinery, electronics, transportation equipment, and fabricated-metal-products industries. This diversification has decreased the local economy's dependence on the forest and food-products industries. Foreign trade is also a growing force in the Oregon economy.

The population of the Portland SMSA (which includes Clackamas, Multnomah, and Washington counties in Oregon and Clark County, Washington) increased by 43 percent between 1960 and 1979, compared with 39-percent growth in the Pacific Northwest and 22 percent in the United States as a whole. Total SMSA population at midyear 1979 was estimated to be 1,190,600. This relatively rapid growth reflects two trends: a shift of population in the region from rural to urban area and an in-migration of population to the Pacific Northwest from other regions.

Employment too has increased more rapidly in Portland and in the Pacific Northwest than in the country as a whole. Jobs in the manufacturing and construction industries increased from 79,200 in 1960 to

143,000 in 1979 but decreased as a percentage of the total employment from 29.8 to 25.9 percent. Conversely, the percentage of employment in the service and trade sectors has grown from 70.2 to 74.1 percent of the total, increasing from 186,900 to 409,300 jobs. This trend is similar to the nationwide shift toward higher concentrations of employment in the service and trade sectors.

In spite of these gains, employment in goods-related industries (manufacturing, mining, and contract construction) is still proportionately lower in Portland than in the country as a whole. The relative percentage of government-sector employment is also somewhat lower in Portland. Employment in the transportation, communications, utilities, wholesale and retail trade, finance, insurance and real estate, and services and miscellaneous sectors, however, is proportionately greater in Portland. In fact, because of Portland's role as a regional warehousing, distribution, trade, and financial center for Oregon, southwestern Washington, and the Columbia Basin, the city has more jobs in these sectors than are necessary to support strictly local needs.

The most significant development, however, is the continuing trend toward greater diversification in Portland's manufacturing sector and decreased reliance on forest- and food-products industries. In 1960 the food- and forest-products industries accounted for about 41 percent of all manufacturing employment; by 1979, the proportion had declined to about 23 percent, although total employment in these sectors has experienced only minimal decreases. Manufacturing growth has occurred in machinery, electrical and electronic equipment and supplies, transportation equipment, primary metals, fabricated metals, and other durable goods. The strongest gains have been made in electrical equipment and supplies, including electronic instruments and communications equipment.

The work force in the Portland area has a reputation for high productivity and stability. The electronics industry views the area as another Silicon Valley, but without the problems of overcrowding and escalating housing costs. From an economic-development point of view, Portland is a desirable market. However, the pressures for expansion and development have also raised concern; no one wants to see the problems of Silicon Valley repeated in Portland. Concern for social issues as well as economic development is characteristic of public-private cooperation in Portland.

Governing Portland: The Commission Form
of Government

Among the seven cities discussed in these case studies, Portland is the only one that has a commission form of government.

Since 1913, Portland has been governed by a city council—more properly, a commission—composed of the mayor and four commissioners. The mayor and commissioners are elected at large in even years on a nonpartisan ballot for staggered four-year terms.

As a council, the mayor and the commissioners enact the legislative ordinances. Individually each functions as the principal administrative officer of a major department of city government. The city's charter says that the five departments should be Public Affairs, Finance and Administration, Public Safety, Public Utilities, and Public Works, but actual functions are assigned to each department by the mayor. Thus the commission form of government provides five elected officials who both legislate for and administer the city government. No chief executive officer is provided for. The mayor is the titular rather than the executive head of the government and shares both executive and legislative powers with the other members of the council. Neither the mayor nor any other single official has comprehensive powers over the city government as a whole. However, the mayor does have the power of budget preparation and of making or changing assignments of bureaus or activities to the commissioners. Figure 6–1 lists the assignments as of January 1981.

The mayor's appointment powers are a rather formidable tool. At one point during his second term, Neil Goldschmidt assigned all functions to himself. The fact is that if a mayor has the energy and capacity, he or she can literally run the show. In the 1960s Mayor Terry Schrunk also assigned all the departments to himself.

Because the mayor is not by charter the executive head of government, he or she must have important skills of organization, persuasion, and cooperation in order to employ executive power. Former Mayor Neil Goldschmidt characterized the mayor's role well: "When the mayor makes commitments, he has to be able to deliver three votes on the council."

In assigning functions to the commissioners, both Goldschmidt and Connie McCready reserved for themselves those functions of executive and administrative control such as budget, planning, computer services, and development in order to have the capability to plan and manage. The current mayor, Francis J. Ivancie, has departed slightly from this pattern by assigning the Bureau of Planning to another commissioner. At the same time he dismantled the Office of Planning and Development and transferred many of its functions to the PDC, which he assigned to himself.

Because executive power is somewhat diffused, the independent and quasi-independent commissions such as the PDC have tended to develop important leadership positions in the community. The PDC, for example,

Department of Finance and Administration (Mayor Francis J. Ivancie)

Office of Fiscal Administration
  Budget Office
  Bureau of Financial Affairs
Exposition-Recreation Commission
Portland Development Commission
Portland Housing Authority
Housing and Community Development
City office building
Bureau of Water Works
Bureau of Hydroelectric Power
Office of Emergency Services
Fire and Police Disability and Retirement Fund Board
Airline Affairs
Public drinking fountains
Sister City Program

Department of Public Works (Commissioner Mike Lindberg)

Office of Public Works Administrator
  City Engineer
    Bureau of Street and Structural Engineering
    Bureau of Sanitary Engineering
  Bureau of Maintenance
  Bureau of Wastewater Treatment
  Bureau of Refuse Disposal
Bureau of Human Resources
City-County Commission on Aging
Comprehensive Health Planning Association (representative)
City-County Health Committee (member)
Metropolitan Human Relations Commission
Metropolitan Youth Commission
Bureau of Personnel Services
Civil Service Board
Energy Office
Business Licenses Division
Bureau of Emergency Communications
Bureau of Electronic Services
Emergency Medical Services
911

Department of Public Affairs (Commissioner Mildred Schwab)

Bureau of Parks
Portland International Raceway
Monuments, except drinking fountains
Pittock Mansion Advisory Commission
Metropolitan Arts Commission
Bureau of Fire
Fire Code Board of Appeal
City Attorney's Office
Office of Cable Communications
Bureau of Planning
Bureau of Buildings
Boards of Examiners

```
Boards of Appeal
Bureau of Traffic Engineering
Taxicab regulations
Telephone, electric, and other franchise matters, including utility rates
Civic Auditorium

Department of Public Safety (Commissioner Charles Jordan)
Bureau of Police
Office of Neighborhood Associations
Office of Justice Planning and Evaluation
Office of General Services
    Bureau of Central Services
    Bureau of Facilities Management
    Bureau of Fleet Management
    Parking Garages
    Property Control Division
    Purchasing and Stores Division
Bureau of Computer Services
Bureau of Risk Management
```

Source: The Mayor's Office, Portland, Oregon.

Figure 6–1. Distribution of Official Business of the City of Portland, January 1981

is an important community agency with distinct powers, resources, and staff.

Public-Private Cooperation: A Matter of Policy

The city's policy documents are grounded in recognition of the importance of public-private cooperation. The Portland Downtown Plan of October 1, 1980, recognizes the partnership role of the private sector in realizing each goal. More specifically, in the March 26, 1980, Economic Development Policy for the City of Portland, one of the major goals is public-private partnership (see figure 6–2).

The climate for public-private partnership does not stop with public-policy statements. The City Club included a number of goals that relate to public-private cooperation in its "Report on a Vision of Portland's Future."[3]

Government and business relationships will improve with creative and flexible approaches to problem solving, including cooperative use of community colleges to train and retrain people for industry.

Business and government will work together to set goals to meet environmental and social needs. Businesses that meet such goals creatively will be rewarded through the tax structure for doing so.

Business owners will understand that a healthy economy includes high-quality social, cultural, educational, and recreational institutions and will support these institutions through financial contributions, loaned executives, and other programs.

It is within such a context that public-private cooperation takes place in Portland.

Selected Examples of Public-Private Cooperation

The examples of public-private cooperation discussed here illustrate industrial, commercial, neighborhood, and downtown development. In some projects, leadership came from the private sector; in others, public

---

The city shall foster a development partnership between the public and private sectors that is responsive to the economic needs of Portland's business and residents.

Goals

A. *The City's Role in Economic Development*

1. To adopt and annually revise an Economic Development Strategy that will respond to citywide economic needs recognized by the City Council and will serve as guidelines for economic development programs. The strategy may include:

   Employment Targets defining the types of new jobs and labor force skills that would be most effective in reducing unemployment;

   Public Assistance Guidelines defining the types of economic development projects that should be carried out or assisted with public funds; and

   Industrial Land Availability indicating whether there is enough vacant or underdeveloped land to permit expansion of existing firms or the location of new firms, and addressing shortages identified.

2. To design and administer programs and projects in order to insure citywide coordination of the development strategy. Coordination and linkage must be maintained between development programs and all major City Departments and agencies.

3. To design the Economic Development Strategy to insure that the City's involvement in economic development is directed to those areas where there is a clearly identified public objective, where it is demonstrated that the objective would not be met without public involvement and the programs are economically feasible.

4. To provide public services and facilities which support the economic activity of business and industry. In addition, the City may support special cultural events which stimulate commercial activity and business in the City.

5. To work with business and industry to collect available information about business activity, employment and other major economic indicators affecting the economy of Portland and the metropolitan region. This information gathering function will be used to supply business and industry with information important to their operations, to identify opportunities and areas of concerns for economic development and to evaluate the impact of past economic development policies and practices.

6. To insure citizen involvement in the policy development and decision-making process on publicly funded economic development projects and activities.

B. The Private Sector Role

1. To initiate economic activity and growth in the City of Portland. The City recognizes that private business and industry have a vested interest in the economic health and stability of the City, and the City will, therefore, encourage and cooperate with existing and new business and industrial organizations.

2. To carry out economic activity and growth within the framework of public laws, policies and plans such as this policy, the Comprehensive Plan, the Energy Policy, the Greenway Plan, the Arterial Streets Policy, and the Downtown Parking and Circulation Policy.

3. To participate in the formulation of public laws, policies and programs.

Source: Excerpt from Economic Development Policy (Portland, Oregon: March 26, 1980).

Figure 6–2. Defining Public- and Private-Sector Roles in Economic Development of Policy in Portland

leadership was more prominent. The common thread is that none of these projects would have succeeded or would be where they are today without the active collaboration of *both* sectors.

The results have been attitudinal as well as economic. For example, the unique agreement with Wacker Siltronix to provide training to Portland residents for over four-hundred new high-technology jobs has spurred interest in using similar training methods in conjunction with other industrial-development projects. Each project has had spinoffs and a real or potential ripple effect. The Transit Mall, for instance, was intended to have a ripple effect on downtown revitalization, as is the performing-arts complex.

It is also important to note that all the projects have had setbacks and experienced difficulties. Momentum for the construction of a performing-arts center languished in the late 1970s. The developer for the Saint Johns waterfront project recently pulled out. Not all downtown development proposals have survived. The proposed Cadillac Fairview (Oregon) development for the Morrison Street Downtown Development Project was withdrawn. The lessons learned from these setbacks are as valuable as those learned from success.

Saint Johns Business District Improvement Program. The Saint Johns neighborhood is located on a peninsula between two rivers. It is roughly five miles from downtown Portland, at the northernmost extremity of the city and the outer edge of development. Because of its small-town characteristics and services, Saint Johns is often considered a town in itself rather than a part of Portland. In fact, early in its history it was a small city.

Beginnings. From its inception, the business-district revitalization program has had the basic ingredients for public-private cooperation. In 1976 Lord and Leblanc, Inc., which had been commissioned to conduct an

economic analysis of the Saint Johns business district, identified two
requirements for development:

> (1) perceptions on the part of entrepreneurs of unmet demand resulting
> from a limited supply of retail and service offerings relative to demand
> and their response to those opportunities; and (2) public actions taken
> to create opportunities.[4]

The Saint Johns Business District Improvement Program highlights
some significant aspects of public-private cooperation at the neighborhood
level:

The importance of cohesive and identifiable neighborhood leadership

The value of a comprehensive approach

The need for a sense of place and identity

The importance of capacity building and availability of expert staff

The Saint Johns neighborhood is bounded by industrial areas, specifically the port area and the largest industrial district in Portland. There
is very little developable land left in the neighborhood other than that
earmarked for industry.

The neighborhood is mainly lower-income working class, with over
10 percent of all families below the poverty level, compared with 6.9
percent in the Portland SMSA.

The area has not changed significantly over the past twenty to twenty-
five years except for the trend toward apartment development. There was
a 68-percent increase in the number of renter-occupied units between
1962 and 1976, compared with a citywide increase of only 22 percent
during that period. Saint Johns has the largest concentration of affordable
housing in Portland.

Since 1972 Saint Johns residents have been organized under an umbrella agency representing seven neighborhoods in north Portland. Originally formed out of the Poverty Program, the North Portland Citizens
Committee (NPCC) has become a recognized representative of the overall
neighborhood's needs and interest. Revitalization is the main goal of the
NPCC effort. In 1974 the city contracted with NPCC to hire a coordinator
and staff for the north Portland neighborhoods. A neighborhood headquarters, Neighbors North, was located in Saint Johns.

The Saint Johns business district, a ten-square-block commercial area,
developed around the turn of the century. Historically it has given the
neighborhood a strong community identity and cohesiveness. It has provided an economic and social core similar to that of a small town. The

surrounding natural setting adds to the sense of being separate from the greater Portland area.

In 1960 the Bureau of Planning completed the Comprehensive Development Plan, Saint Johns Area. This plan acknowledged the potential problems inherent in the expansion of industry adjacent to the neighborhood. Some policy recommendations on physical standards in the business district were part of the plan, including proposals for rerouting traffic, redesigning intersections, improving individual stores, closing some areas to traffic, and creating a mall-like atmosphere. However, due to a change in priorities, these recommendations were never implemented.

Implementation. Saint Johns received little planning or public-agency attention until 1975, when the Community Development Block Grant Program selected it as one of four Portland neighborhoods to receive assistance. Saint Johns was a good choice for attempting a neighborhood-preservation strategy because it was still economically sound, but was beginning to show the very earliest signs of decline. The Community Development Block Grant improvement package initially focused only on residential projects. On the basis of the recommendations in the city's 1960 plan, however, the merchants asked the NPCC and the city for assistance. From an $800,000 Community Development Block Grant to the neighborhood, $62,000 was allocated to the business district for commercial rehabilitation loans and architectural services. The remainder was to be used for housing rehabilitation and public-works improvements.

The Saint Johns Boosters, a business promotional group founded in 1933, formed an eighteen-member Plan Advisory Committee of residents and merchants to work with the city and NPCC in reviewing the plans and providing business and residential input.

From the outset, the city and the community believed it was important to combine business-district improvement with residential-area conservation so that homeowners would not be competing with merchants for improvement dollars. All improvements were discussed at public neighborhood meetings and were assigned priorities.

In December 1975 the PDC, the Bureau of Planning and the Plan Advisory Committee selected the consulting firm of Lord and Leblanc to study the Saint Johns economy and develop a comprehensive plan of action. Countless hours of community input at ten public workshops contributed to the Lord and Leblanc report.

Economic analysis showed that the central problem facing the business district was its inability to capitalize on growth in the area's market demand. The analysis concluded that with expansion and changes, local business could capture a greater percentage of the growing neighborhood market.

The final product of the planning process was a comprehensive program that set the basis for public expenditures in the Saint Johns business district over a five-year period. Because city staff anticipated that implementation of the program would require a range of financing resources, the document also included a description of potential public and private development resources.

During the implementation phase, a number of groups continued to play strong coordinative roles: the PDC as program manger; the Bureau of Planning as technical analyst for certain projects; Neighbors North as community organizer; the Plan Advisory Committee as representative of merchant and resident interest; the Saint Johns Boosters as primary program participants; and the NPCC as the overall neighborhood review body for Community Development Block Grant allocations.

The Business District Improvement Program is designed to improve the appearance, traffic circulation, the economic performance of the Saint Johns business district as both a commercial and a neighborhood center. It includes the following development activities: physical development of commercial, residential, public, and institutional uses of the area; new-business development; and educational development.

The key concept of the program is that physical changes alone will not solve the problems facing the business district. In order to create a stronger commercial center, it is equally important to improve management of business operations and to promote and provide new opportunities for private investment. The city wanted to maximize the benefits of the physical improvements by coordinating them with activities designed to increase the economic strength of the commercial center.

In undertaking a comprehensive approach to the business district, the PDC is combining a variety of financing resources. Approximately $750,000 has been directed to the business district and $1,329,000 to the residential area. Community Development Block Grant funds were the major vehicle for initiating the program; over a two-year period, $662,000 was allocated to the business district. Other funding resources include a National Urban Reinvestment Task Force Grant of $75,000 to provide educational and technical assistance to merchants, a National Endowment for the Arts grant of $10,000 to provide design assistance of commercial rehabilitation, and for the services of a private-sector professional to assist in evaluating the security standards of store designs.

Physical improvements include alterations in common commercial areas such as better traffic patterns, aesthetics, and parking; commercial-rehabilitation efforts by individual businesses; residential-rehabilitation and public-works improvements; and architectural improvements of public and institutional facilities.

The physical improvements triggered some controversies that had the effect of strengthening the overall commercial-revitalization program. For example, the PDC in the process of rerouting truck traffic to industrial areas adjoining the neighborhood, angered the merchants by rerouting trucks through the business district. This opposition to the traffic circulation test stimulated new ideas and enthusiasm for the business district. In addition, the traffic circulation test received extensive press coverage and brought the Saint Johns business district to the attention of Portland residents and potential investors, who subsequently began to inquire about the area.

Other improvements to the common areas included: street closures in selected areas; pedestrian amenities such as benches, planter boxes, and landscaping; improved parking options such as short-term angle parking and strategically located off-street parking; redesigned intersections to direct selected traffic into or around the business district, to provide a sense of entry to the district, and to ease pedestrian movement; and improved street lighting.

Physical improvements fell behind schedule in early 1978, and merchants became disorganized as a result of the constant delays. At one point the Saint Johns Boosters tried to divorce themselves from the improvement program. But even though attendance at improvement association meetings dropped off, there was a continuous dialogue with the city that included business-community representatives.

Another important component of the Saint Johns Business District Improvement Program is the Business Development Program. Funded by a $75,000 grant from the Urban Reinvestment Task Force, it was designed to complement the physical improvements by developing business seminars; a commercial-retail stabilization team; a promotions calendar; promotional events; program information (a business-district newsletter); and an investors' guide.

The commercial-retail stabilization team (CRST) was developed to provide a follow-up to Saint Johns business seminars; its function is to make business expertise available to Saint Johns business operations on a one-to-one basis. Team members include specialists in advertising, marketing, building security, finance, accounting, and other fields. CRST assistance began in March 1978 with a series of advertising consultations. Twenty businesses took part in one-hour appointments with three consultants. Each client was asked to prepare for the meeting, bringing copies of recent ads, a current advertising budget, and specific questions. Consultants followed up on the consultations with letters reiterating major recommendations. As a supplement to a seminar on financial management and accounting, CRST also offered in-depth financial-management assistance. This five-week course was tailored to the needs of Saint Johns businesses by one of Portland's major banks, and the cost to business owners was less than half the usual bank rate.

Through a grant from the National Endowment for the Arts, an architectural firm was hired to assist in developing a design scheme for the entire business district. A series of design workshops was conducted, covering various aspects of commercial-building rehabilitation. Twenty-one business operators subsequently took advantage of personal consultations with the architect. A publication, the *Building Improvement Handbook*, has been prepared to provide area businesses with design guidelines and information about remodeling and financing.

The ongoing need for technical assistance was realized early. In analyzing the role of the Urban Reinvestment Task Force participation, the PDC's 1978 progress report noted:

> Success of the St. Johns program hinges on using a few public improvements to attract new private investment. URTF finances the business assistance portion of the program, which City of Portland believes is essential to stimulate this reinvestment in St. Johns.
>
> [The] St. Johns Business District Improvement Program is an experiment. URTF recognizes the program's experimental nature and has been flexible, allowing city staff to alter the program when necessary. URTF staff have also been personally helpful in guiding the program. Sensitive to the delicate public-private partnership that neighborhood commercial revitalization demands, URTF staff followed program progress closely and suggested careful adjustments when needed.
>
> [The] City of Portland has asked URTF to continue in this role for another year. The proposed 1979 program includes:
>
>> increased use of the many business assistance tools developed during the first 18 months; and
>>
>> development and implementation of a St. Johns investors guide, and a strategy to attract new investment.[5]

The business-development program continued through 1979 and early 1980 much as it was designed. However, in 1980, the Saint Johns Boosters decided to launch out on its own with the Neighborhood Reinvestment Corporation (formerly the Urban Reinvestment Task Force). In the Saint Johns Boosters' letter of application on June 12, 1980, President Wayne M. Hatch characterized the organization's hopes and capabilities:

> The St. Johns Business District has seen many changes with more to come. The partnerships created in our revitalization efforts are unique and have brought many of our projects to fruition. Leveraging the public expenditures to the private reinvestment opportunities has been laborious. We feel we have now identified some of the keys in our grant application.
>
> We also feel it is time the St. Johns Boosters took on the full responsibility as an accountable agent for the grant. The City of Portland and Boosters are continuing our partnership but in a different vein. We have joint maintenance responsibilities and are clarifying our agreement. We are asking in the grant that the City sit as a member of the management

board. The City or its agent also will participate in writing the end of the year report, with our assistance, so that our program may be replicable throughout other commercial districts in this city and other cities throughout the United States.

The grant was awarded, and in December 1980, the Office for Facilitating Improvement by Community Effort (OFFICE) was established to promote the continued revitalization of Saint Johns through new investments. This office acts as a facilitator as well as providing assistance to individual businesses.

Results. The effectiveness of the ongoing public-private partnership in Saint Johns can be measured in terms of both community improvements and improved ways of working together.

The community improvements range from $1.5 million in physical upgrading of the business district, the $1-million Saint Johns Racquet Center, $1.7 million for Cathedral Park, over four-hundred renovated homes, and some $2 million of capital improvements in the residential neighborhood.

Other special projects in Saint Johns include a $13,000 grant to the Portland Recycle Team for rehabilitation of office and warehouse space. As a result of the city's support, the recycling effort is beginning to become financially self-sufficient. A $32,000 grant made it possible to convert an old incinerator building into an Astronomy Center. The Saint Johns Community Center received $125,000 worth of improvements, including replacement of obsolete equipment.

The business-development component of the program has provided a wide range of seminars, training programs, promotional events, and services, but what really is important is that revitalization is taking place. Lord and Associates reported in September 1979 that the benchmark data on Saint Johns Business District through 1977 outperformed the Consumer Price Index for the Portland metropolitan area.[6]

The program has had other important but less tangible consequences.

Promotions have increased. Events are held almost monthly now. Local press attention has grown and several merchants now have organizational expertise.

Enthusiasm among business owners has improved substantially. Seminars, workshops, and consulting assistance renewed merchants' interest in managing their businesses. They have requested future programs, and some now seek aid independently.

The Saint Johns business community is much stronger than in the past. The Booster Club is better organized than in recent years.

Cooperation among merchants pays dividends in joint advertising, promotions, and group decision making about parking, public improvements, and many other issues.

Neighborhood merchants' and residents' pride in Saint Johns is steadily climbing. Citywide and even national attention drawn by Saint Johns' improvments helped arouse local sentiments.

Conclusions. In ''Neighborhood Approaches to Urban Capacity Building,'' Arthur Naparstek and Chester Haskell of the University of Southern Californa write:[7]

> The central prerequisite for partnerships is that *all* relevant actors, be they city officials, business leaders, or community representatives, must be able to interact with each other as peers.
>
> Another crucial factor is that such partnerships are, of necessity, locality based, i.e., they relate to a specific neighborhood or subsection of a city.

The authors could have had the Saint Johns experience in mind.

A key lesson to be learned from the Saint Johns project is the importance of *cohesive and identifiable neighborhood leadership*. The public-sector leaders need to be able to deal with a defined group that can make commitments. In describing the success of NPCC, a case study published by the National Commission on Neighborhoods noted that:

> NPCC seems much more independent than in the days of PMSC [Portland Metropolitan Steering Committee]. Their strong leadership, connected with various networks in the city and the neighborhood, plus the coordination through Neighbors North, has produced a wide ranging and diverse base of support. This has happened by means of a conscious strategy of packaging community resources and leveraging one achievement into clout for another issue.
>
> NPCC spent considerable time developing a relationship with the Portland Development Commission (PDC). Over the years, a *quid pro quo* arrangement emerged between NPCC and PDC. First PDC engaged in a tree planting program. Success there expanded the effort into a street paving (side-stripping) program, in which NPCC volunteers solicited door to door to secure 50¢ per frontage-foot from homeowners and landlords throughout North Portland. This yeoman's effort yielded the community matching funds necessary for the side-stripping project. In addition, the working relationship betwen PDC and NPCC helped influence the decision to use St. Johns as a target neighborhood for housing rehabilitation, and then to expand the boundaries from a restricted six block area to all of St. Johns.

Another interesting source of NPCC's independence is their relationship

with Portland's Office of Neighborhood Associations. In 1975, ONA
contracted with NPCC to hire a coordinator and secretary to help North
Portland groups. They hired Jerry Mounce, a North Portland native with
twelve years of experience in business. By contracting with NPCC to
hire Ms. Mounce, rather than hiring her directly, ONA allowed her to
work independently of City Hall, while at the same time participating
in the ONA communication and influence network. NPCC supported
Ms. Mounce's efforts to work with all organizations in North Portland.
In doing so, she facilitated cooperation among NPCC, the St. Johns'
Boosters (a business group), and the St. Johns Improvement Association
(a group of businessmen who organized in 1975 to plan revitalization
of their business district). This arrangement furthered the working relationship with PDC, which has now plunged into commercial revitalization in St. Johns.[8]

Another important aspect is the value of a *comprehensive approach*.
The multifaceted Saint Johns program allowed for a wide range of opportunities and funding. The program is aimed at improving the business
district *and* the surrounding community and allows for flexibility and
changes as the situation dictates. Because the program is comprehensive,
it has won vital support from the citizens of Saint Johns.

A *sense of place and a district identity* are also important. Portland
has a strong neighborhood identity, and Saint Johns is one of its oldest
neighborhoods. Pride and sense of place provide an important ingredient
to public-private cooperation.

The need for a *capacity-building mechanism* and *availability of expert
staff* cannot be overlooked. The business community was able to develop
its capacity to act and to represent itself more effectively through the use
of many of the components of the improvement program. Those programs
funded by the Neighborhood Reinvestment Corporation were directly
aimed at improved capacity.

Much of the work of ONA is intended to improve capacity of the
neighborhood association. The staff at Neighbors North and the availability of consultants and staff from PDC to work with the community
and business leaders contributes significantly to a successful public-private venture.

In the 1978 eighteen-month evaluation, the program staff stated:

> Having staff available daily in the business district has also contributed
> to the program's success. Developing rapport with small merchants is
> not easy for public employees—or anyone else. Daily contacts build
> familiarity, trust, and finally, good working relationships.[9]

Downtown Portland and the Transit Mall. One of downtown Portland's
salient features is described in a 1981 PDC publication:

Often called the "City of Parks and Fountains," Portland's downtown
has grown up in a setting of parks, fountains, outdoor sculptures and
other artworks, and landscaped pedestrian ways. The famed Ira Keller
Fountain, located adjacent to the Civic Auditorium, is a national land-
mark. Lovejoy Fountain, Pettygrove Park, O'Bryant Square, the Park
Blocks and the newly constructed Waterfront Park all provide a place
for people to lunch, sit in the sun, hear a concert, walk, play, or simply
take a quiet moment out from their busy workday lives.[10]

It was not always so. The growth of regional shopping centers and
the decline in housing stock took its toll on downtown Portland in the
1960s. According to William Naito, vice president of the Portland Chamber of Commerce and developer of Galleria and Old Town, commercial
restoration projects:

> As . . . suburban shopping centers thrived, businessmen became dis-
> couraged with the declining economic situation of downtown, and many
> closed shop. This downward trend continued and worsened when the
> developmental plan for the city, instituted with the Clean Air Act Pro-
> gram and the parking lid, was announced. Retailers who were both
> sharing the risks the City was taking and trying to compete with suburbia
> and its shopping centers, thought that doomsday had finally come to
> downtown.
>
> The trend was for downtown businesses to get out of the area and move
> to newly developed suburban shopping malls where business was boom-
> ing.[11]

Since the early 1970s, however, retail employment has increased,
and downtown development has picked up significantly. Portland's
Transit Mall is a national showcase, and many other downtown developments have received national as well as professional recognition.

Downtown development during the past two decades, especially the
Transit Mall, highlights several vital components of public-private cooperation in Portland.

The importance of open, regular lines of communication between
the public and private sectors

The value of a comprehensive approach

The importance of agreed-upon public policies, plans, and objectives

Beginnings. In 1972 the city of Portland adopted a Downtown Plan that
called for the development of a Transit Mall. The U.S. Department of
Transportation defines transit malls as:

streets reserved for the use of [public] transit vehicles and pedestrians. They are generally located at the intersection of several transit routes in downtown near heavy pedestrian acitivity, such as retail stores, restaurants, and office buildings. Passenger amenities make these malls attractive and may include shelters, benches, plants, and route and schedule information displays.[12]

The Tri-County Metropolitan Transportation District of Oregon was responsible for the design and construction of the mall, which is a $15-million public investment in downtown. Federal sources provided 80 percent of the money. Utility work began in the fall of 1975, and roadway construction began in April 1976. On December 1, 1977, the mall was opened to buses traveling its full length.

The mall forms the spine of Portland's highest-density commercial and retail area. By minimizing the conflicts between auto, bus, and pedestrian traffic, it has tripled the people-carrying capacity of Fifth and Sixth Avenues. It serves as the major transfer point for the public-transit system, allowing easy access of people to buses, and has improved bus mobility by reducing automobile traffic.

The Portland Mall is an integral part of the Oregon Clean Air Implementation Program, which was designed to reduce air pollution in downtown Portland by increasing public-transit ridership and limiting parking and auto access in general in the downtown area.

The key to the mall's success was support from local merchants. Mayor Goldschmidt was aware that nothing is a more visible signal of downtown decay than empty storefronts. He personally visited the major downtown department stores early in his first term to solicit support and to prevent moves from dowtown to suburban locations. In discussing downtown development, he noted that the lack of an organized downtown interest group made it more difficult to deal with the diverse interests of the merchants and owners. Toward the end of his tenure as mayor, before the mayor was appointed Secretary of Transportation by President Jimmy Carter, the Association for Portland Progress (APP) was formed to begin representing downtown interests.

In describing his administration's program to revitalize the downtown area, Goldschmidt referred to downtown as "first among equals" in the hierarchy of neighborhoods.

Mayor Goldschmidt found that there was a need to balance the clean-air requirements with promoting shopper access and with improved transit ridership. Toward this end the City Council adopted the Downtown Parking and Ciculation Plan in 1975. Its major emphasis was to shift available parking spaces from long-term to short-term use and to limit the number of spaces in downtown to the total available in 1973. Parking for residential development and hotels was exempted from this parking "lid." Reliance on public transit for work trips into the downtown area was to be increased.

The plan put every downtown street into one of three categories: auto oriented, pedestrian oriented, or transit oriented. Development regulations indicate what uses are permitted on each type of street. For example, a parking structure cannot have an entrance or exit driveway on a pedestrian-oriented street.

Also in 1975, a particular portion of downtown was turned into a free-fare zone for bus trips; thus was Fareless Square created.

These developments did not take place without protest or difficulty. Bus rates and schedule changes caused confusion and consternation. Construction of the mall disrupted the flow of traffic, closed off streets, and interrupted pedestrian flow. To be able to respond to complaints and to correct deficiencies as quickly as possible, the mayor reorganized his agencies and formed the Office of Planning and Development. Mayor Goldschmidt stated, "I needed to be able to deliver and they needed to trust me to deliver. I wanted all the necessary talent and agencies under my control." The new offices included the Bureau of Planning, Bureau of Buildings, Portland Development Commission, Bureau of Economic Development, and Housing and Community Development.

> By creating the Office of Planning and Development, the mayor hoped to have at his disposal a single governmental unit that could research and analyze the city's business and investment climate, review and analyze requests from neighborhood organizations and the business community, carry out development programs and projects, and help establish a dialogue on development issues both within the municipal government and between the government and the private sector.[13]

He also placed the Bureau of Traffic Engineering under his jurisdiction. "If a mayor can't get a street sign replaced or repaired, who's going to believe he's going to revitalize downtown?"

In discussing downtown development and the Transit Mall, the business community in general regards the mayor's role as key to the project. The mall and the other elements of downtown development were evidence that the city meant business.

The city made other large capital investments in downtown during the 1970s. Figure 6–3 illustrates the impressive range of these development projects.

The private sector responded with clear evidence that it also took the city seriously. Although many of the projects listed in figure 6–4 had been planned prior to the city's effort, the level of private development was unprecedented.

Name of Project	Specific Location	Past Expenditures	Projected Expenditures to 1982	Total Expenditures[a]
Transit Mall	5th and 6th Avenues Burnside to Madison	$15,000,000 (to end of 1977)	—	$15,000,000
Storm sewers	—	474,000	$2,535,000 (possible $1.5 million after 1982)	3,009,000
Water mains	Transit Mall	484,000	—	484,000
Street lighting	SW Park, 9th and Taylor	—	98,000	98,000
O'Bryant Square	SW 9th and Washington	1,356,000	—	1,356,000
Portland Development Commission Waterfront (include closure of Harbor Drive)	—	3,820,000	3,940,000	7,760,000
Parking garages	NW Glisan-Irving, 5th–Broadway	5,350,000	8,115,000	13,465,000
Transportation Center	Skidmore, Yamhill	820,000	220,000	1,040,000
Historic districts	South Auditorium	210,000	1,290,000	1,500,000
South Auditorium Urban Renewal	SW 6th–Broadway, Morrison–Yamhill	23,400,000	850,000	24,250,000
Pioneer Square		—	1,500,000 (set aside in trust fund—actual may be more)	1,500,000
Morrison Street Improvements		—	(funds not yet allocated)	

Source: *Economic Development in Portland, Oregon, Opportunities, Constraints and Policy Issues* (Portland, Oregon: Portland Bureau of Planning, September 1977).

[a]All future expenditures are in 1977 dollars.

Figure 6–3. Major Government Investments in Downtown Infrastructure

Type of Project	Name	Location	Characteristics
Housing	Clay Towers	SW Clay, between 11th and 12th	175 moderately priced units. Waiting for federal funding.
	Lovejoy Village	SW 4th, east of SW Hall	Middle-income housing, 260 units.
	Roosevelt Hotel	SW Salmon and Park	Renovation, low-income, federal subsidy
	Regency Hotel	SW Columbia and Broadway	Renovation and conversion of rooms to studio apartments.
	Rosenbaum Hotel	SW 12th and Washington	Rehabilitation
	Oak Plaza	SW 4th and Oak	Rehabilitation
Retail	Nordstrom	SW Broadway–Park, Morrison–Yamhill	Under construction
Office	PGE's Willamette Center	3 blocks centered at SW 1st and Salmon	3 buildings, largest of which is 17 floors
	Far West Federal	SW 4th and Washington	Under construction
	Orbanco	SW 5th–6th Ave. Main–Salmon	22-story office building
	TN	Quarter block, SW 6th and Oak	12-story office with retail and recreational space
	U.S. National Bank Tower	SW 5th–6th and Ankeny–Oak	38 stories, timetable not disclosed
	Mark's Columbia Square	SW 1st–2nd, Columbia–Jefferson	15 stories, South Auditorium
	Project 1011	SW 1st–2nd, Madison–Salmon	Two 20-story office towers
Cultural	Oregon Historical Society	SW Park and Madison	Expansion to Madison Park Apartments, destroyed by fire, 1972
Hotel	Marriott	SW Front–1st Ave., Clay–Columbia	On PDC vacant block, 502 rooms
Parking garage	Central Plaza South	SW 3rd–4th Aves., Morrison–Alder, SW 9th–10th Ave., Morrison–Yamhill	City operated, 800 cars, eight levels. City operated, 500 cars
Transit	Greyhound, Trailways Stations (Transportation Center)	3 blocks, NW Irving to Glisan, 5th–Broadway Ave.	Site of former Hoyt and adjacent 2 blocks; as of 7/77 status is uncertain.

Figure 6–4. Uncompleted or Planned Downtown Portland Building Construction Projects as of July 1977

In interview after interview, public- and private-sector leaders have emphasized the importance of two-way communication and easy access to decision makers. In many respects the success of downtown Portland is as much a story of successful communication as it is one of development.

Recent setbacks also highlight the value of communication processes. The withdrawal early in 1981 of the Morrison Street Downtown Development proposal by Cadillac Fairview (Oregon) was a disappointment to many in Portland. The development raised concerns and surfaced policy questions for city council. Although this particular proposal was withdrawn, a senior executive of Cadillac Fairview has stated that he would prefer to pursue developments in Portland because the rules are clear to everyone and the process is understandable. "You don't get the runaround from the city."

Results. Development in downtown Portland exemplifies diversity. Moreover, it has been undertaken on an unprecedented scale.

In the retail sector, for example, Meyer and Frank remodeled their store, Nordstrom's located a new store downtown, and many new small shops and restaurants have sprung up. Total retail development has exceeded $15 million. Office space has taken off as well. Over $300 million in office complexes have been built. Fountain Plaza and Willamette center are typical examples of these new complexes. Historic-preservation efforts have been integrated into downtown development. Prominent among these projects are the Failing Building, Pioneer Courthouse, and the Commonwealth Building restorations. Other development projects have focused on housing and convention facilities.

The Transit Mall is an unqualified success. It has cut ten minutes off the average trip through the core of the city. Currently, 40 percent of peak-hour trips into downtown are by public transit, as are 23 percent of all downtown trips throughout the day. Transit ridership has increased by a dramatic 110 percent since 1973. The downtown area is undergoing a boom. Employment and office space are up 50 percent, twice the rate predicted in 1973. The downtown occupancy rate is over 95 percent, and construction is under way on 1.5 million square feet of new office space. Downtown employment has increased from 60,000 to 75,000 people, not counting those who will be occupying the new offices being constructed. As for air quality, carbon-monoxide emissions in the area have decreased 22 percent over a five-year period.

There have been some important policy results as well. The *Portland Downtown Plan* (updated in October 1980) gives direction to downtown development. The Economic Development Policy adopted March 26, 1980, includes a specific section on the central business district (see figure 6–5 for an excerpt). The Updated Downtown Parking and Circulation Policy (adopted October 30, 1980) details the policy on downtown access. And the Downtown Housing Policy October 30, 1980, amplifies the general guidelines contained in the Downtown Plan.

Each of these policy documents was developed and influenced by the work of the citizen's committees and input from the private sector.

Conclusions. The initiative for the massive infrastructure investments in downtown Portland originated with the public leadership. But private-sector cooperation and subsequent investment far outweighed public expenditures. The value of open, easy dialogue among leaders from both sectors was essential in ensuring that development objectives were understood and that trust and confidence were established. Simplifying the processing of permits, reorganizing development efforts, and placing traffic engineering under the mayor's jurisdiction were all efforts to facilitate response to the needs of the private sector. Improved communication had to be backed up by action. The commission form of government gave the citizens of Portland several avenues of communication with their

---

The City Shall Assist in Promoting Retail, Lodging, Office, Residential, and Cultural Opportunities and Facilities in the Central Business District

Goals

A. *Downtown Plan*

To support programs and policies which serve to maintain downtown Portland as the major regional employment, cultural, and business center. The City will implement the 1972 Downtown Plan as updated by Council ordinance, and will carry out the urban development goals of the Comprehensive Plan.

B. *Cultural/Entertainment Center*

To support the development of additional downtown space for performing arts and the development of cultural facilities compatible with other economic development projects planned or projected for the central business district. Development of such space will take into account additional traffic and parking needs, availability of private funding resources and the effect on private investment in complementary projects which enhance the central business district.

C. *Housing*

To support implementation of the Housing Policy of Portland (adopted by City Council, March 1978).

D. *Corporate Headquarters*

To encourage the retention and recruitment of corporate headquarters located in the central business district.

Source: Economic Development Policy for the City of Portland (Portland, Oregon: March 26, 1980).

Figure 6–5. Central Business District

elected leaders, and they have grown accustomed to speaking up and participating.

The variety of programs and sources of funding provided a greater possibility of success in responding to downtown-development needs than reliance on a single approach would have offered. In addition to considerable private investment, downtown development has been funded by tax-increment financing, a special transportation-district payroll tax, federal grants from the Bureau of Outdoor Recreation, Department of Housing and Urban Development Community Development Block Grants, Urban Mass Transit Administration, and National Trust for Historic Preservation.

The vehicles for achieving development were equally varied: retail expansion, office-space construction, increased tourism, historic preservation, park development, construction of parking structures, housing development, and transit improvement. Transportation in its broadest sense was the catalyst for this revitalization.

Wacker Siltronix Corporation. From the outset, the move of Wacker Siltronix Corporation to Portland was tied to a strong jobs-development objective. As an example of public-private cooperation, it illustrates

The importance of public leadership as a broker of interests and a catalyst for the generation of ideas

The necessity of an overall strategy

The value of using several techniques or programs to reach a common objective

The recognition of the intergovernmental nature of some public-private interactions

The importance of allowing the private sector to do what it does best: create jobs

Beginnings. Putting people to work was one of Mayor Goldschmidt's central objectives early in his term. He indicated that retaining the working population was another. Both translated into the retention and expansion of business in Portland.

The problems created by these goals were clear to the Goldschmidt administration. Bringing industry into Portland, thereby creating jobs that might go to outsiders who would move in to take them, would not do much to put the city's unemployed to work.

A 1977 staff report, "Economic Development in Portland, Oregon: Opportunities, Constraints and Policy Issues," noted that this problem was particularly acute with regard to jobs requiring high levels of skills that are not possessed by the city's unemployed work force or not in the city's labor pool.

The answer to this dilemma was the development of a "first-source" agreement with incoming industry, and Wacker became the test case.

Wacker Chemtronics is a German company that has attracted 40 percent of the U.S. market for hyperpure polycrystalline silicon wafers, a critical element in the production of electronic products ranging from watches to computers, from automobiles to satellites. Eager to maintain its position in the competitive American and Far Eastern markets, Wacker decided to construct a new facility in the United States. Within a year, it had narrowed its sites to Portland, Augusta, Georgia, and Houston, Texas.

Company representatives began their evaluation of Portland by contacting the Chamber of Commerce with inquiries about the availability of suitable sites, labor-force characteristics, constructon cost, environment, and energy availability.

In describing his first visit to Portland, Dr. Hans Hermann, Wacker's chief executive officer, noted that what impressed him was the active part the mayor and City Council played in making the company's representatives feel welcome. The city had arranged for various state and port officials and representatives of the private sector to accompany the delegation during its visit.

Subsequently, Mayor Goldschmidt and members of his staff visited the Wacker headquarters in Germany. On this key trip, the mayor was accompanied by a representative of the State Department of Environmental Quality and an electrical building inspector. The state representative examined the German equipment for compliance to Oregon requirements, and the electrical inspector gave advice on wiring-code enforcement. The providing of such expertise was identified by Dr. Hermann as another indication that the city was willing to promote the partnership.

Wacker was very interested in the people of Portland. Several top executives visited the city to walk its streets and visit shops and neighborhoods. Because they knew Portland had a reputation for a productive work force, they were receptive to the idea of a first-source agreement.

Throughout 1977 and into 1978, Wacker representatives considered the three cities, weighing factors such as the cost and reliability of power, environment, availability of raw mterials, labor force, and site and construction costs. Portland rated high in the areas of power, labor force, and the proximity to both customers and critical raw materials. But there were real problems with the site itself, including poor access, inadequate public utilities, and significantly higher land costs. Portland's proposal to Wacker had indicated the city's ability to address these problems was contingent on the successful adoption of an urban-renewal plan for the area, the sale of tax-increment bonds to finance the city's portion of the renewal costs, and the willingness of property owners to sell the parcels constituting the site to the city so that the city would not have to resort to the time-consuming condemnation process.

Indicating its faith in the city, Wacker notified Portland that it was the company's preferred location.

Implementation. Using CETA funds, Portland began a dialogue with Wacker and the Portland Community College to create the First Source Manpower Program. Together they developed the Silicon Technology Training Program, which included recruitment, assessment, training, and placement for twelve production occupations. Training periods were staggered and varied from sixteen to thirty-two weeks, depending on the occupation. Instructors from the college were sent to Germany, where they learned the silicon-wafer-production process at Wacker's Burghausen factory. These instructors later became the supervisors at the Portland plant. All manuals and instructions were translated from German into English for the teachers. Wacker provided the machinery for the program and the technical assistance for installing it. The company's investment in this training program is calculated at $1 million.

Before starting training, participants went through two days of testing and assessment and a physical examination based on an analysis of the physical requirements of each occupation. Where appropriate, trainees received preemployment counseling, prevocational training, instruction in English as a second language, or corrective medical treatment.

Many other features of this industrial-development project provided significant opportunities for public-private cooperation. The city, through the PDC, was able to keep the project moving on the tight time schedule set by the company.

On April 12, 1978, Wacker, the city, and the PDC, the city's semi-independent urban-renewal agency, signed a nonbinding memorandum of understanding authorizing the proposed terms of an agreement. Five days later the PDC adopted the needed urban-renewal plan. The area covered by the plan consisted of 360 acres, 84 of which would be purchased by the PDC and resold to Wacker. Like the Wacker site itself, the balance of the renewal area was characterized by inadequate streets and utilities, circumstances that had prevented the development of this increasingly valuable industrial land. For this reason the plan called for expenditures of $3 million for street and utility improvements.

On May 11, 1978, the Portland City Council approved the PDC urban-renewal plan, thereby giving the PDC the authority to undertake the renewal program. On May 26, the PDC and Wacker signed a formal disposition and development agreement. Because bonds to finance the project had not yet been sold and the site had not yet been purchased, the PDC's obligations were still conditional upon successful completion of these actions and sale of the site to Wacker within sixty days.

On June 7, the City Council adopted the necessary bond ordinance permitting the sale of tax-increment bonds to finance the urban-renewal activities. The proposed serial-bond issue was to be retired over twenty-eight years with funds provided from Wacker's estimated $1 million in annual property taxes.

Unfortunately, voters in California had created a major obstacle to the completion of this bond sale by overwhelmingly approving the Jarvis-Gann 1-percent property-tax limitation measure on June 6. Within two weeks, 200,000 voters swept up in the antitax movement signed a similar initiative being circulated in Oregon. This initiative, which proposed to limit taxes to 1½ percent of value, was quickly certified for the November 1978 election ballot. If approved, it would reduce by 40 percent the amount of tax revenues available to retire the proposed bonds. In response to the California measure, ratings on all California tax-increment bonds had been suspended by a national bond-rating service; and with the success of the Oregon signature campaign, the rating service also suspended all Oregon tax-increment bond ratings and declined to rate the issue already in process for the Wacker project.

As a result of the threat of the initiative legislation and the absence of a rating, no bids were received for this initial bond sale on June 28, 1978.

An alternative proposal utilizing thirty-two-year term bonds was quickly prepared by the PDC. However, proceeding with the revised bond sale would not permit PDC to meet its schedule with Wacker. Moreover, the city's financial advisor recommended that Wacker significantly increase its financial guarantees in order to provide extra security for the bonds.

On July 6, Wacker agreed to an extension of one month to August 17, 1978, for the sale of the site and increased its financial guarantee for completing the project from $1 million to $5 million. The City Council, on July 12, authorized the restructured bond sale for the project.

Even though these bonds were not rated, the city received two bids on August 3, and the council accepted the low bid. Funds from the bond sale were received August 15, 1978. The site was purchased by August 17 and resold to Wacker on that day. Construction began October 1. The initiative petition was defeated by Oregon voters in November 1978, and shortly thereafter, the second bond issue was given an *A* rating by the national service.

Results. The Wacker Siltronix plant began operations in March 1980. By the time of the plant dedication that fall, 450 persons had completed training and were employed at the facility. And today the first-source agreement is still in force. The city has a new industry, one that has already attracted additional secondary industries to the community. It also has a successful procedural model for human development and job training. Wacker has a plant operating to its specification and is planning a major expansion in the next decade.

Conclusions. Public leadership was essential to the success of this project. Wacker management admits that it had a firm offer from Augusta, Georgia, involving a considerably lower price for land. But as Dr. Kimbark MacColl, a local historian, repeatedly pointed out in discussing the Wacker story, the role of the mayor and the city's ability to deliver were deciding factors. Using his staff in the Office of Planning and Development, Mayor Goldschmidt was able to provide the expertise that Wacker management wanted.

The role of the PDC was also critical. This semi-independent development arm of the city, with its staff of approximately one-hundred professionals, had the authority, mechanisms, and track record to respond with the time limits set by Wacker.

The strategy of job development gave focus to, and necessary justification for, the investment of public money and energy in private-industrial development. Moreover, as Dr. MacColl noted, the first-source agreement was an important signal to the citizens of Portland that their city government cared as much about human development as it did about industrial development.

There has, however, been criticism of other aspects of the Wacker project. Mayor Ivancie, for example, believes that industry would have moved to Portland without so many concessions. Nevertheless, no one has argued against the overall strategy.

The city's ability to marshall so many resources, including public financing, CETA, urban renewal, and code enforcement, provided a range of mechanisms for cooperation with the private sector.

The Wacker example clearly demonstrates that there are often many publics in the public-private partnership. In this case the long list included the Port of Portland, several state agencies, Portland Community College, the PDC, the city, and various federal agencies. It highlights the need to assign appropriate roles to each partner. For example, running interference within government agencies can best be done by insiders (that is, political leaders and staff). Creating jobs is best done by the private sector. That is what the Wacker project is all about.

Performing-Arts Center. On March 31, 1981, the voters of Portland au-

thorized a $19 million general-obligation bond issue to build a perform-
ing-arts complex in downtown Portland. This bond issue is to be
supplemented by $6 million of private money to make up the $25 million
needed to finance the project.

As of early 1982, ground had not yet been broken for the center. The
private-financing drive only got under way in July 1981, and there are
still many months of planning, property acquisition, construction, and
outfitting before the lights dim for the inaugural performance in 1983.
Nevertheless, the history of this project illustrates a number of important
components of public-private cooperation:

The importance of public leadership and legitimacy

The value of broad private support

The critical role of timing and chance

The value of a comprehensive approach

The importance of compromise and negotiation

The spinoffs of collaborative effort

Beginnings. In 1976 Commissioner McCready created the Portland Metropolitan Performing Arts Theater Task Force to investigate the need for
a performing arts center and to make recommendations for location and
structure. The task force was composed of private citizens representing
a balance of expertise and interest in the performing arts. Without exception, each member represented more than one perspective or constituency (that is, membership in an important cultural committee and relative
professional expertise). Labor, management, finance, the arts, design,
and construction were all represented.

The task force mailed out questionnaires, conducted a public hearing,
inventoried existing facilities, identified facilities that had renovation or
conversion possibilities, and submitted their findings to Commissioner
McCready on their deadline, March 31, 1977. The group's conclusion
was that there was a need for a theater smaller than the existing Civic
Auditorium. The report called for a second phase, which would require
modest financial support, to focus on an audience survey and to obtain
professional estimates on the use and cost of several potential sites.[14]

One conversion possibility was the Masonic Temple in downtown
Portland. The initial review of the building by city staff indicated that
its size, condition, structural makeup, and location made it attractive. In
1978 a theater consultant's study was funded by the city, and although
it concluded that rehabilitation costs would be higher than originally

estimated, the temple became nearly everyone's choice. Part of the excitement about the site was due to the prospect of renovating a marvelous old rococo, Moorish-style building. The other plus was cost; although expensive, this conversion would still be cheaper than building a center from scratch.

However, after several negotiating sessions between Commissioner McCready and Masonic-lodge representatives, it became apparent that the lodge leadership did not really want to sell. As a result of this setback, the Performing-Arts Center project was relegated to the back burner.

Two events in 1979 changed this situation dramatically. First, Monford Orloff, chairman of the board of Evans Products, announced that Evans was donating one square block of downtown Portland to the city for the Performing-Arts Center. Second, Commissioner McCready was elected mayor by the City Council to replace Neil Goldschmidt. In April 1980, Mayor McCready reestablished the Performing Arts Center (PAC) Committee, instructing it to pick up where the task force left off. She charged the committee not to conduct another study but to design, finance, and build the Performing-Arts Center.

Implementation. The reconstituted committee, like its predecessor, represented a balance of community interests. Three advisory committees were also formed: Design/Construction, headed by John Schleuning, an architect; Finance, headed by Robert D. Scanlan, vice-president of Coldwell Banker; and the Arts Needs and Use Advisory Committee, headed by Mary Folberg, a dance instructor and director of the Jefferson High School Dance Department. The chairman of the PAC Committee was Ronald Ragen, an attorney and former member of the Metropolitan Arts Commission. PAC Committee members were invited to participate in the work of the advisory committees.

Private stewardship of this committee effort has been essential to its success. One month after appointing the PAC Committee, Mayor McCready lost her bid for election for a full four-year term to Commissioner Ivancie. (Although the election was held in May 1980, Mayor McCready continued in office until November 1980.) Other council members supported the need for the center, but the project was seen by many as Mayor McCready's. Therefore, there was fear that when she left office in November, the momentum would be lost. Because a broad range of private interests was represented on the PAC Committee, members were able to go about their task of proposing a site, selecting a design concept, and identifying financing, regardless of the politics of the moment.

In late 1980 the Paramount Theater was identified as the best site for the center. The original estimate to renovate the Paramount and construct two smaller theaters was $20 million, less than the new construction on the Evans Products property. Evans Products generously agreed to allow the city to sell the donated property and use the proceeds as part of the private-funding match for the complex.

Once in office, Mayor Ivancie assigned responsibility for the complex to Commissioner Mildred Schwab. Although there was a time lag in reappointing the PAC Committee, the members continued their efforts as if they had already been reappointed.

The City Council voted unanimously to put the bond issue on the March 31, 1981, ballot. Nationally bond issues were being voted down with regularity. The PAC Finance Committee, sensing that this bond issue would be tough to pass, raised $142,000 for publicity. However, fund raising proved particularly difficult. Backers of the center felt that part of the reluctance may have been due to a particular trait of Portlanders: They have to be convinced that something is a good thing before they will back it. But the bond issue was passed and private donations started flowing in; additional help came both from the Portland Chamber of Commerce and the Association for Portland Progress (APP).

Results. Although no Performing Arts Center exists yet, the project has had a discernible impact.

To begin with, the vision is a few steps closer to realization. A bond issue has been approved by the citizens of Portland, although many, including the mayor, thought it would not pass.

There is a plan for the center that is linked specifically to the objectives of Portland's Downtown Plan as well as to the Downtown Parking and Circulation Policy and the Arterial Street Classification Policy. A report by the Arts Needs and Use Advisory Committee states:

> The proposed Center and the existing Civic Auditorium have the potential, on any given night with three to four cultural events scheduled, of drawing over 6,000 individuals to their surrounding area. With this concentration of people, nighttime activity is directly affected. Furthermore, as a result of high fuel prices, increasing percentages of individuals who work in the downtown area are staying in the heart of the City from 5 p.m. until performance time and/or are staying downtown following the performance for some other form of nighttime activity.[15]

Furthermore, the site is only one block from the Transit Mall. The center is expected to be a stimulus to private development of the surrounding neighborhood. The Committee summarized the intrinsic economic impact of the arts:

> Arts activities help draw and hold people to inner cities, broaden the

tax base and revitalize the economy. Businesses are more likely to stay or relocate in Oregon .if their employees find a vital cultural climate in Portland. Thus, our new Performing Arts Center will be an important key in strengthening Portland's economic health.

Another effect is somewhat difficult to measure, but may in fact be longer lasting. As a result of activities on behalf of the Performing Arts Center, important elements of the private sector have now strengthened their lines of communication and have a track record of working with the public sector. Mary Folberg, chairperson of the Arts Needs and Use Advisory Committee, explains it this way: "We in the arts community know more about the business community and vice versa. They now want to keep us involved." In fact, that is just what is happening. Folberg is a member of the design subcommittee of PAC Committee, and the arts-community input will be available during design, construction, and implementation planning.

Conclusions. The Performing-Arts Center project highlights several key characteristics of public-private cooperation in Portland. First, public-sector leadership must be visible and lend legitimacy to the venture. The commission form of government allows this leadership to come from a particular council member, not necessarily the mayor. The diverse nature of political power requires that someone on the council take the political lead. Commissioner McCready, when she became mayor, gave the arts-center effort an important boost. She sponsored the original study and pushed the next phase after the Masonic-lodge setback. Later, Commissioner Schwab provided the visible council leadership. The PAC Committee membership included important, long-standing associates. City-staff support and contacts were important to the planning process, during which both commissioners also provided help.

Second, the project enjoys broad private-sector support and leadership. The committees reflect a wide spectrum of expertise and membership. Both the Chamber of Commerce and the downtown-based APP support the complex. The private leadership provided by the committee was absolutely critical to ongoing efforts, especially during the mayoral transition and the private campaign for the bond issue.

Third, timing and chance are critical. The Evans Product donation came at the right time to provide the financial spark to continue the push for the Performing-Arts Center.

Fourth, the project took a comprehensive approach. In an article in the *Portland Journal*, Robert Wallace, president of APP and chairman of the board of the First National Bank of Oregon, said: "Rarely are the people of Portland presented with an opportunity to participate in a project with such far-reaching benefits to such diverse segments of our community.'' The Arts Needs and Use Advisory Committee report lists the areas in which this facility will benefit the city:[16]

Economic role of the arts

Tourism

Downtown Plan objectives

Transportation objectives

Civic pride

1-percent funding for graphic arts

Growth of high-quality local artists

Education of artists and audiences

Increased access for audiences

Quite literally, there is something in this project for everyone.

Fifth, there is value in negotiation and compromise. Not all issues have been resolved. For example, equity actors want the little theaters to be union; many of the small theater groups are opposed to this. In order to move ahead on the bond issue, both sides have left the union issue unresolved. Property owners in the area have been approached and have indicated that they are willing to work out arrangements that are acceptable to the furtherance of the project. And Evans Products was willing to change the terms of its gift to allow for the sale and use of the proceeds. This type of willingness to compromise is critical to successful public-private interaction.

Characteristics of Public-Private Cooperation in Portland

The four examples described in this case study illustrate characteristics that fairly accurately portray the nature of the process of public-private cooperation in Portland. What is difficult to assess is the relative importance of each characteristic in predicting success. Furthermore, what works in Portland may not work elsewhere.

The Process

Although the cast of characters differed from example to example, it is apparent that the success of these projects was facilitated by *open and regular communication between the public and private sectors.* The numerous task forces, study groups, citizen- and business-advisory committees, and neighborhood associations promote this flow. In addition, the commission form of government provides for more avenues for access to Portland city government. Each commissioner is a visible administrator as well as a legislator.

The downtown-development effort began with the mayor's making a personal appeal to the major retailers to remain in downtown Portland. Scores of meetings, often on a one-to-one basis, were held to solicit ideas and to support and explain the decisions made. The move by Wacker Siltronix was eased along by personal visits to various Portland delegations to Germany and several visits by corporate management to Portland.

The success of the Saint Johns project was built on communication. The Neighbors North network of community and business leaders, the Saint Johns Boosters, and the PDC and city staff interaction played key roles.

In setting up the PAC Committee, Mayor McCready was careful to include representatives from the city at large to ensure that the total arts community was represented. The balance among financial, artistic, design, labor, construction, and promotion interest has been achieved. The committee network provided these divergent groups with constructive lines of communication.

A comprehensive approach is invaluable in public-private ventures. Success is rarely one-dimensional. It might seem that the Transit Mall has been the key to success in downtown Portland because of its national acclaim, but the mall represents only $15 million out of hundreds of millions of dollars invested in downtown development. Private partners are much more likely to respond to a variety of interests. Downtown Portland revitalization is working because of its multifaceted approach. Historic preservation, public amenities, parking and traffic-circulation improvements, public-transit development, and housing, office and retail development and expansion have all contributed. The Wacker plant is another case in which the comprehensive approach paid off. It was never viewed as just an industrial-development project. Its impact on jobs and employment development broadened its appeal. Similarly, Saint Johns' development was approached in terms of both neighborhood improvements and business development. This enhanced the project's appeal and ensured community support.

The comprehensive nature of the Performing-Arts Center planning process drew on the talents and interests of the entire community. The 1976 task-force study provided guidance on design, location, use, and financing. Furthermore, the committee work tied the Performing-Arts Center to the Downtown Plan, the Transit Mall, the Parking and Circulation Policy, and the comprehensive planning process. Both the Chamber of Commerce and the APP, as well as all the council members, publicly endorsed the center.

Agreed-upon policies and plans are invaluable. It is difficult to discuss downtown Portland without mention of the Downtown Plan because so much of the downtown revitalization has been anchored to it.[17] The value of clearly articulated policies is that they set the foundation for understanding of the ground rules. The Downtown Plan was developed *with* the downtown community, not *for* it. Portland's sense of fair play extends to public-private cooperation, and ground rules are important. The Portland City Club recognized the value of goal-oriented public policies when it commissioned a study of the need for community goals. The charge to the committee stated:

> During recent years, communities and governments have begun to realize there was little consistency in their planning and actions, because of a lack of stated goals and objectives for the community. In recent years, several of our own research projects (such as *Planning for Transportation in the Portland Metropolitan Area* and *Sign Code Revision*) have noted that the lack of community consensus on what we're trying to do makes satisfactory solutions hard to find.[18]

Both downtown revitalization and the Performing-Arts Center have been tied to the Downtown Plan, the Downtown Housing Policy and Program, the Updated Downtown Parking and Circulation Policy, and the Economic Development Policy of March 26, 1980. These policies provide a cohesive basis for public-private interaction and enhance the legitimacy of results that are in concert with those plans.

In a different sense, the Wacker example supports the value of understood public policy. Mayor Goldschmidt looked for and found a policy issue to justify the public expenditure of resources and time to the benefit of the private sector; the first-source agreement became public policy in support of Wacker Siltronix's development. Human-resource development and jobs for Portland residents were the key. The city's Economic Development Policy includes first-source agreements in the statement to provide guidance in the future.

Public-private cooperation often has an intersector nature. The ventures may and often do involve more than one actor from a particular sector. The nature of industrial development in the Portland area is such that the Wacker Siltronix move required active participation of a wide variety of public entities (that is, Office of Environmental Quality of the State, Port of Portland, Portland Development Commission, city of Portland, and Portland City College). The participants in the Saint Johns Business District Improvement Program included Neighbors North, Saint

Johns Boosters, PDC, Neighborhood Reinvestment Corporation, Small Business Administration, city of Portland, numerous community and business leaders, consultants, and private developers. Depending on sources of funding and types of projects, public-private cooperation will often cross may lines of authority and levels of government.

It seems to be the nature of successful public-private efforts to result in *spinoffs and extensions of the collaborative process*. This may be more of a result than a characteristic, however; the examples indicate that participants tend to promote the public-private process in other projects. The value of input from the artistic community in the Performing-Arts Complex use and needs study has not been lost on the financial and design work. Artistic representation is now a permanent part of the process. The jobs-training alliance forged by industry, the city, and the City College of Portland continues to look for new applications. The network formed to implement the Saint Johns Business District Improvement Project is now tackling the Saint Johns Waterfront Project. The basic nature of downtown development is to capitalize on the spinoff effect of successful collaboration.

There is inevitably a *degree of chance and sensitivity to timing involved in public-private collaboration*. Given the complex nature of the process and the multiplicity of actors, it almost goes without saying that timing is important. The Performing-Arts Center concept made little progress until the generous donation by Evans Products and a new mayor came on the scene. Being able to respond flexibly to such opportunities is a sign of effective public-private partnership.

The Private Partner

There are *many private partners* in Portland. From neighborhood-association leadership to large, private developers, they are as diverse and varied as their interests. In describing the leadership climate in downtown Portland in the 1970s, Mayor Goldschmidt bemoaned the fact that there was no single focus of organized leadership; he felt this made his role in public-private negotiations more difficult. More recently, a group with a distinct "downtown interest," the APP has been formed. The Chamber of Commerce is a wider-based organization that attempts to focus interest through its committee structure, but many of the city's professional leaders are not represented. Private-sector leadership is diffused, and that is the way Portlanders like it.

Private participation is selective. Private-sector leaders seem to choose their involvements in accordance with their interests. Some contribute significantly to the arts; others, to historical preservation. Retail leadership is keen on the impact of the parking-space lid on downtown; the Transit Mall draws business participants naturally from along the transit line.

It is always difficult to assess the actual importance of key participants in more recent projects. Nevertheless, it seems clear that *broad private support is critical to public-private partnership in Portland*. At times there was no public leadership in the Performing-Arts Complex project. During the mayoral transition, the committee continued to function "as if appointed." The bulk of the energy and leadership in the project has come from the private sector.

The neighborhood nature of the Saint Johns Business District Improvement Program required significant neighborhood involvement. Neighbors North and the Saint Johns Boosters provided the network for such leadership to emerge. Evidence of such private-sector and community leadership convinced Portland city government the project was viable.

These partnerships also seem to work best when the *private-sector partner is called upon to do what the private sector does best*. In the Performing-Arts Center development, the city staff initiated the planning, but the private participants provided artistic know-how, design criteria, management alternatives, community input, and financing. Wacker Siltronix collaborated with the City College, providing technical manuals, equipment, job specifications, and a full-time employee-development manager. This collaboration was critical to ensuring that the training was on target for the jobs available. Both downtown development and Saint Johns are clear examples of public-private partnership that were designed to use public investments to stimulate private development in order to achieve clear public objectives. In articulating the justification for Portland's Economic Development Policy, the city reached the following conclusions about public-private partnership:

> Private enterprise is directly responsible for about 85 percent of job and income generation in Portland.

> Private investment, supported by focused public investments and decisions, is the key to long-term urban revitalization.[19]

These policy conclusions clearly recognize the appropriate role of the private partner.

The Public Partner

The public sector provides leadership, legitimacy, and a facilitating role to public-private leaderships. On both the downtown development and the Wacker projects, strong public leadership brokered the many sources of funding and government programs to provide the public efforts to stimulate private involvement. In the case of Saint Johns, public provision of the staff support and training was essential to making the partnership work. The public sector is readily suited to providing staff support to such projects. The participation of Mary Folberg, who provided the link to the arts community, in the arts-center project was supported part-time by the city. City-planning staff, PDC staff, and/or consultants were made available in all four projects to ensure the availability of appropriate planning support.

Only the public partner can handle the creative packaging of outside resources. In discussing the nature of urban management in the future, the Future Horizons Committee of the International City Management Association noted:

> In imagining the nature of the job of urban managers in the future, the first conclusion was that, "The prime role of the manager will be as a broker or negotiator—but not a compromiser." The role of broker, according to the committee, "will supplant the traditional role or functions of top management because local government executives must be people who can lead by being led." The leadership will "call on the ability to direct an organization or group of people without dominating. It will call on the ability to help people see more clearly their own desires and goals, and unobtrusively to help them satisfy those desires and goals."[20]

Some Thoughts on the Portland Environment

In some respects, Portland is like any other metropolitan area of comparable size. It can be measured and compared; its rate of growth, analyzed and pondered. But Portlanders believe their city, with its many distinct neighborhoods, is unique. The Saint Johns example clearly illustrates this special sense of place.

Finally, Portland's form of government is unique among those of the other cities studied in this volume, and its impact is somewhat difficult to assess. In theory, government by commission promotes diffusion of executive leadership. Yet many outsiders view the mayor of Portland as a strong leader. Although Portlanders have had several opportunities to abandon this form of government, they have not seen fit to do so.

Acknowledgments

Many people in Portland contributed time and energy to this research effort. The hallmarks of this experience were, above all, friendliness and cooperation. The writing of this case study was itself an example of public-private cooperation. It is only fair to say that the case study could not have been written without the help of the people listed here.

First, I wish to thank the Committee for Economic Development Trustees from the Portland area who provided guidance and reviewed my work. Don C. Frisbee, chairman of Pacific Power and Light Company; John D. Gray, chairman of Omark Industries, Inc.; and Harry J. Kane, executive vice-president of Georgia-Pacific Corporation helped open doors and introduce me to the Portland area. The trustees also provided expert advice in reviewing an early draft of the case study.

I valued both the time and the candid responses from Mayor Francis J. Ivancie and former Mayors Neil Goldschmidt and Connie McCready. The story of Portland public-private cooperation could not have been told without their contributions.

In each project there was one person who provided the institutional memory: For Saint Johns, it was Jerry Mounce of Neighbors North; for the Performing-Arts Center, it was Mary Folberg; for Downtown and Wacker Industries, it was Douglas G. Wright. Special thanks also to Warne Nunn, corporate secretary of Pacific Power and Light Company; Millard McLung and Thomas Vaughan of the Oregon Historical Society; Dr. E. Kimbark MacColl, local historian; Roy Beadle, former editorialist of the *Oregon Journal;* Chris Tobkin of the City Club of Portland; and J. Don Chapman, executive director of Association of Portland Progress.

The field research for this project included site visits during the period from September 1980 to June 1981. Over one-hundred persons were interviewed either in person or by telephone. The field research was conducted by James R. King and George P. Barbour, Jr., of PMC Associates.

Notes

1. Ben Chieh Lin, *The Quality of Life in the United States,* (Kansas City, Mo., Midwest Research Institute, 1970).
2. "Report on a Vision of Portland's Future," *City Club of Portland Bulletin* 60, no. 54 (May 19, 1980):301.
3. Ibid., pp. 294–295.
4. *Saint Johns Business District Improvement Program* (Portland, Ore.: Lord and Leblanc, Georgia Pacific Building, January 1976).
5. *Saint Johns Business District Improvement Program,* Progress Report, (Portland, Ore.: Portland Development Commission, September 1978).

6. Letter report dated September 11, 1979, from Lord and Associates, Inc., 117 Southwest Taylor Street, Portland, Ore. 97204.

7. Arthur J. Naparstek and Chester K. Haskell, "Neighborhood Approaches to Urban Capacity Building," in *Urban Affairs Papers* vol. 3, no., 1 (winter 1981).

8. *People Building Neighborhoods,* Final Report to the President and Congress of the United States (Washington, D.C.: National Commission on Neighborhoods, March 19, 1979).

9. *Neighborhood Accomplishments in Portland, Oregon 1976–80* (Portland, Ore.: Office of Neighborhood Associations, March 15, 1979).

10. *Downtown Program* (Portland, Ore.: Portland Development Commission, March 1981).

11. *Auto in the City* (Washington, D.C.: U.S. Department of Transportation, Office of the Secretary, 1980), p. 48.

12. *Auto in the City, An Examination of Techniques Managers Can Use to Reduce Traffic in Downtown Areas* (Washington, D.C.: U.S. Department of Transportation, 1980), p. 48.

13. *Coordinated Urban Economic Development, A Case Study Analysis,* (Washington, D.C.: National Council for Urban Economic Development, March 1978), p. 23.

14. Portland Metropolitan Performing Arts Theater Task Force, *Task Force Report* (Portland, Ore., March 31, 1977).

15. *A Framework for a Performing Arts Center in the City of Portland, Oregon* (Portland, Ore.: The Arts Needs and Use Advisory Committee, August 4, 1980), pp. 24–25.

16. Ibid.

17. *Goals and Guildlines/Portland Downtown Plan* (Portland, Ore.: Portland City Council, October 1, 1980).

18. "Report on the Need for Community Goals", *Portland City Club Bulletin* 54, no. 5 (June 29, 1963):11

19. *Economic Development Policy* (Portland, Ore.: Portland City Council, March 26, 1980), p. 6.

20. Lawrence Rutter, "Capacity to Lead; The Future of Urban Management," *Urban Affairs Papers* 3, no. 1 (winter 1981):58.

7 Dallas: The Dynamics of Public-Private Cooperation

William E. Claggett

For many years, Dallas has had a reputation as "a city that works." The dynamism evident in Dallas must be attributed to an active and healthy relationship between the public and private sectors. Public-private cooperation over the past fifty years has been based on a set of positive attitudes about the mutually supportive responsibilities of all types of organizations. Moreover, the positive attitudes expressed by business and government about each other are considered more important than any specific project. Indeed, cooperative activities would be extremely difficult to achieve if the necessity and desire to work together had not first been established and become a widely held value in the community.

This relationship has evolved in part from the economic, social, and political structures of the community, which have provided the basis for honest and efficient government and for the tradition of voluntary citizen and business participation in government. Although many of the economic conditions and public and private relationships have changed in the past few years, the basic structure of public-private cooperation is likely to persist and at the very least provide the self-renewing basis for public-private efforts to meet the challenges of the future.

Considering the vitality of the Dallas economy and the continuous history of high-level business leadership, the Dallas case study was organized to analyze and assess processes of public-private interaction in the context of project activities that would represent the full range of public-private cooperation as it has developed in Dallas.

Economic Growth: The Basis for Cooperation

The economic characteristics of a community determine the specific opportunities for cooperation. During periods of economic decline, business and government must search together for ways to revitalize the economy. High-growth communities such as Dallas are presented with the problem of maximizing growth potential while providing for the cultural and aesthetic atmosphere necessary for balanced growth.

In 1980 the Dallas-Fort Worth metropolitan area had the seventh-

largest population in the United States, and the city of Dallas was one
of the few large U.S. cities whose population continued to grow, even
though it did so at a slower rate than occurred between 1940 and 1970.
During those three decades, the population of Dallas increased from
295,000 to 845,000; in 1980, it was an estimated 901,000, a gain of
about 8 percent since 1970. The total metropolitan area has a population
of slightly over 3 million. The growth of new business in Dallas has been
a strong stimulus to population increase. However, Dallas's businesses
are not dependent on companies from other areas for their growth. As
Dallas/Ft. Worth Business Quarterly reported in 1978:

> The Metroplex has reached . . . important threshold economic maturity
> when growth is generated within this area. There are far more manu-
> facturing jobs being created by the expansion of existing area manu-
> facturers and by the birth of new local companies than there are from
> companies relocating in the Metroplex.[1]

A sustained population increase usually indicates a parallel growth
of economic activity; indeed, economic growth fuels population growth.
From its birth as a trading post in the middle of the nineteenth century,
Dallas grew through this trading function, aided by rail- and air-transport
developments. From 1940 to 1960, its economic growth brought its national ranking among cities in insurance activities to third, in banking to
eleventh, in retail sales to fourteenth, and in number of million-dollar
firms headquartered to tenth. In 1980 it is estimated that Dallas ranked
seventh nationally for banking, tenth for retail sales, and third for corporate headquarters.

Dallas is a prototypical postindustrial city. The proportion of its
population in blue-collar industrial jobs is less than the national average;
yet industrial activity is important, accounting for 17 percent of employment. With favorable state enabling legislation pertaining to annexation,
the city increased its land area by 137 percent between 1959 and 1970,
a trend slowed, but not stopped, in the last ten years. This expansion
allowed the city to retain a high proportion of the area's well-to-do
families and a substantial proportion of the business and industrial establishments, as well as to capture a large share of its new economic
growth.

In 1980 the Dallas metropolitan area had the lowest cost of living
among the twenty-five largest U.S. metropolitan areas; this was due in
large measure to a low overall tax burden. Recently, however, Dallas
has experienced a rate of inflation that has exceeded the rate in many
other major cities. The most dramatic rises in costs have been related to
housing, but transportation is also increasingly expensive because Dallas
lacks a highly developed mass-transit system, and most residents must

rely on private automobiles. Although other segments of the consumer price index are rising at a rate comparable to that for the rest of the country, certain key elements such as taxes and wages are expected to lag far enough behind to assure continued expansion of business, industry, and other employment activities in Dallas.

The Roots of Public-Private Cooperation

To many, Dallas epitomizes public-sector managerial efficiency and unfettered private-sector development. In May 1981, the city celebrated fifty years of council-manager form of government. Events surrounding the change from a commission form of government to a council-manager form and subsequent developments in the 1930s established the groundwork for public-private cooperation in Dallas. As the city's economy grew in the 1920s and 1930s, business leaders became concerned with the unpredictability of the commission form of government and its susceptibility to corrupt practices. Several business leaders created an informal group, the Citizens Charter Association, to support a change to a council-manager government. This group also sought to identify and promote those candidates for office who would not only recognize the business community's need for an efficient government but also could provide the infrastructure and services necessary to sustain economic expansion. Although never formally organized, the association was an effective force in local government affairs, operating in an ad hoc manner, well into the 1970s.

Because of a change in City Council election procedures from at-large seats to single-member districts, the Citizens Charter Association became less effective as a political force and is no longer active.

Following their success in installing a new form of government, the business leaders who were instrumental in organizing the Citizens Charter Association also organized the Dallas Citizens Council in 1937 to work for the designation of Dallas as the site for the Texas Centennial Celebration. The success of that endeavor and the manner in which the participants worked through DCC established a pattern of responsible business leadership that survives to this day. Although a detailed analysis and description of the operating characteristics of the Dallas Citizens Council is presented in a subsequent section of this report, it is important to note here that the Dallas Citizens Council membership is made up of the chief executive officers of the largest corporations in the city. Individuals are chosen for their business position, regardless of their length of residency in Dallas or their perceived social status. This has resulted in a changing and growing membership in the Citizens Council, which has been a source of strength and vitality in its oeprations. The Dallas Citizens Council, both directly and indirectly, has spawned numerous public-private projects over the years and has been instrumental in creating organizations that operate as facilitating structures to meet particular aspects of public-private cooperative needs.

The Special Role of Government

With a population of just over 900,000 people in 1980, Dallas is the largest U.S. city with the council-manager form of government, which concentrates administrative and policy responsibilities in the office of city manager. Contrary to popular belief, the City Council of Dallas is not solely a legislative body, nor does it have administrative oversight of the numerous city departments and other operating entities. Similarly, the city manager is more than an administrator. The manager sets policy on numerous issues and advises the council on matters for which the council has statutory and charter responsibilities, including the administrative boards for parks, civil service, and public transit; the staff functions of the city attorney and auditor, and appointment of municipal-court judges. The City Council also has certain review-and-appeals responsibilities and is the legal instrument to conduct public hearings.

It is the city manager who makes the system work, both by design and in practice. The manager appoints the heads of twenty-six operating agencies, information services, planning and staff functions, and public works. With an operating and capital budget of just over $600 million (including revenue-producing services) and more than 13,000 employees, the manager is in effect the chief executive officer and chief operating officer of a major corporation. Indeed, the manager's role is frequently likened to that of a corporate executive, with responsibilities for marketing of services, setting reasonable fees and user charges, hiring and firing, purchasing goods and services, and overseeing financial management and accounting. Moreover, the manager is liable for the services provided.

The similarities between the city manager's functions and those of a corporate executive, in terms of level of responsibility and of technical and administrative skills required for the job, have fostered understanding between the two sectors. People involved in the various management processes of the city see the private sector in a very positive light. It is widely recognized in City Hall that the economic health of Dallas is of paramount importance. This attitude has contributed to the view that Dallas should be a willing partner of the private sector in moving to solve problems, remove roadblocks to growth, and accept a portion of the risk for innovative private-sector projects that have long-term public benefits.

The View from the Private Sector

The general attitudes of the private sector toward the city government are very favorable. A Dallas business profile survey of nearly eight-hundred chief executives and senior officers conducted by the city in 1979 revealed that 92 percent of the firms surveyed believed that the city government had a "positive effect on the Dallas business climate."[2] Thirty-one percent of the sample stated that they had done business with the city, and well over two-thirds of those respondents were apparently satisfied with the way the city conducts its affairs. Dissatisfaction was related primarily to delays in payments and work schedules. Asked to evaluate fifteen different city services relative to their business operations, about one-third of the respondents ranked regulation of utilities, police protection, and fire protection as the most important; street maintenance and bus services followed close behind.

The respondents were also asked to judge whether the impact of city government on the Dallas business climate was very positive, somewhat positive, or very negative. The results were overwhelmingly positive; about 44 percent stated very positive, and about 48 percent stated somewhat positive. With respect to the services businesses would like to see improved, those services they felt had the most impact on their operations received the highest rankings, as one would expect. Street maintenance was the service felt to need the most improvement and for which respondents would increase their taxes to pay the cost of improvements. Police protection was a close second on the scale of services for which the respondents would be willing to pay more.

Overall, the survey results reveal a generally well-satisfied business community. This view is certainly substantiated by the opinions expressed by business and community leaders interviewed by the researchers for this case study. The manager of the public enterprise, the city of Dallas, is seen by the business leadership as one of their own in terms of outlook, technical abilities, and general priorities.

Government Operations Important for Public-Private Cooperation

Interviews with city-management staff and several speeches delivered by the city manager during the course of research for this study pointed to several characteristics of government operations that are particularly important for effective public-private cooperation.

Reputation. A reputation for fairness, thoroughness, professionalism, and competence is seen as being especially important to gaining the confidence of the business community. The reputation of the organization is also noted for its importance in attracting competent and highly qualified staff who further enhance the organization's high reputation. The Dallas city government has an outstanding reputation both locally and throughout the country.

Reliability. The trustworthiness of the city government is important in establishing confidentiality with respect to negotiations or dealings with the business community when there are certainly no questions of impropriety with respect to the public interest. It is critical that some business dealings be conducted outside of the public limelight; yet in many communities, this is impossible to achieve. The Reunion Project could not have developed without confidential negotiations.

Predictability. Business must know how the government will act under certain circumstances and must trust the government's word. Despite obvious limitations to a government's predictability, this is a key feature in helping business reduce uncertainty and minimize investment risks.

Accessibility. City management staff must be available and accessible to the business community. Willingness to meet with members of the business community is the first step in establishing a sense of trust and resolving conflicts through negotiated processes.

Partnership. The city government must recognize and accept a reasonable share of the cost and risk inherent in cooperative ventures with the private sector. This willingness to be a true partner was a key element in reaching the Bryan Place accord.

Follow through. Follow through on commitments is of tremendous importance to the business community. Timeliness of followthrough is also seen as significant because of the importance and cost of time to the private sector (a concept frequently not appreciated by the public sector).

Selection of Projects

The examples chosen to illustrate the extent of collaborative efforts in Dallas represent the full range of public-private activity as it has developed in this city. Of course, they are only a small portion of the total public-private effort in Dallas. Nevertheless, they demonstrate the broad dimensions of what constitutes the healthy working relationship between the two sectors. They illustrate both the diversity and the common threads necessary for successful public-private interaction.

Each project had to meet three criteria:

First, a project or activity had to be one designed to achieve specific economic improvements such as jobs, income, retail sales, and increased capital investment.

Second, a project or activity had to have aesthetic goals such as provisions for the performing arts, architectural design improvements, urban design, park services, and library programs.

Third, a project or activity had to involve an ongoing process addressing those goals that seek to improve the institutional environment for individual and organizational cooperation.

Two projects and a process were selected.

Reunion, a major public-private project, included development of a major hotel, a public park, a municipal-activities center, and transporation links. Its primary objective was to generate economic activity to benefit both the private developer and the general public.

Central Research Library was initiated by the private sector to develop a central research facility. The project stimulated a government response that established broad city policy for cultural-enrichment activities. The objective of this undertaking was to enhance the quality of urban life for Dallas citizens.

Goals for Dallas, an extensive program that has spanned several decades is an ongoing process that provides the basis for improved cooperation through the sharing of information and the building of awareness with respect to community needs. In order to more fully explicate this, the case study focuses on one aspect of the process, higher-education developments, that has been supported, if not initiated by, Goals for Dallas.

Figure 7–1 summarizes the major features of each project: its originators and its key participants, the proposed benefits and any obstacles, and the final outcome in relation to its original set of goals.

Reunion

The Reunion Project is an outstanding example of a positive political, economic, and social response to individual initiative. Reunion is mul-

Illustrative Projects	Who Initiated	Sector Responsibility	Major Participants	Basic Objectives	Key Decisions	Benefits
Reunion	Private developer	*Public* Sports arena; roads; parks; Reunion Tower parking; utilities; 33 acres of land *Private* Hotel; tower; roads; utilities; 20 acres of land	*Public* City manager and his project officer; city attorney *Private* The developer's project officer	*Public* Economic development and rejuvenation of downtown *Private* Economic and civic improvements; return on investments	Contract agreement	Construction and hotel employment, increased tax base, collateral development, increased convention and tourist trade
Dallas Public Library	Business-government leader	*Public* Site selection & provision; design; 3/4 funding; account of private funds *Private* Provision of "margin of excellence," which was 1/4 of total cost; rally and sustain popular support for project	*Public* City manager; library staff *Private* Friends of Dallas Public Library; Erick Jonsson	*Public* Better information services; augmentation of downtown development *Private* Basic library facility to meet emerging needs; bragging rights for world-class reseach library	Creation of the organization; "Friends of Dallas Public Library" for funding purposes. Public-sector accounting procedure to handle funds City Council establishes a cultural-arts policy	Construction of unusual facility of greatly expanded capacity and technological sophistication Established a precedent for public-private cooperation in the cultural arts Led to establishment of Cultural Arts District

Goals for Dallas	Mayor of Dallas
Chiefly an organizing device to coordinate with sectors and individuals to achieve broadly accepted goals	*Public* Officers at all levels take part. Federal, state, and local agencies have commitment funds and personnel *Private* More than 100,000 individuals have had a direct role in committees, fund drive, etc.
General improvement in the quality of life of the metropolitan region Establishment of goals to guide public and private program and investment decisions	Multiple and continued personal commitments of individuals at all levels, public and private
Major facilitating device to focus private efforts on civic needs Information sharing and coordination among individuals and organizations	

Figure 7–1. Characteristics of Public-Private Activities

tipurpose land development sitting on the fifty-acre site in the city's central business district. The project includes a high-rise luxury hotel; a ten-acre public park; a 17,000-seat municipal-activities center; much needed road and street improvements and public-parking facilities; the Reunion Tower that has become a focal point for the downtown skyline and that houses a restaurant and other entertainment facilities; and the restored multiuse Union Terminal Building (see figure 7–2).

The name "Reunion" was taken from "La Reunion" settlement, which was built by some two hundred Europeans in 1854 on what is now

The project	50-acre downtown Dallas development that includes a Hyatt Regency Hotel, 50-story tower, restored Union Terminal Building, parks and pedestrian walkways, municipal sports arena, road network, and public parking.	
Originated	1973	
Participants	Public:	City of Dallas
	Private:	Woodbine Development Corporation
Sector responsibility	Public:	Municipal sports arena, Union Terminal renovation, road network and parking, some utilities, 33 acres of land
	Private:	Hotel, theme tower, some roads, some utilities, 20 acres of land
Cost: Phase I	*Total: $200 million*	
	Public:	$25 million (arena)
		$10 million (roads and parking)
		$350 thousand (public park)
	Private:	$75 million (theme tower, hotel, roads and utilities)
Funding mechanism	Public:	Revenue bonds and sports-arena seat options
	Private:	Equitable Life and First National Bank of Dallas
Opening	Hotel and tower—Summer 1978	
	Sports arena—Spring 1980	
Benefits	Construction jobs	— 425 people employed with $20 million payroll
	Hotel jobs	— 800 people employed with $3.5 million payroll annually
	Increased tax base	— 2700 percent
	Hotel-occupancy tax	— $200,000 annually
	Increased utilization of nearby public facilities, collateral development, increased convention business	

Figure 7–2. Reunion Fact Sheet

the west end of downtown Dallas. As one news release suggested, the project is ''a reunion of old and new Dallas, a reunion with downtown Dallas, and a reunion with Dallas's original transportation hub, the Union Terminal Building.''

Beginnings. The Reunion Project originated in the private sector in 1972, when a development company bought part of the downtown land site, with no specific plan for its development. Knowing that a portion of the adjacent land was owned by the city, the developer contacted the city manager to determine the intended use. The city manager indicated that the land had been acquired in anticipation of future transportation needs but that the city had no other plans for the site. The city also owned the neighboring historic Union Terminal and was interested in its restoration as part of a long-range plan to revitalize the surrounding area as a western anchor of the downtown district.

At this initial meeting between representatives of the two sectors, the possibility of a joint venture was discussed. On the basis of this conversation, the city manager's office prepared a directive stating the city's position on a possible joint project. This directive encouraged the private group to evaluate the property, disregarding land ownership, and devise a master plan for best use of the land. The developer would bear the cost of preparing this plan and the city would provide the support data and any needed technical expertise.

The terms of the city's directive were standard, clearly stating that the city would not be obligated to any action based on the recommendations in the developer's plan. However, on the basis of the informal assurances from the private sector that the planning and subsequent negotiations would be carried out in good faith and in keeping with the best interests of the city, the public sector felt confident enough to call for a master plan. In turn, the pervasive interest and enthusiasm for the idea displayed by city officials encouraged the private investor to undertake the substantial cost of preparing a master plan. Indeed, it was this atmosphere of cooperation and mutual trust that laid the groundwork for what would eventually become a profitable public-private venture.

A planning team hired by the investor to devise the master plan sought to determine those features both sectors considered most important for a development. On the basis of an analysis of the economic and civic goals articulated by the city officials and the businessmen, plus an extensive assessment of potential land use, the planners produced recommendations for an overall design. The project was to include:

A luxury hotel

Entertainment facilities

Renovation of the Union Terminal Building and transit center

A municipal-activities center

Road systems to meet current and projected transportation requirements

Reduced traffic on existing main thoroughfares

Extensive public-parking facilities

Long-term plans for office buildings, retail facilities, and residential space

The overall cost of the project was estimated at over $200 million. The plan stipulated that the developer would use no federal monies and would neither request nor receive any tax abatement or other preferential tax treatment from the city.

Throughout the eight-month planning phase, more than twenty administrators and staff members from the city manager's office worked closely with the planners and the private developer to incorporate the expectations each held for the project. These negotiations were carried out in an atmosphere of privacy and confidentiality in an effort to ensure the candidness and mutual understanding necessary for a successful partnership. Each participant felt sufficiently protected from public scrutiny at this critical stage to openly discuss and resolve such normally sensitive issues as financing preferences and land disputes. As a result, each sector developed an understanding and respect for the principal requirements of, and institutional contraints on, the other.

The master plan was completed late in 1973 and presented to the City Council for its consideration and approval. It was at this time that a majority of the council members were first made aware of the project. Their reaction was generally enthusiastic, but some council members expressed deep concern that city officials had spent nearly a year planning a $200-million joint venture without the council's knowledge.

In response to this criticism, the city manager indicated that the "delicate" nature of the negotiations had made it necessary for the representatives of each sector to conduct their discussions in private. He explained that "the complex relationships of private interests and the city government in working out details made [inclusion of the Council] impossible."[3]

During the next four months, the council debated the plan, and a series of intense negotiations took place to iron out the details of a formal agreement. Issues raised by council members were considered, and the result was an unprecedented forty-three-page contractual agreement between the city of Dallas and the investor. The major points of the contract illustrate the range of issues, provisions, terms, and conditions covered by this complex document.

Construction obligations

Remedies for default

Air rights (leasing and restrictions)

City lease obligations

Adjoining and connecting property use

Street location and access

Licensing

Transfer of property

Use of city property

Financing

Service system tie-in

Approval processes

Provision of open spaces

Utilities

Parking concessions

The contract clearly defined the responsibilities of each sector. The hotel, a theme tower, openspace area, and certain road improvements or construction would be provided by the developer. The municipal-activities center, certain parking and road facilities, and renovation of the Union Terminal Building and transit center were to be the responsibility of the city. The provision of utilities and other service requirements would be achieved through a complex formula designed to ensure that both parties would contribute their fair share. Perhaps the best illustration of the extent to which this agreement set out the exact dimensions of each sector's responsibility and of the formality of the relationship is found in the following clause taken directly from the contract.

It is specifically understood that the relationship herein created between [the developer] and the City is contractual in nature and is in no way to be construed as creating a partnership or joint venture between [the developer] and the City. The obligations of each of the parties hereto

. . . shall be solely the obligation and responsibility of each such party.[4]

The contract also called for transfer of land between the city and developer; 8.7 acres owned by the city were exchanged for 11.3 acres held by the private investor. Although this was not an even trade, it simplified previously burdensome property lines and created tracts of a size that was more appropriate for development purposes. This act of reciprocity further demonstrated the degree of commitment to a relationship between the two parties that ultimately led to a mutually satisfactory outcome.

Results. The outcome of this cooperative effort exceeded the expectations of all participants. Phase I, completed by the private developer in the fall of 1978 at a cost of some $75 million, includes:

Hyatt Regency Dallas, a thirty-story, silver reflective-glass, luxury convention hotel, with 1,000 rooms, an eighteen-story atrium lobby, and a 20,000-square-foot Grand Ballroom

Reunion Tower, a fifty-story tower topped by an observation deck, a revolving restaurant, and other entertainment facilities enclosed in a geodesic dome

Union Terminal Building, a transportation, business, and retail center restored to its 1914 architectural form

Openspace, consisting of ten acres of parks, fountains, and pedestrian walkways

Road network and parking, with an eight-lane divided boulevard encircling the hotel and tower providing access and parking for 2,000 cars

Pedestrian connection via an underground walkway linking the hotel and tower with the Union Terminal Building

Reunion Arena, a 17,000-seat sports complex built by the city officially opened in spring 1980, with final figures indicating the overall costs to be $25 million

Subsequent phases, which will be undertaken as market demand dictates, will include a network of office buildings (some currently under construction), expanded hotel and restaurant facilities, major shopping areas, and residential space.

Conclusions. The most important and unique aspects of the Reunion

Project were the early commitment to a discreet negotiation on the part of the participants and the contractual agreement. From the very outset, both parties followed a set of professional, formal procedures that encouraged candid and sincere negotiation efforts from both sectors. In the early, confidential planning stages, each side was able to gain an understanding and feel for the other's position. They openly discussed and explored the sensitive issues that surround such an undertaking, free from the inhibiting effect of public scrutiny and speculation.

Of course, those confidential, private conditions in which city officials and their private-sector counterparts escape public scrutiny are not without their controversial aspects. Certainly, such arrangements raise significant issues with regard to the public's right to know when their government officials enter into negotiations and what those negotiations entail. Indeed, such questions were raised by City Council members when the master plan was made public. As one local newspaper editorial stated just before council approval was given,

> At issue is determining how much "give and take" is necessary between the City of Dallas and [the developer] before infringing upon other private interests as opposed to public opportunities in a project which has been tagged as vital to development of downtown Dallas. "The whole project has been done in a very unusual manner," said [a council member]; ". . . the point is whether it is good for the entire city."[5]

Certain features of the contract are also important. The advantage of a formal agreement is the security it affords each participant. In this instance the private investor had the assurance that the actions agreed on by the city would be carried out no matter what political uncertainties existed. Moreover, the contractual agreement provided the city with a set of rational planning guidelines that would ensure orderly and healthy economic-growth conditions for the downtown area, again at minimal risk.

The exchange relationship that characterized the Reunion Project generated a set of arrangements that has benefited subsequent public-private interaction in Dallas. The city and other private developers found the contract agreement such a useful instrument that it has become common practice in joint activities. In 1975, for example, one of the area's largest residential developers approached the city with plans to revitalize a portion of the deteriorating inner city by developing a residential neighborhood that would attract middle-income homeowners back to the central city. However, because of uncertainties inherent in purchasing the large amount of inner-city land necessary to undertake such a project, the developer would need certain assurances from the city. On the basis of the success of the Reunion contract agreement and exchange relationship, the city and the residential developer entered similar negotiations. The contractual format was equally successful.

To induce lending institutions to provide the capital necessary to finance such ventures, the city devised the *Areawide Redevelopment Program*. Intended to absorb some of the financial risk associated with non-economic factors, the proposal

> Defined certain conditions that, if allowed to continue, would create an environment detrimental to the health, safety, and welfare of the city;
>
> Designated an area within a two-mile radius of the central city as a special-priority target area;
>
> Invited private developers to undertake housing redevelopment;
>
> Offered and committed the city, as a last resort, to enter into contracts to purchase from the participants property acquired for redevelopment under certain conditions; and
>
> Established a fund to guarantee financing of the city's commitment.

With the city as a buyer of last resort, the risk of failing to acquire enough land for the project was, for the most part, eliminated, and the private developer set out to acquire the necessary property. Some 350 transactions and $7 million later, fifty-five acres had been purchased and construction began. In spring 1980, the first homes in the Bryan Place Project were ready for occupancy. Initial buyer response to this middle-income, inner-city housing was so strong that a waiting list had to be created. This demand is currently being met by the developer with the construction of Bryan Place, Phases II and III.

Central Research Library

The provision of adequate public-library facilities is generally regarded as the responsibility of the public sector. By skillful use of resources from both the public and the private sectors, the city of Dallas will soon provide the general public and the business community with a margin of excellence in library service that it otherwise could not afford. The Central Research Library, which is nearing completion, will double the capacity of the existing library and will provide a link between this city service and the City Municipal Center, a pedestrian mall, and additional public parking in the central business district.

A highly significant bricks-and-mortar achievement in itself, the Central Research Library project is considered even more valuable to the citizens of Dallas because it was instumental in the creation of the city's Cultural-Arts Policy. This document, enacted by the City Council in 1979, asserts the importance of educational and cultural services to the community and includes specific guidelines for public and private cost sharing in the development and construction of cultural-arts facilities. The policy has set a precedent for the participation of both sectors in areas traditionally considered the exclusive responsibility of either the public or the private sector.

Beginnings. As in the case of the Reunion Project, individual initiative set the Central Research Library plan in motion. Two individuals, one from the public sector and one from the private sector, provided the thrust and guidance that has kept the project moving. However, the overall success of the undertaking is largely due to the positive response to the plan by both the city government and the business community.

The need for educational- and cultural-enrichment projects, such as the library, within the central business district was first articulated in the original Goals for Dallas process in 1966. During the goal-setting effort, two civic leaders, who soon became active patrons of the library, together with other members of Goals' education and cultural-arts committees, developed a set of long-range plans for the establishment of a research library in downtown Dallas that would be completed in three separate stages.

Following an established pattern of acquiring land sites in advance of need, the city in 1967 procured a site of 106,000 square feet adjacent to the City Municipal Center. This site could be reached from all parts of the city via the freeway and was located in an area that allowed easy access within the central business district. Armed with an available site for the construction of a central research facility, the library staff alerted the library board to the critical problems of the existing Central Public Library building. The board asked the City Council to help solve the problems of lack of space and the inability of the existing facility to make full use of new technological developments in library services.

The City Council authorized a study of the library. The study reached the following conclusions:

The enlargement of the present building would not be feasible.

The ultimate space requirements for the library would be 600,000 square feet.

The immediate space problem was critical, and an interim solution was proposed.

A new building within the central business district was needed.

In 1972, Capital Improvement Program (CIP) funds amounting to $315,000 were voted for planning a library of at least 600,000 square feet. The City Council formally designated the site acquired in 1967 for this facility and authorized the leasing of additional space as an interim solution (see figure 7–3).

In 1975 the citizens of Dallas voted another $615,000 in CIP funds for a design for the building. The design was quickly approved by the City Council. During the period of design development, the possibility

The project	Ten-story building with two levels below street grade; 650,000 square feet library space; 200 public parking spaces
Originated	1965–1970
Participants	Public: Library Staff, City of Dallas Private: Friends of the Dallas Public Library
Sector responsibility	Public: Site, design, construction, funding (three-fourths) Private: Concensus building, funding (one-fourth), facilitating federal grants
Cost	$34,735,000—construction 2,500,000—furniture, fixtures, equipment 2,398,000—architects' and engineers' fees 365,000—owner's expense
Funding	$ 4,911,000—Economic Development Administration Grant 315,000—CIP 1972 500,000—National Endowment for the Humanities matched by $615,000 in Capital Improvement Program funds, 1975 10,000,000—private funds 25,000,000—Capital Improvement Program, 1978
Opening	Occupancy—October 1981 Opening —April 1982
Benefits	Phase I —Expands room for collections by 85 percent Phase II—Expands each level's capacity by 50 percent Advanced communication and data-processing systems Cooperative local, state, regional, and national linkages Sufficient terminals for computer-based information-retrieval systems Convenient to largest work-force concentration in city Comprehensive plan for citywide cultural-activities development Guidelines and policy for future public-private cultural development

Figure 7–3. Library Fact Sheet

of private funding was mentioned for the first time. A new library facility had been on the city's agenda for almost ten years and was passed over repeatedly because of the expense involved. If private-sector support could be secured, a better facility could be constructed.

In August 1977 the city obtained a $4,911,000 grant from the Economic Development Administration for the underground parking that was integral to the design. The grant specified that monies must be put to use within ninety days of the grant. With the design approved and the money for the lower floors in hand, construction of the project was begun.

Because of the size of the project, it soon became obvious that both the public and the private sectors would have to participate if the library was to meet the needs of both sectors. It had been suggested earlier that the private sector would be responsible for one-fourth of the cost of construction. The city now requested that these monies be assured before it began to promote a bond issue for the completion of the facility. There was, however, no formal mechanism for the collection or transfer of any of these funds to the city.

In 1976 the private sector set about raising the funds for which it had accepted responsibility. A business-government leader who had been instrumental in initiating the project became chairman of the fund drive. To begin the campaign, 150,000 leaflets were included in the monthly statements of one of the largest banks in Dallas. Pledge letters were also mailed. The letters and leaflets detailed the need for, and the benefits to be derived from, an enlarged library-service capability. The pledges allowed the contributor to set up a payment schedule that would terminate in 1984. This solicitation was contingent on the success of a yet-to-be-scheduled bond election. Through 1980, $8,350,308 has been collected from the private sector. The transfer of money from the private sector to the public sector was accomplished through an organization called the Friends of the Dallas Public Library. All pledges were made payable to this organization, which in turn wrote the city a check in the amount of the monies received.

Results. With private support pledged, the city voted $25 million for the completion of the project. The cost of the project had been estimated at $40 million. In order to ensure that this amount would not be exceeded, the construction firm working with the architect and the city agreed on a maximum price for the project. This method will result in the project being completed for nearly $100,000 less than was budgeted.

The project includes:

Seven floors of library space

Over 2,000 individual work areas

Art gallery and bookstore

Restaurants

Public parking

Pedestrian mall

Ramp connecting library and adjacent streets

Nearly 7 million square feet of usable space

Storage for 3 million books

Computers for access to investment information and research material.

Conclusions. In the development of the Central Research Library, responsibilities of each sector were defined as the project progressed and were dictated by its needs. On an informal basis, each sector contributed as needed and according to its expertise. The most obvious contribution of the private sector was the donation of one-fourth of the total cost of the project. Less obvious, but of equal importance, was the use of long-range planning for services usually provided by the public sector.

The public sector was responsible for the selection of the site and the construction of the facility. It also took on the unusual responsibility for the allocation of private funds. Perhaps the greatest responsibility of the public sector was to maintain the private trust that allowed this project to be attempted as a public-private venture. The private sector worked to give the project a positive public image. It initiated the project, built consensus, and provided partial funding. It went on to promote the use of public-private mechanisms to ensure that future projects could follow the guidelines set by the Central Research Library project.

As indicated earlier, in addition to providing the city of Dallas with an excellent research library, this project was instrumental in creating what has come to be known as the city's Cultural-Arts Policy. Because of its roots in the Goals-for-Dallas process, in which the need for downtown cultural-enrichment facilities was set forth, planning for the library provided an opportunity for the city government to take a comprehensive view of the cultural environment. In doing so, it became evident that the cultural arts have a strong economic impact in Dallas. They enhance business opportunities, provide employment, and stimulate outside interest. City officials also recognized that increased patronage of the city's cultural activities meant that their institutional settings had been outgrown. To meet this growing interest, policy guidelines were formulated setting the levels of public-private participation in the development and implementation of cultural arts facilities. The City Council adopted these guidelines in 1979. The Cultural-Arts Policy sets forth five basic principles:

The city of Dallas will assist qualified arts organizations in providing needed facilities in accordance with a carefully conceived and approved plan.

Site selection, planning, and design will be performed or approved by the city. Facilities developed under this program will be constructed, owned, and maintained by the city.

The cost of acquisition of sites will be shared 75 percent by the city and 25 percent by the cultural-arts institution.

The cost of construction will be shared 60 percent by the city and 40 percent by the cultural-arts institution.

The city will determine program support for each organization each year as a part of the general budget process.

Today plans are underway to provide a permanent home for the Dallas Symphony Orchestra and the Civic Opera, together with other activities in a "cultural-arts district" of downtown. These plans have won the support of both public and private organizations. A recently passed cultural-arts bond election has brought renewed enthusiasm from throughout the city and has resulted in a parcel of land for the site of the new Museum of Fine Arts being donated by a local corporation. In addition, the city recently announced that major landowners in the arts district have agreed to work with the city in preparing an overall plan for future development. Included in the cooperative effort will be absorption of outside-planning costs; agreement on building heights, setbacks, landscaping, and building-design guidelines.

Goals for Dallas

The Goals-for-Dallas Program was first proposed in 1964 by the mayor, who was also one of the city's foremost business leaders. It was formally launched in December 1965. The creators of the program recognized that a city has a major impact on nearly all aspects of the life of its citizens, an impact derived from the way the various parts of a city interact with individual and collective economic, social, cultural, and political interests. They also saw that public officials and others whose actions would shape the future of Dallas did not have any overall community goals to guide their day-to-day decisions.

Goals for Dallas was thus conceived as a process whereby citizens could consider alternative future directions and reach consensus on specific goals and steps to achieve them. The privately funded process was initiated by creation of a twenty-seven-member citizen planning committee that developed operational and organizational details. The first goal-setting effort resulted from the deliberations of eighty-seven people from the greater Dallas area who met in conference for three days to debate issues framed in reports by selected local essayists, who in turn were supported by experts from throughout the United States. The conference resulted in the first publication, *Goals for Dallas*, in 1966, which set eighty-six goals in twelve areas of broad concern. These were, in order of presentation:

The government of the city

The design of the city

Health

Welfare

Transportation

Public safety

Elementary and secondary education

Higher education

Cultural activities

Recreation and entertainment

The economy of Dallas

The *Goals for Dallas* document also contained the background essays and supplementary information. It was widely distributed and used as a basis for a series of neighborhood meetings, held over a three-year period, to refine the goals, establish priorities, and assess methods proposed for their achievement. In all, thousands of individuals volunteered many more thousands of hours to set directions for the future of the city and its surrounding region.

What became known as the first Goals-for-Dallas cycle was completed in the early 1970s with designation of a number of agencies to take reponsibility for specific goals. A second cycle, now nearing completion, was begun in 1976. This cycle involved a review of the previous goals, assessment of steps taken, and development of a new set of 205 goals. In this second cycle, more attention has been focused on implementation. Seventeen task forces were established, one for each goal category. These task forces eventually became Achievement Committees, which oversee and report on steps taken for each of the 205 goals.

Planning for a third cycle is under way. Because each cycle adapts to changing conditions and builds on what the previous efforts demonstrated as strengths and weaknesses of the process, it is anticipated that the third cycle will involve the agencies and individuals charged with implementation more in the process of generating the goals themselves, along with specifying implementation steps. In addition, ways are being sought to involve a larger number of citizens more directly and to develop ways to place greater reliance on established neighborhood organizations. Goals for Dallas is an ongoing public-private effort to articulate community goals and in the process improve the environment for individual and organizational cooperation. Although it is difficult to establish a clear causal connection between the process, a specific goal, and a related outcome, it is nevertheless widely acknowledged by business and government alike that the process has been instrumental in facilitating many developments. Goals for Dallas represents an important mechanism for sharing and building awareness with regard to specific community needs.

The many educational-system improvements that have been effected over the past fifteen years and the parallel formulation of education-related goals through the Goals-for-Dallas process illustrate this point. Education was selected by the researchers because of the needs expressed by the private sector for an expansion of higher-education opportunities, the private sector's work with public bodies, and the public sector's positive response.

For many years, Dallas business leaders have stressed the important link between high-quality education and economic growth. By the mid-1960s, the Dallas economy had grown to a point where it was clear to many citizens that higher education in Dallas needed significant reinvigoration. There was special concern about the need for improved graduate education and research, medical education and health care, and post-secondary-school community education.

The 1966 *Goals for Dallas* document elaborated twenty-four goals related to education, many of which were broad in statement but supported by specific suggestions for achievement. Many of these goals are well on their way to realization, and although Goals for Dallas has not been solely responsible for their achievement, there is no question the program established the favorable conditions under which these projects have been realized.

Graduate Education and Research

The most conspicuous result of the goal of making Dallas a first-rate educational center has been the creation of the University of Texas at

Dallas (UTD), a component of the University of Texas system. Its establishment is a monument to public-private partnership. Founded in 1961 as the Graduate Research Center of the Southwest, this distinguished, privately funded, non-degree-granting research facility was given to the state of Texas in 1969 with the understanding that a university would be established. In a little more than a decade (1969–1981), that goal was realized.

In 1966 participants in the Goals-for-Dallas process agreed that Dallas needed outstanding universities with graduate programs. In seeking the most effective approach, they asked such questions as:

> Does the answer lie in building up Southern Methodist University or other private schools? Should North Texas State University, Texas Women's University and Arlington State College be joined to form a strong state system? Ought the State of Texas build a brand new university in the North Texas area, or a new graduate school?[6]

By 1969 the question had been answered. Three distinguished business leaders who had been instrumental in the creation of the original Graduate Research Center of the Southwest urged Goals for Dallas to establish a University of Texas at Dallas. Through personal donations and strong individual support, UTD was founded; the personal contribution by these three individuals was in excess of $15 million.

Community organizations were mobilized to offer support for a legislative bill to create UTD. The Dallas Citizens Council and the Chambers of Commerce of Dallas, Fort Worth, and Arlington, as well as many corporate representatives, sent supporting resolutions to the Texas State Legislature. The Goals-for-Dallas program developed detailed projections of the need for graduate-level education. Trustees of the privately developed and endowed Southwest Center for Advanced Studies offered that relatively young institution's facilities, and the legislature created the new university in 1969. Graduate classes in the physical sciences began the following year. By 1975 graduate programs in arts and humanities, management sciences, and the social sciences were added, along with upper-division undergraduate programs for all parts of the university. In 1975 enrollment was 3,365; by 1981, it was nearly 7,000; and it is still growing.

Private philanthropy and public commitment characterized the cooperative effort that created UTD. Goals for Dallas provided a forum for working out an emerging recognition of a greatly expanded need for higher education and legitimized the university's specific form. Other major facilitating bodies whose membership was engaged in the Goals program lent their support to the venture. UTD plays a role in urban development in that its presence is cited as an attraction for firms considering relocation to Dallas from other parts of the country. Built on a concept of community service, the university has many programs of service to business and industry, and its cooperative programs and activities in research and teaching are steadily increasing.

Medical Education and Health Care

The model of public-private cooperation evident in the development of UTD was not new to the Dallas area. The Univeristy of Texas Science Center had its roots in the small, private Southwestern Medical College, which had been formed in 1943 by a group of prominent Dallas residents. This group had previously founded the Southwestern Medical Foundation (1939) to promote medical education and research in the region, and the creation and direction of the Medical College was one of its first major accomplishments. The foundation subsequently offered the equipment, library, and certain restricted funds of the college to the University of Texas if the university would locate its new branch in Dallas; this was done in 1949.

The Southwestern Medical Foundation was instrumental in this transition through its leadership and its ability to raise funds. The foundation's board of trustees has consistently been made up of influential Dallas citizens with considerable wealth and political power. In 1970 and 1971, the foundation spearheaded a drive to raise $7.5 million of local money to be matched with $12.5 million from University of Texas system funds and $20 million in federal funds. When the drive was over, the local contribution of funds exceeded the original goal by more than $2 million, a clear testimony to the dynamism and leadership of the community.

Many of the foundation's trustees were also active in Goals for Dallas, and it is no coincidence that the Goals proposals of 1966 and 1969 included recommendations for health-care education. In 1966 the general goal for health read:

> The physical well-being of its citizens is a major Dallas goal. Without health the individual cannot attain fully his potentials for his own benefit or the benefit of the community. The problems of health are complex and interrelated but their solution is a challenge we must meet to have the kind of city we envision.[7]

Goal 2 of the more specific goals reads:

> Seek to build Dallas's hospitals, Southwestern Medical School of the University of Texas and related institutions into a great medical center

to enhance medical knowledge through research and to improve medical services.[8]

By 1969 that goal had been fully articulated in highly specific terms. The relevant section of the Goals document is highly illuminating with regard to both the Goals process and the dynamic network of interrelated interests in Dallas.

Goal Two

Interpretation: A great medical center with a broad cooperative program is essential because of the changing patterns of medical care, the increase in federal government health programs and the need to meet the community's health problems more efficiently. All the city's hospitals and major health-related institutions should play significant roles in the coordinated programs of the center and their research activities should be recognized and encouraged.

To Achieve the Goal: SMS, hospitals and other health-related agencies and facilities in the community should become part of a Dallas Medical Center which would have an integrated health program with common objectives, rather than becoming a geographical grouping of institutions.

The Dallas Medical Center should be established under the leadership of the Health Panel of the Community Council of Greater Dallas. In cooperation with the regional health planning agency in the North Central Texas Council of Governments, the Health Panel should seek the coordination of health and hospital programs and facilities on a community-wide basis.

A strong medical school must serve as the nucleus of a medical center and SMS, already strong, is undertaking a master plan to develop into a Life Sciences Center—a health professions campus including schools in medicine, dentistry, nursing (with Texas Woman's University), pharmacy and the allied health professions. The plan also calls for the addition of fundamental teachings including the social and behavioral sciences.

As an initial step toward developing a community-wide program the existing Southwestern Medical Center Council should be strengthened to provide leadership for achieving a workable, integrated program for its members. These include the Dallas Country Hospital District, SMS and Texas University regents, Children's Medical Center, Callier Hearing and Speech Center, St. Paul Hospital and representatives of city and country governments and of the two daily newspapers, the *Dallas Times Herald* and the *Dallas Morning News*.

To achieve this Goal a continuing effort to develop community awareness of the advantages of such a Center should be undertaken by the Community Council, Southwestern Medical Foundation, Dallas Chamber of Commerce, Dallas County Medical Society, SMS and Dallas Hospital Council.

Then by December 1969 agreement among Southwestern Medical Center institutions on common objectives and relationships should be sought by Southwestern Medical Center Council, Dallas County Commissioners and Community Council. At this same time the Community Council, Dallas hospital administrators, SMS, County Medical Society, City and County health departments and Hospital Council should develop a cooperative program among the community's health institutions to coordinate patient-care facilities and education of personnel.

Continuing efforts to develop support for approval of the medical school's Life Sciences Center by the State Legislature and Texas college Coordinating Board should be undertaken by the Chamber of Commerce, Dallas County Legislators, SMS and the County Medical Society. Then in June 1969 and on a continuing basis the Southwestern Medical Foundation should determine availability of private funds for the first phase of the Center.

At this same time the Dallas County Hospital Board and County Commissioners should seek to raise additional funds for the Parkland Hospital expansion. An investigation of the possibility of state support for Parkland Hospital and additional support for SMS should be conducted on a continuing basis by Southweatern Medical Foundation, County Commissioners, Dallas County Hospital District and State Legislators from Dallas County.

Costs and Progress: The first phase of developing the Life Sciences Center is estimated to cost about $40,000,000, with financing from local, state, and federal funds. In the last session of the Legislature the Dallas County Hosptial District was authorized to sell additional revenue bonds to permit funding totaling approximately $20,000,000 for expansion and renovation of Parkland.

A number of Dallas hospitals, health institutions and SMS carry on significant medical research activities.

Construction should start during 1970 on the $5,220,000 Neuropsychiatric Institute on the SMS campus. It will include a community health center.

The creation of The University of Texas at Dallas will strengthen the new as well as ongoing health-related programs in the Dallas area.[9]

By 1975 the first stage of the Health Science Center was completed and the buildings dedicated. More than $50 million was eventually spent on a complex that is designed to train medical scientists and allied-health professionals. Four buildings and 1,200,000 square feet of space were created, including a five-story bioinformation center that served as the main teaching facility for an entering class of two hundred graduate students. Other elements of the Health Science Center have been developed since 1975, increasing the investment substantially.

At all stages of its development, the Health Science Center has been stimulated and supported by strong individuals who have worked through facilitative structures, such as Goals for Dallas, to organize support for specific objectives. It is clear that the need for this major health facility was recognized before Goals for Dallas came into existence, but it is equally clear that the Goals process helped to focus interest on the goal of improved health-care training and to generate broad support.

In 1981 the Health Science Center had some 2,100 students and health-care-training facilities that are among the finest in the world. There are founteen buildings, a full-time faculty of 674, a medical library of 161,630 volumes (excluding microforms), and a medical computer-research center.

Post-Secondary-School Community Education

Awareness of the community's increasing education needs became apparent to all in Dallas with development proposals made in the early 1960s. Private firms had carried much of the responsibility for postsecondary technical education by providing on-the-job training, but it became obvious that a more formal and more general educational arrangement was needed. Much of the push for junior-college education came from the Dallas business community; indeed, the Dallas Chamber of Commerce spearheaded a drive to support the establishment of Dallas County Junior College. Although earlier proposals had come from the educational community, a greater realization of the need for skilled manpower by the business community was required before this need could be met.

In 1965 Dallas community leaders encouraged local state legislators to vote for the establishment of a community-college district in Dallas. A petition with 60,000 signatures was presented to the State Board of Higher Education, and subsequently, the state legislature approved the plan for a community-college district with four campuses. Dallas County voters authorized the district and approved a $41.5-million bond sale to support the project. By early 1966, when the first *Goals for Dallas* document was published, the community-college-district concept was expanded from four to seven campuses; by 1979 classes were being held in all seven institutions; and today more than 41,000 credit students and 30,000 community-service students are being served. These enrollments are double those projected in the 1966 Goals document.

The purpose of these junior colleges is to provide technical and vocational training to post-secondary-school students, as well as academic preparation for students who intend to go on to earn a baccalaureate degree elsewhere. The importance of this role for the junior college has taken on additional meaning as the Dallas economy has developed an increasing dependence on a more highly educated work force than would come from traditional vocation-technical education programs.

In 1973 the Goals program again served as a facilitative mechanism for another major educational development in Dallas. The Dallas County Community College District Foundation was formed "to provide means for friends of the District to make donations and contributions to the colleges." The foundation was strongly promoted by the same Goals-for-Dallas group that promoted the community-college program.

The community-college development is an excellent example of the facilitative role of the Goals process and of the Dallas style of public-private cooperation: An idea was formulated on the basis of existing needs. A major private-sector figure was put in charge of developing that idea. Other major support was generated through the legitimizing auspices of Goals for Dallas. The public sector was invited to take part in something of great magnitude and obvious importance. A "margin-of-excellence" support mechanism, in this case a foundation, was created to develop special financial sources to supplement the public funds. Stability was guaranteed through the selection of a chancellor with full backing and supplementary salary support from the private sector.

Organizational and Individual Roles

Facilitating Structures for Cooperation

Organized activities that provide the means by which one sector pursues goals beneficial to both constitute facilitating structures. In Dallas a number of civic organizations play a vital role in the development of many economic, cultural, and political programs. These organizations provide a forum in which the common interests of the city's business, professional, and government leaders may be explored and supported. Among other things, these groups endeavor to

Produce and maintain an overall urban environment conducive to successful, ongoing commercial activity

Ensure business-community awareness of those influences that may alter the positive atmosphere necessary to sustain growth

Serve as a link between the individual and policy-setting entities

In Dallas, these facilitating structures generally fall into three categories: broad-policy groups, place-oriented organizations, and special-interest or project-focused organizations. Any particular organization can fit all three categories, but one is usually dominant. The broad-policy groups are perhaps the most difficult to define; yet they are also the most important in establishing the overall tone and direction of public-private interactions in a community. They may take the form of a metropolitan-planning council, a chamber of commerce, a committee of one hundred, and the like. Place-oriented groups tend to be concerned principally with the development or improvement of a particular locality and the issues of concern to the social or economic institutions within specified geographic boundaries. A neighborhood-improvement association or an area association of businesses would fall into this category. The focus of special-interest organizations is on a specific issue, project, or program. Because it has a membership with a uniform commitment to a particular set of concerns, the life cycle of a special-interest group may only coincide with the life of the issue for which the group was formed. The special-interest or project-focused organization may also include private corporations operating on a specific public-private activity. An example might include a corporation's entering into a contract with a city for the provision of specific public services or to develop a project plan in conjunction with public interests and needs.

Public-private organizations in Dallas have four primary categories of operating characteristics: purposes, decision and management style, membership, and communications.

Under the category *purposes,* the operating characteristics included the following:

Facilitative, with a particular focus on communications and coordinative processes

Informative and analytical

Promotional

Fund raising

Planning development

Project focus, with limited organizational life

Process focus, with an interest in the institutionalization of the public-private activity

Advocacy

Decision and/or *management style* characteristics include:

Open or closed processes

Participatory (rather than exclusive) processes with respect to the organization's membership

Directive (rather than consensual) processes with respect to the membership and to correlative groups

Deliberative (rather than reactive) in response to specific issues

Reliance on standing committees as opposed to ad hoc structures

Operating with task forces, either formal or informal

Collaborative with respect to other groups

Negotiatory in approach to resolution of conflict

The *membership* category includes the following characteristics, and is élitist in the sense that each of the following categories can in fact operate to exclude otherwise interested or qualified parties:

By invitation only

Self-selecting through the sharing of common interests, business, or professional activities

Determined by place of residence or business

By occupation or profession

Communications includes the following characteristics:

Reliance on informal or word-of-mouth processes

Published newsletters

Periodic publication of operating reports

Press releases or personal interviews for public record

Formal announcements

Open minutes

Open records of proceedings and documentation of activities

Occasional analytic reports on matters of public interest

Facilitating structures can be defined according to these characteristics to the extent that they can be discerned. Figure 7–4 shows how the operating characteristics can be arrayed according to the range of interest. Thus, for example, groups whose primary interests are focused on broad

Operating Characteristics	Range of Interests		
	Broad Policy Issues	Place Orientation	Special Interests or Project Focus
Purposes	Facilitative Promotional Fund raising Informative Process focus Planning interest	Promotional Informative Planning Facilitative Project focus Advocacy	Advocative Informative/analytical Project focus Fund raising Promotional
Decision and/or management style	Closed Exclusive in decision Consensual Deliverative Task forces (internal) Collaborative	Open More participatory than exclusive Consensual Reactive Standing committees Collaborative	Closed Exclusive processes Directive Reactive Ad hoc task forces (formal) Negotiatory
Membership	Invitation Occupational similarity or separateness Élitist	Self-selection Residence or business location Unrestrictive	Self-selection Occupational Unrestrictive for special interests and restrictive for individuals on limited projects
Communications	Informal Personal interviews Closed records Occasional public reports	Formal (business base) Newsletters Published reports Informal (social-neighborhood base) Open minutes Press release	Newsletters Published reports Press releases Formal announcements Minutes and records tend to be closed unless common interest is an avowed public concern

Figure 7–4. Principal Focus of Facilitating Structures and Operating Characteristics

policy issues rely principally on informal communications to achieve their purposes. This is a highly effective technique because of the homogeneity of the membership and the frequency of regular informal contacts among the members as they pursue their independent business and recreational activities. This is not the case with groups whose interests are geographic or whose only concern is a special issue or project; such groups require formal communication processes and planned regular meetings.

In Dallas the most active and effective organizations have been those with broad policy concerns or those with a focus on special interests or a particular project. Partly because Dallas is a relatively young city undergoing very rapid development, facilitating structures with a place orientation have not achieved positions of influence that are observed in older communities.

Broad-Policy Groups

Because a city's broad-policy groups are the most influential of its civic organizations, their membership is generally highly selective, usually limited to top business, social, and religious leaders. The purpose of such groups is to be aware of, and active in, those issues connected with the general welfare of the city. Several Dallas organizations meet these criteria, but one stands out as the premier civic-policy group: the Dallas Citizens Council.

Dallas Citizens Council

The Dallas Citizens Council has had more influence on the social, economic, and political development of Dallas than any other extant organization. It was formed in 1937 to meet the challenge of a difficult economic period. Dallas had won the right to host the official Texas Centennial celebration but was having problems raising the necessary money. In an effort to bolster the city's financial position in this and other matters, several of the area's bankers invited one-hundred prominent businessmen to join them in forming a corporation dedicated to educational and civic goals. All these businessmen responded enthusiastically, and the organization was granted a fifty-year corporate charter. This charter stated that the organization would

> study, and confer and act upon any matter which may be deemed to affect the welfare of the City of Dallas, the County of Dallas, or the State of Texas and . . . support any educational or civic enterprise deemed to promote such welfare.

At the same time a parallel organization was formed, the Citizens Charter Association (CCA). This group, which had many of the same members as the council, was organized to select and promote acceptable political candidates for city offices, usually from within its own ranks.

Although it had a small core of dedicated members, CCA was most visible in election years. For nearly twenty-five years, it was quite active and exercised great influence in city elections. However, because of its rather loose structure, changing political and social conditions, and some formidable opposition in the 1960s, CCA faded from existence, whereas the council has flourished.

Decision and Management Style

Dallas Citizens Council currently has a thirty-four-member board of directors and a nine-member executive committee. It is this inner circle of members that actually decides who will be invited to join and what issues will be addressed. The entire group, now numbering some 240, meets once or twice a year; the directors and the executive committee meet regularly.

Because the board of directors and executive committee meetings are closed to the public, the precise nature of their policy framework is a subject of speculation. However, their decision criteria are based on a broad, finely developed sense of what is good for Dallas. This highly subjective measurement technique is applied to each issue or project under consideration by the board.

The decision-making style of the Dallas Citizens Council is best described as a forced consensus. That is, when the executive committee agrees to support an issue, it is a unanimous decision. There may be some disagreement among individual members from time to time, but when a position is formally taken by the group, there are no dissenting opinions expressed. More important, council policy and practice preclude the organization from taking a negative position on a public issue. The group acts positively or not at all.

For example, many credit the council's efforts as being at least partially responsible for the peaceful integration of the city's business and public institutions in the 1950s. Given the experiences of other cities at the time, the executive-committee members were convinced that resistance to integration efforts would perpetuate a set of unhealthy social and political conditions and spell economic disaster for the city. Therefore, a subcommittee called the Dallas Alliance was formed to meet with black groups, white groups, and business, religious, and civic leaders to pave

the way toward a more peaceful integration than might otherwise have
been expected.

Membership

Membership in the Dallas Citizens Council is by recommendation of
another member only and is limited to chief executive officers of the
largest firms in the area. Individuals are thus chosen for their business
position, regardless of length of residency in Dallas or perceived social
status. Moreover, prospective members must meet other, more subtle
qualifications. For example, a nominee must have previously displayed
a "sincere interest" in Dallas and a "willingness to assume a leadership
role in the community at large."

The council's founders were adamant about allowing only the top
echelon of business to participate. They wanted only those who could
speak instantly for their firms in both financial and policy matters, without
having to secure the approval of a board of directors. In fact, one of the
original members wanted to name the group the "Yes or No Council,"
but he was overruled.

Communications

Communications among council members is quite informal and generally
person to person. Records are maintained, but not for public inspection,
and reports are rarely issued. When the executive committee decides that
an issue should be addressed or some action taken, the appropriate individual members are personally contacted to accomplish the council's
objectives. Moreover, in keeping with its traditionally low profile, the
flow of information out of the council is generally removed from its
organizational context. That is, when information is passed on to other
organizations or the press, it is done by an individual, not on behalf of
the organization.

New Directions

During its forty-five years of existence, the Dallas Citizens Council has
undergone few structural changes. Its membership is still limited to chief
executive officers, it still adheres to the educational and civic goals set
forth in its original charter, and it still manages to exercise influence over
the civic and economic affairs of Dallas. However, a notable change in

the organization occurred in 1976, when it hired a full-time professional director. The director's function is to keep the executive board informed of and active in those social, economic, and political developments critical to the positive and dynamic environment of the city.

Some observers have suggested that with the hiring of a full-time director, the role of the council has begun to change. Whereas in the past the organization depended on individual initiative to introduce and explore issues, this is now the responsibility of the director. Many see this as the initial step toward removing the business leaders of Dallas from the day-to-day activities of the city. This new structure may not diminish the role of DCC, but it will change its way of operating.

Contributions

Some observers suggest that DCC as an organization is not a powerful entity but rather that the individual members hold the power. In some instances, this is true, but the organization has provided the crucial institutional framework that has motivated and mobilized these very powerful individuals. The fact that the council chooses not to take an active role in those issues it cannot support is itself an important contribution.

Perhaps the most important contributions that the council has made to Dallas are

The spirit of cooperation and the working relationship its members have maintained with the city government, fostering trust and the inclination of both sectors to participate in public-private activities

An enthusiasm for a wide variety of programs considered strategic to the vitality of Dallas

A willingness to commit the personal and professional resources necessary to carry out those programs

The role of the council in any of the examples discussed in this case study is difficult to define specifically. For instance, its presence was never apparent in the Reunion Project. Yet, because of the active participation in planning-and-development programs by its members over the years, city officials were accustomed to responding flexibly and did so to the private developer's proposals throughout the Reunion negotiation process. Thus, although it may be difficult to relate the final outcome of many joint ventures in Dallas to efforts of the council, there is no question that this group has served to articulate and promulgate the concept of using the combination of public and private assets to enrich the economic and cultural environment of the city.

Dallas Alliance

The Dallas Alliance grew out of community efforts to resolve the difficult problems of integration. In the late 1950s representatives of DCC and minority groups organized a task force to formulate and implement a plan to ensure the peaceful integration of the city's restaurants and hotels. This group now functions formally as the Tri-Racial Committee. On the basis of the success of this effort, programs were devised that integrated all the city's public-service facilities on the same day, with very little public attention or opposition drawn to the event. This experience contributed to the foundation, in the 1970s, by DCC of the Dallas Alliance to prepare desegregation plans for the public schools. The organization is now independent and is wholly funded by individual contributions.

Although its members represent a cross-section of the citizens of Dallas, many of its strongest supporters also belong to DCC. Priorities of the Dallas Alliance include such quality-of-life issues as criminal justice, education, and neighborhood rejuvenation.

This group represents the city's principal forum for convening the full range of business, professional, and government leaders and developing programs that seek to improve the formal processes of government-business relations. In addition, Dallas Alliance is committed to the broad participation of neighborhood organizations in public-private cooperative activities.

Place-Oriented Organizations

Place-oriented groups limit themselves to issues of a regional nature or a particular area of social or economic development, often relying on geographic boundaries to determine the scope of their interest. Place-oriented organizations have a project orientation rather than the mere process or conceptual concerns of the policy groups. These organizations are more open than broad-policy groups and generally have less selective criteria for membership. For example, the second-ranking officers of large corporations and the chief executives of smaller firms are often members. However, the two types of organizations usually share some membership, providing an informal flow of information between them and establishing mutual interests.

Central Business District Association

Membership in the Central Business District Association (CBDA) is open to anyone having an interest in the central business district, but it consists mostly of the vice presidents of large corporations and presidents of smaller companies that operate there. The organization employs a full-time director whose function is to identify issues that affect the commercial residents of the district or its environment. The group has a seventy-five-member board of directors; the twenty-five-member executive committee is the policy-setting entity.

CBDA's decision style is much like that of the broad-policy groups, one of forced consensus. Because of their mutual interests, members of the executive committee are likely to have similar views regarding issues that have an effect on the social or economic vitality of the central city. Consequently, consensus is not difficult to achieve.

CBDA has experienced little structural change in its twenty-five-year history. However, several significant functional changes have occurred. Over the years the director and many members of the executive committee have worked closely with city officials on both long-range planning and development programs. As a result, the advocacy role of the organization has unofficially evolved into one of advisory status for the local government.

When the group was founded, it took a very active role in many issues. For example, in the early 1960s, CBDA initiated and supported the proposal for the Dallas North Tollway, a much-needed alternate roadway running from North Dallas into the downtown area. However, this activism waned drastically over the next decade. During that period, the organization simply responded to issues, rather than initiating them. Recognizing in the mid-1970s that the central business district needed an organization that was active as well as reactive, the executive committee once again sought to become a leading force in the policy concerns of the area. Today CBDA seeks to anticipate relevant policy questions and initiate action rather than support the activity of others.

Dallas Chamber of Commerce

Membership in the Dallas Chamber of Commerce is open, but most of the roster is made up of the presidents of all the larger corporations in the city. It too has a full-time director and makes policy decisions through an executive board. It conforms as well with the established pattern of Chambers of Commerce elsewhere, with its main function being to support and promote the Dallas area.

Single-Interest Groups

As in most large cities, there may be hundreds of special-interest groups. In Dallas at any given time there are historic-preservation leagues, voters' groups, tenant associations, neighborhood organizations, health-care groups, and so on. Occasionally, these groups will coalesce to provide a more unilateral approach to the issues they address.

One example of such a coalition is the Dallas Community Council (DCC). It serves as a clearinghouse for groups active in health-and-welfare issues. An outgrowth of the Dallas Council of Social Agencies, the Community Council has a paid staff of forty and a full-time director. Through its staff, which has strong minority representation, this organization can present an accurate picture of the health-and-welfare concerns of the various member groups. The flow of information between the council and member organizations is the same as in other civic groups; the staff or director initiates an activity, then passes it on to the executive committee, where it is considered, and finally recommendations are made to the board of directors for approval.

The Community Council has been active in the Dallas area for many years and was pivotal in the creation of the Martin Luther King Community Center and the Callier Speech and Hearing Clinic. The Community Council, as well as such groups as the United Way with its affiliates, provides a focal point for business on a broad range of social voluntary actions.

The Role of Facilitating Structures in Public-Private Activity

The participation of facilitating structures in public-private efforts is discernible at different levels. For instance, as indicated in figure 7–5, the role of the broad-policy groups (specifically DCC) was not immediately evident in Reunion. Although members were not involved in the day-to-day operational details of the project, the group had an undeniable impact on Reunion's success. Because of its commitment to the social and economic well-being of the city, DCC was instrumental in articulating the need to further develop and revitalize that portion of downtown Dallas. Moreover, through its close association with city officials over the years, DCC set the stage for the spirit of cooperation and mutual respect that characterized Reunion. Without the encouragement derived from these previous relationships with the private sector, the city might not have been as open to or flexible in the contract agreement with the developer.

On the other hand, DCC's role was quite clear in both the Central

Facilitative Organization	Illustrative Project		
	Reunion	Public Library	Goals for Dallas
Broad Policy Groups	Not immediately evident but, Tacit approval Acceptance Legitimation (after the fact) Information dissemination Facilitative	Initiated Leadership in planning and implementation Financial support Promotion Consensus building	Leadership Active participation in planning and implementation Consensus building
Place-oriented organizations	Approval Promotional support	Approval Financial support Promotion	Tacit approval Lower-level supportive participation Implementation assistance
Special-purpose organizations	Initiated Funding Promotion Management and policy decisions Implementation	Approval Promotion Financial support	Lower-level supportive participation Implementation assistance

Figure 7–5. Organizational Roles in Partnership Activities

Research Library and Goals for Dallas. The membership contributed strong leadership and management to the private side of the partnership in the library project. It also provided the financial support (both personal and from business sources) that guaranteed the public sector's participation.

In Goals for Dallas, the role of broad-policy groups was formidable. DCC—or perhaps more accurately, its members—furnished authoritative leadership in the planning and strategy activities as well as ardent participation in the implementation of specific goals.

Similar variations in the level of participation in these projects can be observed among the place-oriented and special-interest organizations. For example, in Reunion, it was a special-interest group, the development corporation, that was the primary facilitating structure. It initiated the project, contributed major funding, provided the private-side management, and carried out implementation strategies.

The role of these two types of groups is less apparent in the Central Research Goals for Dallas projects. In each case, special-interest groups and place-oriented organizations offered some financial assistance, promotional activity, and lower-level supportive participation, but leadership was almost exclusively left to the broad-policy groups or their members.

The Roles of Individuals in Cooperative Activity

Dallas business leaders are expected by their peers to participate in public affairs and to accept leadership responsibilities for community activities. This tradition has become so engrained in the business atmosphere over the years that individual businessmen have internalized the expectation and consider it their civic role and an integral part of their business responsibility.

However, there are also roles played by the individual members of these facilitative structures that are distinct from the roles of the organization. Although organizations impart certain characteristics or identities to their individual members, the individuals also bestow certain characteristics on the organizations. In many instances, a group such as DCC lends its strength, through association, to its members, but very powerful individuals often lend their strength to the organization.

The same general classification system applied to facilitating groups can be used to categorize individuals and their roles in public-private relationships. Specifically, they may be identified as: statesmen, individuals interested in regional issues, and individuals with special project interests (see figure 7–6).

Statesmen

Individual business leaders who are concerned with maintaining and expanding all aspects of city life in Dallas may be defined as statesmen. In their different public and private roles, such men and women address broad-policy issues dealing with commerce, industry, cultural affairs, education, health care, water supply, recreation and so on. Statesmen are generally among the most successful business leaders in the area and tend to be chief executive officers or board chairmen of the largest companies. Because of their power and influence, they can mobilize and tap both the human and the capital resources necessary to effect the changes they seek.

As would be expected, statesmen are usually members of broad-policy groups, but often it is their presence as individuals rather than as part of a civic organization that solidifies public-private cooperation. Although statesmen seldom take a visible role in policy formulation, they have an immense wealth of experience and contacts on which to draw, and both are employed to facilitate action.

There is no conspicuous evidence of the role of a statesman (or statesmen) in the Reunion development; perhaps the absence of any opposition to the project attests to the tacit approval of these individuals. Moreover, in special development projects such as Reunion, there is no requirement for statesmen; the developer provides that role. Yet there is little doubt that Reunion benefited from actions of statesmen in other public-private ventures. These individuals built a tradition of reliability and trust between the two sectors that greatly facilitated the spirit of cooperation found throughout the project.

In the Central Research Library project, the role of the statesman is far more evident. One individual with a history of civic involvement was responsible for initiating the project, assembling the private-sector financial commitment, and gaining widespread public support for the joint venture.

The Goals for Dallas education activity relied heavily on the participation and funding provided by several statesmen. These individuals furnished both their financial support and guidance to persons responsible for implementing projects consistent with the educational goals. Their actions demonstrate the benevolent character of the statesman who seeks out the participation and representation of the whole spectrum of the city's population. Without question, this program succeeded because of those individuals who gave their time, money, and encouragement to it.

In summarizing the role of the statesman in our case studies there are several lessons to be learned;

Statesmen can be members of any type of facilitative organization,

Individual Role Characteristics	Illustrative Projects		
	Reunion	*Public Library*	*Goals for Dallas (Education)*
Statesmen	Presence not observable, but gave tacit approval and facilitated activities of others	Initiation and planning Financing Promotion and Advocacy	Active participation in the program Funding assistance Planning and guidance
Place-oriented/regional interest actors	Presence virtually unnoticed	Acceptance Promotion of the need Financing	None observed
Special-interest or project focus	Initiation Funding Acceptance Management Promotion	Limited (this function provided by statesmen) Professional library leadership	None observed (this function provided by statesmen)

Figure 7–6. Individual Roles in Partnership Activity

but given their overall interests, they generally hold membership in broad-policy groups.

Special development projects do not require the presence of "external" statesmen as this role is filled by the developers.

In order for a public-private activity to gain broad appeal, it must have the active support of a statesman-type individual from either the public or private sector.

Place-Oriented or Regional-Interest Actors

Individuals interested in regional issues might be described as "budding statesmen." They either are in the process of developing or have already developed the skills of a statesman, but they exercise those skills only when an activity falls within their regional or neighborhood boundaries. For this reason, they often become active in a project only after it has been initiated; and when the activity is a special development project (such as Reunion), their role is never one of leadership. However, once a project has been introduced, regional-interest individuals will take a very active role in influencing its location within their regional boundaries, as well as assisting in the financial arrangements, promotion, and advocacy.

In the case of Reunion, the role of the regional-interest actors is virtually undetectable. However, these individuals provided strong financial support to the Central Research Library project and promoted acceptance of it throughout the city.

Special-Interest Supporters

Individuals who have a very limited and narrowly focused interest in a particular program or project are often responsible for the initiation, acceptance, and implementation of an activity. They assume the role of statesmen in special development projects.

The developer was the first to propose the Reunion Project and filled the private-sector leadership role throughout the planning and implementation process. In the case of the Goals-for-Dallas education program and the Central Research Library, there was no evidence of the presence of active special-interest individuals. Perhaps the strong presence of statesmen in these projects precluded the need for leadership on the part of special-interest actors.

To conclude, it should be reiterated that the role of the individual is sometimes distinct from that of the facilitative organization with regard to our case studies. While the strength of an organizaton such as the Dallas Citizens Council is undeniable in a project such as Goals for Dallas, we must also look beyond the role of the organization to the individual actors to fully determine the scope and elements of a public-private relationship.

*New Directions in Urban Management and
Implications for Public-Private Cooperation*

The challenges facing the city of Dallas today are substantial and will cause changes in a number of the mechanisms that have served the city so well in the recent past. Difficult problems facing the city include shrinkage of the fiscal base because of the mismatch between the inflation levels for revenues and for costs. Other problems and challenges relate to district representation rather than at-large representation on the city council, transportation problems, and an aging housing stock and infrastructure. However, all these challenges present opportunities for improvement, and some of the new directions in urban management in Dallas that will affect public-private cooperative activities are already evident.

Infrastructure Development. Infrastructure should be developed in accord with economic growth of the community. However, it is perhaps more important for the future that infrastructure maintenance and, to a more limited extent, replacement, receive proper attention. A deteriorating infrastructure can have serious effects on the quality of life in a community, as some older communities have recently experienced.

Maintenance of Existing Levels of Economic Activity. The Dallas city government maintains the view that a growing and vital economy reduces pressures for increased public expenditures to assist persons who might otherwise be unemployed. As the city ages, however, it will be increasingly important to maintain existing levels of economic activity by retaining businesses already in place.

Partnership Development. Again as the community ages and growth rates slow down, there will need to be a greater reliance on partnerships, and public-private ventures of the future will require even more involvement from both sides.

Privatization. Greater reliance on the private sector to provide public services is a nationwide trend in urban management. As privatization efforts expand, Dallas managers may be placed in competition with the private sector. This may not only improve the delivery of the particular services but may also have unintended secondary benefits in the form of more cost-conscious management of public activities.

Performance Contracting. The new development in this area involves the negotiation of a contract between the city and a private developer or provider of a particular service to reach a contract agreement that is binding on all parties. In several public-private cooperative activities, Dallas has used a contract to formally define the responsibility of each sector. The contract has the advantage of binding the city to a course of action with specified steps; this can reduce uncertainty and risk for related private-sector investments. Greater use of performance-contracting techniques will also lead to changes in methods of urban management because there will be a greater need for individuals with negotiating skills and contract-management capabilities.

The Public Entrepreneur. As city life becomes more complex, there is a growing need for urban managers with entrepreneurial skills. The public entrepreneur is the individual who can spot opportunities to package public programs and leverage the public investment with private-sector participation to achieve previously determined public-sector goals.

Strategic Planning. In an era of shrinking public revenues from existing sources, more attention must be given to applying concepts of strategic planning to government. Negotiated priorities among various government departments, interest groups, neighborhood organizations, and the business community will become an important element of local government. Creative financing and new definitions of public-private responsibilities will be major aspects of public strategic planning processes.

This is not an exhaustive list of new directions in urban management evident in Dallas. However, these examples illustrate the continuing special role that government will play in promoting a variety of public-private cooperative activities. It is clear that Dallas intends to improve its ability to play the role of a full partner.

Conclusions

Public-private cooperative activities in all communities are nearly limitless from the perspective both of time and function. To observe them and define them is a matter of personal attitude. One person's cooperative venture is another's sinister cabal. A person's attitude is probably determined in part by whether or not he or she is part of the process. In Dallas, public-private cooperation has for the most part involved a set of positive attitudes about the mutually supportive responsibilities of all types of organizations. The positive attitudes expressed by business and government about each other are considered more important than specific cooperative ventures or projects. Indeed, cooperative activities would be extremely difficult to achieve if the necessity and desire to work together had not first been established and become a widely held value in the community.

Because the cooperative attitude of the business and government communities has been so prevalent, the *processes* through which specific cooperative activities have emerged are seen as being more important than particular projects. Thus analysis of public-private cooperation in Dallas leads to a sense of collectivity in public-private processes that is not evident when assessing particular projects or accomplishments. Individuals are seen to act largely without reference to any participative organization and may or may not have the tacit approval of community-wide or other interest groups. Yet there is the distinct impression that the individual operates within a relatively impartial but beneficient framework of cooperation. The leadership of Dallas, both government and business, has sought to create a climate for unity of purpose and action. On really important matters, as they view them—bond programs for capital facilities, the creation of a special transportation district, or the bond program for a fine-arts center, to name several—the leadership speaks in one voice. Dissenting views are generally not aired, although dissent is not discouraged at the appropriate time and in the appropriate setting.

The following are the most frequently noted characteristics of public-private cooperation in Dallas mentioned by the business, government, and community leaders interviewed for this case study. Although this list is not all-inclusive, the characteristics apply to all types of cooperative activities.

> Maintaining, improving, and expanding nearly all aspects of city life (commerce and industry, education, health-care facilities, cultural affairs, transportation, taxation, water supply, parks and recreation, and so on) are seen by all business, government, and community leaders as important to the high quality of life in Dallas and to the city's continued growth.

> The private sector in particular perceives the quality of life in the city, of which the business climate is a part, as a matter of interest

to the overall health of the economy and thus of vital concern to each business and business spokesperson.

Individual business leaders are expected by their peers to participate in public affairs and to accept leadership responsibilities for communitywide activities.

Tangible or development projects that have a public-private cooperative character primarily involve private-sector representatives acting on their own behalf.

The organization of private-sector individuals working in association on a public-sector problem aims primarily at facilitating the actions of other individuals or organized entities.

Organized facilitation of public-private interactions tends to be ad hoc and is more likely to be initiated by private interests or by individuals acting in a private capacity.

The city government is viewed as a willing partner in all types of projects that promote or enhance the vitality of the community.

Both public and private organizations have developed a cadre of professional managers with technical and administrative capabilities in common, allowing for more effective intersector cooperation.

If the city government accommodates the development interests of a private-business concern or individual, the terms of the accommodation are made available to all parties with similar cooperative needs.

Openmembership organizations with interoccupational or multi-interest memberships are of relatively recent origin and are a response to the recognition that problems involving pluralistic interests require codeliberation of diverse organizations.

Organized cooperative public-private activities are usually triggered by some event or emergent need, with institutional or individual roles differentiated along the lines of a broad-policy focus, orientation to a specific location, or focus on a special limited interest or project.

Acknowledgments

The authors of this chapter wish to thank the citizens of Dallas—public and private, past and present—for their many contributions to programs that have made Dallas a showcase for public-private cooperation. Without their efforts, this report would not have been possible.

More directly, many individuals contributed to the analysis and the conclusions about the dynamics of public-private cooperation in Dallas. Over fifty persons were interviewed during the course of the study. Included were leading figures in business and industry, government officials, directors of not-for-profit voluntary and community-service organizations, education and religious leaders, and others involved in civic affairs. We wish to thank all of those who contributed valuable insights and information about the nature of public-private relations in Dallas for their generosity of time and spirit.

Because so many Dallas citizens contributed to the success of the projects and processes described in this document, decisions about whom to mention in a particular circumstance became impossible to make. If we noted one individual for his efforts, then we surely would have to mention others who may have been equally important, even if in a secondary role. And if we mentioned others, who would we unintentionally omit whose contributions were also critical? Therefore, we made the easy decision and concluded that we would not mention any individuals by name. We intend no slight and trust that persons involved in these projects will understand that their roles are known and that their efforts on behalf of the larger community are fully appreciated.

Because this study was commissioned by the Committee for Economic Development, we wish to depart from our "no-name" policy at this point and acknowledge the contribution to this study of the three CED Trustees from Dallas: Mark Shepherd, Jr., chairman, Texas Instruments Incorporated; L.S. Turner, Jr., executive vice president, Texas Utilities Company; and Honorary Trustee Stanley Marcus, consultant, Carter Hawley Hale Stores, Inc. While the conclusions and views expressed in this report are solely the responsibility of the authors, the Dallas CED Trustees were very supportive throughout the study and aided immeasurably in the authors' understanding of events.

This report was prepared under the direction of William E. Claggett, president of William Claggett Associates. Assistance with interviews, analysis and preparation of project summaries was provided by Linda McCormack and John W. Sommer. Major assistance in analysis of public-private cooperative processes, presentation before the CED subcommittee and in final-report preparation was provided by Sunny Johnston. Finally, appreciation is extended to Eileen Tollett for her typing and support services under difficult and often trying conditions created by the authors.

Notes

1. J. Rees, "Manufacturing: A Good Dynamo," *Dallas/Ft. Worth Business Quarterly* (May/June/July 1978), p. 15.

2. City of Dallas, *Management Services Research Report: 1979 Dallas Business Profile Survey* (Dallas: Office of Management Services, 1979).

3. Henry Tatum, "Private Dealings of Project Leave Councilmen Cold," *Dallas Morning News* (October 13, 1973).

4. City of Dallas, Master Agreement Among the City of Dallas, Hunt Investment Corporation (Dallas: Woodbine Development Corporation, and Ray L. Junt, individually, April 29, 1975), p. 34.

5. "Union Terminal Project Sparks Council Questions," *Dallas Morning News* (February 15, 1974).

6. *Goals for Dallas,* Dallas, Texas (1966), p. 196.

7. Ibid., p. 3.

8. Ibid., p. 9.

9. Ibid., pp. 36–37.

8

The Atlanta Public-Private Romance: An Abrupt Transformation

M. Dale Henson and
James King

On October 27, 1981, the citizens of Atlanta elected a new mayor to a four-year term. This election marks the beginning of what it is hoped will be a new era in public-private cooperation in the city. The new mayor, Andrew Young, is Atlanta's second black to serve in this office. Although he won the election without the support of the business community, most business leaders feel they can work effectively with the new administration, and plans are already underway to form constructive relationships with the new mayor.

This case study can be instructive both to the citizens of Atlanta in their pursuit of public-private cooperation and to other cities faced with significant shifts in the balance of political power within their communities. This is a study of complex problems associated with such a transition and how the business community attempted to deal with what it perceived to be a hostile attitude toward its interests on the part of public-sector leadership. The Atlanta story demonstrates that public-private cooperation is not easy. It also demonstrates that changes in the political base of a city require continuous and lengthy negotiations to bring about a new balance of interests that reflect concerns often overlooked in the name of economic progress.

The lessons recorded here can help leaders in both sectors gain a deeper understanding of the need for patience, understanding, and tenacity as they pursue their individual and collective objectives. Conflict is inevitable and compromise is required. This is a story of both. It is also the story of how Atlanta once again proved its ability to cope with adversity and come out a winner.

The Atlanta Economy: Two Decades of Transformation

During a relatively short time span, about twenty years, an agrarian Southeastern economy was replaced by a new industrial-technological society. This fast-paced change has forced (and is still forcing) Atlanta to quickly develop the complex management apparatus necessary to give direction to this regional transformation.

Being the key southeastern city is not a new role for Atlanta. Founded in 1835 at the intersection of two railroads, it developed as a distribution center, channeling goods and money between the largely rural economies of six or seven states and the rest of the country.

Although some industries were developed during its first 125 years, until the 1960s, Atlanta essentially functioned as a pipeline in the regional economy. The economy of Atlanta, unlike those of most American cities, was not built on a water port, raw materials, or cheap labor. It was based primarily on a unique ability to respond to the economic organizational demands of the emerging rural market and to assist in the channeling of huge investments by national and international interests into the region.

Bypassed by the first Industrial Revolution, the Southeast, with Atlanta as its hub, is attempting to accommodate and manage a century's economic progress within two or three decades. The primary economic forces—transformation from an agrarian to an industrial society, information-based technological changes and new patterns of mobility to the Sunbelt—are joined by the large challenge of accommodating the correction of historical racial imbalances in the economic, social, and cultural life of the region and the nation.

During the 1960s and 1970s, Atlanta made a quantum jump in economic growth, advancing from its traditional role as a regional distribution, transportation, financial, and professional-services center to that of a large metropolitan area with a considerable set of national and international economic responsibilities. Although the proportion of manufacturing jobs is relatively low, the economy is well diversified and affords a variety of jobs and lifestyle opportunities. This growth has also spawned entirely new industries such as the convention business.

Beginning with internationally acclaimed architect John Portman's Hyatt Regency Hotel in his downtown Peachtree Center in 1967, thousands of new downtown-hotel rooms have been added, and over 3,000 additional rooms have recently been announced.

The state of Georgia joined the privately financed hotel developers in advancing the Atlanta convention business by constructing the 725,000-square-foot Georgia World Congress Center in downtown in 1976. The facility allows the handling of much larger trade shows than was previously possible. Studies have shown that during its first three fiscal years of operation, this facility returned a net profit of $15.5 million. During fiscal 1979, the center was one of the few in the nation that had operating revenues in excess of operating expenses; it actually returned a $350,000 operating-expense appropriation to the state. The state is now planning to double the size of this facility.

In 1961 Atlanta's John Portman provided one of the initial spurs to increased demand for downtown-hotel rooms by building the twenty-two-story, 2-million-square-foot Atlanta Merchandise Mart in the Peachtree Center complex. His plans call for a 50-percent expansion of this mart. In addition, Portman's 1.2-million-square-foot Atlanta Apparel Mart opened in November 1979 adjacent to the Merchandise Mart, further enlarging Atlanta's role as a regional and national commercial center. These facilities lend enormous support to the hotel industry, which in turn supports and is supported by the convention industry. As a result of these developments and skillful promotion, Atlanta is consistently ranked among the top convention cities in the country.

Atlanta had considerable excess office inventory when the 1974 recession hit but was able to work this off by 1979–1980. New downtown developments include the 1.4-million-square-foot, fifty-two-story Georgia-Pacific Corporation headquarters structure scheduled to open in July 1982. (The firm is moving its corporate headquarters back to Georgia from Portland, Oregon.) Approximately 1,200 employees will occupy about one-half of this space. Two blocks south, Marathon U.S. Realties has a 600,000-square-foot, nineteen-story atrium office tower under construction; and a few blocks southeast of this, the state is completing construction of its 850,000-square-foot, twenty-story twin towers that will house 2,500 to 3,000 employees.

Southern Bell Telephone and Telegraph Company began moving 3,600 employees into its new $100-million, forty-seven-story, 2-million-square-foot headquarters on the northern edge of downtown in February 1981. Georgia Power Company's striking new 760,000-square-foot, twenty-four-story headquarters on the edge of downtown in the Bedford-Pine redevelopment area was completed in early 1981. Coca-Cola moved into its new twenty-six-story, 600,000-square-foot corporate-headquarters facility located near the downtown area in early 1980.

Even with these impressive recent downtown developments, the strongest growth continues to the north, where millions of square feet of new office and retail space are being constructed. Downtown Atlanta is finding it increasingly difficult to compete with this upscale northern-perimeter area, where many national firms have located their regional operations because it is free of the congestion and problems of the inner city.

Despite its rise to the status of a national city, Atlanta is still not a national-headquarters city; only three of the *Fortune* 500 industrials are headquartered here (Coca-Cola, Gold Kist, and National Service Industries, to be joined by Georgia-Pacific in 1982). However, at last count, 431 of the *Fortune* 500 have some kind of operations in the city.

Two additional huge public investments have enormous implications for Atlanta's economic future: the opening of Hartsfield Atlanta International Airport on September 21, 1980, and the opening of the first 11.2 miles of the rapid-rail service in 1979. The 2.2-million-square-foot new airport terminal is the world's largest, with 138 aircraft positions, providing efficient service for the world's second-busiest airport (after Chicago's O'Hare). Atlanta is the eighth city in the country to be served by a rapid-rail system (to consist of fifty-three miles upon completion).

In the 1970s *metropolitan* Atlanta's population passed those of Milwaukee, Newark, and Cleveland, moving to sixteenth among the nation's 288 standard metropolitan statistical areas. The *city*, however, continued to lose population, declining 4 percent during the 1970s to 425,000, twenty-ninth among American cities. The city's population is now over 66 percent black, eleventh among the nation's cities in number of black residents and eighth in the proportion of blacks, and exceeded only by Washington, D.C. (over 70 percent), among the cities with total population exceeding 400,000.

These statistics, however, fail to tell the complete story of the difficult shifts in public-private relationships that characterized Atlanta's transition. Change did not come easy, and the process of achieving the level of economic development described here was fraught with difficulty (see figure 8–1).

The Atlanta Public-Private Romance: 1960s Style

The Context for Collaboration

During the late 1950s the once-in-a-generation changing of the business-civic leadership was underway. The older leaders had guided the affairs of the city for four decades and were ready to turn power over to their sons and other successors. For example, Robert W. Woodruff, who brought the Coca-Cola Company to its international prominence and who possessed the largest personal fortune in the South, was turning operations over to J. Paul Austin and others in the company. Ivan Allen, founder of the Ivan Allen Company and a long-time member of the power structure, turned his company and civic affairs over to his son, Ivan Allen, Jr.

Virtually all the power heirs were close friends or acquaintances, most having been born and raised within a few miles of each other. Most had attended the same schools and churches and belonged to the same

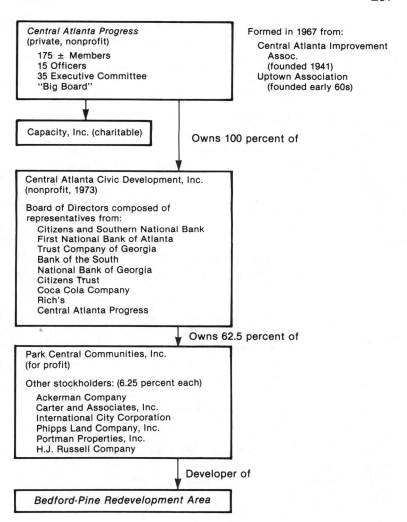

Figure 8–1. Organization of Central Atlanta Progress and Its Subsidiary Groups

clubs. They were white, business oriented, generally not political, well bred and educated, and totally committed to their city.

There were only a handful of them: presidents of the five major banks, Georgia Power Company, Southern Bell Telephone & Telegraph Company, and Atlanta Gas Light Company; chief executive officers of the largest Atlanta-headquartered firms such as Coca-Cola; heads of the leading retail establishments such as Rich's; managers of the Atlanta regional branches of a few larger national firms such as Sears Roebuck; and heads of some of the locally based businesses such as Ivan Allen Company, Haverty Furniture Company, Adair Realty, and a few other realtors.

This was the business-civic leadership, the power structure, as the 1960s began. It was generally progressive, cohesive, and highly efficient. It was also undemocratic by definition. But these leaders got things done, and much of Atlanta's national acclaim during the 1960s reflected their dedication and achievements.

Throughout Atlanta's development during this century, the Chamber of Commerce was the seat of power. As in other cities, the members of the power structure cut their teeth on various posts in the United Appeal, Community Chest, Boy Scouts, and the like and were elected to the chamber board of directors at the same time that they entered the top positions in the business mainstream. Ivan Allen, Jr., had various offices in the chamber and was groomed to become its president.

Anticipating the heavy responsibilities of this, the top-power post in Atlanta, Allen had started planning his recommended program of action about two years before he became president. During 1960 he consulted with his peers in the power structure and assembled what became known as his Six-Point Program to "guide the city through the decade." This program was summarized in chamber literature as follows:

Schools: The Atlanta Chamber of Commerce must take a bold and firm stand on this issue. It must clearly set forth to the public at large and the business community in particular the full implications of the Little Rock, Norfolk and New Orleans stories. It should officially endorse the majority report of the Sibley School Committee (favoring keeping public schools open) and actively work for the passage of the necessary legislation in the January session of the General Assembly. Atlanta's public schools must stay open, and the Chamber should provide its share of vigorous leadership in seeing that they do.

Expressways: The Atlanta Chamber of Commerce must use its every facility to press for a definite step-up in the tempo of local expressway construction. To this end it should lend its full and continuous support to local, state and federal agencies in all possible ways. Although the Chamber takes pride in what has been completed, it must at the same time insist that progress has not been fast enough and that a substantial acceleration in the expressway program is absolutely essential to the health and well-being of the Atlanta community.

Urban Renewal: The Atlanta Chamber of Commerce must vigorously support the city's urban renewal and housing efforts across the board. More specifically, it should: (a) urge and assist in a speedup of activity by the city and its agencies handling the current program; (b) encourage private capital to take advantage of the unprecedented development opportunities in urban renewal projects; (c) press for a further expansion of urban renewal (including an expanding program of finance) in the years immediately ahead; and, (d) work with all agencies concerned in locating new housing for the Negro population.

Auditorium-Coliseum, Stadium: The Atlanta Chamber of Commerce should strongly support the construction of an auditorium-coliseum and a stadium. Finance and building plans should be readied, sites selected, and an operating organization set up as rapidly as possible. The public wants these facilities, and there is no time to lose.

Rapid Transit: The Atlanta Chamber of Commerce should take the lead in pressing for a practical, large-scale rapid-transit system for Atlanta. The scope and timing of the project calls for an immediate start at concrete planning and programming. The only alternative is even more expressways than now projected at five times the cost per mile and even further expansion of automobile traffic loads, with a breakdown in central traffic circulation by the end of the decade.

"Forward Atlanta": The Atlanta Chamber of Commerce should establish and vigorously carry out a three-year "Forward Atlanta" program of education, advertising, and research to carry the Atlanta story over the nation. This program should be supported by a minimum budget of $500,000 per year, raised from the Atlanta business community. Only through such a campaign can Atlanta hope to stay on top in the years ahead. [1]

Of course, Allen could not have foreseen how closely this program would follow through the 1960s. For one thing, he had no idea that he would be mayor during most of that decade. Nor did he realize that a great deal of the program would be accomplished without direct assistance from City Hall. In effect, the unanimous acceptance by the Chamber of Commerce of this program when Allen became its president in January 1961 and his election as mayor the following year made this program an official city plan, although it was never formally accepted as such by the Board of Aldermen.

The Election of Ivan Allen, Jr.

Early in 1961 there was increasing talk about the possibility of Allen running for mayor, from both the black and the white leaderships. As president of the Atlanta Chamber of Commerce, he had already negotiated successfully with the black and white communities over desegregation in the city. *Atlanta Constitution* editor Eugene Patterson's column in March 1961 was a stirring summary of how the community generally felt about Ivan Allen, Jr.

At first Ivan Allen, Jr., was a mystery to most observers of the political and civic scene. It was difficult for those who did not know him well to grasp and hold onto and finally to believe that his motives were entirely altruistic. Why would a native white Atlantan who had enjoyed all the privileges of his position in a white-dominated society want to engage in the required street combat of the times? To subject himself and his family to personal abuse? Why did he not simply sit on the sidelines in his insulated comfort and watch the action?

He had in fact nothing to gain personally but the deep satisfaction of helping hold his city together during the most critical times since the Civil War. He was, and is, the personification of the altruistic man. This essential character is further strengthened by the fact that no cracks have been found during those twelve years since he left office (even by his most severe critics) to detract from his superior leadership.

In his inaugural address to the Board of Aldermen in January 1962, Mayor Allen described the public-private partnership that had guided the city during the 1940s and 1950s, when William B. Hartsfield was mayor, and that he intended to carry forward into his administration:

> Let me state here and now that I think the first rule of thumb for any of the things that must be done in Atlanta is this: that in any area where private enterprise can and will undertake a project, this must be done. This must be encouraged and endorsed and expected. Your city administration will enter the picture only when it has determined that private enterprise cannot undertake those services and provide those facilities that Atlanta must have.[2]

Mayor Allen retained the excellent department heads that he had inherited from the Hartsfield era. He added only his personal secretary and several assistants. Thus one of the most important features of a smoothly operating public-private partnership was retained and enhanced: The stability that ensures not only continuity of administrative practices but solace and comfort to the private sector in its dealings with City Hall.

The building of Atlanta Stadium is perhaps the best example of the city's unique public-private partnership during the sixties. Early in his first term in office, Mayor Allen had attempted to generate interest in building a stadium because he thought Atlanta was ready for major-league baseball and football. In the spring of 1963, a sports editor from the *Atlanta Journal* called the mayor and told him that an owner of an American League team was threatening to move his club away from its home city because of a poor season at the gate and was going to be in Atlanta looking at possible stadium sites.

The owner was not interested in the three sites he was shown and was ready to go back home unless the mayor had something else to offer.

Mayor Allen reviewed a map of the city and declared that he had the best site in the world: an urban-renewal area within a few blocks of downtown that was being cleared of its decaying slums. The team owner agreed with the mayor and told him that if he would build a stadium, the team would come to Atlanta.

Mayor Allen took Citizens & Southern Bank head Mills Lane to the area and showed him around. According to Mayor Allen, the following conversation took place.

"How bad do you want this stadium, Ivan?"

"Bad."

"You've got it. Tell you what, if you'll recreate the Old Stadium Authority and appoint the people I recommend and make Arthur Montgomery [head of the Atlanta Coca-Cola Bottling Company] chairman and me treasurer, I'll pledge the full credit of the C&S bank to build it. And if that's not enough to get it done, you and I can't get it done."[3]

Lane contracted with two local architectural firms to draw up the plans for the stadium. At that point there was no agreement with the prospective team, and there had never been a meeting with the Fulton County commissioners or with the Atlanta Board of Aldermen on the matter. Mayor Allen warned Lane that he had no security, that he should not get in too deep, that he should take some steps to protect himself and the bank. Lane reportedly answered, "You go back over to City Hall and run the city's business, and let me run this show."

On the basis of a verbal understanding that the team would come to Atlanta for the 1965 season, construction was begun. The normal time to build a stadium of that size is easily two or possibly even three years. Mayor Allen, Lane, and Arthur Montgomery had committed themselves to having it done within one year, paying a $600,000 premium. The stadium was completed during 1964, but the team could not make it to Atlanta for the 1965 season. On April 12, 1966, the stadium was jammed for the season opener for the new Atlanta Braves.

The mayor had carried his Chamber of Commerce Six-Point Program to City Hall in 1962 and, with the partnership of his power-structure peers, accomplished a remarkable number of his stated goals:

Schools: Atlanta's public schools did stay open. It was not a uniformly smooth transition, but no one stood in the doorways being refused admittance, and there was no violence.

Expressways: It was considered vital to the economic well-being of downtown Atlanta that the expressway system be completed as rapidly as possible. Six legs of the interstate system intersected in the shadow of the state capital in downtown Atlanta, one of only five cities in the country that enjoyed that distinction. The Chamber of Commerce had a committee that did nothing but monitor progress on the construction and exerting whatever influence was available for expeditious completion.

Urban Renewal: The urban-renewal programs that started in the late fifties continued; some of the cleared land was utilized for the new stadium. Although Mayor Allen enthusiastically welcomed all federal programs, Model Cities, Economic Opportunity, Head Start, and so on, the clearing and redevelopment of urban-renewal areas was not a model of progress.

Auditorium-Coliseum, Stadium: A civic auditorium and adjacent exhibition hall were built on urban-renewal land as was the new stadium, all during the 1960s.

Rapid-Transit: The Chamber of Commerce's rapid-transit committee was headed by Richard Rich of Rich's department stores, one of Atlanta's premier civic leaders. He and his committee members were instrumental in supporting the continued planning for a rapid-transit system for Atlanta. In addition, Mills Lane of the Citizens & Southern National Bank was a leader in the formation of the Action Forum, which it is said was formed for the express purpose of assisting in the passage of the public referendum that authorized the one-cent sales tax to start construction of the Metro Atlanta Rapid Transit Authority (MARTA). This referendum was passed in 1971.

"Forward Atlanta": The multimillion dollar Forward Atlanta Program went forth as Mayor Allen suggested. The business community raised $1.5 million for the first three-year phase and after reviewing the progress made during its implementation, renewed the program for two more three-year periods during the 1960s.

That Atlanta did not suffer the severe racial disturbances experienced by other cities during the sixties is high tribute both to Mayor Allen and to the city's business and civic leadership. It was an extremely volatile period, and Atlanta contained all the ingredients for enormous fireworks: the headquarters for most of the civil-rights organizations and the white-racist groups, a population within the city limits that was approximately 50 percent black, and the status of a converging point for all activists who entered the South.

Although there had been some token desegregation earlier, the city was almost totally segregated when Mayor Allen took office. In his first day in office, Allen ordered all the signs in City Hall designating "white" and "colored" for bathrooms and water fountains removed. From that day forward, the mayor pulled and pushed a sometimes reluctant white business community toward acceptance of desegregation. The white-business power structure was thoroughly pragmatic. They could see what was happening in other southern cities such as Birmingham and Little Rock and did not want their city similarly smeared. In large measure they were fearful that it would not be good for business, rather than being touched by a high sense of justice. Nevertheless, under the leadership of Mayor Allen, the white power structure and the emerging black power structure were able to acquiesce and compromise through the turbulent decade, and Atlanta enjoyed the greatest growth in its history.

However, by 1969 the balance of political power in Atlanta had shifted, and public-private relationships were destined to change.

The Changing Balance of Political Power

Despite the obvious accomplishments of the Allen administration and sincere attempts to provide a context for racial harmony, demographic changes were having their effects on the city's political base. The mayor and the business and civic leadership were effective in dealing with the well-established black power structure. However, Model Cities, the poverty program, and other federally funded efforts were producing a new kind of leadership that was based in the neighborhood and was activist in its attitude. These new leaders were seeking a piece of the action and had federal guidelines requiring citizen participation to back up their claims.

For example, in Atlanta, as in other cities throughout the country, community organizers were active in mobilizing constituencies against the very type of projects that more traditional public-private interests favored such as freeways that cut through low-income neighborhoods and urban-renewal projects that displaced the disadvantaged.

Their idea of progress derived from a perspective different from that of many (if not most) of those who had previously run the city. They were not impressed with the ability of the public and private sectors to get things done, particularly when they felt that things "got done" at the expense of low-income residents.

These new leaders were quick to see that community action alone would not produce the results they were seeking. Clearly, the way to effect change was through the political process, and voter-registration drives became as important as low-income housing and social services.

The Election of Sam Massell

These changes in the political base of Atlanta, along with a more aggressive attitude toward the exercise of power by the black community provided the setting for alterations in the traditional relationships between the public and private sectors. Those alterations were to have a dramatic effect over the next twelve years. According to a study by the Voter Education Project, *The Atlanta Elections of 1969:*

> Since 1953, at least, Atlanta's mayors had been chosen by a coalition composed of virtually all black voters, most of the middle and upper-middle class whites who live on the northside of the city, and a minority of whites elsewhere . . . . The previously successful coalition of black and northside whites was shattered in 1969 . . . . Upper-middle class whites and the city's traditional ''power structure'' lost their former position of influence . . . .

In that year a new coalition of blacks, neighborhood-based organizations, liberal whites, and organized labor combined to elect Sam Massell mayor over the business-backed candidate. This election marked the beginning of the transition toward a new era in public-private relationships that proved more difficult than anyone might have imagined at the time.

Massell became a candidate in 1969 after Mayor Allen declined to run for another term. Although Sam Massell, a young realtor, had been vice mayor under Allen for the past eight years, he was not the choice of the Atlanta business community. The power structure supported the Republican candidate, Rodney Cook, a moderate, an alderman, state representative, and insurance executive whose political philosophy meshed with theirs. Despite the urging of the lame duck Mayor Allen, the black leaders would not accept Rodney Cook as a candidate.

The black leaders, including Dr. Martin Luther King, Sr., Jesse Hill (an insurance-company executive), Reverend Sam Williams, Ralph Abernathy (Dr. King's righthand man at the Southern Christian Leadership Conference), and Senator Leroy Johnson, the first black Georgia representative since Reconstruction, were fascinated with the strong showing in Los Angeles made by Tom Bradley, a black candidate, against incumbent Mayor Sam Yorty. Their feeling was that if Bradley could do so well, there was a very real possibility that a black mayor could be elected in Atlanta. After all, Atlanta's population was 40 percent black, compared with only 25 percent in Los Angeles, and between 1961 and 1969, the proportion of Atlanta's black registered voters had increased from 29 percent to nearly 41 percent. The black community had always gone along with the white power structure, accepting its moderate candidate. But now, inevitably that close coalition was no more.

In the end the black community split its vote between two black candidates and forced a runoff between the two white candidates, Cook and Massell. A new coalition, composed of labor, liberals, and blacks won the race for Massell. This coalition also elected Maynard Jackson as the first black vice mayor in the city's history, and black representation on the Board of Aldermen increased from one to five (out of eighteen).

Massell readily admits that he did not court the business community during his administration. Although a successful businessman in his own right, he was never a part of the private power structure, nor did he choose to be. His personal style was to work one-on-one with selected members of the business community to get things done for the city. He points with pride to the Omni complex, MARTA, and the development of the new airport as examples of his ability to work effectively with business leaders on a project-by-project basis. Those close to his administration agree and state that there were few occasions when Mayor Massell was unable to get the support of the business community that he needed to meet specific objectives.

What Massell did not do well was participate in or give proper attention to social relationships that are part and parcel of public-private cooperation in Atlanta. He was much more comfortable eating lunch at his desk in City Hall than in one of the private clubs frequented by many influential members of the business community. Similarly, he generally turned down invitations to important business-sponsored functions in favor of working late in his office on the details of his administration. Unfortunately, this behavior was seen by many members of the business community as an affront to their stature and importance. Mayor Massell was seen by some as an upstart young liberal who had not paid his dues and was therefore suspect with regard to his support of business community objectives. This opinion was of course influenced by the new constituency he was seen to represent.

But Mayor Massell did not always side with the new coalition that had elected him. In some quarters, he was viewed as overly responsive to the business community and its interests. The Massell administration was therefore characteristically transitional in that it apparently pleased neither side despite a good record in running the city and meeting many community goals.

This conflict in style and lack of communication strained relations between the public and private sectors and laid the groundwork for further change in the 1973 election.

The Election of Maynard Jackson

In 1973 Maynard Jackson successfully challenged Sam Massell, who was seeking a second term. This was seen by most, including Massell, as a natural outgrowth of the new power base that had been formed in 1969. Voter registration in the black community had increased substantially, and neighborhood organizations were stronger. In addition, Jackson had gained considerable recognition and political acumen as vice-mayor.

What was perhaps surprising was the support Jackson received from the business community in his mayoral race. His supporters included some of Atlanta's leading business executives: J. Paul Austin, chairman of the board of the Coca-Cola Company; Richard Kattel, chairman of the board of Citizens & Southern National Bank (successor to Mills Lane); John Portman; and Augustus ("Billy") Sterne, chairman of the board of the Trust Company of Georgia. These members of the white power structure joined prominent blacks including contractor Herman Russell (currently president of the Atlanta Chamber of Commerce); W. L. Calloway, an established realtor, and Jesse Hill, head of Atlanta Life Insurance Company and president of the Atlanta Chamber of Commerce in 1978, in forming the "kitchen cabinet" that Jackson used as an advisory body during his campaign.

Not only was the predominently white power structure prepared to accept a black mayor; it was also willing to work for his election. No one was naive enough to think it would be an easy transition, but all were hopeful that a new, progressive coalition could be forged between downtown and City Hall.

What they were not prepared for was the unrelenting support for the goals of the black community and the neighborhoods that the new mayor would bring to the office. Nor were they prepared for the aggressive style with which he would pursue these goals over the course of the next eight years. Few (if any) business leaders expected a return to the public-private romance of the 1960s when the mayor was considered an extension of the business community. However, they did not expect the polarization between the public and private sectors that characterized the Jackson years.

Clearly, the business community, including Mayor Jackson's backers, both black and white, felt left out of the creation of a new working relationship with the mayor and what he saw as his primary constituency. They were also concerned about what they considered poor appointments and a hostile attitude toward the business community and its objectives.

During the Jackson terms, relations between the public and private sectors deteriorated to the point that representatives of these sectors found it difficult even to talk with each other. Mayor Jackson felt that, as the first black mayor of Atlanta, he had a mandate to be responsive to the needs of the black community and neighborhood organizations that had supported his election to office. In addition, he was sincerely dedicated to these goals, although he had never been poor or particularly active in the civil-rights struggles of the 1950s and 1960s.

Most members of the business community understood these objectives and supported them in principal. But they underestimated the expectations that the black community would place on the mayor to be their advocate for change and the pace at which these changes would be demanded.

The election of Mayor Jackson, however, was not the only vehicle through which changes in political power were taking place. The new city charter and the rise of neighborhood power were also indications that the demands of blacks and low-income groups would have to be recognized and dealt with in the 1970s.

A New City Charter

For a hundred years Atlanta had operated under a weak-mayor form of government. Although the chief executive supposedly had figurehead power, Atlanta had not experienced a weak mayor for decades. William B. Hartsfield and Ivan Allen, Jr., had governed with the full support of the business community. Sam Massell was not generally regarded as a strong mayor, but he had been adept at getting what he wanted from the Board of Aldermen, which maintained administrative authority over the city departments.

The new charter, which became effective with the inauguration of Mayor Jackson in January 1974, separated previously mingled executive and administrative functions. The mayor was given direct authority over the city departments and the new president of the City Council, appointing the council committees and chairpersons. Previously all twelve aldermen were elected citywide, although they were qualified from wards. The new charter provided that twelve of the councilpersons were to be elected by district and six members chosen citywide.

At the same time that Jackson was elected in October 1973, voters threw out most of the lawyers and bankers who had dominated the board and elected eight new councilpersons with no previous legislative experience.

Mayor Jackson had the considerable task of reorganizing City Hall, reducing the number of departments from twenty-six to nine, and installing his own choices as department heads.

Rise to Power of the Neighborhoods

The neighborhood movement cut its teeth in the early 1970s on the issue of whether an interstate highway (I-485) should be constructed through some very stable and desirable neighborhoods near the downtown area. The highway was vigorously opposed by the Citywide League of Neighborhoods. Most of the downtown-business power structure supported the construction of the new thoroughfare, including Central Atlanta Progress, which thought it would be economically beneficial to the center of the city. After months of hearings and confrontations, the city administration opposed the highway, and Governor Jimmy Carter halted it in 1973.

Flushed with this first major victory, the neighborhood groups quickly enlarged their membership base, and new groups were formed throughout the city. Their power was significantly increased when Mayor Jackson took office and by the provision of the new city charter calling for the election of council members on a district basis.

Mayor Jackson had always espoused a deep commitment to the neighborhoods. He tried to assure the business community that bringing neighborhood representatives into the policy process would not exclude business participation. Rather, he proposed amending the traditional two-sided government-business relationship to include what he called "the grassroots community," whether black, white, middle class, or poor.

Jackson's strong support of the neighborhood movement was nourished by the establishment of twenty-four Neighborhood Planning Units throughout the city whose views and recommendations must be considered on all programs affecting each respective planning unit. These organizations provided a legitimate voice for the community in decision making as well as a fertile base from which aggressive community residents could build a power structure to lift them to elective office. During the city elections of 1977, five new council members were elected from these neighborhood power bases, and a special election selected a sixth.

The impact of these changes in the political power base cannot be overestimated. They collectively set the context for public-private relationships and contributed to the concerns of the business community regarding their future role in shaping the goals and objectives of the community.

Although these major changes would have been sufficient to create serious problems with respect to effective communication and cooperation between the public and private sectors, the transition would have been substantially smoother had it not been for a major real-estate recession in 1974, the year Maynard Jackson took office.

Beginning in 1974, Atlanta was trounced by the worst recession experienced since the 1930s. Essentially, it was a real-estate depression thrust onto the city by an unexplained euphoria that would not let lenders and investors refuse to fund most kinds of real-estate development proposed for Atlanta. As a result of this overbuilding, foreclosures were announced almost daily, developers went bankrupt, some of the larger banks with heavy real-estate portfolios were thoroughly shaken, and architects, construction workers, real-estate agents and brokers, and anyone associated with the real-estate development industry were on the streets looking for almost any kind of work. It was an extended bath; in the spring of 1977, three years after its beginning, there were still 8 million square feet of office space vacant in the metropolitan area, 30 percent of it in the immediate downtown district. Thousands of condominium units were auctioned off at less than fifty cents on the dollar, and many of the major office buildings changed hands several times.

It was a sharp and steep plunge from the nationally acclaimed "top of the heap" achieved in the 1960s and early 1970s, and it had an adverse psychological impact not only on business leaders but also on the community as a whole. It also had an impact on the feasibility of many of the goals of the Jackson administration. For example, the promotion of minority businesses, a major objective, would have been far easier to achieve in the context of economic expansion. Similarly, finding employment for blacks and other low-income individuals would have been less difficult in a growing economy. Moreover, the acceptance of these goals by the business community and its energetic commitment to their attainment would have been far more likely if it had not had its own problems just staying in business.

It was clear that the business community needed to develop new ways of dealing with the mayor and City Hall. It was also clear that new institutional mechanisms would be needed to bridge the gap that was developing within the community over the definition of progress in Atlanta.

Central Atlanta Progress

Formation

Central Atlanta Progress (CAP) was formed in 1967 by the merger of the Central Atlanta Improvement Association and the Uptown Association.

The Central Atlanta Improvement Association had been organized in 1941 to represent the interests of the business and property owners in the immediate vicinity of the center city. This organization concentrated largely on public-works improvement such as street and parking improvements and construction of viaducts over the downtown railroads. It also was instrumental in the passage of bond referenda. Although the membership consisted of the most influential downtown firms and top community business leaders generally headed the organization, the seat of the business-power structure remained the Chamber of Commerce.

The Uptown Association was founded in the early 1960s by the chairman of the First National Bank, which had just completed a major new office building in an area about two miles north of the center of downtown, and the regional head of Sears, Roebuck, whose major retail-catalog facility was located in the same general area. They were concerned about generally deteriorating conditions in the area and pushed for public improvements, primarily street widenings. The association never developed into much more than a quiet neighborhood business group.

During the 1960s Atlanta began its greatest building boom, and the famous Forward Atlanta national promotion program was launched under the auspices of the Chamber of Commerce. As the area blossomed into what *Business Week* described as "the Cinderella city of the 1960s," it became apparent that the central business district had far outgrown its old boundaries, that the larger area could be better served by a single organization. In 1967 the Central Atlanta Improvement Association and the Uptown Association were merged to form CAP, a private, nonprofit corporation.

CAP immediately launched the forerunner of a continuing series of public-private partnerships, the Central Atlanta Study. This comprehensive planning effort was funded by a U.S. Department of Transportation grant and matching funds contributed by the city and CAP. In its last year (1969) under the leadership of Mayor Allen, the city contracted with CAP to produce the plan. This policy and administrative arrangement formed the pattern for several other city-CAP planning-and-implementation projects that continue to this day. A seven-member policy committee guided the effort, cochaired by Mayor Massell, Alderman Wyche Fowler, and CAP President John Portman.

But although CAP was led by some of the city's most powerful and influential businessmen, it was still essentially a technically based research-and-planning organization whose executive director was a professional planner. The Chamber of Commerce was still the organizational instrument of power.

Change

By 1973, it was obvious that the city was facing a new order of problems and opportunities that could fundamentally and permanently change the old paternalistic pattern of public-private cooperative efforts. For one thing, there was a very good chance that the city would have its first black mayor before the year was out. Although Atlanta's community power structure generally viewed itself as progressive on racial matters, the business leaders knew there would be a period of adjustment of substantial proportions to a predominently black city administration, which appeared inevitable.

In addition, a new powerbase was emerging: the neighborhoods. During 1973, a storm of protest over the proposed construction of major auto thoroughfares through older, stable neighborhoods was launched by those neighborhoods. The forces favoring the highways, which included the business leadership and CAP, were defeated when then Governor Jimmy Carter canceled the proposed federal-state program. (Today new homes are being constructed on strips of neighborhood land that had been condemned and cleared for these highways.)

It is impossible to determine whether a conscious decision was made by CAP leadership to strengthen its capability to meet these and other new problems, but the beginning of an enlarged, more visible, and more powerful role in the affairs of the city began with the recruitment of Dan E. Sweat, Jr., to the top professional staff post of CAP in April 1973. Harold Brockey, head of Rich's, Atlanta's largest homegrown chain of department stores (now owned by Federated), probably played an influential role in enticing Sweat away from his position as executive director of the Atlanta Regional Commission, the official overall planning agency for the area. Sweat had also been chief administrative officer to Mayors Allen and Massell.

Steeped in the political wherewithal to "get things done," Sweat brought to CAP a vigor, a force, and not a little impatience that remains characteristic of the organization to this day. He is regarded, along with his "bosses," as one of the most influential people in the city. He changed the nature of the top staff position at CAP from that of simply implementor of policy to that of full participant in setting policy.

The mayor and City Council members dealt directly with Sweat on most matters, and the CAP Board of Directors seemed to fully approve this procedure. Some observers said that the CAP board wants Sweat to handle these direct communications, that they do not want to. be forced to deal with what they consider to be inept members of the City Council or with the mercurial disposition of a mayor who never bothered to return their phone calls.

After Sweat's arrival at CAP, the organization swiftly became the base of business power in the city, the position that had been held by the Chamber of Commerce for almost a hundred years. There was no fight, no challenge to this transition. It was so smooth that it was hardly noticed even by the participants.

Organization

Membership in CAP, (about two hundred in early 1981) is limited to the chief executive officers of private business firms and commercial-property owners in Atlanta. The only requirement for membership is a willingness to work for the collective interests of the downtown economy. CAP prides itself on being the reservoir of power and fast action, admitting that its process is not very democratic. In 1981 there were few blacks and only one woman on its 102-member board of directors. CAP is not apologetic about this: It simply points out that there are very few women and blacks in corporate positions of power and therefore eligible to sit on the board.

Overall policy is set by CAP's fifteen officers, who meet monthly; the executive committee of thirty-five that meets quarterly; and the larger board of directors that meets annually. The operating budget of about $300,000 is financed primarily through membership dues, although general fund raising is sometimes utilized for special projects, along with some foundation support. The city also contracts with CAP for special projects. CAP operates "lean and mean" as described in the February 1981 *Business Atlanta* magazine. There are only six staff members in addition to Sweat; two are vice presidents in charge of projects, and the other four are supporting staff.

CAP operates with no standing committees; task forces are created for special projects and are dissolved at their completion.

Inner-City Housing

In 1973 CAP continued its intimate involvement with efforts to produce downtown housing for moderate- and upper-income families by jointly funding (with a federal grant) a "back-to-the-city" housing study. The Central Atlanta Housing Policy Committee, consisting of representatives of CAP and the city, was established to guide this year-long study. The motivation for encouraging the return of middle- and upper-middle-income people to downtown was initially direct economic self-interest. But the involvement was quickly broadened to a leadership role in the development of policies and action programs to generate balanced housing for the entire central-city area.

The report and recommendations were presented to the City Council and the mayor in mid-1974. Specific goals were detailed: increased housing-stock rehabilitation and new housing starts, with emphasis on an increase in the proportion of units for middle- and upper-income families. Public reorganizational changes were recommended along with implementation strategies, reflecting a recognition that "no sustained involvement by the private sector in housing and community development can be expected without some public sharing of risks and responsibility for a coordinated program—the state, local government, and private business community must take a larger, more direct role in housing. Support of the federal government, however, is still an essential element."[4]

Transition Role

CAP's role in the Atlanta transition has been difficult at best. Both the organization and its president made front-page news in their controversies with Mayor Jackson and his staff. However, they have continued to keep the lines of communication open and to work out problems between the public and private sectors on a case-by-case basis. Perhaps of more importance, CAP is seen as a friend by many of the City Council members and a number of neighborhood leaders. Many would argue, in fact, that without CAP, the economic progress that has been made over the last twelve years would have been impossible. In any case, CAP has proven to be a necessary element in Atlanta for linking diverse interests and providing staff capacity during a period of major political and economic change.

In playing this difficult role, CAP has managed to get both sides to "hang in" during the transition period. In this way, CAP has placed itself in a key position for providing a forum for negotiation and compromise between the business community and public-sector leadership both now and in the future.

Prior to the recent election, for example, CAP's president and members of the CAP board worked with *both* candidates for mayor and their respective staffs to develop a comprehensive agenda for the 1980s that could be endorsed by public- and private-sector representatives. This is particularly significant in light of the fact that one of the candidates, Sidney Marcus, had the strong backing of the business community. Primarily because of its role as facilitator, CAP felt confident that the business community could work effectively with either candidate. Moreover, this process helped to ensure that a spirit of cooperation would be adopted at the outset of the new administration.

Atlanta Chamber of Commerce

The Atlanta Chamber of Commerce began to lose its position as the seat of the downtown power structure in 1973 when CAP began its activist role in negotiations and programs on behalf of the central-city area. The reasons for this shift are complex and must be evaluated both within the context of the political, social, economic, and racial changes occurring in the city and in terms of the personalities of leaders.

The chamber had been the acknowledged business powerbase at least since 1925, when the first Forward Atlanta Commission was formed to promote the city on the national level. During the remainder of that decade, the business community spent nearly $1 million on an unprecedented advertising and public-relations program predicated on the then-novel theory ''that a city can be sold just as merchandise and services are sold.''

Business leaders knew that they faced the difficult tasks not only of getting across the manifold assets of Atlanta to the national, industrial, and investment communities but also of dispelling some of the false illusions harbored about the South in general.

Ivan Allen, Sr., served on the Forward Atlanta Commission during that period and was chairman of the industrial-development sales effort conducted through the chamber staff.

Ivan Allen, Jr., was president of the chamber in 1961, when the decision was made to launch another Forward Atlanta Program. The chamber raised and spent millions on advertising, public relations, and business solicitation, taking credit for the massive 1960s building boom in Atlanta, and retaining its position as the seat of business power.

The Chamber of Commerce had always been the official economic-development arm of the city. Like Mayor Hartsfield before him, Mayor Allen routinely referred all such matters to it, never creating an economic-development arm within the city-hall administration. The chamber–city-hall relationship was smooth on all issues with the exception of a brief Civil Rights Bill disagreement.

With the election of Mayor Jackson in 1973, this relationship changed. Jackson formed the Office of Economic Development under the Department of the Mayor. He also founded the quasi-public Atlanta Economic Development Corporation to coordinate Atlanta's economic programs and projects. With these actions, the mayor further removed City Hall from the Chamber of Commerce-based economic programs.

Coincident with these changes, the board of directors of the Atlanta chamber departed from its tradition of top business-executive leadership by bringing in, late in 1974, a new top executive with extensive background in the public-service sectors. His goal was to seek out the broadest possible community consensus and encourage greater participation by community members in organizations that stressed a unified approach to goal-setting, action planning, development, and implementation.

Thus the Chamber of Commerce began its transition from the center of downtown business power to a broader-based organization striving to serve many constituencies across an enlarged geographic area. Not all business leaders agreed with this dispersion of energies or with specific measures taken. Among those measures were:

The sale of *Atlanta Magazine,* a slick, nationally acclaimed city publication started by the chamber in 1961 at the beginning of the Forward Atlanta Program.

The move of the chamber's offices from the Commerce Building, which is only one block from the center of the city, to the nearly bankrupt and consistently troubled Omni International office/retail complex, which is several blocks west of the center city. This complex is regarded by some as a poor psychological setting for a community-promotional organization.

The creation of a number of area councils throughout the metropolitan region that deliberate independently of the chamber's board of directors and that are intended as a device to bring the region's smaller business firms in outlying areas into an active role with the chamber.

This changing style is also evident in the advertising and public-relations campaign conducted by the chamber. The successful Forward Atlanta campaign of the 1960s was fired by the slogan "the City Too Busy to Hate" (started by Mayor William B. Hartsfield) and was always upbeat and directed to the national business interests outside Atlanta.

The 1974–1977 recession rocked the city, dispelling the recession-proof theory espoused by city advocates, and was concrete proof that the recently experienced rate of growth would not continue. Despair was thoroughly prevalent when the chamber then began its city-oriented media campaign with the slogan "Look Up, Atlanta," which, however well intended, signaled to the national investment community that the city was well aware of its problems.

In mid-1981, the chamber coordinated a public-service television, radio, and newspaper campaign with the slogan "Let's Keep Pulling Together, Atlanta," which promotes the courage of the city in the wake of the shocking murders and disappearances of black youths. The campaign started when Coca-Cola representatives asked Mayor Jackson what they could do to help promote a feeling of unity in the city. Reportedly, about $150,000 in business cash is being leveraged into a $2-million effort through donations of ad-agency time and efforts by the large corporate clients.

The chamber seems to have lost some of its traditionally close co-operation of the local press. In the 1960s the press never publicly disagreed with the Chamber leadership; it was always brought in at the beginnings of all programs and issues, and disagreements were worked out before-hand. Now, however, the press does not hesitate to disagree.

Some Post-1970 Facilitiating Structures

Research Atlanta

Research Atlanta was formed in 1971 as a nonpartisan, nonprofit cor-poration for the purpose of researching and publishing studies of various critical public-policy issues affecting metropolitan Atlanta. This privately supported organization originally developed fact sheets on a number of public issues. By early 1981, more than eighty studies had been published on topics ranging from economic development, taxation, and public fi-nance to housing, public education, and government structure.

No public monies are accepted for Research Atlanta. The board has established an endowment of $135,000; the interest is used to help pay office expenses. Donations from private contributors finance the remain-der of the operating budget. Five report topics are initiated each year by the Project Selection Committee, which is made up of members of the thirteen-person Board of Directors. Draft reports are forwarded to the relevant public officials and are published only after they have given their endorsements and any significant disagreements have been resolved.

Leadership Atlanta

Leadership Atlanta was founded in 1969 by the Atlanta Chamber of Commerce and the Florence C. and Harry English Memorial Fund. The program provides civic and social education to future leaders in Atlanta businesses, government, and community organizations.

Of the first class of fifty, thirty were drawn from Atlanta firms that believed their nominees had the capability of becoming president of the company in the 1980s. These businesses paid the tuition for their nom-inees submitted from the community at large, government, churches, and community organizations. These students were judged to be on the verge of becoming civic leaders.

Participants begin meeting in October of each year for a ten-month series of seminars, lectures, and field trips. Subjects include economy and government, education, ecology, crime, poverty, urban transporta-tion, health services, and labor. Practical experiences offered include cruising in police cars at night and tours of various neighborhood centers.

An effort is made to achieve a sexual and racial balance in all the classes and the number of black men and women of both races has increased substantially.

Officials praise the value of the commonality of experiences gained by Leadership Atlanta graduates. They also consider it important that these graduates will continue to communicate as they come into contact with each other in various business and civic efforts through the years and thus will be able to work together more productively as they mature in the community.

Action Forum

Action Forum was started in the late 1960s by Mills Lane. He recruited W.L. Calloway, an established black realtor to assist in selecting those to be invited to participate. Calloway and his friends invited about fifteen blacks; Lane recruited the same number of whites. All participants except City Council member Q.V. Williamson were, and are, from private businesses.

The membership is a cross-section of community leaders. They meet on a Saturday morning once a month to freely discuss key issues facing the city. There are no officers, and no minutes are taken. It is up to each member to act on the issues discussed in his personal and business dealings outside of Action Forum.

Action Forum claims some credit for influencing the passing of the referendum that authorized the current 1-percent sales tax being used for construction of MARTA, and many believe that Action Forum was, in fact, organized primarily for that purpose.

Action Forum is not generally regarded as being an effective mediating instrument. It is virtually impossible, however, to measure the value of the frank interchange of ideas and open discussion of community problems among this racially balanced group of community leaders.

The Urban Study Institute

The Urban Study Institute was founded in 1979 to monitor the state budget process, identify inequities in state-spending formulas and the distribution of burdens for specific programs, and bring these matters to the attention of the relevant public and private institutions.

State Senator Paul D. Cloverdall, an Atlanta insurance executive and chairman of the Fulton County senate delegation, personally orchestrated the creation of the institute. With political and financial support from both the city and Fulton County, he approached the Atlanta Chamber of

Commerce, which quickly agreed to finance the organization's budget, originally through contributions from individual members and later from the chamber budget. The Metropolitan Atlanta Community Foundation provided some initial funding, and later the Atlanta Board of Education joined as a budget participant.

The institute began operations in January 1980. An executive director was recruited from the staff of the City Council and is now assisted by three professional staff members. Areas to be researched are generally identified by the Board of Directors, which consists of the chairman of the Fulton County senate and house delegations and the Fulton County Commission, the mayor, and the president of the Atlanta Chamber of Commerce.

The institute claims credit for identifying and successfully claiming $2.2 million in new revenues from the state to Atlanta and Fulton County and the equivalent of $1.25 million in services from the state, which now operates the juvenile-detention center in Atlanta. The institute is currently working on the budgeting aspects of Grady Hospital and mental-health programs.

The Greater Atlanta Project (GAP) was born in crisis. The rapidly rising crime rate in Atlanta during the 1970s and the growing national perception of Atlanta as a center of violent crime prompted a number of Atlanta organizations to form a coalition through which communications could be established with the Department of Public Safety, the Metropolitan Atlanta Crime Commission, and the local and national public. The coalition consisted of the Atlanta Chamber of Commerce, CAP, the Atlanta Convention and Business Bureau, and the Georgia Hospitality and Travel Association. The business members of these organizations obviously had the most to lose by the increasingly adverse local and national publicity on crime in Atlanta; the latter two groups would be affected especially severely if huge convention business were jeopardized.

GAP selected two aspects of the problem on which to focus its resources: assisting the city in fighting crime head on and conducting a campaign to promote Atlanta locally and nationally in the hope of correcting the magnified perception of the crime problem. In October GAP entered into a $65,000 contract with a professional public-relations firm for a six-month effort.

During the period from October 1979 to April 1980, the four-member organizations unilaterally continued to work with the city on a large number of aspects of the crime problem. Meanwhile the public-relations firm conducted a survey of executives in charge of business relocation and convention planners throughout the country to ascertain the extent to which Atlanta's reputation had been tarnished and to provide background for a public-relations campaign. Surveys of corporate executives were simultaneously conducted in New York, Chicago, and Washington, D.C.

On the basis of these surveys as well as queries of city leaders, the public-relations firm prepared news releases and fact sheets, assisted the Bureau of Police Services in local press communications, and set up a two-day trip to New York by the mayor and prominent Atlantans to meet with the media.

At the conclusion of the public-relations contract in April 1980, GAP expanded its membership to include the Atlanta Business League, a predominently black business organization. Joel Goldberg of Rich's who had been instrumental in the formation and conduct of GAP, agreed to officially head the effort. The group's name was changed to the Atlanta Business Coalition. The top *staff* executive's of the member organizations now meet twice a month to discuss and deal with problems facing the city, but the top *business* executives are not directly involved in these meetings. Only issues common to the five organizations are entertained. These are subsequently brought to the attention of the boards of directors of the members by their chief executives.

Some of the achievements of the Atlanta Business Coalition are that it:

Pushed for the expansion of the World Congress Center in Atlanta (a state-financed $80-million expansion of this major meeting center);

Pushed for a hotel-motel tax;

Assisted in the preparation of "Goals for the 1980s" being conducted by Research Atlanta;

Assisted in the "Block Parent" program, which provides for participating businesses to display an emblem indicating children should report there if they are accosted by strangers (This is a direct result of the murder of black children in Atlanta.); and

Printed and distributed brochures addressing the question of crime and how to protect oneself from it.

Bedford-Pine Urban-Redevelopment Project

The Bedford-Pine Project consists of a 278-acre urban-renewal area near downtown Atlanta that was earmarked for new residential, commercial, and retail development. It is the most ambitious public-private development partnership in the city today and could have a more enduring, positive effect on the inner city than any other effort in its history, with the exception of the partially opened rail rapid-transit system.

Bedford Pine has been plagued with delays, frustrations, and considerable public controversy. That portions of it are at least under construction is a tribute to the unshakable commitment, innovative talents, and perhaps most of all, tenacity of CAP and its subsidiary, Park Central Committee, Inc. (PCC).

Beginnings. Buttermilk Bottoms was part of Atlanta's old Fourth Ward. Some say its name was derived from the thick milky puddles that were created when rainfall mixed with the light-colored clay soil. It was a largely thrown-together community of ramshackle wooden-frame apartments, duplexes, and older homes converted to apartments. Most of its streets had never been paved, and the area was poorly drained and regularly flooded. There were approximately 2,800 dwelling units in 1,200 structures, only 50 of which met minimum living standards. Inspectors had found one structure housing fifty families sharing two bathrooms.

Buttermilk Bottoms, along with the area to the east, was designated by the city as an urban-renewal area in 1963, and property acquisition began by the Atlanta Housing Authority (AHA), the city's designated redevelopment agency. Early on Mayor Allen led the development of a new civic center within this area on the site of the old community elementary school. The families being displaced organized an active citizens group and participated in the design of an acceptable neighborhood-development program in 1968. Under that plan a new elementary school was built within the redevelopment area to replace the school that had been razed. In addition, a recreation center and a park were constructed.

A 311-unit public-housing project was completed by AHA in 1972 to house some of the people displaced by the razing of the neighborhood. The remaining displaced families (approximately 2,000) were dispersed into other public-housing projects throughout the city, principally near downtown.

The AHA completed disposition on sixty-eight acres of the larger redevelopment area in the early 1970s. Developments on this acreage included the Mercer University School of Pharmacy, a professional building for the Georgia Baptist Hospital, Butler Street Baptist Church, a substation of Georgia Power Company, a park-recreation center, and five miniparks.

In April 1972 Atlanta was chosen as one of twenty-three cities to participate in the Department of Housing and Urban Development's Project Rehab to rehabilitate 1,000 units of moderate-income housing in the inner city. Between 600 and 700 units were found in the Bedford Pine urban-renewal area along Boulevard and Parkway Drive. Two local development firms won the contracts, and work was begun on the HUD-subsidized rental units. The total estimated cost was approximately $13 million. (As of May 1981, these rehabilitations were virtually completed.)

By the early 1970s it became apparent that the Neighborhood Development Program adopted in 1968 had severe flaws. It was determined that the area originally designated for light-industrial purposes had evolved into a higher land-use category, too expensive for industrial use. In addition, intensive efforts to attract developers to build low- and moderate-income residential units were failing, even though Atlanta was in the midst of its nationally acclaimed ''go-go'' building boom. Developers, lenders, and investors locally and throughout the country seemed to believe there was no end to this euphoric state of affairs. With very profitable projects throughout the city and in the rapidly growing suburbs, developers had all the work they could handle. At this time there was no private-sector involvement in Bedford Pine.

HUD Spurs Development. In January 1973, in anticipation of the shift from the old urban-renewal to the community-development block-grant program, HUD cut off all funds for property acquisition in Atlanta unless the land to be acquired could be disposed of within one year. AHA received a year's extension to complete acquisition *contingent* on having the property under contract of sale by June 30, 1974, *and* having an assurance from at least one prospective purchaser to bid on the property.

During the summer of 1973, AHA, pressured by HUD to act swiftly, advertised for proposals for the development of a 78-acre tract in the larger Bedford Pine urban-redevelopment area, which originally consisted of approximately 278 acres. This request did not dictate what the projects should be, but it encouraged proposals with a strong housing content, and simply specified that only one-hundred subsidized units were required.

AHA had been charged with failure to exercise its responsibility even at this early date by not setting specific public goals for Bedford Pine. Rather, AHA left the larger portion of goal setting to the developer-bidders, who, according to some officials, were the least qualified.

The downtown-business community had long been aware of the vital importance of intown housing to the maintenance of a viable city. Prior to 1973 the Task Force on Housing, chaired by Paul Austin (of Coca-Cola) and John Portman, had studied the possibilities of replacing some of the poorer residential communities with some moderate- to high-income housing. At that time, Coca-Cola was investing millions of dollars in its new world-headquarters complex, which was separated from downtown by Techwood Homes, the oldest public-housing project in the nation, built in 1937, and Portman was continuing his heavy investments in the

Peachtree Center. With the appointment of the highly regarded public administrator Dan Sweat to the presidency of CAP, this organization moved even faster into planning intown housing.

When first advised of AHA's plan to ask for development proposals for Bedford Pine, CAP attempted a considerable amount of public persuasion, urging prospective bidders to plan a strong housing program. CAP was not satisfied that a qualified developer could be persuaded to enter what was sure to be a drawn-out process; the track record of developers attempting to work profitably on public projects was not good. Therefore, CAP moved quickly to form a subsidiary, for the specific purpose of responding to the AHA request for development proposals.

PCC was first set up as a nonprofit organization, but AHA took exception to this status, maintaining that it must be for-profit and have a track record in order to qualify as a redeveloper.

The executive director of AHA called Sweat one morning and requested that Sweat have his six PCC-board-member developers, who were to be the guiding force behind PCC, at the AHA offices that afternoon to meet with the AHA board. The purpose of this meeting was for CAP to show that these major Atlanta development firms were truly united and would stand behind a PCC proposal on Bedford Pine. In effect, CAP was called on to dispel the notion that PCC was just a ''paper'' organization. (It was and still is, in a sense, just that.) By some miracle, all six top executives were in Atlanta on that day, and all six showed up at the meeting. From that time forward, AHA accepted PCC as a qualified developer.

A major challenge for PCC was to arrange the financing for the preparation of the plan, pay operating expenses, and acquire the acreage if its proposal was accepted. The resulting solution was one of the many great stories of the abiding civic commitment of Atlanta's downtown financial institutions. All six of the largest downtown-based banks agreed to provide the necessary line of credit ($10 million) for these purposes; all six are represented on the Board of Directors of the nonprofit parent of PCC, Central Atlanta Civic Development, Inc.

From the date of this commitment in late 1973, when the monies were beginning to be drawn down, until the execution of the land-disposition agreement and first sale of property in May 1978, these banks carried the project without the slightest hint of withdrawing the loans, which amounted to over $2 million at that time.

PCC prepared a broad development plan for 4,500 housing units, including the specified minimum number of subsidized units. This proposal was submitted to AHA in October 1973.

PCC Selected as Redeveloper. From the six bids received, AHA selected the PCC bid for $11 million. This bid was secured by a $1-million commitment for planning and disposition. The assignment was subject to the preparation of a final comprehensive development plan that would be acceptable to AHA, the Project Area Committee (PAC), the City Council, and the mayor. Subsequent approvals were also required from the Atlanta Regional Commission, HUD, and the Council on Environmental Quality. In addition, PCC was required to submit an acceptable environmental-impact statement on the project. PCC was given until June 30, 1974 (six months), to prepare an acceptable plan.

PAC is a neighborhood citizens advisory group that HUD mandated should be consulted on the project. The activist head of this group, Ted Clark, wrenched a major concession from AHA: The plan must receive the PAC stamp of approval before it could be submitted to the City Council and/or the mayor for approval. This move was later sincerely regretted by PCC and, some say, by AHA, although that agency never admitted it. The concession gave PAC veto power over the plan and gave Clark considerable personal power.

AHA provided funding for a full-time professional planner to advise PAC during all the negotiations. Some feel that AHA simply shifted its responsibilities and subsequent pressures to the PAC, which was not professionally qualified to conduct the detailed planning.

Negotiations, proposals, counterproposals and threats (primarily from Clark) began in earnest; all were reported almost daily and in detail in the local press.

The June 30, 1974, deadline for submitting an acceptable plan was extended until the environmental-impact statement was prepared. A local legal-aid attorney sued to amend the environmental-impact statement in accordance with the new plan. PAC head Ted Clark brought in PAC as a friend of the court, and the scope of the statement was expanded to include social environment—health, employment, housing, daycare, and other social services. Thus the final plan had to agree with the environmental-impact statement. The court ruled that the sales agreement transferring the land to PCC could not be consummated until HUD approved the expanded statement.

This delay was not protested by PCC. Early in 1974, Atlanta began its march into its deepest real-estate recession since the 1930s. The developers and bankers who put PCC together were having severe problems of their own and could not have easily proceeded with the development of Bedford Pine even if the impact statement had not been required. PCC continued with the development of the plan during 1974 and early 1975 while the statement was being prepared and PCC investors were busily taking care of their own recession-induced problems.

The major point of dissension between PAC and PCC concerned the number of low- and moderate-income housing units to be included in the development. PAC insisted that half the units be set aside for the poor, which meant subsidies. Also PAC wanted these subsidized units integrated fully into, and indistinguishable from, middle- and upper-income units in the project, even scattered throughout the same buildings containing the market-rate units. PCC, being composed of developers and lenders, was aware of the difficulties of marketing such mixed apartments, particularly in the upper price levels. And one of the principal objectives of PCC and its parent, CAP, was to lure middle- and upper-income residents back to the city.

In addition, PCC did not want to give the impression to developers, lenders, investors, or particularly renters and homeowners that Bedford Pine was some sort of social experiment. They feared that this would put a stigma on the entire development.

It is significant that Mayor Jackson took office at the precise moment, January 1974, that the controversy over the Bedford Pine project started heating up. Even though the mayor maintained a hands-off stance, it was inevitable that a considerable portion of the general public, as well as of the metropolitan business community, viewed the torrid confrontation as an introduction to a black city administration.

PCC Plans Accepted. In late 1974 Mayor Jackson attempted to break the PCC-PAC-AHA deadlock by appointing a negotiating team with the agreement from the parties that there would not be a break in the talks until an agreement had been reached. Although the goal was to lure middle- and upper-income residents back to the city, an agreement was finally reached that 25 percent of the housing units should be subsidized. On March 27, 1975, the PCC plan was finally approved by all the parties, providing for 3,000 housing units, high-rise and mid- and low-rise, with 25 percent as family units and two-thirds of all the units available for owner occupancy. The plan also allowed for 2.6-million square feet of office space, 250,000 square feet for a community shopping center, and 150,000 square feet for convenience retail uses and public-private and commercial recreation facilities.

During these negotiations, the environmental-impact statement was being prepared. Although the court ordered HUD to prepare the statement, it was actually put together by PCC at a cost of about $300,000. The ten-pound document was finally approved by HUD on November 8, 1976, after two years of processing. It contained a lengthy set of provisions for social services by PCC and for the funding of a shopping center to be turned over to PAC. The approval of the EIS was the signal that AHA was then legally able to execute an agreement for the sale of land to PCC.

Over the next three years, the land-disposition agreement was negotiated between PCC and AHA with continuous and vigorous intrusions by PAC. The resulting document, four-hundred pages long, is an extremely technical treatment of staged takedowns, transferable development rights, and a long list of social obligations that PAC and AHA extracted from PCC.

Although PCC is not technically a "redeveloper" and does not intend to become one in the strictest sense of that term, the intricate details of the circumstances under which it can take down specific parcels of the seventy-eight-acre tract, and for what purposes, had to be spelled out. Furthermore, PAC insisted on compliance with a seemingly unlimited number of community wishes and demands.

PAC wanted PCC to guarantee 650 units of low-income housing *whether or not federal, state, and local subsidies were available.*

PAC and AHA wanted review over architectural design.

PAC wanted parks, open space, and recreation facilities guaranteed, even if public financial assistance was not available.

PAC and AHA wanted PCC to submit plans for landscaping, grading, pedestrian, and bicycle paths for review and approval.

PAC wanted PCC to provide seed money for the development of a shopping center to be operated by a community-development corporation, with profits to be used for community services.

PAC wanted PCC to give first preference in employment to current and former residents of the area and require its contractors and subcontractors to do the same.

PAC wanted PCC to provide space and resources for a health-maintenance center and child-care center.

AHA wanted to approve the location and form of the art to be provided in Bedford Pine. One-half of 1 percent of the total cost of development is being set aside for art.

PAC and AHA wanted to approve graphic-design systems, exterior lighting, people-moving systems, waste-collection systems, safety and conservation programs, and so on.

During the summer of 1975, PCC hinted that it was ready to take PAC to court rather than make any further concessions. Under urban-renewal law, PAC must concur in plans for redevelopment unless it has withheld its approval unreasonably. Whether unreasonable or not would be decided in court. Mayor Jackson then assumed the role of mediator in the deadlock and called a meeting on November 22, 1975, for representatives of PAC, PCC, AHA, and the City Council.

PCC was hoping that the mayor could pull PAC in line with their proposal, but PAC maintained that the mayor could not force it to settle for anything. HUD said the meetings could be illegal because the press was excluded. PAC said that it wanted the press excluded because PCC controlled the press and would use it as a tool to bully PAC. Jack Traver, owner of the *Atlanta Journal* and the *Atlanta Constitution,* was a member of the executive committee of CAP.

Throughout early 1976, AHA, and PAC continued to haggle over the terms of the disposition agreement. In August 1976, PCC publicly threatened to cancel its plans entirely, accusing the city of failing to carry out its commitments for infrastructure improvements in Bedford Pine. At that time PCC had spent over $500,000 in planning and negotiations, paid by the original stockholder investments, a loan of $400,000 from the Atlanta Civic Enterprises Foundation, and draws on the bank loans.

In January 1977 HUD announced a grant of $3.5 million to be used for streets, sewers, lighting, landscaping, sidewalks, and the like in Bedford Pine. The city was to spend an additional $1.2 million.

On January 29, 1977, Ted Clark publicly blasted PCC for reportedly trying to reduce the number of housing units from 2,250 to 1,850 and for other purported violations of the agreement.

Meanwhile work continued slowly on the public improvements to which the city and AHA were committed, with the widening, upgrading, and relocation of streets and the construction of a major new connecting street through the project. PCC was soliciting the interest of qualified developers for specific projects within the overall urban-redevelopment area. This was most difficult because PCC did not yet have control of the property and could not easily negotiate land costs for residential development until the dimensions of the land writedown resulting from a substantial commercial-office land sale were known. Furthermore, the controversy frightened potential developers. Nevertheless, PCC was successful in setting up a meeting with an executive of one of the country's largest supermarket chains to explore the possibility of this firm's becoming a tenant in the proposed community shopping center, in which PAC would play an ownership role. But after meeting Clark, the executive reportedly left and could not be persuaded to return.

City Pushes for Action

Exasperated by the protracted negotiations, George Berry, the mayor's highly respected chief administrative officer, addressed the City Council,

"The time comes in every project that somebody has to get tough and crack the whip. This time has arrived with Bedford Pine." He encouraged the city to give PCC, AHA, and PAC until March 31, 1978, to resolve their differences. If they failed to do so, he recommended looking for another developer. As of this time, Mr. Berry said, the city had invested $18 million in the area, including the Civic Center, and PCC had spent approximately $800,000 on planning.

PCC President Joseph G. Martin immediately replied, "For the City to say we need to be pressured to do something we've broken our backs on for four years is preposterous." Clark replied, "If cracking the whip means something inferior to what we had planned—we say the hell with George Berry."

Meanwhile, Georgia Power Company had completed its detailed planning for its new corporate headquarters, which called for some modifications to the Bedford Pine development plan. The City Council tentatively approved these changes in February 1978. But PAC objected to them because they reduced the amount of office space in the project and allowed Georgia Power Company to develop the twenty-two-acre site as it chose.

Early planning was also under way for three other projects.

Atlanta Area Presbyterian Home had earlier submitted a letter of intent to build a twenty-two-unit high-rise for the elderly. PAC had threatened court action to block the sale. In addition, the Presbyterian congregation were reluctant because of the perceived neighborhood problems. When a physician attending a convention was slain in a robbery attempt on a nearby street in June 1979, the project was withdrawn from consideration.

Developer Joel Cowan and contractor Herman Russell both members of CAP, were planning a 150-unit residential high-rise.

A local joint venture (Landmarks Group and John Laing-American) was investigating a residential development of about 700 units.

The *Atlanta Constitution* editorial of April 14, 1978, stated that "Bedford Pine has become a model of bureaucratic bungling and delay." Clark again publicly threatened court action if the City Council approved changes in the comprehensive plan to accommodate Georgia Power Company, but four days later, he withdrew his objection.

PCC planned to complete the land-disposition agreement with AHA on the entire seventy-eight-acre tract *simultaneously* with the closing of the sale of 17.5 acres to Georgia Power Company. Thus PAC's opposition to Georgia Power's plans was holding up the entire Bedford Pine development.

This time Clark was insisting on a clarification of goals for minority participation in the Georgia Power construction contracts. PCC had already agreed with AHA there would be 20-percent minority participation, but this provision was omitted from the PCC-Georgia Power Company land-transfer agreement. Georgia Power had maintained that it would adhere to federally mandated minority participation. Frustrated time and time again, the company hinted that it might pull out.

Clark now introduced a new wrinkle into the negotiations. He wanted Georgia Power Company to pay PAC a consultant's fee to help in finding minority contractors to work on the $62.5-million office facility. Georgia Power offered $1,000 a month, which Clark called an ''insult.''

Finally, nearly five years later after PCC was awarded the bid to be the redeveloper, the Bedford Pine land-disposition agreement with AHA was executed, and PCC sold development rights to Georgia Power Company for $14.5 million. PCC agreed to pay AHA $11 million over a ten-year period. Georgia Power also bought an adjacent 4.5 acres from Genuine Parts, an Atlanta-based automotive-parts firm that had previously occupied the site and had moved its new headquarters outside the city.

Georgia Power's purchase of the development rights was not only crucial for the planned residential components (by allowing residential land write-downs) but also provided a substantial anchor to the near-downtown portion of Bedford Pine. The company had demonstrated an unusually strong civic commitment to downtown and to the project. It is unlikely that a private developer would have tolerated the protracted negotiation or been able to afford the expensive delays.

Clark tried once more to stop Georgia Power by charging that changes in the development plan made a new environmental-impact statement necessary. He also accused PCC of making a profit on the transaction and said that the land-transfer documents were illegal. But HUD replied that these charges were unwarranted.

Georgia Power Company's handsome 760,000-square-foot, twenty-four-story office tower was completed in early 1981. The 67,000-square-foot roof of an adjacent three-story structure contains solar collectors for heating, cooling, and hot water. Energy consumption for the entire complex is only about 55 percent of the average for conventional structures.

Plans for Condominiums Announced

Charles Ackerman, a successful Atlanta developer, unveiled his plan for an $18-million nonsubsidized condominium development in Bedford Pine. It would contain 561 units priced from $50,000 to $80,000, with the first phase consisting of 62 units on six acres of the twenty-three-acre tract.

Reportedly the land was to be acquired for $650,000, or a very attractive $0.65 per square foot.

In presenting his plan to a closed meeting of the City Council, AHA, PAC, and PCC, Ackerman asked for permission to build fewer housing units on the tract than the 980 called for in the master plan. His contention was that the market would not respond to high-rise units on the site. Ackerman asked for approval by August, with construction to begin in December 1979.

PAC responded by vowing to fight the project, charging it was "economically exclusive" because it made no provision for low-income residents. (In fact, there were already approximately 1,385 subsidized-housing units in the immediate surrounding area.)

The city applied for a $3-million UDAG grant to provide low-interest mortgages to low- and moderate-income residents. This application was later denied.

Over a year later, in September 1980, AHA passed a resolution easing the requirement for firm commitments for low-income subsidies on the Ackerman project. The provision was that if government-subsidized mortgages for low-income families are *not* available, Ackerman can sell the units with conventional mortgages, at prevailing rates, market prices of $65,000 to $95,000 a unit.

In October 1980, RGR Realty Corporation of New York began work on its $13.5-million Bedford Place residential project, which had been announced in August 1979. The first phase of this project consists of a 144-unit high-rise tower and a 44-unit low-rise, all to be rented on the open market at $269 to $573 a month, and 68 low-rise units to be subsidized. Two more phases are planned for this development. To assist RGR, the city applied for a $7-million UDAG grant to be used for underground parking; it received a $2.34-million grant.

Ackerman obtained title to the three-acre first phase of his development in April 1981, two years after his announcement. Construction began immediately, and firm contracts or reservation deposits have reportedly been received on 17 of the first 28 units at prices ranging from $60,650 to $108,750. A total of 568 units are planned. Given the character of the surrounding residential neighborhoods and the crime problem, real and perceived, this is a risky venture at best for market-rate housing in those price ranges. But despite these uncertainties, construction financing was provided by the three local banks who are members of the original consortium that provided initial financing for PCC.

Outcomes

Significant development of the Bedford Pine project area is underway despite the problems and delays. Those closely associated with the project feel that the current plans are feasible and that development will proceed at a reasonably rapid pace.

PAC still exists, but it has for the most part been replaced by other neighborhood organizations and individuals with a direct stake in the development, and Ted Clark has apparently lost his leadership role. A community-development corporation under the guidance of a public-private board of directors is working closely with PCC on the development of a shopping center.

Those involved in the years of negotiations have varying views on the process. CAP and PCC staff feel that the delays were unnecessary and that most, if not all, of the objectives sought by PAC could have been achieved without the confrontational techniques introduced by Clark. Neighborhood leaders, although not comfortable with Clark's style, are convinced that some of the confrontation was necessary for the achievement of their objectives. All agree, however, that the mayor and AHA could have provided more leadership and decisiveness at critical points.

Some city officials expressed surprise that the project has come as far as it has. One City Council member felt that such an experimental project would take time to develop and was not surprised at the difficulties experienced.

Whatever their views, however, city officials, neighborhood leaders, and PCC staff are confident that the project will be a success and do not anticipate any further major confrontations or delays.

Whether the project should have taken so long is, of course, a subject for debate. There is no question that it exacerbated public-private sector differences and resulted in considerable frustration. It also became a focus of attention for continuing and expanding the breech between City Hall and the business community. It did, however, create the basis for continuing cooperation between PAC and the neighborhood. The development of this trusting relationship could well be the most important consequence of the Bedford Pine project in terms of future cooperation between the business community and the new power bases in the community.

Public-Private Cooperation: What Community Leaders Think

Any assessment of public-private cooperation during the Jackson administration must take into account the selective perceptions of those most involved. In this case, it is important to record not only the views of the business community but also the views of public officials and neighborhood leaders.

The Business Community

Members of the business community appear to be unanimous in their belief that public-private cooperation hit rock bottom during the tenure of Maynard Jackson. They cite as the primary causes of deteriorating relationships his poor administrative ability (which they see as reflected in the appointment of unqualified persons to key positions in City Hall as well as to boards and commissions), his attitude toward the business community in general, and his almost exclusive promotion of the goals of the neighborhoods and the black community. They feel that he failed to reflect the needs and objectives of the entire community and virtually ignored the interests of the business sector.

It most certainly was not the election of Atlanta's first black mayor that produced this negative assessment. Rather, this collective judgment comes from pragmatic business leaders who know how to get things done and who were consistently shocked and dismayed by what they saw as the lack of experience and talent in important positions.

Business leaders also complained that they could not get through to the mayor and to that substantial number of business leaders who supported Jackson in his quest for the City Hall seat. It appeared that Jackson had simply turned his back on them and their interests.

Early in 1974, CAP made an effort to resolve the problem. It was decided that major problems as seen by the business structure should be outlined and discussed. These problems and *perceptions* of problems were presented to a large, by-invitation gathering of major Atlanta employers and civic leaders, who were given the draft of a letter that was tough and to the point.

The letter stated that some business operations "have moved and more are considering moving for other than economic or management reasons." It listed fourteen reasons cited by businesses for these moves, including "perceived racial split in leadership, growing racial imbalance of the labor force, fear of crime, . . . schools lack racial and income mix, level of educational achievement, walking around at night is unsafe, entertainment is isolated and oftentimes dangerous to reach, drunks and derelicts on the streets, white flight from the city, perceived attitudes of mayor as anti-white, dilution of the partnership between government and business in Atlanta which resulted in a major communications-action vacuum."

The mayor was told in advance that Harold Brockey, chairman of the board of Rich's Department Store and chairman of CAP, and Dan Sweat, president of CAP, were preparing to present him with a letter.

Shortly after Brockey and sweat hand delivered the letter, it was reported in the press as being an "attack" by the business community on the administration. Later the mayor said that the meeting had been cordial and constructive, and he charged the *Atlanta Constitution* with being "the most negative of all the media."

Front-page headlines on September 25, 1974, said, "Jackson says he seeks city hall business accord." This was Jackson's first public reply to the so-called Brockey letter. He stated that it was time to reforge the progressive partnership between business and downtown that had been broken by Mayor Massell. He promised the business structure that he would repair the alliance, but made it clear that he would expand the partnership to include grassroots representation.

In November 1974 the mayor accompanied Atlanta Chamber of Commerce president Bradley Currey on a business trip to Chicago, painting a picture of harmony between the business community and City Hall. Jackson was quoted at that meeting as saying that the published reports of the feud were grossly misrepresented. On returning to Atlanta, Jackson had a "Pound Cake Summit" meeting every two or three weeks to discuss substantial issues with the business community.

On March 23, 1975, a controversial series of newspaper articles, entitled "A City in Crisis," began appearing in the *Atlanta Constitution*. The seven in-depth articles were prefaced as follows:

> Throughout the sixties, Atlanta was Camelot, spared serious racial turmoil and blessed with experienced leadership, the city became a great center of commerce and a mecca for emerging blacks. Today, political power has shifted. New leadership wrestles new problems, there are tensions among the people. Camelot has faded. What's happening to Atlanta? Will the dream survive?[5]

John Portman summarized much of the feeling of the business community in one of these articles as follows:

> We have developed a lack of trust in the business community towards city government, a lack of trust in the city government towards the business community, a lack of trust of the city government towards the press, and it is perceived that the press doesn't trust the other two. Everybody is standing off—and we were really going in this town once![6]

As late as August 1976, the chairman of the Community Relations Commission charged that Jackson was giving the business leaders "very limited opportunities in decision-making." The mayor's answer was, "I will not cater exclusively to the old-line establishment leaders of

Atlanta commerce whose wishes were often granted by past administrations.''

Business leaders felt that Jackson had let them down. Mills B. Lane was asked if he would go out on a limb to build Atlanta Stadium under current circumstances. He replied, ''No, I would not do it again today. I do not have the confidence that the city and the county governments would perform.''

Many business firms also resented the tough minority requirements on contracts for the city, and many refused to participate in submitting proposals. The mayor enforced joint-venture contracts on all construction at the airport, as well as on other projects, and there was considerable controversy over this policy during the entire construction period.

The public-private partnership was not materially improved during Mayor Jackson's second term, which ended in December 1981. Many businesses left the city. Nevertheless, businesses have made substantial investments in the downtown area. In December 1975 Atlanta voters approved a $18.9-million bond issue for a new public library, which is now open. In September 1976 the state-financed, $35-million World Congress Center opened in downtown Atlanta, and an $80-million expansion approved by the Georgia General Assembly in 1981, and in 1980 Atlanta's main airport the Hartsfield International Midfield Terminal opened.

But despite these impressive developments, the business community still had negative perceptions of City Hall. These strong views can be at least partially explained as a response to the personality and style of Mayor Jackson. He was indeed an imposing figure. His demeanor was one of ''quiet intimidation,'' and his articulateness was interpreted by some as arrogance. This particular style was not well suited to please Atlanta businessmen, especially those who had supported him in the election.

In addition, inability to gain access to the mayor regarding matters of importance to the business community left them with no opportunity for serious discussion of the issues and the development of joint solutions.

However, the most important deficiency appears to have been the mayor's selection of key personnel to run his administration. Members of the business community believe that high-quality staff are necessary for public-private cooperation and were impatient with the lack of experience and competency they feel characterized Mayor Jackon's major appointments.

This combination of factors created an environment that prevented public-private cooperation on issues of substance and left the business

community with no course of action other than to withdraw its support
and openly criticize the mayor and his administration.

Mayor Jackson

As might be expected, the mayor did not agree that public-private cooperation deteriorated during his tenure. In a recent article in *Business
Atlanta,* a publication of the Atlanta Chamber of Commerce, Mayor
Jackson cited what he felt to be the many accomplishments of his administration, including streamlining of government operations, keeping taxes
down while maintaining a double-A bond rating, development of the new
airport on schedule and within budget, many public improvements, the
creation of the Atlanta Economic Development Corporation, assistance
to small business, the opening of MARTA, and significant private investment in the city. According to the mayor, these successes would
not have been achieved without cooperation between his administration
and the business community.

However, in defending his record, the mayor also drew attention to
the fact that his goals were not necessarily in harmony with those of the
private sector in all cases.

> When I began my first term as Mayor in 1974, the city and its gov-
> ernment were undergoing great change.
>
> With Atlanta's "new" black and white voices came new agendas and
> new implementing procedures. A true measure of our success since
> 1974 is that these new agendas substantially were fulfilled while we
> maintained our traditional goals of fiscal soundness, economic progress,
> harmony and justice. . . .
>
> We have succeeded as an administration, however, not because of a
> slavish, unquestioning adherence to downtown dicta, but because of a
> stubborn holding to the belief that the best government is an open
> government, an honest government, a responsive government, an ef-
> ficient and productive government that seeks to serve all of the people.
> We have had our failures and disappointments; yet we all can look back
> on the last eight years with encouragement because, most of the time,
> 99% of the time, we were constant to that belief. On this point, despite
> certain incorrect perceptions, the facts back us up.[7]

Mayor Jackson's defense of his administration in these terms highlights the conflicting objectives that became a major point of contention
between him and the business community. It is not that business was
unprepared to assist in meeting these goals; rather it felt these goals were
the only goals the mayor was seeking to achieve. Public-private part-

nerships must be grounded in a spirit of give-and-take. They must involve willingness to negotiate and bargain toward solutions that produce outcomes desired by all sides. The business community was willing to come to the table with the new black and neighborhood leadership that the mayor wanted to include in the process, but it believed that it was to be excluded.

Public Officials

Elected and appointed public officials interviewed in the course of this research were not quick to defend the mayor's efforts to work with the private sector. In addition, they were in general agreement that the mayor had made some very poor appointments.

One former public official, now in the private sector, pointed out, however, that the problem of competency had as much to do with who had left as it did with who was appointed. In his opinion, most of the experienced people in City Hall during the Allen administration had reached retirement age around the time Mayor Massell left office, and their departure left the Jackson administration with little in the way of experienced staff and institutional memory.

Others were less charitable in their assessment. One high-level official in the Massell and Jackson administrations stated that the mayor was too easily sold on the notion that energetic people could perform complex management functions even though they had little or no experience. Another viewed the appointments as simply a manifestation of Jackson's inexperience as an administrator and his lack of attention to the day-to-day details of running the city.

Nor were these public officials entirely sympathetic to the views of the business community. One appointed official stated that the business leadership had no understanding of the complexities of being mayor in a modern city and little appreciation of being a black mayor with a new and demanding constituency. He also said that he felt the historical political position of business in the community prevented many private-sector leaders from accepting the mayor as a peer in their relationships.

Elected officials felt that much of what Jackson had tried to do in terms of serving the black community and enhancing the role of the neighborhoods would have been done by anyone who happened to be mayor during that period of political change, particularly in terms of minority business-expansion goals. They did, however, feet that the goals of the mayor could have been achieved with less rancor if it had not been for his intimidating style and appearance of aloofness to the interests of the business community.

On balance, these officials believed that much had been accomplished in spite of the differences between City Hall and the business community. Some felt strongly that the local press had been a major contributor to poor relationships by continually sensationalizing conflicts between the public and private sectors and generally presenting a negative image of the city.

Although reluctant to give the mayor high marks, these officials did suggest that to blame all the problems on the mayor would be a disservice, that it was necessary to recognize the political and economic changes taken place during the period and the need for understanding and constructive action by both private-sector leadership and public-sector representatives.

Neighborhood Leaders

Neighborhood leaders expressed mixed feelings about the performance of the mayor. They felt strongly that he had done much for the black community and for neighborhood organizations through his policies for expanded minority business opportunity and citizen participation in the decision-making process.

They did agree, however, that cooperation between the mayor and the business community had not been good. Some saw this as a mistake; others felt that it was a necessary step in the process of change. All hoped that relationships had now reached a point where collective action could replace the confrontation and considered CAP a good mechanism for meeting this objective.

These leaders agreed with the contention that the mayor had made some bad appointments, but they were more concerned with the fact that a number of key staff members were recruited from outside the city than with their questionable level of competence. They felt that qualified individuals could have been found in Atlanta who would have been in a better position to know and understand the needs and objectives of the community.

All in all, the neighborhood leaders felt that Maynard Jackson had done what he had been elected to do. They did, however, think that his approach to the issue of public-private cooperation could have been more outgoing without losing sight of the goals he was pursuing on behalf of his constituency.

These comments tend to indicate that in general, Mayor Jackson lived up to the expectations of the black community and the neighborhood organizations that supported him. But they also indicate the sensitivity that has developed over the past eight years regarding the need for public-private cooperation in meeting their needs.

Few, if any, would contend that continued confrontation is necessary or desirable. Through all the adversity of the past decade, blacks and neighborhood organizations have gained the experience and understanding necessary to deal with the business community on equal footing and are looking forward to the opportunity to do so. The transition period may indeed finally be over.

Acknowledgments

Atlanta's business, civic, and political leaders have always been generous contributors of their time, resources, and knowledge to efforts that could affect the well-being of their city. Their response to the development of this report was no different.

Particular credit must be given to Dan Sweat, president of Central Atlanta Progress and his staff for assistance in tracing the evolution of Bedford-Pine and advice in selecting those figures, public and private, that cast the brightest and most penetrating light on Atlanta's public-private experience.

Notes

1. Ivan Allen, Jr., with Paul Hemphell, *Mayor: Notes on the Sixties* (New York: Simon and Schuster, 1971).

2. Ibid.

3. Ibid.

4. Central Atlanta Progress, *Case Study on Downtown Housing* (unpublished paper, Central Atlanta Progress, 1979), pp. V–87.

5. *The Atlanta Journal and Constitution* (March 23, 1975).

6. Ibid.

7. "Business Atlanta" (October 1981), p. 82.

Index

About the Contributors

George P. Barbour, Jr., is president of PMC Associates in Palo Alto, California, specializing in program evaluation and performance measurement for local, state, and federal agencies. He is also a member and former chairman of the Council on Municipal Performance in New York. Before joining PMC, Mr. Barbour held a number of positions with the city of Palo Alto, including director of service management systems, Development Center of the International City Management Association.

Mr. Barbour is the author of numerous articles on government management and productivity. He is a graduate of Saint Mary's College in Moraga, California, and received the master's degree in public administration from American University in Washington. Mr. Barbour has lectured at Stanford University, Golden Gate University, California State University at Hayward, and San Jose State University.

John Brandl is professor of public affairs at the Hubert H. Humphrey Institute of Public Affairs of the University of Minnesota in Minneapolis. He has been associated with the University of Minnesota since 1969, and from 1969 to 1976 he served as director of the School of Public Affairs.

Dr. Brandl is currently serving his second term as a member of the Minnesota House of Representatives. He has held a number of other government positions including service as deputy assistant secretary of the U.S. Department of Health, Education and Welfare. He has also held faculty positions at several universities in this country and abroad; among them are Boston College, Harvard University, the University of Wisconsin, the University of the Philippines, and the University of Sydney.

Dr. Brandl is a former member of the Board of Directors of the Citizens League of the Twin Cities and is the author of numerous articles on government issues. A graduate of Saint John's University in Collegeville, Minnesota, Dr. Brandl received the doctorate in economics from Harvard University.

Ronnie Brooks is manager for community development for Dayton-Hudson Corporation in Minneapolis. Prior to that, she served as president of the Center for Environmental Conflict Resolution of the Upper-Midwest Council. She also served as the coordinator for the Negotiated Investment Strategy Project for Saint Paul, which involved intergovernmental negotiations to coordinate public- and private-sector development activities. Before joining the Upper-Midwest Council, she was special assistant to the governor of Minnesota in the area of legislative and budget programs. She has also served as director of majority research for the Minnesota State Senate.

Ms. Brooks is a graduate of the University of Michigan and received the master's degree in political science from Michigan State University.

Pastora San Juan Cafferty is director of the Hispanic Studies Program at the National Opinion Research Center in Chicago and is also professor at the School of Social Service Administration and the Committee on Public Policy Studies of the University of Chicago. Dr. Cafferty also serves on the board of the Kimberly-Clark Corporation and is a member of the Chicago Bar Association Advisory Group, the Metropolitan Housing and Planning Council, and the Aspen Institute for Humanistic Studies Committee on the Third Sector.

Before joining the University of Chicago, she served as special assistant to the general assistant secretary of the U.S. Department of Housing and Urban Development, as special assistant to the Secretary of Transportation, and as an instructor at George Washington University.

Dr. Cafferty is a graduate of Saint Bernard College and received the master's degree and the doctorate in American history from George Washington University.

William E. Claggett is professor of public policy and management at the University of Texas at Dallas. In addition, Mr. Claggett is director of a university project to develop regional and national programs that respond to the need for people trained in public-private management. Mr. Claggett has served in the capacity of special assistant for business affairs and urban policy in the office of the U.S. Secretary of Commerce. He has also worked as a consultant in public management and policy development for numerous state, federal, and local governments.

Mr. Claggett was formerly director of the San Francisco consulting firm Public Affairs Counseling, senior vice-president of the Real Estate Research Corporation, and director of the urban-affairs group for Arthur D. Little, Inc. He is a graduate of Harvard University.

M. Dale Henson is president of Dale Henson Associates, an Atlanta-based economic-development consulting firm that he founded in 1970. While most of his activities have been with private developers, lenders, and investors, he has also developed revitalization plans and programs for urban areas. Mr. Henson has directed urban-redevelopment studies involving public-private partnerships in several Atlanta inner-city neighborhoods and has developed strategies for revitalization in a number of other cities.

He has served as a member of Regional/Design Assistance Teams sponsored by the American Institute of Architects in Rockford, Illinois, and San Bernardino, California; as a consulting analyst for the International Downtown Executives Association; and as a resource team member for the National Main Street Center program of the National Trust for Historic Preservation. Mr. Henson has also worked with the U.S. State Department on private-economic-development strategies for Northeast Brazil.

Mr. Henson received the bachelor's degree and the master's degree from the Georgia Institute of Technology.

James King is vice-president of PMC Associates in Palo Alto, California, a firm specializing in research, consulting, and training for local, state, and federal agencies as well as private-sector clients. Before joining PMC in 1976, Mr. King held a number of posts with the city of San Jose, including director of the Office of Intergovernmental Affairs and executive assistant to the city manager, and director of the Office of Policy Research. From 1969 to 1971, he served as director of the City Demonstration Agency and assistant to the mayor of New Orleans. Prior to that Mr. King was special assistant to the assistant secretary for Model Cities and Intergovernmental Relations at the U.S. Department of Housing and Urban Development.

Mr. King is the author of numerous articles on public policy and management improvement and is a frequent speaker on these subjects.

Katharine Lyall is currently vice-president for academic affairs for the University of Wisconsin system. Before joining the university in 1981, Dr. Lyall was professor of political economy and senior research scientist for the Center for Metropolitan Planning and Research and also director of the Graduate Program in Public Policy for The Johns Hopkins University. From 1977 to 1979, Dr. Lyall served as deputy assistant secretary for economic affairs for the U.S. Department of Housing and Urban Development. She has also served as executive director for the Committee on Evaluation Research at the Russell Sage Foundation and as assistant professor of economics at the Maxwell School at Syracuse University.

Dr. Lyall is the author of numerous articles on national and international political and economic issues. She is a graduate of Cornell University, and received the master's degree in business administration from New York University and the doctorate in economics from Cornell University.

William C. McCready is associate professor of sociology at the School of Social Service Administration at the University of Chicago. In addition, he is Program Director for the Center for the Study of American Pluralism at the National Opinion Research Center. Dr. McCready is the author of a number of publications and articles on ethnic America, and he is the editor of the research journal *Ethnicity*. Before joining the University of Chicago, Dr. McCready taught at Loyola University and Saint Xavier College.

He is a graduate of Saint Mary of the Lake College, and he received the master's degree in sociology from the University of Chicago and the doctorate from the University of Illinois.

Shelby Stewman is associate professor of sociology at Carnegie-Mellon University and is the author of numerous publications in the areas of manpower and labor and organizational demography. His work is applicable to policy decisions and human-resource planning in such areas as equal-employment opportunity, forecasting labor costs, career development, and the aging of work organizations. Other work includes a focus on urban concerns, such as public-private partnerships, the delivery of urban services, and integrating budget and labor planning for cities.

Dr. Stewman is a graduate of Ouachita Baptist University, and he received the doctorate in sociology from Michigan State University.

Joel A. Tarr has been affiliated with Carnegie-Mellon University since 1967, where he is currently professor of history and public policy. Since 1975 Dr. Tarr has been the director of the Carnegie-Mellon Program in Technology and Humanities, and since 1977 he has been codirector of Carnegie-Mellon's Ph.D. program in applied history and social sciences.

Dr. Tarr is the author of numerous articles and books on history and public policy, including *A Study in Boss Politics: William Lorimer of Chicago* and *Retrospective Technology Assessment*. Dr. Tarr is a graduate of Rutgers University and received the doctorate from Northwestern University.

About the Editors

R. Scott Fosler is vice-president and director of government studies for the Committee for Economic Development. In addition, Mr. Fosler is a member (and former president) of the Montgomery (Maryland) County Council. Before joining CED in 1974, Mr. Fosler served as assistant to the executive director of the National Commission on Productivity. Prior to that he was a senior staff member of the Institute for Public Administration.

Mr. Fosler is currently vice-chairman of the Washington Metropolitan Area Economic Development Advisory Committee, and vice-chairman of the Board of Directors of the Washington Council of Governments. He also chairs the steering committee on Intergovernmental Affairs and Local Determination for the National Association of Counties, and is a county representative on the state-local coalition. Mr. Fosler is currently representing the United States in an international project comparing public-private partnerships in ten countries sponsored by the Organization for Economic Cooperation and Development.

Mr. Fosler has a degree from Dickinson College and received the M.P.A. from the Woodrow Wilson School of Public and International Affairs at Princeton University.

Renee A. Berger is an independent consultant on urban affairs and director of community partnerships for the President's Task Force on Private Sector Initiatives. Until December 1981, she was a senior research associate with the Committee for Economic Development. In addition, Ms. Berger has been selected by the Organization for Economic Cooperation and Development to design a discussion framework for the first international seminar on public-private partnerships. Her public-private research has also included consulting work for the American Enterprise Institute, the Charles S. Mott Foundation, and the Aspen Institute. Ms. Berger has also served as a research associate for the Academy for Contemporary Problems and has done management consulting for the U.S. Department of Housing and Urban Development. She has taught public administration and urban policy at the State University of New York at Buffalo, George Washington University, and the Washington Institute.

Ms. Berger is the author of a number of articles on urban issues. She has a bachelor's degree in English and a master's degree in planning from the State University of New York at Buffalo.